In Nonna's Kitchen

Maria Kennol

April 2015
12

Also by Carol Field

—

Celebrating Italy

Focaccia

The Hill Towns of Italy

The Italian Baker

Italy in Small Bites

In Nonna's Kitchen

Recipes and Traditions from Italy's Grandmothers

CAROL FIELD

HarperCollins*Publishers*

Photographs of Gisa Sotis, Giulia Tondo, Annita di Fonzo Zannella, and Andreina Pavani Calcagni by Serafino Amato. All other photographs by the author or the families of the women.

HarperCollins books may be purchased for educational, business, or sales promotional use. For information please write: Special Markets Department, HarperCollins Publishers, Inc., 10 East 53rd Street, New York, NY 10022.

FIRST EDITION

Designed by Joel Avirom
Maps by Paul Pugliese

Library of Congress Cataloging-in-Publication Data

Field, Carol.
    In Nonna's kitchen: recipes and traditions from Italian grandmothers /
Carol Field. — 1st ed.
        p.   cm.
    Includes bibliographical references and index.
    ISBN 0-06-017184-7
    1. Cookery, Italian. 2. Italy—Social life and customs.   I. Title.
TX723.F53   1997
641.5945—dc21   96-47958

98 99 00 01 ❖/RRD 10 9 8 7 6

CONTENTS

Acknowledgments

—

This book would not even exist were it not for all the wonderful Italian grand-mothers and great-aunts and their daughters, granddaughters, nieces, and grand-nieces, daughters-, and sons-in-law I saw in Italy. I am deeply grateful to all the families for their help and hospitality.

The list of people who helped me in Italy is amazingly long. It must begin with very special thanks Marina Colonna, Mary Taylor Simeti, and Anna Tasca Lanza for their warm hospitality and wonderful help. Others who were extremely kind and helpful to me include Enea Angelucci and his wife, Teresa Stoppoloni; Franco Azzali; Danilo Baroncini and Susan Lord; Kinta Beevor; Rolando Beramendi; Massimo and Patrizia Biagiali; Professoressa Franca Bimbi; Nadia Calestani; Professoressa Marlis Z. Cambon; Giovanni Minuccio Cappelli; Shirley Caracciolo; Bruno Ceretto; Sammie Daniels; Alessandra del Boca; Rosetta Dorigo; Nicole Douek; Daniela Falini; Patience Gray; the Guerra family; the Lancellotti family: Ida, Emilio, Francesco, Angelo, and Zdena; Carla Lionello; Antonio Marella; Terenzio Montesi; Giuseppe Morandi; Lina Morasini; Maria Rosario Stoja Muratore; Giovanna Passannanti; Prof. Luisa Passerini; Paola Pettini and her enchanting family; Anna Maria Petrocchi; Graziella Picchi; Michaela Rocca; Marcello Salom; Franco Santasilia; Sofia Savelli; Grazia Sotis and her family; Alfredo Talin; Ilario Taus; Cav. Angelo Tomassetti; Leonardo Tondo; Marc Van Put; Franca Virga; Baronessa Gucchi Winspeare.

Thanks to great friends and traveling companions in Italian adventures: Ed, Nancy, Corby, Fred, and Faith.

Esther Prigioni and Katherine Vaz are two special friends to whom I will forever be grateful for their amazing generosity and help.

I can't imagine what I would have done without the advice and suggestions and referrals of Linda and Marisa Bassett, Claudio Cambon, Linda Connor, Carla Deykin, Maria Teresa di Suvero, Paola Sensi Isolani, Elisabetta Nelsen, B. K. Moran, Corby Kummer, Rose Scherini, Amy Smith, and Paula Wolfert. Special thanks to Fran Gage, who gave me her questionnaire and list, and to Carol Helstovsky, whose bibliography was a great help to me. Profound thanks to my wonderful readers and listeners Whitney Chadwick, Mary Felstiner, Diana Ketcham, Cyra McFadden, Jean McMann, Diana O'Hehir, Annegrete Ogden, and Alison Owings.

Profound thanks to my wonderful testers, Farina Achuck, Maxine Bloom, Maria S. Carey, Susie Farnworth, Joe Frescatore, Cyra McFadden, Colleen McGlynn, Beth and Bruce McLean, Jean McMann, Tasha Prysi, Peggy Rash, Gretchen Shopoff, Carol Sinton, and the remarkable Vaz women, Elizabeth and Katherine.

Special thanks to the Italian Trade Commission in New York and Franco Vitulli in Rome and to everyone at the Oldways Preservation Trust in Boston. And to Arlene Wanderman in memoriam.

Susan Friedland has been an enthusiastic and understanding editor and Fred Hill, as always, an attentive and thoughtful agent. Joel Avirom has once again given a book of mine its handsome design. I am deeply indebted to the intrepid Carla Lionello, who miraculously organized everything for the photographs for the cover, and to Serafino Amato for his wonderful pictures. Sharon Silva, an extraordinary copy editor, is a true heroine.

I am extremely grateful to some very special people who saw me through this book with amazing care: Ellie Coppola, Julie Freiberg, Sally Lilienthal, Jean McMann, Carie Matthias, and Cynthia Wardell.

Special love to John, who has lived through the adventures and eaten his way through yet another book, and to Alison and Matthew, who are always supportive and enthusiastic and full of good suggestions.

In memory of

my grandmother, Erma Arnstein
1887–1978

my mother, Ruth Hart
1917–1977

my mother-in-law, Gladys Field
1903–1997

1

LE NONNE

La nonna, la nonnina: every Italian has a grandmother story. "My grandmother used to make a treat for me by packing a thimble with moist chestnut flour. I watched her press it down hard and then put it into the hot embers of the fire," remembers a very old Tuscan handyman, "and when she pulled it out after a few minutes, she tapped sharply on the top and out fell a perfect little mound. It was my snack, something special for me to eat." Said another: "I remember watching my grandmother brush her teeth with a sage leaf." These grandmothers, *le nonne*, are the keepers of memory and the providers of many of the sacred moments of everyday life. Many of today's Italian grandmothers, women in their sixties, seventies, eighties, and even nineties, still live with a strong attachment to the kitchen and still think about cooking as their own grandmothers and great-grandmothers did, which is why what they cook is called *la cucina della nonna*. They are the link to an earlier time in the country's past and their food is the comfort food of home, an amazing panoply of genuine dishes passed from older generation to younger in the course of daily life. When people say a dish reminds them of their grandmother's food, they are not likely to be referring to an extravagant collection of ingredients or a complicated dish. *La cucina della nonna* is based on simple ingredients that are available to almost anyone: a ripe tomato, a few branches of rosemary, a small bunch of basil, a loaf of country bread, a handful of rice or dried beans, some olive oil, a bit of pasta, Parmesan cheese, some freshly grated bread crumbs.

Most of these older women were born and have lived in a time when seasonality ruled life, when tradition and culinary folklore were clear and unchanging. As if engraved in the beams and stones of the house were the givens: the women made the food and baked the breads that nourished the family. They hung braids of garlic and hot red peperoncini from the beams of the ceiling to dry. They put up jams and sauces and ragùs to preserve the taste of summer through the entire year and set them in glass and terra-cotta containers on the shelves of pantries and storerooms. They kept many kinds of dried beans, lentils and chickpeas and other legumes, piles of nuts, and tubs of lard. Branches of grapes that remained on the vine until their flavors were deeply concentrated were wrapped with grape leaves and smoked in the fire of the chimney or hung to dry on long wooden dowels and saved for gifts at the end of the year. Women were the custodians of copper and bronze pots, of terra-cotta casseroles, and of special polenta paddles. They carried inside them a lexicon of domestic knowledge—they knew where wild foods might be safely gathered, how to sow and harvest beans and at what phase of the moon, how to fatten up a pig, and how to keep alive the natural yeast with which they made their bread. And though many of them were illiterate, they taught their daughters and granddaughters what they knew, for if a village were to learn a girl couldn't cook, she would never find a husband. According to tradition in Piedmont, bread is so important that a girl wasn't considered ready for marriage until she could make the dough for the family and bring it to the communal oven for baking. Such secrets and know-how passed from mother to daughter, and mythologies were kept alive through the pleasures of the table.

Those pleasures—the food, the folklore, and the incredible diversity of local dishes—vary not only from region to region and from city to city but from town to town, from hillside to hillside, and to tiny fractions of villages where citizens live on tongues of land that jut into the sea or on remote rocky terrain that climbs high into the mountains. Because Italy did not become a unified country until 135 years ago, it has essentially remained a collection of regions with individual culinary identities. The simple food of daily life and the special dishes prepared only on the *festa* days of the villages are genuinely localized tastes that form a profound part of each person's heritage and sense of identity. "When I want to talk to my grandmother," a young woman said to me, "I use her implements and I cook her dishes." In many cases these women are the last generation who have a repertory of family dishes with their idiosyncratic flavorings and techniques, who know and use local greens and herbs, whose food is deeply rooted in family history and is an expression of regional tradition. They are the connection to a way of life that is gradually being lost in Italy, and when they are gone, that link will disappear with them.

The changes in the country were strongly brought home to me when I happened to meet Sofia Savelli, who lives with her family in the tiny town of Pergola, in Le Marche, a region of central Italy, whose undulating green hills and silent valleys recall the stillness and quiet of an earlier time. Fashionably thin in her chic miniskirt,

Sofia is in her early twenties and works in an office in the nearest big town. She still lives at home and freely admits she doesn't know how to cook. "I don't even have a grandmother I could introduce you to, but I'm going to take you to meet our neighbor, Lina Morasini. She knows how to make everything," Sofia says as we climb into the car. After bumping along the road a bit, we arrive at a property with petunias the color of bougainvillea, fruit trees in blossom, a kitchen garden and fields, and even a wood-burning oven in a nearby small shed. The dog, lying lazily in the sun, bestirs himself to bark until Lina, her husband, daughter, and daughter-in-law appear at the bottom of the staircase. Just a glance at the property suggests that Lina probably still cooks the way country women did a generation or two ago. And a visit to the large room where she keeps the jams, condiments, and sauces she has put up during the year confirms that hunch. The shelves are full of jars of preserved eggplant and mushrooms, of olives marinating in olive oil, fruit jams, a puree of fresh tomatoes called a *passata*, tomato sauces cooked with vegetables, and a dense paste of tomatoes that have been boiled in a cauldron and then dried in the sun.

"Here, try this," she says, opening a bottle of preserves made from Golden Delicious apples and *mosto*. It is sweet and fragrant with the flavor of apple. "It takes a full day to make. Some people say they can do it in three hours, but they have to use a lot of sugar that way and it doesn't keep as well. Or taste as good," she adds quietly.

The secret ingredient is the *mosto*, freshly squeezed grape juices boiled slowly for hours into a thick syrup. It is a natural sweetener, like honey, with a flavor somewhat like concentrated raisins. Sofia looks mystified. She has never heard of mosto before. "There's nothing unusual about it," says Lina, with some surprise. Not long ago every family had its own grapes with which to make mosto. Lina's mother and grandmother always made it and she is only following their example as she cooks what the season produces and preserves everything she can to tide the family over through the long winter months.

A tour of Lina's cantina turns up a huge wooden cask of wine made from their grapes as well as a chamber filled with the sweetish smell of the prosciutto, salami, and sausages hanging from the ceiling like fragrant stalactites in a cave. Because there was no real refrigeration in the past, most women made food that could keep for long periods of time. The pig, that highly regarded animal, furnished the meat for a year of eating. From its well-fed body came sausages, salami, prosciutto, pancetta, and zampone, enough to flavor the dishes of an extended family for many months.

"My family were *contadini*, country people, who worked for a landlord and I saw that the padrone's family made food that wasn't part of our lives. Almost everything we ate we grew or my mother made. She had a great reputation for making jams and baking. Remember her *bigné*?" she asks the two women, who nod enthusiastically in response. "She learned to make them from her mother. They were both rich and light. She cooked them in the wood-burning oven and then filled them with pastry cream."

Sofia drove me back to the town of San Lorenzo in Campo in Le Marche, where I went to talk with Efresina Rosichini, a robust, big-boned grandmother who cooks in her family's restaurant. She didn't have any *mosto* but she did have *saba*, which is just mosto boiled down into an even thicker concentrate. She went to her pantry, opened a jar with contents as dark as espresso, and let me taste its rich, earthy sweetness. Throughout central Italy, women her age continue to make *saba* at home and use it instead of sugar in their baking, but only in Le Marche are they prohibited from selling it. Sofia would have been stunned. First *mosto* and now *saba;* she might not know how to cook, but she has never even heard of these ordinary ingredients. And one was contraband? Efresina answered hesitantly, looking around to see if anyone was listening. "It used to be that immediately after a baby was born, its body was massaged from head to toe with *saba*, because we thought it would give strength for life. But no one thinks like that and we certainly don't talk about those things anymore." *Saba* can be made at home, but it cannot be bought for use in superstitious practices.

The number of women of a certain age in Italy, grandmothers, great-aunts, and great-grandmothers like Efresina and Lina, is diminishing, and as they disappear, the *mosto*, *saba*, and similar local specialties that they take for granted are vanishing as well. It is not really surprising that Sofia had never heard of simple ingredients that her own grandmother would have made and used without a second thought. In the space of fifty years, Italy has been transformed from a predominantly agricultural country to an industrial and urban society. The great shift came after the Second World War, from which Italy recovered with surprising swiftness. The world of agriculture changed radically with the abolition of the *mezzadria*, the centuries-old system of sharecropping which gave half the crop to tenant farmers and half to the landlords. Freed from scratching out a living, some of the contadini remained on the land, but many more left to pursue opportunities in the cities. In the south great estates were broken up and land was given to the peasants, although many did not remain on it. With these changes, a shift took place as the rich were obliged to make sacrifices and give up some of the privileges they had assumed were their inalienable rights. Then came the economic boom of the decade between 1957 and 1967 that made Italy the seventh-richest economy in the world. Newfound prosperity allowed many people to improve their lot and it created a much larger middle class than Italy had ever known. In a fairly short period of time people who had lived with no electricity, no plumbing, no telephone, and no means of transportation had the means to buy those as well as mixers and food processors for their kitchens. That transition is instantly visible in how differently women live now from the days when nonne were always in the kitchen, presiding over ovens and rustic stone fireplaces in which copper pots full of the warming soups of winter simmered slowly. It was not long ago that by early morning most of these legendary nonne might already have made the bread and the sweet ring-shaped coffee cakes for grandchildren who would arrive later in the day. They would have fed the courtyard animals, picked the vegetables in the kitchen garden, perhaps even gone into the fields to work or pull up radicchio, wild greens, and mushrooms for their salads, vegetable tarts, and *frittate*. Slices of quince, fat ripe peaches, or golden apricots might be bubbling slowly in a deep pot soon to become the jams and preserves for spreading on bread at breakfast or for filling a *crostata*, the latticework tart that is the archetypal comfort dessert in Italy.

Despite these changes, many of today's Italian grandmothers, those in their fifties as well as those in their seventies and eighties, still cook *la cucina della nonna*. They may use their modern equipment to make the dishes they set before their families, but those dishes are the same ones their mothers and grandmothers made. They are the true culinary heritage of the country, although many of them did not even exist before the eighteenth century when the diet of modern Italy was set. So many pastas and polentas, soups, *pizze*, and vegetable dishes depend on ingredients that Columbus brought back from America that it is almost impossible to imagine what Italian grandmothers were making before they had potatoes and peppers. What did they do without the corn that became the ubiquitous polenta of the north, the tomatoes that gladden the heart of every southern Italian, and the white beans that may have given the Tuscans their nickname, *mangiafagioli*, bean eaters?

Everywhere I went in Italy the women I saw shared a passion for food. Their backgrounds and homes varied immensely but their devotion to the food of their families, of their villages, towns, and cities was unmistakable. They range from my friend Anna's aunt Lina, an aristocratic Sicilian woman in a navy Chanel suit with a skirt short enough to show off her sensational legs, who rushed into the room, arms outstretched, shrieking, "*Sono nonna, sono nonnissima*" to much shyer, more modest country grandmothers who spoke in dialect—they didn't know Italian—and could only talk with me, a stranger and foreigner, in the reassuring presence of the men in the family.

Some of the women come from the north of Italy, others from Tuscany, Umbria, and Le Marche in the center, and still others from southern Italy and Sicily. They come from cities as large as Naples and Rome and from villages with fewer than 250 people; they come from the mountains, they come from the seaside, and they come from hilly landscapes where grapes and olives and a rich variety of agriculture flourish. Some of the women grew up in dire poverty and never went to school, others grew up in immense comfort in wealthy aristocratic families, and a number came from middle-class families of varying means. What they ate reflects the reality that for centuries there were essentially two types of diets: the varied cuisine of the aristocrats and the food of the poor, which was based on whatever ingredients were available. Local variables, such as the type of vegetables, the wild greens in the fields, the availability of pasta, polenta, or rice, and the imagination of the cook, created the flavors in those dishes. In every case the food the women cook, the dishes they learned from mothers and grandmothers and aunts, is a profound link to their pasts and it reflects intimate family history inflected with regional and social nuances.

The dishes that these women cooked for me ranged from delicious gnocchi prepared in a kitchen no more than four feet wide, where the biggest counter space may have been the sill under the window, to custardy desserts made in an enormous kitchen with interconnecting rooms, multiple sinks, tables, and refrigerators. An old woman who still cooks on a very old wood-burning stove served me pasta made with eggs from her chickens and a voluble and passionate grandmother living in Chianti served her Vin Santo as an aperitif and then produced exceptional examples of every course of a meal.

In almost all cases the women worried that the immense portions they served weren't enough, so when seconds were inevitably offered, there they were at your elbow, strongly encouraging you to eat more, even though it was clear that more succulent courses would follow. Mild demurrals would be tolerated but refusals on the part of a guest would seem callous, thoughtless, perhaps even denigrating to the glorious food filling the platters and bowls on the table. Yes, a husband or grandfather might be struggling to keep his waistline and the woman herself might eat very little, but guests and sons and daughters and grandchildren were expected to plunge energetically forward, thrusting spoons into soup, forks into ribbons of pasta and the grilled meats and stews that followed. A recipe that would elsewhere serve eight was perfect for five at a grandmother's table.

Perhaps Italian women have a wisdom about food encoded in their DNA. So many of them simply shake out the contents of the cupboard into the pot or the terrine and produce extraordinary soups and stews. They know how to make very fine curls of Parmigiano-Reggiano with a potato peeler and how to slice artichokes mere micrometers thick using a *tartufaio*, the special implement for slicing truffles. They know to soak dried beans with a little flour or baking soda to soften their skins and to add a pinch of sugar when the acidity in tomatoes needs balance. They go mushroom hunting with open-weave baskets so the spores will fall back to earth and reseed themselves. They coax intense flavors from the most humble ingredients: root vegetables, stewing hens, cornmeal, fava beans, little-known innards. These women have divined ways to keep pears, lemons, and melons fresh through the winter.

Almost everyone in Italy has memories of being with a grandmother in the kitchen. Remembering her white-haired nonna using two tablespoons to shape the dough for *bigné al forno*, Paola Pettini sat at her long dining table in Bari surrounded by a collection of colorful antique majolica plates and bowls on the walls and sighed audibly. "There were fragrances in her kitchen that I'll never forget," she said, a distant expression in her eyes, explaining that it is the perfume, the aromas, the wonderful smells that give these memories such force. Gianna Modotti, a warm and thoughtful woman who immediately wants to put everyone at ease, grew up with her grandparents in the Carnia mountains of Friuli and remembers waking up in her second-story bedroom, smelling the aromas floating up from the kitchen. All the cooking was done on the fire. "The soups and meat and desserts changed as the seasons changed and they were different depending on what time of year it was." She remembers her grandmother preparing the snails she collected in the season when they were plentiful and frying the frogs her grandfather caught, dipping them in eggs and bread crumbs and cooking them till they were golden and crunchy. "My memories have remained with me forever because I lived them intensely and I still remember all the flavors."

Such women still exist in all of Italy, although in diminishing numbers. Pia Zoli Maestri, a tiny dynamic woman with a seemingly endless supply of energy, was born in 1917 outside Piacenza in Emilia and grew up in a thirteenth-century medieval fortress-castle with a moat and drawbridge around it. She was immensely observant and loved spending time with the contadini families who worked for her family. As a result she knows everything about what it was like to run a household during a time of war when there was no soap, no butter, no flour. She and her sister made bread, made soap, made cheese. There were no freezers or refrigerators, but there were boxes, some as big as armoires, constructed with a faucet connected to the interior. Country people put snow on the shelves inside what was essentially an improvised ice chest, layered them with straw, and kept perishables that way. When the snow melted, they could turn the faucet and let out the water.

"*Ho vissuto molto, nata in campagna.* Being born in the country, I have seen a lot and I lived the life of a contadina even if we weren't. My sister and I learned by watching the people around us. We learned to do everything. We made butter by shaking whole milk, shaking and shaking it in a bottle until it coagulated. We put the butter on a block of ice and fed the milky liquid that remained to the pigs. We made ricotta cheese. We even made soap from leftover pork fat that wasn't good for cooking or eating. We put it in a pot, added caustic soda and a little something to give a nice fragrance—tiny pieces of leftover soap, usually—and we stirred it very slowly over a low fire until it was done."

For all the years of this century until the end of the Second World War, scarcity was the norm for many people. Times were difficult and food was not always plentiful. Even so, most nonne say the same thing: "*Si stava meglio quando si stava peggio*—We were better off when we were worse off." "Even though we worked hard all the time, we had fun," Nella Galletti remembered. "We always sang when we reaped the wheat and we had a contest with our scythes to see who could cut the most the fastest. And at night, people often sat together in front of the fire, the women knitting or making lace, men playing the accordion or talking, telling stories, and we loved to sing and dance." Women picking grapes during the harvest in Piedmont sang from hillside to hillside, sometimes in competition, sometimes in antiphonal response to verses from across the valley. Everyone agrees that life is much easier now, but, as one woman said, "People aren't as good-natured and I don't hear anyone singing anymore." They remember the warmth and connection from a sense of community that prosperity has done nothing to encourage.

In the country women worked as hard and as long as men. They carried everything on their heads, from bundles of grass or hay wrapped in a bedsheet to large jugs of water and faggots of wood. On top of all their other work, they bore and raised their families, fed and nursed them. All those who were part of the sharecropping system called the *mezzadria*, which prevailed in Italy until the early 1960s, lived from their agriculture, subject always to the whims of the seasons and the owners of their land. Under this system children didn't go to school for long, but were dispatched to help in the fields when they were very young; women went to town only for rare festivities or to buy, perhaps, shoes. The people were attached to the land, although until the end of the Second World War, days of work were not guarantees of a minimum decent diet.

The women, especially the stoic countrywomen, have a deeply impressive dignity and bearing. If the lives of Italians can be divided between well-being and poverty, and between poverty and eating to keep hunger away, as one woman thoughtfully proposed, the difference might be measured by whether bread was freely available at every meal. In most families bread was the first food, the most basic food, the one constant that always appeared upon the table.

Meat, and especially beef, on the other hand, was abundant only in middle-class and aristocratic households. Many people saw meat three times a year—at Christmas, Easter, and at the celebration of the town's patron saint—rare moments of plenty in a life marked by scarcity. What meat there was usually came from the household pig, its meat preserved and conserved in an amazing variety of ways to be eaten in small portions or as flavorings through the entire year. Beef found its way to table on a plate only when the animal had outlived its usefulness in the fields and made its final sacrifice by offering itself up for many meals, and then it had to be cooked long enough to become tender. Milk-fed veal, sometimes even chicken, was served only to babies and sick people; an old saying has it that "when veal and a person appear at table, one of them must be sick."

And if someone was sick, a nonna made food *in bianco*, literally white food, comforting and soft food cooked in broth to encourage a return to well-being. "The *riso in bianco* was neither a Tuscan dish nor a complicated one: large-grain rice, well cooked but not overcooked, and seasoned with a lot of fresh butter and grated Parmesan," writes Aldo Buzzi in *A Journey to the Land of the Flies*, remembering the miraculous dish made by his aunt Anna's cook. "It was absolutely white, with shades of light azure, and very good. Perhaps it depended on the quality of the rice. Perhaps on the butter or the Parmesan. Perhaps Assunta had a secret. I have tried several times to make it but have never succeeded in getting the same delicacy." *Pollo in bianco, pesce in bianco, riso in bianco*: from sickness to health, from the nursery to the dining room to great feasts in the countryside and in city villas, women have nursed their families through difficult times.

In her novel *Umbertina*, Helen Barolini described the way of life of an Italian woman in a poor family: "She knew of the struggle to eat, and the occasional joy of a feast day. She knew the patterns of life; everything was as ordained and set as the square kerchief she folded over her head and the black felt caps her father and brothers wore—these were their badges, as the hats of the gentry were theirs. Men were over women in her world, and the rich over the poor. Over everyone was God. . . It was God's will that girls should marry and work for their husbands and bear children, so life could be endlessly repeated." Country wives never sat at table but stood and served the men. Wives of workingmen were permitted to sit but never had time. Only middle- and upper-class women in the city took their meals at table with the others.

Some women are fortunate enough to possess the small kitchen notebooks kept by their grandmothers with old family recipes written in black ink in a spidery hand. They keep them carefully in a separate drawer, and some still use them, for they are the source of family dishes that pass from generation to generation. The pages of these small notebooks are simple annotations of domestic life, but they are also the dreams and memories of a world that is quickly disappearing. Some of today's nonne have written their recipes on a few cards banded together or have tossed pages into a drawer. Opening a handsome cabinet and pointing to the pages inside, Vanna Corbellani Camerlenghi laughed. "My archive," she said, pulling out a few sheets of paper and riffling through them.

Much more rarely will a woman pull a single treasured cookbook out of a drawer because there were very few important cookbooks published in Italy until recently. Pellegrino Artusi's *La scienza in cucina e l'arte di mangiar bene* (*Science in the Kitchen and the Art of Eating Well*), published at the end of the nineteenth century, was the first cookbook written for middle-class families that unified Italian cuisine, although its dishes were almost entirely from Romagna and Tuscany. Over a million copies have been sold, making it the most successful book in Italy after *Pinocchio*. Ada Boni, the most important Italian cookbook writer of this century, wrote *Il Talismano della Felicità*, a book of sumptuous dishes for a middle- and upper-class audience, which carefully and methodically outlines the steps of preparing a multitude of dishes. *Il Cucchiaio d'Argento*, a cookbook written by a group of women, is the other book that *le nonne* might have, although few of them referred to any books at all. Most contented themselves with memories of meals eaten, days spent in the kitchen watching a mother or grandmother move through the rich and endless procession of tasks that produced the flavors that forever define emotional access to a deeply felt way of life. It is a way of life for which many people are now profoundly nostalgic.

The women who still have their family recipes in written form utilize them in different ways. Some refer to them and use them to pass on the food of home to the next generation. At her daughter-in-law's urging, eighty-five-year-old Giovanna Passannanti brought out the carefully kept recipe book begun by her grandmother in Partinico in Sicily in the nineteenth century and continued by her mother in the earlier part of this one. She sighed as she read about *agnellino al forno*, baby lamb and potatoes baked until they have a golden crust, and the *torta con un ripieno di mandorle tritate*, an exceptional lemon-flavored chocolate and almond tart. Franca Virga is completely devoted to her mother-in-law, who taught her how to cook all her husband's favorite dishes—some from the little black book—and passed on many of the secrets of the kitchen, such as flavoring chicken dishes and meat broth with allspice—a long-standing Partinico tradition—and washing anchovies with vinegar to get rid of their smell.

Laura Mansi Salom grew up in Palazzo Mansi in Lucca with three cooks in the kitchen. Twice a day her family ate multicourse meals that included two first courses, an elaborate *piatto di mezzo*, or "in-between course," a main course, dessert, and four or five different wines. She has carefully preserved all the complicated recipes from her family, writing them in her contemporary script so that they are much easier to read now. She still makes a few of them for major parties but exults, "We've had a revolution! We eat a lot less now—I eat a first course and a salad for lunch and that's it. Often I eat in the kitchen with my grandchildren and instead of all those waiters, we're on our own. Even at great dinners, I don't want to stay at table for hours and hours—no more five- or six-course meals in my house—and I only serve two wines, not a different wine for each course.

"World War II brought about the big changes. Waiters didn't exist anymore, and we had to learn not to eat when there were so many shortages. But when the war was over, my grandparents wanted everything to be the same as before. They wanted to eat the same dishes and the same number of courses. And my grandmother returned to driving around the top of the walls of Lucca every morning in the horse-drawn carriage. I'm happy to have lived the other life, but I don't have the spirit or desire to relive it. I prefer the life of today—it's so much more easygoing, more dynamic." Elegant and extremely chic, Laura Mansi Salom is seventy and still cares deeply about traditional food. "I know what the best food is, but I try to simplify everything. I go to the pastry shop and order the puff pastry so the effect is the same as what we had once, but I'm not doing all that work and neither is the now nonexistent pastry chef. You have to know how to order and coordinate dishes and that's true for both rustic and elegant meals."

Life in Italy has always revolved around the kitchen. In traditional Tuscan *cucina*, the word for kitchen, also means house; *la cucina della nonna* means the food handed down from grandmothers but it also refers to the fireplace and the hearth over which these women have presided. The kitchen has always been the most lived-in room, the warmest part of the house, and the smells and the flavors, the colors, and the smoke of the cooking existed in a kind of theater in which mothers and grandmothers presided over the daily dramas and rituals of their families. This is where families exchanged news, gossiped, told stories, where women often prepared food for an extended family of twenty or twenty-five people. If the kitchen was the center of women's kingdom, the fireplace with its hooded chimney was the focus of its existence. "There used to be *ottomila fuochi*, eight thousand fires, here," an old woman said to me as we bounced along on a bus in Le Marche, meaning there used to be eight thousand households, each one identified by the smoke escaping its chimney, evidence of the fire inside where food was being cooked and warmth was enveloping the house. A quick glimpse would put the current number at no more than four or five hundred.

For centuries cooking in Italian houses was done in an iron, brass, or copper pot that hung from a sooty chain in the fireplace over embers that burned continuously. Into the pot with its boiling salted water went *strutto* or *lardo* to flavor a slow-cooking soup or polenta, or beans to enhance stews and the thick sauces into which people dipped their bread. Potatoes, corn, onions, beets, and other vegetables were buried and cooked under the ashes. Women once did most of their cooking on the brick or stone hearth fired by whatever wood was cut from nearby trees. Once the floor was hot, the ashes were swept away and many kinds of food, from focaccia to Amalia Ceccarelli di Ridolfi's *crescia di Urbino*, a simple dough rolled extremely thin and folded again and again with lard spread between many layers, were cooked directly on the scalding stone. Other times hot embers were spread right over the breads or meats (they were brushed off before serving), although women also covered the food with a concave cast-iron top and piled live coals over it. This method of cooking between two fires has almost entirely disappeared, and the roasting or baking that is done in its place confers an entirely different taste.

Cooking on the hearth, *sul focolare*, in Italian, becomes *s'l'arola*, in the dialect of Le Marche, from the Latin *areola*, for small area. Adele Rondini, a seventy-five-year-old native of Le Marche, an artist and teacher who has written twenty-four books, makes the irrefutable and touching point that in poor families the kitchen really became a little altar on which everyone made sacrifices. She describes her own childhood kitchen in Le Marche with its tall and spacious fireplace, a large hood sheltering the hearth, and a food warmer with its latched door containing the ashes that were destined for the washing. There was a squat and paunchy country oven and a range made of a dark metal. Before gas ovens were available, her family, like most others, used to cook on the hearth or on a *fornello*, a one-piece stove top with one or more cabinets underneath that held the coal or wood for heating. When the temperature needed to be raised, someone waved a straw fan over the coals or blew through a tube to make the dormant ashes glow red. The family oven reminded her of a ship with many portholes allowing glimpses of the red-hot fire inside, and she still remembers the rabbits and capons, turkey, and lamb cooked in it. They were placed on a raised sand-filled slab, and she swears that they had a special taste that was entirely different from any food cooked today in regular ovens. "Food is fascinating. I love stories about its traditions and how food used to taste because it was cooked differently. It's just like dialect; dialect is the juice of language, its flavor and taste and inflection, and it is disappearing. Whenever you lose one or the other—a dialect, a way of cooking, a kind of ingredient—you lose the essence of local tradition. You really lose a part of culture."

Like Adele Rondini, most grandmothers learned to cook before there were refrigerators or modern stoves with individual burners, in many cases before either gas or electricity was available. Some of them began their mornings collecting wood with which to light a fire and walking substantial distances to get water from a well. But no matter what the obstacles, the women cooked the comfort food of Italy, the stews and hearty soups, the pastas, risotti, polenta, and beans that gave their families the energy with which to work hard every day of their lives. Women took whatever was growing in the kitchen garden and the fields, stored in the larder or plucked straight from nature, and with imagination, frugality, and a deep-seated knowledge of local ingredients created an entire cuisine. The dishes they made are the essence of what we admire and love in Italian food.

Most kitchens were simple. There was usually a stone sink under a window, a deep wooden *madia* which held the flour and natural yeast for bread baking, and chests in which glasses and plates were kept. On the wall hung shelves for tin-lined copper pots and earthenware pots and pans, soup bowls and ladles, and for the mortar and pestle in which women ground salt and made simple daily condiments like the mixture of garlic, parsley, and *lardo* pestled together to serve as a sauce for pasta. They hung baskets with bread and crackers high enough to frustrate whatever mice and insects might forage for sustenance. There was usually a wooden table for eating, although many families kept warm while they ate by sitting on long narrow benches set on two sides of the fire. Heating was rudimentary at best. In many houses it came only from the fireplace, which was large enough to contain chairs or low benches at the sides where people took turns sitting to get warm. Families that could afford prodigious quantities of wood kept water at a constant boil on the stove top, making steam that was carried through a tube to heat the whole house. To overcome the cold at night, people often scooped embers left from the fire into a brazier which they slid between the icy sheets to heat them before bedtime.

In the country, the kitchen was center of a kingdom that included the threshing floor, granary, stalls, hen coops, pigpens, well, and wood-burning oven, while in the city there was a pantry and wood storage as well as a place for all the accoutrements of making bread and cooking. Many of these women lived close to the earth and raised most of what they ate. For them organic wasn't a movement; it was a way of life. Traveling markets selling provisions might arrive in small towns once or twice a week, but otherwise people relied on growing, cooking, and preserving what they produced.

Of necessity they lived without waste. They burned the cuttings from vines and trees in their wood-burning ovens and fireplaces. They used the ashes from those fires for washing laundry, for polishing copper, for preserving salami, and for rubbing the rinds of cheese. They used the fat of pigs for making soap. They ground corn into polenta, but they used the leaves to stuff mattresses and to roll the tobacco for their homemade cigarettes. Once wheat had been harvested in the fields, women and their children made a second foray to glean whatever had been overlooked, collected the sheaves that remained, took them to the mill to be ground, and then carried the flour home to make their loaves of daily bread. Angela Padrona, one of eight girls and a boy growing up near Monopoli in Apulia in the 1930s, described going to one of the great farm properties after the harvest of grain to collect the remaining ears of wheat, one by one, all day long under the hot sun.

For hundreds of years women all over Italy have baked huge rounds of country bread and served them three times a day as sustenance for their families. In Tuscany a saltless loaf was set upon the table, in Alto Adige and Trentino it was rounds of rye, in

Sicily people sat down to durum flour loaves studded with sesame seeds, while in Apulia the bread was huge crunchy crusted wheels whose porous interiors were the warm color of wheat. Women baked these breads in a wood-burning oven, if they had one at home, in the communal oven, or they invented a kind of rudimentary oven by placing the dough directly on the scalding hearth and covering it with a concave top over which hot embers were strewn. The breads rose higher under the protection of the cover and became lighter as they cooked. No matter which kind of bread they eat, Italians know that bread is the most sacred of all foods. Wasting bread is considered such a sin that when someone dies, that person is immediately sent to Purgatory where an inventory is taken of how much bread he or she might have wasted during a lifetime. For every crumb wasted, the punishment is always the same: collect an equivalent number using only the eyelashes to pick them up.

Women in the country made a number of loaves of bread for their families once a week, using natural yeast saved from the previous week's bake, and they left them to rise while they worked in the fields or took care of the daily chores. In houses that didn't have wood-burning ovens, the women shaped the risen dough, placed the loaves on a board, and carried them on their heads to the communal oven. They baked a first piece as a kind of pizza or focaccia to make sure the oven was hot enough. Sometimes they would embellish it with onions on top or a bit of tomato, cheese, and herbs and then drizzle it with oil. That first piece—called *cacciananze* in Le Marche or *faccia vecchia* in Sicily—was often given to the children as a way of pacifying their hunger and their impatience. A bread doll, called *la pupa di pane,* was often the only gift a mother or grandmother could give her small children every once in a while.

Women speak dreamily of the bread of their childhoods. One woman remembered, "My mother made 75 or 80 pounds a week! And the bread was so good that we will never taste its like again." Another reminisced: "I still remember my mother burning vine and olive branches in the outdoor oven and then swabbing the floor with twigs dipped in rainwater to make steam. She filled the oven—and it was big!—with large big flat rounds of bread. When it was time for them to come out, we gathered around to watch her pull the door away and slide them out, one by one. I swear there isn't a smell in all the world as good as bread just out of the oven. And no bread that you buy tastes anything like it."

Lina Morasini's mother also made bread once every ten days, not just for the nine people in her family, but for the workers who helped out as well. The flour was kept inside a big wooden chest called a *madia* with space on one side for the natural yeast, a big ball of dough left from the previous week's bread making. She beat tepid water and natural yeast directly into the flour and kneaded it energetically for a long period of time. Before going to bed, she always made the sign of the cross over the top of the dough, closed the top of the *madia*, and left it to rise during the night. Next morning she added more yeast and water to the dough and then beat them together and kneaded them as long as she had strength. She covered the dough to protect it and let it rise again before cutting and shaping it. "I remember she always wanted the loaves to slump a bit; that meant they were ready to go into the wood-burning oven. She always made extra loaves. People were so happy to exchange wine for home-baked bread," Lina said.

Pia Zoli Maestri remembers making bread with 30 pounds of flour at a time, using yeast left from the baking of the week before and a little commercial yeast bathed in water. With help from a couple of other women, she and her sister made an enormous mass of dough. "It was a lot of work to knead and cut, but once the wood-burning oven was hot enough, we removed all the ashes and branches and put the first round of bread inside. On top of the loaf we put a single feather from a chicken. If it fell off forward, toward the mouth of the oven, the oven was too hot; if it rose and turned over in a backward somersault, it was just right."

Memories are not always so rapturous. A woman in the mountainous north remembered her mother's rye bread being so hard that after ten days it practically required an ax to cut it. Pure wheat was a luxury, so bread for the poor was often made of a mixture of grains. Nella Galletti, who has lived her whole life in the same few miles of the Umbrian countryside, remembers how hard it was to make bread when precious wheat was almost unavailable. Her family's bread was often made with three parts cornmeal and only one part flour, so the dough shredded easily and didn't rise much. "My mother used to make pizza by mixing boiling water with cornmeal and salt. She kneaded the dough a lot before forming it into balls, flattening them, and stretching each piece of dough over a cabbage leaf and stacking them, dough and cabbage leaf, one on top of the other. She made a big fire in the wood-burning oven and slid in this multi-tiered pizza and covered it with the hot embers so it cooked from the bottom and the top at the same time. It took a long time until they were done. "*Era buona, ma anche c'era fame*—The pizza was good," she said thoughtfully, "but then, there was also hunger."

Country women made many flat breads that took little time because they didn't have yeast and could be slapped on a griddle or disk and cooked in the fireplace. The *piadina* of Romagna—sometimes called the tortilla of Italy—is made by stretching a simple unleavened dough into a thin circle, placing it on a griddle-like terra-cotta disk, and cooking it in a hot fire, turning it once so both sides blister evenly. In nearby Emilia, women once made little round *tigelle* by filling scalding hot terra-cotta disks with the dough, stacking them one on top of another, and leaving the dough inside to cook as the disks cooled. Lately those terra-cotta disks seem to have been replaced by attached flat iron plates, the Italian equivalent of a waffle iron. It was once easy to buy lightly crunchy cornmeal-and-wheat *focaccette di Aulla* from hawkers and vendors in that little Lunigiana town in western Tuscany, but Rina Ramponi, lamenting their demise and the poor products made in their stead, says, "What focaccette we eat, we make at home in the fireplace." She spreads a small bit of leavened dough inside a number of hollow disks that have first been heated to scalding in the fire, stacks them one on top of the other until all the dough is used up, and then thrusts the entire stack back into the fireplace to finish cooking. "Shall I admit it? Today's metal disks are really better than the terra-cotta ones we used to use." All of these simple flat breads are served hot with fresh ricotta, *raviggiolo*, or buttery stracchino cheese or prosciutto, salami or coppa, or, in the case of the tigelle, a spread made of finely chopped garlic, rosemary, and *lardo* or pancetta.

Like their mothers and grandmothers before them, the nonne have built an entire cuisine on leftover bread. Bread is first eaten when it is freshly baked, but with time, the loaves change. They dry out or become stale. Then the bread can be grated for bread crumbs, grilled for crostini and bruschetta, turned into bread salads, bread soups, or dumplings. It can be layered in minestrones; Luisa Cappelli's ultimate ribollita is merely yesterday's soup layered and boiled with yesterday's bread. Stale bread can be the architectural platform holding up the *cappon magro,* an elegant and complicated Ligurian dish, but it is also the thickener in simple country soups. *Sopa mata, zuppa matta, suppa cuata*: every region has its own version of bread-thickened soups and salads. *Panzanella* is bread salad in Tuscany but becomes *cialda pugliese* in Apulia and *caponata dei marinai* in Naples. *Pancotto* in Lombardy is slices of bread cooked in broth, seasoned with nutmeg, and served with grated Parmigiano-Reggiano cheese. Pancotto in Abruzzo in the south gets its flavor from a bay leaf, pancotto in Apulia adds potatoes and arugula, whereas in Calabria it has tomatoes, parsley, bay leaves, peppers, garlic, and celery. Pancotto in some form or other feeds the young, the old, and the just plain hungry in the entirety of Italy from Valle d'Aosta to Palermo. As individual as the regional food of Italy is, bread—and leftover bread, in particular—is the great unifier, the one constant that connects the food of aristocrats and peasants, city dwellers and country people, Italians living in the north and the south.

Until fifty years ago, geography played an immense role in the diet of each region. Transport of ingredients was almost unheard of, so what wasn't grown locally simply wasn't available. In a mountainous area where the land is stingy and the climate one of endless winter with minuscule harvests, there is not much hope for agriculture. Many residents had to make do with what they could grow, shoot, hunt, or trap. Snails and frogs, the natural products of the land and its rivers and internal canals, were the staples of the poor. Wheat won't grow at high altitudes, so buckwheat made the pasta of the Valtellina, and rye was turned into the bread of Alto Adige and Trentino.

If that was the past, what of the future? In the last fifty years, the period within which many of these women grew up, married, and had families, Italy has changed radically from a primarily agricultural country to an industrialized urban society. Large families have been replaced by nuclear families with one or, at most, two children. People who were once peasants and tenant farmers now own their own land and farm their own crops, using modern methods and modern machinery. And the women who cooked the food, who celebrated the great harvests in this humane and harmonious landscape, keeping alive the great traditions of the past, do so less frequently today.

A centuries-old continuum is being broken. Everywhere I went, inquiring about women who still lived with traditional values and cooked the dishes of their childhoods and their families, people told me again and again "there used to be a lot of them, but now we're almost out," as if they were a disappearing commodity or a nonrenewable resource. And indeed they are. Most women are no longer consigned to the extremely hard life of earlier decades. They have their own homes now and do not want to return to an existence of unending and exhausting work. Who could wish otherwise for them? These women can now go to the beauty parlor, watch soap operas on television, send their children to university, and have a different self-image. "Sorry," many of them said, "we don't qualify. We're all *signore* now."

But if women's lives have changed, what is to become of the culture embodied by and embedded with the culinary habits of the grandmothers' time? Italy remains a deeply food-oriented culture, but patterns that were once taken for granted are disappearing.

Gone are the great harvests of the past. Where it once took thirty people four days to thresh the wheat, now the harvest is brought in in a single day with one tractor. And since workers no longer spend days in the field, they are no longer fed a massive celebratory meal of fettucine in goose broth, crispy roast goose, and a great ring-shaped cake flavored with marsala to celebrate the end of their labors.

Gone are the days when sheep wandered the hillsides, cutting the wild grasses as they went. Of course the pecorino cheese made from their milk was perfumed by the grasses and had its own memorable, if irreplaceable, taste.

Gone are the pigs that were raised to be massive when they reached maturity. Now pigs are grown to weigh 275 pounds—just enough for well-developed haunches with which to make prosciutto, but certainly not enough for the *lardo* and *strutto* that flavored the baking and the dishes of yesterday.

Gone are the days when nursing mothers stayed in bed for eight days, eating only pigeon broth. No longer does the mother of a new mother arrive for her first visit carrying a fat chicken or capon and a mountain of vermicelli cradled in her apron. Meals celebrating weddings, baptisms, and first communion that were always cooked at home are now held in restaurants.

Yes, the Italy of the childhood and early adulthood of these nonne has changed immensely. No matter how passionate they may be about the food of their families, some of today's grandmothers are more than happy to cast their vote with new products and technology. A number of them have set aside their rolling pins for pasta machines and their food mills for food processors, have installed microwave ovens, and even the most meticulous among them have succumbed to electric polenta pots with a motorized arm that stirs continuously. Nonstick pans now appear in many kitchens, although most women of a certain age had long ago created natural equivalents. Heavy cast-iron pans grew black from being used on the fire. In lieu of washing them, women cleaned them with ashes and wiped them with a rag and over time they were seasoned and as resistant to sticking as new Teflon-lined pots.

If fewer and fewer women are living according to the old patterns, what of their daughters, whose generation has seen the world change so dramatically? The younger women have gone to work. The size of Italian families has shrunk so radically that the Italian birth rate is now the lowest in the Western world. Perhaps there are already more grandmothers than grandchildren. Italian women used to live where they were born, unless they moved to where their husbands came from, and there they stayed. Now many people have become internal immigrants, moving from region to region within the country. Families are fractured, regional roots are disturbed, and many of the nonne of yesterday have left their posts at the stove. The postwar economic boom and the riches of the eighties have brought material plenty to Italy in a way never known before. "And that's why," one woman said to me, "you're going to have trouble finding the women you want. There are now grandmothers who wear bikinis and go to plastic surgeons."

Quite a change from a time when children stood mesmerized, watching their grandmothers making pasta, forming various shapes with their rapidly working fingers. Now the tortellini and orecchiette that they eat are likely to come from the local *pastificio* or *salumeria*. And the special dishes that are made only for holidays are also disappearing from celebratory tables. And when they are gone, who will remember not only the recipes but the secrets of their making?

Italians recognize that the threat of the loss of this knowledge is serious. While the French are dealing with the same problem by sending chefs into the schools to teach children about French food, school districts in various parts of Italy have created projects that encourage children to interview their grandmothers about what they ate when they were young, what they cooked when they were married and raising families, how they celebrated and what they ate at the great agricultural moments in the calendar as well as the religious holidays. The children filled out questionnaires with their grandparents' answers and brought them back to their grammar schools in Fabriano and Ancona in Le Marche, in Rimini in Emilia Romagna, and Arezzo in Tuscany, and they have collected and published them in books. These books are sweet and touching, full of wonder and respect on the part of grandchildren and of unexpected information from the grandparents, who speak with nostalgia and deep feeling of the past and with pride of their new way of connecting with the youngest members of their families. The books have names like *Sapori Perduti* (Lost Tastes) and *Sul Filo dei Ricordi* (On the Path of Remembrances). Their authors are listed, in one case, as *Progetto Ragazzi 2000–Progetto Genitori* (A Project of Kids 2000 and Their Families). Whether prompted by such programs or moved by the same spirit, other women of grandmotherly age have written to their local school systems, volunteering to help with such a project for their own communities. A public health agency in Rimini interviewed old people in rest homes and recorded their memories of the food of their youth.

The unavoidable question remains: Even with the recipes and remembrances of the nonne in these pages and many others who still exist, how can we possibly hope to re-create the tastes of the past? Crops are raised differently now and ingredients inevitably taste different. Women once cooked only what grew in season, but freezing and transporting ingredients over long distances have broken open the rhythms of life. Peaches are now available in January and radicchio in summer; no one has to wait for Easter to eat milk-fed baby lamb. Fewer Italian women cook in terra-cotta casseroles, fewer still use pots scooped out of smooth *pietra ollare*, a natural stone ideal for long, slow braising and stewing. Wood-burning ovens, which give food an entirely different texture and flavor than today's electric and gas ovens, are purely optional these days. There can't be many women who still light a glowing fire on the hearth behind a revolving spit laden with meat and game birds that turns slowly, operated by a system of cogs and gears and pulleys with stone weights anchoring the rotating skewers. *Lo spiedo*, the word for that device, an implement of the past, is now much more likely to describe someone who is slow-witted and picky. Thinking about that old spit, a Florentine laughed. "We Tuscans roasted like that so much that when we cook a roast on top of the stove we call it an *arrosto morto*, literally a dead roast, because it just sits immobilized in a pan and doesn't revolve on a spit the way we expect." What that implies of course is that even if we start with the same recipes, the food they produce tastes different.

No one knows this better than the grandmothers. But they also know that no matter how rapidly Italian life is changing, the heritage of food, the legacy passed through generations of their families, remains deeply important. Italy remains a food-centered culture, a culture in which food carries the emotional weight of people's feelings, memories, and sense of self.

Yes, women are busy working and yes, food is prepackaged for convenience and even the vegetables for a *battuto* come precut and frozen ready for a quick thaw and sauté. Anyone can make minestrone from a box of premeasured ingredients just by adding a cube of bouillon. And yes, they can even go to immense supermarkets for once-a-week shopping. In return, many dishes are slowly being consigned to memory. Nearly forgotten food has begun to have a veil drawn across it, like a hidden secret.

Yet *la cucina della nonna*, the comfort food of home, is staging a comeback throughout the country. Even though Italy has become a land of change and accelerated options, where almost half of the men no longer return home for lunch, where Nutella, a chocolate and hazelnut spread in a jar, has become the afternoon snack (*merenda*) of children, where television is erasing regional differences and fax machines are speeding up life, even so, people are looking backward as they look ahead. Recent romantic television spots even show patient wives cooking *la cucina della nonna* and serving it in a rustic setting to a huge group of family members. The ads are playing on a gnawing sense of loss, a yearning for life as it was once lived, deeply rooted in the connections of family and food, of the earth and the seasons. As women no longer work their alchemical magic with food and as dishes that give meaning and definition to their lives are being subtly changed or disappearing altogether, people sense that their emotional landscape is being altered. Some women regret the loss of community, of solidarity, which they knew in their lives. As much as Italians love the energy and material pleasures of contemporary life, they may well be nostalgic for the tastes of home. No one wants life to change so swiftly or dramatically that they will acknowledge, when it is too late, what one Italian immigrant announced with deep feeling: "The stones in the street will cry when we are gone."

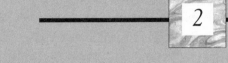

MATERIA PRIMA

Basic Ingredients

*O*pen the door into the kitchen of any Italian grandmother, and you're likely to find a spotless room with herbs on the windowsill, everyday implements like ladles and whisks, a cheese grater and colander hanging from a rack, an espresso pot on the stove, a bowl of coarse sea salt and a jar of olive oil on the counter, perhaps an arc of pots on the wall, and a wooden table with a pull-out drawer holding all of the eating implements. What you will not find are special measuring cups or spoons; these women use espresso cups and wineglasses, coffee spoons and ladles and most of all, they rely on their eyes and their noses and their hands, the preferred tools of true cooks. Their bowls may be mismatched, there may be just a few pots and pans, and the oven may have no thermometer or gauge (high, medium, and low are the choices) but should you ask how they know when a dish is properly cooked, the answers may range from a blank stare and shrugged shoulder (translation: it is obvious) to suggestions that a knitting needle or single reed from a whisk broom plunged into the interior should come out clean.

It is the rare Italian grandmother who cooks from a written recipe. These women already know what they are doing. They measure *all'occhio* (by eye), they scoop up *un pugno* (a handful, literally a fistful), and they pour *al dito* (by the finger). "How much is *due dita*, two fingers?" I asked a nonna as she poured wine into a sizzling pan, and she replied by laying her index and third fingers together, placing them parallel to the bottom of a drinking glass, and pouring until the wine reached the top of the upper finger. Aha—no more worrying about Pyrex cups.

Does it matter that one woman's handful probably holds more than another's or that one has much thicker fingers than another? That the flour varies from region to region, so the amount of liquid it absorbs would vary as well? Not to them. It is all part of the innate knowledge of le nonne. They know how to buy pale green and pink tomatoes for salad and red ones that are at the perfect point of ripeness for sauce. They can detect minute differences between one artichoke and another and have been known to chastise a greengrocer roundly for even suggesting they accept what they can clearly see is an inferior peach. Just watching the women as they shop at a greengrocer is convincing evidence that many of them have keen, well-trained senses that inform them exactly which pieces of fruit and which vegetables are destined for their tables.

They know when to be demanding and when not. Many dishes are built on whatever is in the garden and the pantry. No zucchini? Make the minestrone without them. Extra potatoes? Add them to the soup as a thickener. Need greens? Go into the fields and pick them. Have an aged chicken? Toss it into the pot: "*Gallina vecchia fa buon brodo*—An old chicken makes a good broth." Writing recipes for their food struck many women as absurd. "There aren't recipes," one said, "there are ingredients."

They can also be extremely specific: use meat from a pasture-fed lamb that weighs no more than 17 pounds; you must have white spring onions, or, even more astonishing, dip a knitting needle into olive oil and let twelve drops fall onto the plate. And sometimes: no garlic! Giovanna Dolfi-Zenzi Lusignani described the traditional *latte in piedi*, literally "milk standing on its feet," an ancestor of crème caramel, by giving its recipe: Beat 20 egg yolks with 20 tablespoons of sugar. Bring 1 liter of whole milk to the boil, add the egg mixture and vanilla, pour into a buttered high-sided baking dish, set them in a bagna maria in a very warm oven—just under 400°F.—and bake. Its name depends on a good cook: if the custard is cooked well, it keeps its shape when unmolded; if not, everyone can watch it descend in an unceremonious slump. And how does Giovanna tell when this incredibly rich dessert is done? Not with a toothpick, but with a single straw plucked from a small whisk broom made of reeds from the nearby river, a plant whose seeds are used to make face powder.

Sometimes making an ingredient can be as much work as producing the final product. Giuseppina Ianné Piazza, who lives in Valledolmo, Sicily, used to make panettone by first creating wheat starch. Imagine—she started by soaking flour in water, changing the water twice a day for eight days, then putting the soaked flour through a vegetable mill and discarding the water. Only at that point, once she crumbled the remaining flour, did she have the starch that allowed her to start on the recipe itself.

There are ingredients, such as eggs, that were once so precious that an entire range of alternative dishes was created without them. *Pasta matta*, crazy dough, is a pastry dough that gets its name because it is made with flour and water and salt, but no eggs. *Sopa mata*, crazy soup, is just bread and water or broth flavored with whatever vegetables grew nearby—beat no eggs to thicken its interior, please. During times of hardship and certainly during war, when women sold their eggs for necessities, they figured out how to make a frittata without eggs: flatten cooked potatoes with a fork, add some wild greens and wild mushrooms, and sauté.

Once-common ingredients have become hard to find, even in Italy. In the past when only the rich had sugar, grandmothers made natural sweeteners from the grapes and figs that grew almost everywhere. They simmered freshly pressed grape juice in huge pots for a long period of time until it was reduced to a syrupy liquid (*mosto*) or they concentrated it even further until it was 20 percent of its original volume and formed a thread when tipped from a spoon. It was then known as *sapa*, *saba*, or *vincotto di uva*, depending on where it was made. Overripe fresh figs can also be mashed and boiled for several hours to produce a comparable fig syrup. Each of these gave a different and deeper sweetness than sugar.

In the same spirit of frugality, when country people took honey from their beehives, they put the combs in a big basket and weighted them down to keep the wax in. Then when they washed the basket what remained was *acqua mielata*, honeyed water, which they used to sweeten their cookies and cakes.

Some of the country's most important ingredients didn't even exist until the eighteenth century when the fruits and vegetables that Columbus brought back from America were truly incorporated into the country's eating patterns. What did Italian grandmothers do before they could make sauces from sweet juicy tomatoes, before they had polenta, which, like pasta or rice, became an Ur-dish to be flavored with anything that was on hand? What took the place of the white beans that are the basis of soups and hearty filling minestrones? The grandmothers of today's grandmothers inherited a gamut of ingredients that Italy now takes for granted.

Of course they had basic foods that have been in Italy for centuries. Some of these grow only in a single region or even in a collection of small valleys, further intensifying the individuality of the dishes grandmothers produce. *Mele in pietre*, a winter apple that takes months to mature, grows only in Le Marche where it is cooked in *crescia sfogliata*, a strudel-like dessert that uses fruit left over from the winter. The pastry is filled with the winter apples, walnuts and hazelnuts, dried figs and raisins, and apple or quince jam and then baked in a wood-burning oven. Women often give it as a gift at Christmas. Other singular tastes belong to individual areas. Tuscans can't imagine some soups and mushroom dishes without the taste of *nepitella*, a spiky-leafed member of the wild mint family, while Romans insist on *mentuccia*, a slightly different wild mint that is similar to pennyroyal, for their artichokes. Piemontesi believe *erba di San Pietro*, a small plant known as St. Peter's grass or cost-mary, is essential to a good frittata.

Some ingredients come already packaged and ready for use. A number of sausages in Brescia and Parma depend on a spice packet containing coriander seeds, cloves, cinnamon, star anise, and caraway seeds all ground together. Women in Chianti and the Maremma making the traditional *cinghiale al sugo dolce forte*, boar in a sweet and sour sauce, go to the grocer to buy spices that are premixed and ready to give the meat its characteristic taste. A grandmother in Lucca once refused to give me the secret of a special tart that she makes, although she dropped hints that it depended on a mixture called Tuscan spices, which turned out to be suspiciously similar to those used for panforte. And every nonna in Italy names lievito Bertolini, a vanilla-scented baking powder that comes in a small envelope, as a basic ingredient in desserts.

Some ingredients can no longer be found. Morena Spinelli in the Tuscan town of La Panca reminisced about tiny eggplant with an emphatic flavor that simply aren't grown anymore in Chianti. And tiny sweet fish from the Arno before it became polluted. "And the cooked apples we bought during festivals—we used to save the peels, dry and hang them for the beautiful aroma that took away kitchen smells." Eighty-seven-year-old Ines Pernarella reminisced about the goat's milk ricotta once made by shepherds near the hill town of Monte San Biagio in southern Lazio where she has lived all her life. Many women remembered the incredible drink their mothers and grandmothers made for them when they came home from school. An egg yolk, sugar, and milk were beaten together for a very long time, a mixture to which chocolate was sometimes added, and sometimes the mixture was cooked to a zabaglione-like state.

Some foods have been replaced by packaged alternatives. Ornella Reneglio remembers making pasta at home in Piedmont when she was a child and drying the strands over the backs of chairs. There was one pasta recipe and two shapes: long or short. When Agnesi spaghetti appeared commercially—and that didn't happen until late in her childhood—it came in long boxes and the grocer insisted on breaking the long pasta in half when he sold it.

While it is not unusual for women to continue to make pasta at home, it is rare indeed to find many who make the domestic equivalent of bucatini or hollow spaghetti. Women in the Albanian community of Ururi in Molise still mix an egg, two and a quarter pounds of semolina, water, and salt into a dough, knead it well, and then roll small pieces of it around the thin metal spoke from an umbrella. With amazing deftness they quickly pull the spoke out, leaving the interior hole that characterizes the pasta. The metal umbrella spokes of the past are in great demand—contemporary ones are useless since they are made of plastic and have squared edges—so women buy any old umbrellas they see at the traveling market, take them apart, and save the spokes to give as presents. Sicilian countrywomen roll the dough around a knitting needle called a *busa*, while southern Italian women have traditionally found that soaking, then drying, the thick strong wild grasses called *disa* will do the same trick.

Antonia Morelli lived with her daughter Graziella Picchi in the country near Pesaro in Le Marche during World War II. Her intimate knowledge of the topography was accumulated over the decades she had spent in the fields, and when the war came with its food shortages, she saved the lives of many people around her with her knowledge of what wild grasses, greens, mushrooms, and herbs could be picked and eaten.

Andar per erbe, to go hunting for wild greens, was once considered the province of the poor, who collected such spontaneously growing plants as rucola, cicoria, frond-like agreti, and tiny greens such as *strigoli*, which are the size of the tip of a shoelace, and they combined them with pasta or grains to make their daily food. When it comes to cooking, country families often have more poesia and fantasia than actual ingredients, but they know how to use every part of an edible product. Their imaginations create delicious combinations. Women in Apulia pick and cook fava beans and serve them topped with swirls of wild cicoria sautéed in olive oil. Next day they beat any left over favas into a puree. They turn it into *maccù*, a cross between a thick soup and polenta that is flavored with borage, or toss it with boiled *lambascioni*, wild hyacinth bulbs that are similar in taste to wild onions.

Ironically, what the poor once picked for free now arrives on Italian tables at great expense. Those who are learned in the lore of the countryside can pull up vine shoots or hops and eat them boiled, sautéed, or in a frittata; they can find poppy shoots which make a delicious vegetable or salad; eat tiny roots of delicate *raperonzolo* raw or stirred into risotto, pasta, or savory tarts; and serve *valerianella* with eggs and salami. *Stringoli*, *cicerbite*, wild asparagus, lamb's tongue, miner's lettuce, and *malva* are available free to anyone who recognizes them in the fields; others pay dearly when they arrive at local markets during their brief seasons.

Women have long believed in slow cooking. A soup pot bubbled all day long. Stews simmered for hours. Bread rose and was baked in rhythms that fit the woman's day. Southern Italian women put the *ragù* on the fire at dawn and left it to cook from sunup to sundown, making it possible for a family to return home from a long day's work and find food ready for dinner. That long slow simmer was part of the cooking of the *piatto unico*, one dish that becomes a two-course meal, or even two meals, like the Neapolitan Genovese, for which meat was cooked for hours in a sauce that became the *ragù* served with pasta, but the roast itself was removed and returned in a successive course or as the centerpiece of the next day's dinner.

Perhaps the nonne learned a lesson from the miracle of fishes and loaves. They certainly know how to serve numbers of people with very little at hand. Renata Marsili can get twenty-eight pieces from a single chicken and two extra thighs. Morena Spinelli makes a grand picnic by digging a hole in the earth, building a fire, cooking a sausage or part of a rabbit and augmenting it with salad and bitter greens picked in the woods. *Acquacotta*, "cooked water," the rustic broth of the Maremma served over bread, was originally made with water, an onion, perhaps a little garlic, a piece of bread, some herbs from the field, especially mentuccia, and, for flavoring, a drizzle of olive oil and a squeeze of unripe grapes, the vinegar of the poor. And was it difficult to gather the ingredients? An old saying has it, "*Mi manca la mentuccia, l'olio e il sale; farei l'acquacotta se ci avessi il pane,*" which means, "I don't have any mentuccia or oil or salt, but I'll make acquacotta for you if you have the bread." And was it precious? Workers covered the dish with an upside-down pan so the aromas wouldn't evaporate.

Many of these women learned to cook at a time when there was no refrigeration. They continue to make sauces and preserve the fruits and vegetables of summer and fall to last through the dark cycle of winter months. They put up tomatoes in August—several days' work produces the sauces, the sun-dried and canned tomatoes that flavor the dishes of an entire year—and they dry herbs at the same time. They leave figs in the heat of the late summer sun to dry slowly, leave some wine grapes on the vine to concentrate their flavor, and hang table grapes or lay them on cane mats to intensify their sweetness. They pick olives and press them into oil sometime between November and January and when that is done, every woman has her own formula for putting olives in brine, in oil, or for dry curing them until they are as wrinkled as an old person's face.

Women have always had strategies for keeping ingredients that were available only in their season. Butter used to be made during the months that men milked the cows and made cheese on the dairy farms of northern Italy, but once the cheesemaking was over in November, the dairies closed until spring. Ida Marverti Lancellotti described taking 7 or 8 pounds of butter produced at the last possible minute, melting them over a very low fire, and continually skimming off the foam until all that was left was clarified butter which she poured into large glass jars and used through the long winter.

She also preserved eggs. Beginning in May when they were plentiful, she checked each egg for cracks by knocking one gently against another and then packed them into huge wide-mouthed glass containers. Next she poured in pure quicklime, a material usually used for construction and for whitewashing, and boiled it until it liquefied and became a keeping agent for the eggs. The jars were kept in a cool place all summer long so the eggs would be on hand through the winter.

Giulia Tondo has fresh oranges from her garden in Rome even during the winter. She picks them when they are ripe, puts them in a tightly woven wicker basket that looks like a gigantic laundry hamper, and fills it with cold water, which she changes every week. Steeping them in this manner keeps them fresh for months. When Giovanna Passannanti still lived on her family's property in the Sicilian countryside, she strung nets high in the air, filled them with freshly picked melons and branches of pears, and they kept well through the cold winter months.

In southern Italy, small clusters of meaty tomatoes, each about the size of a cherry tomato, grow on vines that need very little water. At the end of the season, bunches of these *pomodorini* are harvested, hung from a nail on a well-ventilated wall of a house, and kept ready to be picked, a few at a time, and then used and cooked like fresh tomatoes through the entire winter.

Regardless of the geography to which they belong, many of the traditional recipes of the grandmothers have similarities that cross regional boundaries. Rich or poor, Venetian or Sicilian, every one of these women has pots and pans made of terra cotta, stone, bronze or copper, not the enameled iron or metals or nonstick materials that have crept into many kitchens today. And they have at least three essential implements in their kitchen: long-handled wooden spoons—the *bastone* used for polenta may be almost the length of an oar and the size of a club—a mortar and pestle in which to pound ingredients to release their flavor, fragrance, and essential oils, and a *mezzaluna*, the two-handled, curved chopping knife used to mince food without pureeing or crushing it. Many women prefer the easy rocking motion of a mezzaluna to the staccato rhythm of a knife and always use it to chop the vegetables and herbs that form the base of many sauces.

Many of their dishes were made with the chickens and rabbits women raised in the courtyards of their houses. The impressive gamut of greens with which they cooked may differ from one region to the other, but vegetables there always were, for countrywomen planted them in their *orti*, kitchen gardens, and foraged for them in the fields. And what of the polentas, pastas, and bread-based dishes of every day that become different only when inflected by local herbs, flavorings, and vegetables, and, of course, by the traditions of centuries and by the imagination of the cook? The names of many dishes refer to who cooked them and how—*alla contadina* (the countrywoman's way) or *alla lucchese* (in the style of the cooks of Lucca)—or who shot them—*alla cacciatora* (the hunter's way)—or fished them—*alla marinaia* (the sailor's way). These are the dishes cooked by generations of Italian women who have cadged tastes from the fields and squeezed flavor from the simple ingredients of a country rich in agriculture. They have served them in times of plenty and times of hardship to sustain their families. Through wartime and times of deprivation as well as years of prosperity, generations of Italians have been nourished and provided for by their nonne, the legendary grandmothers of Italy.

A Few Major Ingredients Used by the Grandmothers and Their Wisdom About Them

—

CHEESES

Formaggi Freschi. Soft fresh cow's milk cheeses include buttery stracchino, taleggio, and crescenza from farmhouses in Lombardy. Serve them at room temperature. They are wonderful eaten with greens and toasted walnuts, served simply with bread, and baked into vegetable tortes or *Polpette di Pollo* (page 216).

Mozzarella di Bufala. Buffalo mozzarella is made from the milk of buffalo that roam the plain outside Naples. The milky white cheese has a delicate, lightly tangy flavor that sets it apart from any other. It squeaks when you cut it and then has a slightly shredded texture. Regardless of what you read, most mozzarella in Italy is now made of cow's milk, for buffalo are rarer and rarer. Try to use imported mozzarella or any of the various mozzarellas made by expert cheesemakers, such as Paula Lambert in Dallas or Bellwether Farms in Sonoma, California. Whatever you do, be sure to avoid the bland tasteless balls that are labeled as mozzarella in American supermarkets. Eat mozzarella at room temperature—it is particularly irresistible sliced with tomatoes and fresh basil leaves and drizzled with olive oil. See the Source Guide to Ingredients.

Ricotta. Ricotta cheese is soft and delicate with an enticing fresh taste. It is used for many pasta fillings, vegetable tarts, pizza rustica, and innumerable desserts. Italian ricotta is often made of sheep's milk and is one of the finest ingredients in the country's vast repertoire, its soft pale golden curds dazzling the taste buds with the slightest tang. If you are lucky, you can find sheep's milk ricotta produced by Bellwether Farms or Mozzarella Company in Dallas; see the Source Guide to Ingredients. You can also compensate by mixing 1 ounce of goat's milk cheese to 15 ounces of cow's milk ricotta. Under optimal circumstances, whole cow's milk ricotta should be weighed or measured and then drained, but it should always be pressed through a sieve or whirled briefly in the processor to aerate it. Buy the best ricotta cheese, preferably made with whole milk, at a cheese shop or delicatessen. *Ricotta salata* (salted ricotta) is firm ricotta that has been salted and aged. It can be grated or sliced.

Semisoft Cheeses. The semisoft cheeses include bitto, the special cow's milk cheese of the Valtellina; nutty, slightly buttery fontina from the Val d'Aosta; and sweet, mild provolone and tangy scamorza from southern Italy, semisoft cheeses that are served at table as well as used in cooking.

Pecorino Cheeses. Sheep's milk cheeses from central and southern Italy, Sardinia, and Sicily range from fresh and delicate farmer's cheeses to piquant aged grating cheeses that are sprinkled on top of pastas and stirred into pasta fillings. Caciotta or pecorino toscano is a young, lightly creamy cheese; pecorino sardo is saltier and sharper, and aged pecorino romano is definitely assertive and meant for grating. Sicilian pecorino is eaten in three definite stages: as freshly made tuma, unsalted and still creamy; as a month-old full-flavored table cheese; and finally as a grating cheese. Grated pecorino cheese is often served with highly flavored southern Italian dishes that are made with strong greens.

Parmigiano-Reggiano (Parmesan Cheese). A saying in Emilia Romagna counsels, "Never leave the table if you haven't yet had the taste of Parmesan cheese in your mouth." It is impossible to imagine Italian food without Parmesan cheese, true Parmigiano-Reggiano, made from the milk of cows grazed only in a precisely delineated area of the provinces of Parma, Reggio Emilia, Modena, Bologna, and Mantova. It is made into wheels of golden straw-colored cheese that are aged for at least one and often for two to three years. Yes, it is expensive, and yes, it is absolutely worth it. The mellow salty taste of the cheese with crystals that break on your tongue adds incomparably to many dishes. Do not use it indiscriminately, but set it on the table whenever you are serving pasta (not, however, any with seafood sauces), minestrone from Milan or Genoa, and most dishes from Emilia Romagna. Buy a chunk of the cheese and grate it yourself when you need it so that you get the full impact of its flavor. Use a vegetable peeler or tartufaio to slice thin curls of it. Whatever you do, do not discard the rind. Genoese nonne always put a piece of the rind into their minestrones; it softens and yields up its slightly nutty taste and adds a creamy texture. Others have been known to add a bit to meat broth as it cooks.

Grana padano, a grating cheese which is made in many valleys of northern Italy, is very similar to Parmesan cheese, but it is made outside the delineated Parmigiano-Reggiano zone. It is the most commonly used for cooking and grating.

To store chunks of the hard cheeses, such as Parmigiano-Reggiano and grana padano, wrap them in butcher paper or a brown paper bag and then in plastic. Plastic alone encourages mold. If the cheese has become hard, wrap it in a moist tea towel and then in plastic and put it in the refrigerator; check on its state every day, moistening the towel as needed, until it has softened.

OLIO D'OLIVA (OLIVE OIL)

The dusty gray-green trees dotting the landscape of much of Italy produce the green and dark purple olives that are harvested sometime between late November and January. Once people have stripped the olives from the trees by hand, they are immediately taken to a mill, called a *frantoio*, where they are crushed by two giant stone wheels standing on end, turning and crushing the fruit into a paste. The paste is then spread on flat mats that are stacked and then pressed down slowly and gently, without using any chemicals or heat, until the oil, the fruity runoff, gradually pools and then is collected, filtered, and poured into containers. This is the much sought-after unrefined extra-virgin olive oil whose flavor and aroma add immensely to the food with which it is cooked or served. There are some people who consider unfiltered extra-virgin olive oil with its deep green cloudy color the best oil of all.

The finest extra-virgin olive oil must have perfect taste, fragrance, and texture; it must also have an acid content of less than 1 percent. The second quality of oil called pure olive oil or just olive oil comes from second-grade olives whose flavor, color, or odor has imperfections; it may be extracted by heat or chemical processes. The pure oil is essentially tasteless, colorless, and odorless; a little extra-virgin oil may be added to give the oil some personality. Contrary to what you may think, it is not necessary to pay a fortune for extra-virgin olive oil. I assure you that most Italian grandmothers do not. There are some very good low-priced oils, some preferable for cooking and others for drizzling over food just before it is served. It pays to taste to find the ones you like and to keep more than one bottle on hand.

Extra-virgin olive oil is a critically important ingredient in many Italian grand-mothers' kitchens. It flavors crostini and bruschetta, is drizzled over soups and pastas, is rubbed on fresh fish and vegetables before they are grilled, and is often the medium for sautéing and for flavoring breads. It may be the first ingredient in a pan for a sauté and the last as the finishing touch on a plate of beans or a mixture of greens.

Almost every region in Italy now produces olive oil and almost every person in Italy now uses olive oil, although they certainly didn't before the Second World War. Even people who live in big cities somehow always seem to have a personal source, a special grower or a connection to one for the olive oil that they use in their kitchens and on their tables. Many women swear they use nothing but olive oil in cooking, serving, and even in frying because it is a natural conductor of heat—it has such a high smoking point that it seals in flavor—and provides a crisp exterior.

Oils from different regions complement the foods with which they are cooked and served. Oils from Liguria, Lake Garda, and the region around Lucca are light and delicate; the oils of central Tuscany and Umbria are fruity and fuller-bodied; olive oil from Chianti is famous for its peppery bite; and olive oils from the south may be more assertive and full-flavored, although some oils from Puglia and Molise have the smoothness and fruity flavor of their more famous northern relatives. The flavor of olive oil is critical to almost every savory dish; its smooth texture and mellow taste provide the finishing touch which can make all the difference. The simpler the dish, the more imperative the need to use the best oil. Keep olive oil in a cool dark place, preferably stored in a dark glass container, and use it within a year to a year and a half.

HERBS AND CONDIMENTS

Hillsides and kitchen gardens bloom with large and fragrant sage leaves, with glossy rosemary, fragrant oregano, slightly peppery marjoram, and several kinds of basil, including the amazingly aromatic tiny-leafed Genoese variety. Basil, sage, and flat-leaf parsley must be fresh, and I urge you to use fresh herbs whenever you can. Italians use fresh European bay leaves, milder and less assertive than the California variety, and I hope you will search farmer's markets and local sources to do the same. If you can't find fresh bay leaves, use dried French or Turkish ones. If you use dried rosemary, dried oregano, or dried whole sage leaves (don't even think of using the powdered variety), use about half the amount you would if they were fresh. Oregano is always dried in Sicilian recipes; use an imported brand such as Peloponnese.

Some especially important, if lesser-known herbs, include nepitella, a variety of wild mint that grows all over Tuscany, which is delicious with mushrooms. Mentuccia, its cousin in Lazio, is pennyroyal, a delicately flavored, slightly different wild mint that traditionally flavors Roman artichokes. Use twice as much fresh oregano as mint to approximate nepitella and twice as much marjoram as flat-leaf parsley and a pinch of mint for mentuccia. A saying in Le Marche: *"L'insalata non è bella se non c'è la pimpinella"* ("A salad isn't beautiful without burnet") in Tuscany becomes: *"L'insalata non c'è bella, se non c'è la salvastrella* [purslane]."

Emma Grassi Bensi in Panzano couldn't imagine that I didn't know just what to start chopping when she said "always use *odori*." Many savory recipes in Italy begin with *odori* or a *battuto*, finely chopped vegetables and herbs. The mixture is usually sautéed with olive oil bathing the bottom of the pan (in the north a little butter may be included) and then is known as a *soffrito*. Sometimes the vegetables go into cold oil, sometimes the oil is warmed before the sautéing begins. In Tuscany odori are diced onion, carrot, celery, parsley, and herbs such as rosemary, sage, or nepitella. Emma knows them as well as her own name and automatically picks them from the garden, but the herbs may vary by region. They are so essential to every region's cuisine that greengrocers all over the country usually tuck a handful of parsley, a few stalks of rosemary, and perhaps a fresh bay leaf or two into the package, knowing that they will likely be necessary. Sometimes garlic is called for—although not as often as most Americans assume—and pancetta may be part of the package of flavorings. The meat or other ingredients are added once the vegetables just begin to take color.

IL MAIALE (PORK PRODUCTS)

The pig is the savior of the wintertime and the savor of many dishes, although today's pig is but a shadow of his plump ancestors. In the last fifty years, pigs have been reconfigured for culinary reasons. Lean Yorkshire pigs have replaced local breeds, and pigs are killed when they reach 275 pounds—just beyond the point at which they develop a lean prosciutto, but long before they produce a layer of fat thick enough for lard. Pigs were traditionally raised on farms or in the countryside, eating acorns and chestnuts from trees in the woods, but now a great preponderance are raised industrially and fed an entirely different diet. As a result, they not only taste different than pigs that have been raised privately but the texture of the meat is different as well.

Lardo. There is really no translation for lardo; it is like pancetta and the white rind of the prosciutto, in that it is the preserved white fat of the pig. It was once used as a major flavoring in the *battuto* and in many simple rustic recipes, but in these days when fear of calories and cholesterol are so powerful, olive oil has taken its place. When lardo is listed as a menu item, it refers to the white fat from the pig's rump that has been cut in small sections, rubbed with dry sea salt and numerous mountain herbs, sometimes covered in brine, and always aged for months. It is sliced extremely thin and served with bread or with raw sliced tomatoes.

Pancetta. Although it is not smoked, pancetta is the Italian equivalent of bacon. It comes from the belly of the pig and its creamy white fat is streaked with a little meat. It is laid out flat, flavored with cracked black pepper and cloves, perhaps a little cinnamon and nutmeg, then rolled up like a salami, and cured in salt. Pancetta is used in numerous Italian recipes, often as part of the initial sauté of the *soffrito*. Alas, most American pancetta is so unlike the Italian original that, with few exceptions, you would do better to substitute a high-quality salt pork, or, better yet, a tiny bit of prosciutto and the snowy white fat from its rind. Be sure to taste anything you cook before you add salt, since salt pork can be very salty. I depend on Hobbs pancetta from San Rafael, California, which is an excellent product. You can order pancetta by mail and freeze it in small pieces. See the Source Guide to Ingredients.

Strutto. Strutto is lard, rendered pork fat, that has been used by women for centuries for frying and making pastry. It gives an incomparable crispness to fried food and an unbeatable flaky texture to pastry doughs. As a cooking fat, its contribution to both taste and texture cannot be duplicated. The purest lard is called leaf lard; pork back fat is the second choice. Ask your butcher for help in finding it. To render it, cut the pork fat into small pieces, put it in a deep, heavy-bottomed saucepan, cover with a small amount water, and set it over low heat. Let it cook until it has become a transparent liquid. Skim off the pork cracklings—they are delicious by themselves or you can bake them into bread—pour the lard into a ceramic container, and let it sit at room temperature until it cools and solidifies into a creamy white substance. Keep it in the refrigerator or freezer. If you opt for a commercial lard, taste it carefully. Lard should have no taste and no odor. Many traditional grandmothers insist on using lard, but fear of cholesterol and calories has scared many cooks, even nonne. Some nonne substitute margarine. Ironically, lard actually has less cholesterol than butter.

SALE (SALT)

Italians almost universally use sea salt from the Mediterranean to flavor their food. Salt is a preservative—prosciutto, *baccalà* (salt-dried cod), anchovies, and capers last for months because they have been preserved with salt—but it is also the first and major seasoning in every dish.

In the kitchen, women keep a bowl or jar of coarse sea salt, *sale grosso*, by the stove—they toss handfuls of it into the water for pasta and potatoes, for instance—but they put fine sea salt, *sale fino*, on the table. Crystals of kosher salt are less salty than sea salt; iodized salt has been washed and magnesium has been added so it won't clump and will pour freely. Crystals of natural sea salt are pure—they are, after all, what remains when seawater has evaporated—they are rich in minerals and have a clean taste. Many grandmothers keep their fine sea salt in a shaker with grains of rice so it can pour easily.

POMODORI (TOMATOES)

Each area of Italy has its own preferred tomatoes. Grandmothers use fresh tomatoes in the summer and early fall when they are ripe, sweet, and at the height of their flavor; otherwise they use canned tomatoes or the sauces they have put up when the tomatoes were at their peak. Small, meaty, and flavorful Pachino tomatoes, a favorite in the markets of Puglia and Sicily, are a new early variety, bred to appear before other tomatoes are available. Plum-shaped San Marzano tomatoes with their meaty pulp are most popular for sauces and for any dishes that need long, slow cooking as well as for tomato concentrate and the extract that was once routinely made in the south and Sicily. But there are more, each with its own flavor and characteristics: round and fat Venturas; heart-shaped *cuor di bue*, beefhearts; ripple-topped Florentines; ribbed Genoese tomatoes, *costoluto Genovese*, a late-ripening tomato that also appears in America in August and September; and long thin Romas. In the south clusters of cherry tomato–sized *pomodorini* are harvested and hung on a nail hammered into a well-ventilated wall of a house, and they can be used all winter long.

How to choose? Just watch an Italian grandmother in action at the market. First her eye sweeps across the wooden crates to check the selection, then it returns for a more critical look, followed sometimes by a few questions before she makes a final selection. Italian customers know the cardinal rule: no touching. Grandmothers in smaller towns where they are known seem to have been granted an exemption. They almost always choose pale green and/or lightly pink tomatoes for salad and ripe red-fleshed ones for cooking, but no matter what tomato they have cooked, they almost routinely add a bit of sugar to a tomato dish after tasting it for sweetness, even though Italian tomatoes tend to have less acidity than ours.

Pomodori in Scatola (Canned Tomatoes): Whenever fresh tomatoes at the height of their flavor are not available, Italian grandmothers use canned tomatoes, preferably whole San Marzano plum-shaped tomatoes in natural juices. Some of the best canned tomatoes come from Italy—try cubed tomatoes from Pomi, which use no citric acid in the preserving, or San Marzano–style plum-shaped tomatoes that may or may not come from Italy. California tomatoes, such as the organic ones packed by Muir Glen, are also excellent. Many women add a pinch of sugar to the canned tomatoes to balance their acidity. Italian nonne also use *passata*, tomato puree, in place of chopped tomatoes.

Concentrato e Estratto di Pomodoro (Tomato Paste and Tomato Extract): Tomato paste comes from cooking all the water content out of tomatoes, leaving a pure paste that, in the best of all worlds, tastes solely of the sweetness of tomato. Le nonne often use a little bit of tomato paste, sold in tubes of single and double concentrate, to add color, not taste, and to thicken the sauce. Choose double concentrate for stronger flavor. Tomato extract is a bright red, deep-tasting tomato concentrate that has the clean flavor of fresh tomatoes. It can be made by drying the tomatoes in the sun and then cooking them—a process that takes three days—or by leaving them raw and letting the paste concentrate, which takes a week. To come as close as possible to tomato extract, Anna Tasca Lanza, who makes her own at Regaleali, her estate in Sicily, recommends using three times as much sun-dried tomato paste as the amount of tomato extract called for.

3

ANTIPASTI

Before the Meal

CROSTONE CON FUNGHI
Crostone with Mushrooms

CROSTINI CON LE FAVE
Crostini with Pureed Fava Beans

GRANA SOTT'OLIO
A Grana Cheese Spread

OLIVE NERE CONDITE
Oil-Cured Black Olives Flavored with Orange Zest, Garlic, and Olive Oil

CRESCIA DI MONTEFELTRO
Flaky Disks of Dough from the Montefeltro Family of Urbino

INVOLTINI DI MELANZANE
Eggplant Rolls with Mozzarella, Prosciutto, and Basil Leaves

PETTOLE RIPIENE
Bread Fritters Flavored with Sweet Peppers and Capers

SALVIA FRITTA
Fried Sage Leaves

POMODORI SECCHI IMBOTTITI
Sun-Dried Tomato Sandwiches

POLPETTINE DI TONNO E PATATE
Crispy Deep-Fried Tuna and Potato Balls

GNOCCHI FRITTI
Light and Airy Crisp Fritters

CROSTONE CON FUNGHI

Crostone with Mushrooms

—

Serves 4

&veryone in Luisa Cappelli's immediate and extended family is passionate about food and cooks magnificently. This recipe, from her brother's mother-in-law, is a perfect light dish for brunch, lunch, or Sunday night supper. Cut the crostone in small pieces and they become exceptional crostini for an antipasto platter.

4 large slices of country-style bread, cut ½ inch thick

7 ounces fresh porcini or portobello mushrooms or 1 ounce dried porcini and 6 ounces brown mushrooms, preferably cremini or portobellos

1 stick (4 ounces) unsalted butter

Salt

6 eggs

Freshly ground black pepper

2 tablespoons hot milk

4 very thin slices of ham, preferably Italian

Preheat the broiler. Put the slices of bread on a baking sheet, set them in the broiler, and lightly toast on both sides, about 4 minutes a side, until they become pale golden outside but remain soft inside. Don't let them dry out. Keep warm.

Clean the fresh mushrooms with a mushroom brush or a moist cloth. If you use dried porcini, soak them in warm water to cover for 30 minutes, drain, and squeeze out the excess moisture. Luisa uses a mezzaluna to cut them in small dice, but a knife will do just as well. Melt ½ stick of the butter in a large heavy pan, add the mushrooms and a little salt, and cook over medium heat for 10 minutes, until they are tender and have released all their liquid. Set aside to cool to room temperature.

While the mushrooms are cooking, beat the eggs in a large bowl with salt and pepper. Off the heat beat in the remaining butter in very small flakes. Don't worry if they aren't well incorporated; they will melt during the cooking. Add the mushrooms to the eggs and return the mixture to the pan in which you cooked the mushrooms. Set it over very low heat and cook as for a very slow scramble, mixing with a wooden spoon until the eggs coagulate like a cream. Remove from the fire and add the hot milk very slowly, stirring continually until the mixture forms a cream that is not too dense.

Trim the ham to fit the pieces of bread and put a slice on each slice of warm bread. Spoon a little of the mushroom and egg cream on top and serve immediately on a warm platter.

BREAD (*Pane*): Be sure to have a country loaf, a hearth bread with a crisp crust and a porous interior, of the type often referred to as Italian or French bread. Remember that when it becomes stale, the bread is embarking on a new phase of its existence in which it can be sliced and grilled as bruschetta and crostini, diced as croutons, laid at the bottom of a bowl of soup, indeed incorporated into every part of the meal from primi to dolci— don't miss bread pudding for dessert. Slices of stale bread soaked in vinegar provide a base for crostini toppings and also keep sauces from separating.

Profile of *Luisa Cappelli*

 It is easy to imagine Luisa Cappelli rocking the cradle of one grandchild, teaching another one Latin, painting the shutters, putting up olive oil and exceptional Vin Santo, and cooking a delicious meal, almost all at the same time. Pacing through the living room pointing out portraits of the generations before her, she exudes nervous energy. Words rush from her in a torrent, memories and stories tumbling out as if they had been dammed up for a long time. Short and lithe with glowing pink skin stretched over high cheekbones and stylishly cut short gray hair tucked behind her ears, she is elegant even in the clothes in which she putters on the property and makes order in the house. Deeply religious and deeply connected to her family, she writes books for her grandchildren and makes up nursery songs for them. A letter her granddaughter left under her pillow says, "*Nonna, grazie per esistere.*" ("Grandmother, thank you for being alive.")

Born in Tuscany and married to a Genoese, she lived until recently in Genoa with her three children—two daughters and one son—and six grandchildren. She was widowed after a marriage that was a great love story, with immense joys and sadnesses. One rough spot: when she was thirty-seven and he was forty-five, she unexpectedly became pregnant. Her husband wouldn't speak to her for five days. "*Sono anziano*—I am ancient," he said; "how is there time for fatherhood in my immensely demanding life?"

When Luisa's mother produced her brother, Luisa's grandfather was a good deal more outspoken. "It's lucky you had a son; otherwise you'd have to have kept producing children until you had a son, even it if meant you were on your way to menopause." The grandfather, a handsome prepossessing man with an elegantly trimmed white mustache, commanded everyone, banging his walking stick on the ground and announcing, "*Il padrone sono io.*" He was insistent that a son be the firstborn. "See," says Luisa, gesturing toward an ancient cypress that must have been forty feet tall. It was planted when her brother was born. For her, she says, "not even a root." Women counted for little and had no power. Luisa's mother brought incredible possessions and wealth to the marriage, but it made no difference. She still had to ask her hus-

band for everything, even for permission to buy a pair of shoes. In the family the children spoke in the "*lei*," the impersonal third-person singular, to parents and grandparents as a mark of respect. For Luisa, even at sixty-eight, it is still an enormous emotional leap to be able to give the "*tu*."

During World War II, the family lived in Florence in a villa with a huge garden and Renaissance bronzes. Once during the threshing of the grain, Luisa's mother hid a suitcase full of jewelry in one of the many mounded sheaves of wheat. When she went to excavate it, it was nowhere to be found and it took a long search, "like playing hide and seek," Luisa remembers, to find it. They hid all their belongings in a huge building on the Via Guicciardini, a street that the Germans bombed in its entirety as they withdrew from the city. They lost everything. The grandfather died shortly thereafter at eighty-four.

Of the four family homes she has known during her life, she has chosen to stay in the beautiful Tuscan country house set on a vine-covered hillside outside Panzano in Chianti where her grandfather and father were born and lived. She left everything in Genoa—children, grandchildren, the house of her married life with all its possessions—to be in the huge house that holds what she calls "the baggage of my memories." She lives with a mixture of melancholy and the comfort of being embraced by family history, surrounded not only by her husband's collection of modern paintings by such artists as Picabia and Sonia Delaunay but also by many beautiful family antiques, shelves of leather-bound books, and walls and bureau tops full of family photographs. She walks in a garden defined by huge terra-cotta pots holding lemon trees; cypresses dot its periphery.

When she decided to make the Tuscan house her permanent home, she worked for fifteen days straight to get the kitchen in order. It is the essence of a fine country kitchen with its great old beams, charming blue-and-white ceramic tiles with a rosy pink dot at their center, and the handsome sixteenth-century wooden wardrobe in which she stores plates and silverware. She kept all the equipment of earlier days: an old chestnut roasting pan with its perforated bottom, pans with 4-foot-long handles, even a very old-fashioned coffee grinder with its simple manual mechanism. She makes cold-pressed extra-virgin olive oil from her olives and leaves it in large terra cotta containers that glow with the patina of age. New rules require the holding tanks to be stainless steel, but she put her foot down and said absolutely not! "Oil has been put up since 1400 and always stored in large terra-cotta jars. I put up the oil, and I will not change!" As she talks her hands are constantly in motion, pointing to the old stove, scooping up dried beans and letting them fall through her fingers, pulling out drawers and extracting antique implements from cabinets. She opens the big wooden top of one of the containers and the deep rich perfume of the oil fills the space. It is only a step or two to the barrel-vaulted stone cantina where she stores her blond, soft-edged Vin Santo. She still makes the aromatic, aged amber-colored dessert wine as it was made 100 years ago, and she serves it not only at the end of a meal, as is de rigueur in Tuscany, but chilled, as an aperitif. "It is wonderful with pigeon pâté," she said, or even, I think, with the rustic Tuscan equivalent, her *crostini di milza*, crostini made with calf's spleen that tastes very much like liver.

Every summer Luisa gives a huge party in the garden for which she cooks for two days straight and serves food at tables under large white canvas umbrellas. The offerings, many and various, are made with the same precision and dynamism visible in other facets of her life. She is full of confidence in her recipes and stories about members of her family who are also phenomenal cooks. When making the pheasant dish she loves, *fagiano alla senese*, she admonished, "Set them in the pan, one next to each other, like fiancés." Asked to describe the flavorings in the sausage that go over the top, she looks exasperated. "They're sausages from Falorni," the famous butcher in nearby Greve in Chianti, "ask him." "Use the very best white wine, even better than what you'd use at table, and don't quite burn it all off."

Her recipes come from various family members, all exceptional cooks. Luisa Cappelli's mother-in-law is from Piedmont and couldn't even make coffee when she was married in 1918. To rectify that egregious problem, the first thing that her fiancé did was to send her to Prato to learn to cook pure Tuscan food. For the next two decades she became an obsessed cook and since she had two maids, it was not a problem that it took her two days to make lasagne. Her husband loved to eat and insisted that all the food that came to their table be made at home. And it was. She made galantinas and two weeks before Christmas every year, she began the arduous preparations of stuffing a capon with a filling of meat, hard-boiled eggs, truffles, and pistachio nuts. It was understood that she had to have dishes ready for the times when her husband would call from the office to say he was bringing people home with him for lunch, but once he arrived unexpectedly with guests and realized with a glance that the lasagne on the table had not been made by his wife's hands. "*Portami il sallacino*" ("Bring me the salted herring,") he commanded, refusing to countenance, much less touch, the alien pasta.

Luisa learned to cook from her mother-in-law and still makes her ultimate ribollita, which, when cooked in all its complexity, takes a full three days. Her instructions are both detailed and nuanced: "Cut the softened rind of a prosciutto into pieces and put them in a big, big, big earthenware pot with soaked cannellini beans. . . . Take all the vegetables imaginable and possible, sauté and add them, and cook with just the veil of a simmer. . . . Cover the pot with a hermetic seal and don't even peek until at least an hour and a half have gone by. . . . Toss in the salt at the precise moment that you turn off the heat and the boiling stops. If they sit for a few hours, the beans get even better." Once, when a doctor had to decline a dinner invitation at the last moment, she sent him a tureen of the ribollita and he, in turn, showered her with a massive bouquet of flowers.

Luisa's passions—food, family, religion, poetry—and her immense energy and depth draw people to her. When her husband was in the hospital near the end of his life, a sixteen-year-old boy in a nearby bed was so entranced that he wrote poetry for her. Four years later, they are still corresponding.

CROSTINI CON LE FAVE

Crostini with Pureed Fava Beans

—

Serves 6 to 8

ere's Nella Galletti's Umbrian twist on traditional Tuscan bruschetta. She uses dried favas instead of white cannellini beans, and with that one tiny regional difference produces a distinctly creamy and nutty spread for lightly grilled bread. Crostini are served as little appetizing tastes at the beginning of a meal, but make two or three different types and you'll have the centerpiece of a Sunday supper, a light lunch, or part of a buffet.

> 1½ cups plus 2 tablespoons (8 ounces) dried fava beans
>
> 1 medium onion, roughly chopped
>
> 1½ teaspoons sea salt
>
> 2 to 3 tablespoons fruity extra-virgin olive oil, plus extra for drizzling (optional)
>
> 8 slices of country-style bread, cut ½ inch thick and halved
>
> 3 large garlic cloves, cut in half and lightly crushed
>
> 2 tablespoons finely chopped flat-leaf parsley

Soak the dried favas covered with abundant cold water overnight or for 12 hours before you plan to cook them. Drain and slip them out of their skins. If the skins cling too tightly, cook the beans in boiling water for 5 to 10 minutes, drain, and peel.

Set the skinned beans in a saucepan with the onion and just enough water to cover them. Turn heat to medium, bring to a boil, and add the salt. Immediately lower heat to a simmer, then cover and cook until the water has almost evaporated and the beans are tender but not mushy, about 30 minutes. Check to be sure there is enough liquid; if the water has evaporated, add more.

Drain the beans, reserving the bean cooking water, and puree them in a food processor or blender with 2 to 3 tablespoons extra-virgin olive oil. Taste for salt.

Preheat the grill or broiler and grill or broil the bread 4 to 5 minutes until lightly browned on each side by setting the slices 4 to 6 inches from the heat source. While still warm, rub each slice with some of the crushed garlic, letting it release its fragrance into the bread; then bathe each with a little of the bean cooking water and spread a bit of the fava puree over each. Drizzle with a little extra olive oil, if you want, and sprinkle parsley over the top. Serve warm, if possible.

TIP: Nella says that cooking soaked, skinned dried fava beans in water no hotter than is comfortable for your hand tenderizes the beans, but the cooking time is 10 to 20 minutes longer. To puree the beans, you will need to use ¼ cup more olive oil.

GRANA SOTT'OLIO

A Grana Cheese Spread

—

Makes 1 cup

When women in the area just outside Parma make a cheese spread, they have a choice. They can take a freshly made cheese that has developed cracks as it sits in the circular wooden mold, indicating some hidden defect, and add some dry Malvasia wine and a little cream, or they can use a lightly aged grana and just mix it with olive oil. A perfect recipe: two ingredients produce a simple topping for antipasti or a mid-afternoon *merenda* or snack. Who could want more?

> **3 cups (12 ounces) finely grated grana cheese**
> **10 to 12 tablespoons light olive oil, preferably Ligurian**

Place the cheese in a bowl. Work 4 to 5 tablespoons of the oil into the grated cheese by massaging it with your fingers and mixing it in very well. Cover and leave at room temperature for 7 to 10 days. The mixture will become very dry. Add 1 to 2 more tablespoons of oil, mix in well, and transfer the mixture to a sterilized jar. Cover with the remaining olive oil. The mixture keeps in the refrigerator tightly covered for at least a month.

OLIVE NERE CONDITE

Oil-Cured Black Olives Flavored
with Orange Zest, Garlic, and Olive Oil

—

Makes 2 cups

Nella Galletti

When Nella Galletti's mother made this delicious antipasto, she started with large black uncured olives, washed them well, and then put them in a wood-burning oven at the lowest possible heat where they dried for 2 or 3 days until they were dry and deeply grooved with wrinkles. Only then did she rub them with olive oil to soften their skins. My approach is much easier: start with oil-cured black olives and toss them with flavors to make them spicy, perfect to nibble with chips of Parmigiano-Reggiano cheese and a glass of wine. They will keep well tightly sealed in the refrigerator for several weeks.

> 1 orange
> 1 small garlic clove
> **Freshly ground black pepper**
> **2 cups (12 ounces) oil-cured black olives**
> **Extra-virgin olive oil (optional)**

Peel the orange with a vegetable peeler or orange zester, being careful to remove only the zest of the orange rind and none of the white pith. Chop the zest into tiny, tiny dice.

Smash the garlic clove with the side of a large knife to remove the skin and chop into very tiny dice. Several hours before you plan to serve them, mix together the orange zest, garlic, pepper, and olives to let their flavors mingle. Leave them at room temperature. If the olives seem at all dry, massage them with just enough olive oil to permeate their skins. Cover them well and they will keep in the refrigerator for several weeks.

To store them longer, cover them with just enough oil to cover and keep them moist.

VARIATION: Add ½ tablespoon slightly crushed fennel seeds.

VARIATION: Add the diced zest of 1 fragrant lemon, such as a Meyer lemon.

Olives: Every grandmother to whom I spoke had her own recipe for putting up olives. That doesn't necessarily mean that they have their own olive trees or even that they live in the countryside. They need only go to the greengrocer any time in the late fall when crates of various types of ripe olives appear for sale. Annita di Fonzo Zannella in Lazio does pick her own olives before they become too ripe (so they won't go soft in the brine) and puts them in water for 2 months, then changes the water and adds 1⅓ ounces of coarse salt for every 2½ pounds of olives. Ausilia d'Arienzo in Molise, on the other hand, adds 2⅔ ounces of salt to every 2⅛ pounds of very mature black olives and leaves them for 40 days in a glass jar without any water. Then she boils water, cools it to room temperature, and adds 1 quart to every 4¼ pounds of olives. When it is time to eat them, she drains as many olives as she needs, dips them into finely minced dried oregano and *peperoncino* (red pepper flakes), and puts them out on the table. The aunt of Giovanna Passannanti's friend Rosalba pits and fills white Sicilian olives with a mixture of toasted bread crumbs, chopped almonds, lemon juice or vinegar, and a thread of olive oil; sprinkles them with sugar and cinnamon; lets them sit for a day; and then watches them disappear.

Black olives that are preserved in brine appear frequently in Italian recipes. Use Italian olives if you can find them—small Ligurian olives, such as Taggiasca, any of those put up by Colonna in Molise, or Gaetas from southern Italy. Use Niçoise olives or Moroccan olives, but stay away from tasteless pitted black olives from California or Greek kalamatas, which are too assertive for many Italian dishes. Brined green olives may come from Liguria or Molise; large, sweet and tender Ascolane olives come from Le Marche, and there are even larger cracked olives from Greece. French Picholines are also fine. Black oil-cured olives are often flavored with herbs.

CRESCIA DI MONTEFELTRO

Flaky Disks of Dough from the Montefeltro Family of Urbino

—

Makes 12, serves 8 to 12 people

This wonderful little flat round of dough has all the flakiness and delicacy of puff pastry without requiring any of its complicated folds or turns. It is made only in the region called Le Marche, where I learned it from Amalia Ceccarelli di Ridolfi in Falconara Marittima on the Adriatic coast near Ancona. She, in turn, learned it from her mother, who was a cook for the great families of Urbino.

I saw Amalia cook her crescia on a grill directly over the coals, but I have also seen it cooked on a stoneware griddle set over a flame tamer. I find I have my greatest success when I heat a ridged cast-iron griddle to fiery hotness and cook the crescia in 3 or 4 minutes. Serve this delicate multilayered treat with fresh figs, paper-thin slices of prosciutto, and shards of Parmigiano-Reggiano cheese in the summer; let two toasted walnuts take the place of the figs in the winter.

> **4 cups (20 ounces) unbleached all-purpose flour**
> **¾ teaspoon sea salt**
> **3 eggs**
> **¼ cup olive oil for the dough, plus ¾ cup for brushing the dough**
> **¾ cup milk**
> **Sea salt for sprinkling**

Place the flour and salt in a large mixing bowl and make a well in the center. Beat together the eggs, ¼ cup of the olive oil, and milk, pour them into the well in the flour mixture, and mix until they come together as a dough. Move the dough to a lightly floured work surface and knead for about 3 to 4 minutes, or until the dough is firm and velvety. Flatten the dough, brush both sides with olive oil, cover with a kitchen towel, and let it rest for 20 minutes.

With a rolling pin, roll the dough into a 16 × 9-inch rectangle that is slightly less than ¼ inch thick. Brush it lightly with olive oil and then roll it up. Using the palms of your hands to roll the dough, stretching it as you work, roll it into a log that is 24 to

28 inches long. Cut the log of dough into 12 equal pieces, each about 2 to 2¼ inches wide. Shape into a ball by first pinching the cut edges together and then rolling it roughly into a round the size of a lemon. Set the first one aside to rest, cover it with a towel, and repeat with the remaining pieces. Finally, flatten and use your rolling pin to roll each ball into a circle that is about 5 inches in diameter. Brush each one well with olive oil.

Set a ridged cast-iron griddle over the highest possible heat on your cooktop. It is ready when a drop of water dances on the surface. Place 1 crescia on the griddle and turn it four or five times during the few minutes that it cooks, brushing the surface with olive oil each time you turn it and poking it with a fork to deflate any air bubbles that form. Remove after 2 to 3 minutes when it is as blistered on both sides as a tortilla and has pronounced brown grill marks. Brush it with olive oil one final time, sprinkle with a pinch of salt, and serve hot.

INVOLTINI DI MELANZANE

Eggplant Rolls with Mozzarella, Prosciutto, and Basil Leaves

—

Serves 6 to 8

I don't know if this is what Neapolitans eat when they go to heaven, but I'm sure that anyone still on earth finding it as a first course or a vegetable side dish would be rhapsodic. The genuine, pure flavors of the best Italian ingredients are combined when a slice of lightly sautéed eggplant holds a single slice of fresh mozzarella, a sprinkling of Parmigiano-Reggiano cheese, and a thin slice of prosciutto. Set them on a wash of tomato sauce, if you want, and bake only until the cheese melts.

Use the dark purple oval eggplant, not the round globe ones, for these delicious Neapolitan treats. You can use either prosciutto crudo or cooked ham in the roll-ups.

> 2 (about 1 pound) oval purple eggplants, firm and glossy
> Coarse sea salt
> About 1 cup leaves of fresh basil
> 8 ounces best-quality mozzarella

Extra-virgin olive oil for sautéeing
1 to 1¼ cups (4 to 5 ounces) freshly grated Parmigiano-Reggiano cheese
4 ounces prosciutto slices, trimmed to fit the eggplant slices
Salt
Freshly ground black pepper

Peel and cut the eggplants horizontally into ½-inch-thick slices. Sprinkle them with coarse salt and leave to drain in a colander for 1 hour. Pat dry.

Preheat the oven to 350°F. and lightly oil a large, deep baking pan.

Clean the basil leaves with a damp paper towel. Slice the mozzarella the same thickness as the eggplant slices and then again to fit on the eggplant.

Warm the olive oil in a large, heavy sauté pan and sauté the eggplant slices very briefly until they are lightly golden and soft. Remove from pan to a work surface. On each slice of eggplant place 1 basil leaf, 1 slice mozzarella, ½ teaspoon Parmigiano-Reggiano cheese, 1 slice prosciutto, and salt and pepper. Roll each up and fasten with a wooden toothpick.

Place the eggplant slices in the prepared baking pan, sprinkle them with the remaining Parmigiano-Reggiano, and bake for 20 to 25 minutes, until the mozzarella cheese melts. Let the eggplant rest briefly before serving.

VARIATION: Spread a wash of ½ to 1 cup tomato sauce over the bottom of the baking dish. Giovanna Passannanti makes a quick tomato *salsina* by adding a tiny bit of hot water to the best double-strength tomato extract.

PETTOLE

Fritters Flavored with Sweet Peppers and Capers

—

Serves 6 to 8

Everywhere I went in Apulia, women offered me pettole. I ate them on the great farms called *masserie*, I ate them in people's homes, and I ate them in the simplest possible situations. And why not? Pettole are simply little rounds of bread dough flavored with any number of ingredients—the choices are almost limitless—and then fried in bubbling hot oil where they swell in size and become crisp and golden. A perfect accompaniment for a glass of wine or an antipasto platter.

If your dough has risen before you have time to finish the process, don't worry. Press the dough down, allow it to rise again, and proceed.

1 small (about 4 to 8 ounces) Yellow Finn or Yukon Gold potato
½ sweet red pepper
2 tablespoons capers, preferably salt-cured
¾ cup plus 1 to 2 tablespoons warm water, 105° to 115°F.
½ teaspoon active dry yeast
2 cups (10 ounces) unbleached all-purpose flour
1¼ teaspoons sea salt
Extra-virgin olive oil for frying
Salt for sprinkling

Boil the potato. As soon as it is cool enough to handle, peel the potato and mash or press it through a ricer. Set aside to cool to room temperature. Peel the sweet pepper with a vegetable peeler and remove the ribs and seeds. Cut the pepper into small dice to measure ¼ cup. Rinse the capers and set them in a bowl of cold water for 15 minutes. Drain well and chop the capers roughly.

To make the dough for pettole, pour the water into a mixing bowl, sprinkle the yeast over the top, and whisk it in. Let it stand until it becomes creamy, about 10 minutes. Stir in the riced potato, flour, and salt in two additions, and mix until the dough comes together but is still noticeably moist and soft. Turn the dough out onto a lightly floured work surface and knead for 7 or 8 minutes, until the dough no longer sticks to the surface. Then flatten the dough, sprinkle the peppers and capers over the surface, leaving a 1-inch margin all around, roll up the dough, and knead them in for a minute or two.

Rising: Place the dough in a lightly oiled bowl, cover with plastic wrap, and let rise for at least 2 hours. If it more than doubles, do not worry.

Shaping and frying: Keep a small bowl of water nearby. Using a teaspoon, a melon baller, or your fingers, scoop out a large olive-sized piece of the dough. Moisten the palms of your hands and roll the dough into a ball. Continue until all the dough is used up.

Pour the oil to a depth of 1½ inches in a deep, heavy pan and bring it to 375°F. for frying. If you don't have a thermometer, test the oil by dropping a tiny piece of the dough into the oil; if it bubbles vigorously, the oil is ready. Gently slide the pettole, one by one, onto a slotted spoon and into the oil. Be careful not to crowd the pan. Fry until well puffed and golden, 5 to 8 minutes. Drain on absorbent towels, sprinkle with a little salt, and serve immediately.

FLAVOR VARIATIONS:

- Knead in ½ cup parboiled and chopped cauliflower.

- Knead in ¼ cup finely chopped tomato and ¼ cup finely chopped onion.

- Knead in pieces of 2 or 3 anchovies, well rinsed and filleted.

- Knead in ¼ cup (1 ounce) freshly grated Parmigiano-Reggiano cheese, 1 minced garlic clove, 2 tablespoons finely chopped flat-leaf parsley, salt, and pepper.

SALVIA FRITTA

Fried Sage Leaves

—

Serves 4 to 8

One warm October afternoon in the countryside of the Veneto, Fausto Maculan gave us an excellent tour of his winery in Breganza and then invited us home for lunch in the seventeenth-century house where he was born and grew up. His mother, Pina Maculan, her sister, and the nurse who has been with the family for 50 years, made these delicious appetizers as a prelude to a spectacular meal.

Pina Maculan

Look for large aromatic sage leaves. Italians frequently fry sage leaves (and eggplant slices, zucchini blossoms, even the hearts of Treviso radicchio) as an appetizer or antipasto, something delicate to nibble with a glass of wine. The batter envelops the sage leaf, which is done in a flash, absorbing no oil at all.

> 1 egg
> 2 tablespoons all-purpose flour
> Salt
> 2 tablespoons beer
> Vegetable oil for frying, preferably sunflower seed or canola
> About 30 large leaves of fresh sage

Beat the egg in a mixing bowl, sift in the flour, and stir in the beer to form a slightly stiff batter. If it is too soft, add a little extra flour. The batter should be like a light tempura batter.

Pour the oil to a depth of ½ inch in a large frying pan and heat to 350°F., until a drop of the batter bubbles and dances when dropped into the oil. Dip the sage leaves into the batter, slide them into the oil, and cook, turning once, until they are golden. Drain on absorbent towels and serve immediately.

VARIATIONS:

FRIED ZUCCHINI BLOSSOMS: Do not wash the blossoms, just open and lightly clean their interiors with a moist paper towel. Sprinkle salt inside and fry as above.

FRIED EGGPLANT SLICES: Cut 1 eggplant in half, sprinkle with coarse salt, and let it drain in a colander over a plate for 1 hour. Drain, pat dry, and cut very, very thin slices, with a mandoline, a food processor blade, or, preferably, an electric slicer, using great caution. Make the above recipe adding 1 more tablespoon of flour and fry as directed.

TIP: Never add oil once you've begun frying eggplant slices. Start with an ample amount of *very* hot oil; otherwise the eggplant will absorb too much oil.

POMODORI SECCHI IMBOTTITI

Sun-Dried Tomato Sandwiches

—

Makes 15 sandwiches, serves 4 to 6

*S*ee," says Giovanna Passannanti, "Sicily has such incredible ingredients that it is easy for us to make fabulous food." Point proved with this extraordinary addition to an antipasto.

You have a choice of sun-dried tomatoes for this dish: you can buy them already plumped in oil or you can refresh them yourself in warm water. Taste your sun-dried tomatoes to be sure that they are not overly salty and look them over to be sure they are without holes.

> 30 sun-dried tomatoes
> ⅓ cup fine dry bread crumbs
> 2 garlic cloves, minced
> ⅓ cup grated pecorino cheese
> 2 to 3 tablespoons finely chopped flat-leaf parsley
> 4 to 5 tablespoons extra-virgin olive oil

If you are using dry-packed sun-dried tomatoes, soak them in warm water for 10 to 20 minutes to reconstitute them; pat them dry. If you are using sun-dried tomatoes in oil, barely pat them dry.

(continued)

In a small bowl combine the bread crumbs, garlic, grated cheese, parsley, and 2 tablespoons of the olive oil. Place half the tomatoes skin side down on a clean work surface. Pat 1 teaspoon of the mixture over the top of each, and cover with another sun-dried tomato, skin side up, to make a sandwich.

Warm the remaining olive oil in a large sauté pan and very gently sauté the tomato sandwiches for a minute or two on each side. Drain, pat them dry on paper towels and serve at room temperature as part of an antipasto or as an informal appetizer with a glass of wine.

DRIED TOMATOES (*Pomodori Secchi*): In the south, tomatoes are split in half, sprinkled with sea salt, placed on woven reed mats, then laid on roofs of houses and dried in the intense heat of the sun over the space of a week or two. Then they are put into widemouthed clay containers and immersed in extra-virgin olive oil, perhaps flavored with a little garlic and oregano. In the north, where the sun is not as strong, women dry tomatoes in the oven after the bread has been cooked and the heat has dropped to a very low temperature, leaving them to wrinkle and concentrate their flavors very slowly, 6 to 8 hours.

POLPETTINE DI TONNO E PATATE

Crispy Deep-Fried Tuna and Potato Balls

—

Serves 6 to 8

*A*dd these to your antipasti or hors d'oeuvres repertoire: little round creamy potatoes flavored with tuna and the bite of capers, two indigenous tastes of Sicily, fried to have a lightly crunchy exterior. The recipe is from the notebook of Giovanna Passannanti's grandmother from the nineteenth and early twentieth century, but it would be completely at home on the menu of a contemporary Italian restaurant.

1 pound boiling potatoes

7 ounces best-quality canned tuna packed in olive oil, drained

1 egg

2 full tablespoons freshly grated Parmigiano-Reggiano cheese

About ⅛ teaspoon freshly grated nutmeg

Freshly ground black pepper

1 teaspoon sea salt

2 tablespoons capers, preferably salt-cured, well rinsed and drained

1 tablespoon finely minced flat-leaf parsley

All-purpose flour

Olive oil for frying

Boil the potatoes in salted water to cover, then peel when cool enough to handle and pass them through a ricer into a bowl. Set them aside to cool to room temperature. Beat in the tuna, egg, cheese, nutmeg, pepper, and salt and mix well until you have a thick paste. Stir in the capers and the parsley. Use a teaspoon or melon baller to shape the mixture into small rounds. Sift the flour onto a dinner plate and roll each ball in the flour to coat the exteriors very lightly.

Pour the oil to a depth of 1½ inches into a large, deep frying pan and heat to 350°F. Test by dropping a tiny bit of the dough into the oil: it should dance in the oil and turn golden almost immediately. Use a slotted spoon to slide a few polpettine at a time into the pan and fry until they are golden on both sides, about 3 to 4 minutes.

(continued)

Drain on paper towels. Repeat with the rest of the polpettine. Serve immediately.

VARIATION: For potato pancakes with the bite of capers, make thin patties of the mixture and sauté in a little olive oil.

GNOCCHI FRITTI
Light and Airy Crisp Fritters
—

Makes about 8 dozen

*I*da Lancellotti has fried mountains of these airy crisp fritters in her lifetime. When she and her husband took over his family's osteria in Soliera outside Modena in 1976, she routinely made as many as 500 at a time and served them for breakfast with a quartered onion, crispy pork cracklings, sliced prosciutto and salame, chunks of Parmigiano-Reggiano cheese, and lots of Lambrusco wine.

Men came by for a little pick-me-up around 7:30 A.M., after two or three hours of work, bringing with them bread they had bought at the bakery and mortadella, salami, and hard-boiled eggs from the delicatessen; some even brought kidneys from the butcher shop and cooked them in the tiny kitchen. And always they drank lots of white wine and vermouth. Retired men arrived as well, and at midday the workers returned for coffee. Later they all played cards and bocce, eating gnocchi fritti and other salty snacks and slaking their thirst with lots of Lambrusco. And so life went until Ida, her husband, her sons and daughter-in-law and grandchildren turned the osteria into a restaurant in the seventies sometime after a man arrived one morning in the early sixties and asked for a brioche and cappuccino. They looked at him as if he were an extraterrestrial. She laughs now, but then there wasn't even any milk on the premises, and Ida had to fly out the back door to buy some. It was the symbolic end of an era. In time the bocce and card games disappeared, but Ida, cuoca straordinaria, never gave up making gnocchi fritti even after she began cooking more complex dishes rooted in local tradition.

Ida's prowess with gnocchi fritti is legendary. She made immense quantities for the celebration of her first son's birth in 1947 and says that even on noncelebratory occasions, kids often sit down and eat 20 to 30 at a time!

Ida is firm in her conviction that you have to have just the right ambiance when you are making these gnocchi fritti. When she made them for me she closed the doors to the kitchen and warned that drafts could cause problems. She is convinced that the warmth of her hands makes the recipe work for her while it may not turn out as well for someone else.

There usually isn't much salt in these fritters because they are always eaten hot with prosciutto, any kind of salami, other salty, highly flavored pork products, and cheese. If you are serving them with a different accompaniment, you might want to increase the salt to at least 2 teaspoons.

> 2 cups (10 ounces) pastry flour
> 2 cups (10 ounces) unbleached all-purpose flour, preferably stone-ground,
>   plus extra for shaping
> 1 teaspoon baking powder
> 1½ teaspoons sea salt
> ¾ to 1 cup milk, room temperature
> 3 tablespoons sunflower or canola oil
> ¾ cup sparkling water
> Grapeseed or canola oil for frying

Mixing: To make the dough by hand, put the flours and baking powder in a bowl with the salt, make a well in the center, and gradually work in the milk, oil, and sparkling water. You will have to mix and knead it for 10, 15, even 20 minutes until it is as soft and tender as pasta dough.

To make the dough in a heavy-duty standing mixer, place the flours, baking powder, and salt in the bowl, pour in the milk, oil, and sparkling water and mix for 5 minutes with the paddle. Change to the dough hook and knead for at least 3 minutes. The dough is very soft and tender when it is ready.

If you use a food processor, place the flours, baking powder, and salt in the work bowl with the steel blade in place. With the motor running, pour the combined milk, oil, and sparkling water down the feed tube and continue until a dough is formed. Take it out of the work bowl and knead on a floured work surface for about 5 minutes, until it is soft and tender.

(continued)

Rest: Cover the dough with a kitchen towel and let it stand 45 minutes to 1¼ hours. Ida Lancellotti's mother told her that the dough is ready when you see little bubbles under the skin. She is right. You really do see them.

Shaping: Divide the dough into 10 equal pieces. Cover the pieces you are not using with a kitchen towel. Keep extra flour nearby so you can dip the strips when they feel sticky. Using a rolling pin or a pasta machine, roll the pasta dough to ⅛-inch thickness. Ida uses her rolling pin, which is 3 feet long and looks like a baseball bat, and she first dips each piece of the dough in flour so it won't stick. If you are using a rolling pin, you should follow her example. I think it is easier to use a pasta machine and roll the dough down to the setting numbered 3. Lightly flour the rollers. Start them at the widest setting, flatten the dough, and guide it through the rollers. Repeat, then crank the rollers down to the next, narrower setting. Shortly after you begin rolling, you will have to cut the dough in half because it gets very long in no time. Continue rolling the dough until you have guided it through setting number 3. Be sure to keep extra flour on the board to counter any stickiness. The dough initially resists the rolling process, but ultimately it relaxes and feels very satiny.

Lay one strip of dough on your work surface and cover the ones you are not using. Use a crimped ravioli cutter to cut 4-inch-wide strips on the diagonal across the dough. Repeat, cutting on the diagonal in the opposite direction to produce lozenge shapes.

Frying: Pour the oil to a depth of 1½ inches in a deep fryer and heat it to 375°F. Using a slotted spoon, slide one or two gnocchi in at a time, being careful not to crowd them, or they will change shape and no longer look like lozenges. The dough should bubble and puff up immediately when it enters the oil. Cook, turning, until both sides are golden brown, 2 to 3 minutes. Drain on absorbent paper and eat immediately.

4

MINESTRE E ZUPPE

Soups

BRODO DI CARNE
Meat Broth

BRODO DI POLLO
Chicken Broth

BRODO MATTO
Crazy Broth

PASSATELLI
*Country Soup with Strands of Bread Crumbs
and Parmigiano-Reggiano Cheese*

MINESTRA COI CECI
Chickpea Soup with Tiny Pieces of Pasta

CUTURIEDDU
Rustic Lamb and Fennel Soup

ZUPPA DI PESCE
Fish Soup

GRAN FARRO
Farro and Bean Soup

L'ULTIMA RIBOLLITA
The Ultimate Ribollita

PANCOTTO PUGLIESE CON RUCHETTA E PATATE
Bread Soup with Arugula and Potatoes

MINESTRA DI FUNGHI E PATATE
Mushroom and Potato Soup from Friuli

CREMA DI ZUCCA E PATATE
Smooth Creamy Pumpkin and Potato Soup

ZUPPA CON LE ZUCCHINE
Zucchini Soup with Ribbons of Sweet Basil

ZUPPA VERA CONTADINA
A True Country Soup

BRODO DI CARNE

Meat Broth

—

Makes 3 to 4 quarts

*E*ugenia Azzali is not unusual in combining an assortment of beef and poultry and vegetables to make her meat broth, but she is very fortunate because her duck is homegrown and her garlic, onions, celery, and carrots are raised organically by her son. Even the eggs for the tagliatelle that float in the broth come from their chickens, providing a taste so deep and rich that visions of what life was once like in the Italian countryside floated in my head for days.

To make a good meat broth, you must put all the ingredients together in a deep pot, cover them with cold water, and only then turn on the heat and bring to a simmer. Serve the meat with a green sauce (page 243), and use the duck meat in an elegant ravioli filling, or serve it minced in a tomato sauce over pasta.

2 to 3 pounds beef pot roast, preferably the point of the rump

4 pounds lean duck, whole capon, or free-range chicken, cut up

1 garlic clove, unpeeled, lightly crushed

1 large onion, cut in half

2 celery ribs with leaves, roughly chopped

1 large carrot, roughly chopped

1 fresh tomato or 1 small canned tomato, drained

Salt

Put the pot roast, duck, and all the vegetables in a very large stockpot and add enough water to cover by 2 to 3 inches. Partially cover and slowly bring to boil, skimming any foam that rises to the surface. Reduce the heat to a simmer, cover, and cook for 3½ to 4 hours, skimming off any foam as necessary, until the broth is concentrated. Strain through a colander lined with cheesecloth or paper towels into a large bowl. Allow the broth to stand at room temperature until it is cool. Place in the refrigerator for several hours or overnight, until the fat comes to the surface and soldifies. Scoop up and discard the fat. Season with salt to taste.

You can use the broth immediately, set it in the refrigerator for 2 to 3 days, or freeze it for up to 3 months. If you store it in the refrigerator, boil it for 10 minutes before using.

VARIATIONS: Every grandmother gives her own touch to meat broth. Some add a tomato, some a bit of lemon zest, others a few mushrooms. One told me she put a chunk of Parmigiano-Reggiano rind into the pot, and two Sicilian women always add 3 or 4 allspice berries for flavor.

Profile of *Eugenia Azzali*
—

There are three front doors in Eugenia Azzali's house in Piadena, a tiny village in the countryside between Mantua and Cremona, because three families used to live in it, sharing the six rooms. Now all those rooms belong to Eugenia, a large woman with a soft round face and small eyes that often close against the strong light. She lives with her son Franco, better known as Miciu, a farmer who played the butcher in Bernardo Bertolucci's film *1900*, slaughtering the pig and cooking and serving it up in a great multitude of dishes.

When she was a girl, Genia, as she is called, could feed four people with a single hard-boiled egg by mashing it with olive oil, vinegar, and salt and making a liquid into which to dip the polenta that her family ate every night for dinner. She had never had a whole egg to herself until she married and went to live with her husband's family. They raised corn and ate polenta twice a day, and Genia assured me that while polenta may have been the food of the poor, during World War II if you had polenta you were rich.

For many years Genia, her husband, Pierino, and their two sons lived and worked inside a *cascina*, one of the many monumental brick-and-stone farms sprinkled across the flat plain of Lombardy. The tile-roofed farms were enormous; just the building housing the cows could be several hundred feet long with an open patchwork of brick that allowed air to circulate and dry the hay stored on the upper level.

Each farm enclosed an entire agricultural world with cattle and the dairy cows that gave milk for butter and cheese, fields of corn and wheat, orchards, and vegetable and herb gardens. Pierino worked the fields sowing, cleaning, and gathering, but he also milked cows and gave the milk to the *bergamini*, country people who tended the cows and cleaned the stalls and got their name because they originally came from Bergamo. Genia harvested tobacco leaves and she collected big bundles of corn on the giant brick terrace that served as the threshing ground for grains. She picked reeds and wicker that grew at the river's edge and made brooms with them. Her memories of sounds and smells from those years include the music of milk hitting the empty bucket when a cow was being milked; the susurrus of grain being sifted through a strainer; the brush of the broom sweeping together the kernels of newly threshed corn, and later, once they had dried, the scraping of the wooden bucket against the paved courtyard dividing polenta between the family (25 percent) and the padrone (75 percent). Men and women spent evenings together not in their homes, where burning wood for warmth was much too expensive, but in the stalls, heated by the breath of the cows. The women sewed while the men talked.

Everyone worked the land with animals, with hoes and spades and plows. Both men and women were often on their hands and knees, selecting, planting, and picking plants. How incredibly hard they worked and how long they worked—every day of their lives during the cycle of the agrarian year. During an arduous harvest, all they were given to eat at noon was bread and stracchino *piccante*, buttery stracchino cheese with a peppery bite.

Yearly contracts granted them the right to live in cascine without rent. Their salaries were paid in a quart of milk daily, in 6 *quintali*, about 1,320 pounds, of wheat annually, 1,700 pounds of corn, and almost 1,800 pounds of wood for heating and cooking. They were given a kitchen garden large enough to grow their own fruits and vegetables and to raise chickens. Eugenia used some of the wheat they were given to make dough for the bread that she took to the oven at the big farmhouse to be baked. They ate their country loaves with *puccin*, a dish made of spring onions and celery sautéed in oil with potato or cabbage and a bit of tomato conserve stirred in; if they were lucky enough to have a little meat, it was added as well.

The day I came to visit Genia, her leg was hurting so badly she spent half the time lying on the couch, her large round face contorted with pain. I was unnerved as she moaned, but Miciu called a very old spindly cousin to keep her company, and we all sat in the kitchen, laughing and eating and even singing later on. From time to time Genia would shout out a comment and join in the conversation and slowly everyone else's voices rose in response.

Miciu cooked on the fornello, a very old-fashioned stove that he and Genia still use. The burners on top were heated by logs of wood burned inside one inner compartment. What a lunch he made in consultation with his mother! There were flat ribbons of fresh pasta using five of the eggs he had collected earlier that morning mixed with the best organically grown, stone-ground wheat available. He combined meat and home-grown duck for the broth in which the pasta floated and he picked spinach that was still warm from the sun when he cooked it for us. And what made the *torta al burro* we ate for dessert so golden? Flour milled from their corn, of course.

Miciu cares deeply about tradition. He is keeping the ways of his grandparents alive by raising pigs and making his own salami and sausage, by raising free-range chickens, pheasants, and turkeys, and by growing the crops organically without any pesticides or commercial fertilizers so they preserve the tastes of the past. There were four of us at table in the kitchen—Miciu, Giovanni Morandi, a photographer, and Nadia Calestani, principal of a local school, a threesome who have been extremely close friends for decades. For two days I became the fourth—we went to friends in the city and countryside, to organic growers who are impeccable pasta producers. We ate a frittata made from Miciu's eggs, a taste so fresh, so quintessentially eggy and delicious that I shall never forget it.

Giovanni Morandi brought videos of his films on the rituals of the countryside—we watched the pig being killed and turned into enough salami and sausage to feed a family for a year, although it is too humid in Piadena to cure prosciutto or lardo. We watched the entire harvest of corn from seeds through the drying, and we saw a rural festival with its local band. Genia sat up and announced that they had no band when her husband died, because he asked instead that everyone be given a glass of wine. We also had wine at lunch and grappa too—no wonder there was so much singing afterward.

Watching the films of the rigors of the agricultural life, Miciu remembered cold winter days in the Mantuan countryside beginning with boiling broth and a huge dollop of red wine, a drink to give energy and restore the soul. Because he is so dedicated to preserving the old ways and is well aware of changes in taste over the years, he told me that as an experiment he once cooked half a piece of meat on the wood-burning stove and half of that same meat on the gas range. The difference in flavor and texture, just from those two different methods, was immense, which only confirmed how hard it is to duplicate the tastes of another time.

Things have changed immensely since Genia first married. Most cascine have been abandoned and the farmworkers have scattered, many driven to the cities where they found work as concierges, porters, and manual workers. Genia and Miciu, however, have stayed on the land and Miciu has been an organic farmer for thirty years, raising and selling pigs, partridge, turkeys, chickens and their eggs, as well as fruits and vegetables. He is doing his best to help a large nearby cooperative that is in charge of organic production in Italy and itself produces vegetables, poultry, and wheat that is made into pasta. Forty years ago the area was intensely cultivated with vines and the fields were used for cows that gave milk for dairy products. Now, Miciu laments, European Economic Community directives have made cows worth more to their owners dead than alive because the EEC has substantially lowered the approved quotas of production of milk and cheese for Italy. By paying dairy farmers large sums to destroy their cows, they have essentially transformed the area. It is now planted with corn and with sunflowers, which are used for their oil and seeds. Miciu is well aware that the organic cooperative attracts huge numbers of visitors from schools, and he is hopeful that the farmers will succeed in enticing others to return the land to organic production. Meanwhile he and Genia continue to live on what they produce, buying only their bread. They may no longer inhabit the self-contained world of the cascina and there may not be any cows to keep them warm, but they still eat in rhythm with the seasons not because they have turned their back on modern conveniences, but because they believe that such a way of life is healthier for them and the land. Careful economy and a respect for nature permeate their lives to the point that Miciu and Genia heat their house not with expensive imported gas or oil, as most people do, but with wood from their trees, which they burn in the old stove, creating hot water for the steam that circulates in the pipes.

BRODO DI POLLO

Chicken Broth

—

Makes 4 quarts

*N*o book about Italian grandmothers would be complete without a recipe for chicken broth, the delicious base for all manner of soups, risotti, and chicken and vegetable dishes. New mothers in Le Marche once ate tiny pasta squares floating in chicken broth made from chickens furnished by friends and relatives. The chickens themselves weighed only 2 pounds, but they produced fresh eggs for breakfast that were so delicious that they remain embedded in the memories of many women to this day.

One grandmother I met pierces one of the onion slices with 3 cloves to intensify the flavor of the broth and you may choose to follow her example.

When the broth is finished, remove the chicken and eat it hot with *Salsa Verde* (page 243), or take the meat off the bones and use it to make *'Ncip 'Nciap* (page 218), or *Polpette di Pollo* (page 216).

4 quarts water
1½ teaspoons coarse sea salt
1 chicken, broiler or roaster, 4 to 6 pounds
2 red onions, peeled and quartered
2 celery ribs with leaves, cut into 2-inch segments
2 carrots, washed but not peeled, cut into 2-inch segments
7 sprigs of flat-leaf parsley

Bring the water and coarse salt to a boil in 7- or 8-quart stockpot. Place the chicken in the water with the onions, celery, carrots, and parsley sprigs; bring it back to a boil, skimming off any foam, reduce the heat to a simmer, partially cover the pot, and cook for 1½ to 2 hours, depending on the size of the chicken, until tender.

Remove the chicken and set it aside. Strain the broth into a large bowl through a colander lined with cheesecloth or paper towels. Allow it to cool and then skim off the fat. You can use the broth immediately, keep it in the refrigerator for 2 to 3 days, or freeze it. If you store the broth, boil it for 10 minutes before using it.

TIP: Numerous nonne say the same thing: to make a good meat or chicken broth, put all the meats and chicken in a deep pot with vegetables, cover them generously with cold water, and bring to a boil. To poach chicken or pieces of meat, as for bollito misto, bring the water to a boil and then add the chicken and meat.

BRODO MATTO

Crazy Broth

Makes 4 cups

Why crazy? Because it's ridiculously easy to make. Once you've discovered this trick for making tasty broth, you won't worry when you don't have any on hand. Italian celery is smaller and tastier than ours, so I use the leafy tops to add flavor. I sometimes add a carrot and onion as well.

> 4 cups water
> 3 ribs celery with leaves, very roughly chopped
> 4 bouillon cubes, either chicken or meat, very preferably without MSG
> 1 carrot (optional)
> 1 onion, quartered (optional)
> Salt (optional)

Put the water, celery, bouillon cubes, and optional carrot and onion in a saucepan and simmer for 20 minutes. That's all. Taste for salt. Nonna Lucia Rossi Pavanello removes the vegetables, but you might want to press them through a food mill or puree them and return them to the broth.

Nonna Lucia cooks her fine ribbons of homemade pasta in the broth and produces fantastic soup in minutes.

Passatelli

Country Soup with Strands of Bread Crumbs and Parmigiano-Reggiano Cheese

—

Serves 4 to 6

*S*everal nonne in Le Marche wanted to show me how they made passatelli. I was more than willing as long as the instruction included tasting, since I knew that passatelli were strands of a mixture of Parmesan cheese, bread crumbs, and eggs flavored with nutmeg and lemon rind and pressed directly into steaming chicken soup.

Elvira Bettini

Efresina Rosichini, Elvira Bettini, and Adele Rondini, three women from Le Marche, all use handfuls or lumps as their standard measurements for this recipe so I had to do a bit of translating to divine precise equivalents. Two of the women use a bouillon cube to deepen the flavor of the soup—if you follow their lead, be sparing with the salt—while Efresina adds an entirely new dimension by infusing the broth with the earthy taste of porcini mushrooms.

Passatelli are pressed through a special Italian ricer with holes the size of the tip of a ballpoint pen; a regular ricer is much too fine. The larger disk of a food mill, a spaetzle maker, and the coarse disk of the versatile potato ricer available in The Baker's Catalogue and the Williams-Sonoma catalogue are excellent alternatives. See the Source Guide to Equipment.

Pass freshly grated Parmigiano-Reggiano on the side.

½ cup (2 ounces) freshly grated Parmigiano-Reggiano cheese
⅓ cup fine dry bread crumbs
Grated zest of 1 lemon
A dusting of freshly grated nutmeg
1 egg
1 teaspoon unsalted butter, room temperature
6 cups meat or chicken broth (preferably homemade), all fat skimmed off
1 meat or chicken bouillon cube (optional)
Salt

(continued)

Place the grated cheese and bread crumbs in a mound in a bowl. Grate the lemon zest and nutmeg directly on top, and make a well in the center. Break in an egg and with a fork or wooden spoon, incorporate the dry ingredients as well as you can. Stir in the butter until it is well combined and then start kneading, using the palms of your hands, until the mixture is as tender as pasta dough. Cover the bowl with plastic wrap or a towel and let it rest for 1 to 2 hours.

Bring the broth to a boil in a large heavy pot. Add the bouillon cube if you are using it. Press the passatelli dough directly into it through the coarse disk of a food mill, ricer, or spaetzle maker. Elvira describes the strands, which are about the length of a finger, as looking like silkworms in search of mulberry leaves. Be sure to let the strands fall all over the entire surface of the broth so they are well distributed. Let them simmer for no more than 2 minutes, then turn off the heat and allow the soup to rest for 2 or 3 minutes more. Taste for seasoning and serve immediately.

VARIATION: Soak 1 ounce dried porcini mushrooms in 1 cup of the chicken or meat broth for at least 30 minutes. Drain them in a sieve lined with cheesecloth or two layers of paper towels. Squeeze the porcini, letting any extra moisture fall into the broth in which they soaked. Wash them in several changes of cold water and chop them roughly. Strain the broth through a sieve layered with cheesecloth or paper towels before using.

MINESTRA COI CECI

Chickpea Soup with Tiny Pieces of Pasta

—

Serves 6 to 8

*N*ella Galletti was nostalgic as she remembered making and eating this delicious bean and pasta soup on the days that she and her husband went into the fields to strip ears of corn from their stalks. She didn't have to buy a single ingredient except the salt. "We had chickens, but I usually saved the eggs they laid. When I put one in the pasta it was a special occasion, but now I always buy the tiny dried pastine that are made with eggs."

This nourishing soup is almost as thick as a stew. You could easily serve it with a fork. Countrywomen like Nella used to sprinkle a tiny bit of flour in the soaking water to soften the hull of the bean, although they now use baking soda, which has the same effect and works in less time.

2½ cups (1 pound) dried chickpeas

2 teaspoons baking soda

3 tablespoons extra-virgin olive oil

1 medium onion, diced

2 garlic cloves, minced

2 branches of fresh rosemary

1 tablespoon tomato paste dissolved in a little warm water

Salt

Freshly ground black pepper

4 cups chicken broth or 4 chicken bouillon cubes
    dissolved in 4 cups hot water

4 quarts water

1 tablespoon coarse sea salt

12 ounces quadrucci, pastine, or other tiny pasta

Freshly grated pecorino romano or Parmigiano-Reggiano cheese

(continued)

About 12 hours before you plan to make the soup, put the chickpeas in a large bowl and add cold water to cover them by 3 inches. Add the baking soda to soften their skins, and leave for at least 12 hours.

Drain and wash the beans very well under running cold water. Place them in a 5-quart pot and cover with 3 inches of fresh cold water. Bring to a boil and cook at a steady simmer over low heat until they are almost soft, 1½ to 2 hours.

While the beans are cooking, warm the olive oil in a sauté pan with the onion, garlic, and rosemary and sauté over low heat only until the garlic is pale golden. Add the dissolved tomato paste, salt, and a bit of pepper and simmer for 10 to 15 minutes more. Set aside. Discard the rosemary branches and add contents of the sauté pan to the beans when 30 minutes of their cooking time remains.

When the beans are cooked, drain them, reserving 1 cup of the cooking liquid. Add the chicken broth to the reserved bean liquid and mix in well. Stir this broth mixture into the beans.

Shortly before you are ready to serve the soup, bring a large pot with 4 quarts of water to a rolling boil, add the coarse salt and the small squares of pasta and cook until al dente, about 4 to 6 minutes. Drain the pasta, stir it into the bean mixture, taste for salt, and cook for 2 minutes to incorporate well. Serve immediately with grated pecorino cheese.

Cuturieddu
Rustic Lamb and Fennel Soup
—
Serves 6

*P*aola Pettini, a cooking teacher in Bari who is dedicated to preserving the dishes of Apulia, worked for many years with a countrywoman she knew only as Antonia da Bari, Antonia from Bari. When Antonia reached her eightieth birthday, Paola honored the occasion by collecting and printing recipes for the dishes of Antonia's family in a small booklet so they would not be lost to posterity.

This rustic soup, which is part of that heritage, is a typical springtime dish in northern Apulia. It is thick and nourishing, full of the flavors of lamb and fennel, and it can easily be served as a meal in a bowl. Old people dip their slices of stale bread into the mixture to soften and permeate them with the flavors of the soup, but I'd grill slices of the best crusty country bread I could find and set them in the bottom of the bowl.

2 pounds lamb riblets

4 cups chicken broth, preferably homemade

4 cups water

⅔ cup finely chopped wild fennel fronds or ⅔ cup finely chopped cultivated fennel tops and 2 teaspoons fennel seeds, lightly crushed

½ cup coarsely chopped flat-leaf parsley

⅛ teaspoon red pepper flakes

1 spring onion or ½ white onion, finely sliced

2¼ pounds (about 4) meaty vine-ripened tomatoes, peeled, seeded, and chopped

½ teaspoon sea salt

6 slices stale country-style bread

Freshly grated pecorino cheese (optional)

Trim the riblets of all their fat. Put them in a 4- or 5-quart pot, preferably terra-cotta, cover them completely with the chicken broth and water, and bring to a boil. Skim off the foam during the first 15 minutes of cooking, then add the fennel, parsley, red pepper flakes, onion, and tomatoes. Let the mixture simmer over very low heat until it is as thick as a rustic soup and the meat is tender, about 2 hours.

Remove the riblets from the pot, take the meat off the bones, and return the lamb meat to the pot. Let the mixture simmer for 15 more minutes and then add the sea salt to taste at the very end.

Chill the soup in the refrigerator to make it easy to skim off the fat before serving. You can make this a day ahead and reheat it.

While the mixture is simmering, preheat the broiler. Place the slices of bread on a broiler pan 4 to 6 inches from the heat source and toast lightly until golden on each side. Serve the soup with a slice of grilled bread at the bottom of each soup bowl. You may sprinkle a little grated pecorino cheese over the top if you wish.

ZUPPA DI PESCE

Fish Soup

—

Serves 6 to 8

*G*isa Sotis makes this fish soup with red mullet, which gives it a wonderful strong flavor and a lovely color. Red mullet, *triglia* in Italy, really isn't a mullet at all, but a bright red goatfish with firm, tasty flesh. Since the mullet is so difficult to find, I've substituted small mackerel, trout, or even shrimp with entirely satisfying results.

FISH BROTH

> 8 cups water
>
> 1 large onion, quartered
>
> 1 large carrot, roughly chopped
>
> ¼ cup chopped flat-leaf parsley
>
> 3 garlic cloves
>
> 5 black peppercorns
>
> 1 bay leaf
>
> 2 pounds sea bass fillets, in chunks

SOUP

> ⅓ cup extra-virgin olive oil
>
> 3 garlic cloves, minced
>
> 3 tablespoons minced flat-leaf parsley
>
> 1½ pounds vine-ripened tomatoes or about 7 canned tomatoes, seeded and roughly chopped, plus about ⅓ cup of their liquid
>
> 8 ounces shrimp, peeled and deveined, or small red mullet, filleted
>
> 6 to 8 slices of country-style bread
>
> Extra-virgin olive oil for brushing

Pour the water into a soup kettle or large heavy stockpot. Add the onion, carrot, parsley, garlic, peppercorns, and bay leaf, bring to a boil, turn the heat down to simmer, and cook for about 20 minutes. Strain the liquid and return it to the pot. Gently place the pieces of sea bass in the broth and simmer until the fish is tender when pierced by the point of a knife, about 10 to 20 minutes, depending on the thickness of your fillets. The fish should no longer be pink inside. Remove the fish with a slotted spoon and keep warm. Reserve the fish broth.

To make the soup: While the bass is cooking, warm the oil over medium-low heat in a large, heavy sauté pan with the garlic, parsley, and tomatoes. Let the mixture simmer for about 5 to 7 minutes, then add the shrimp and cook until they turn pink, about 3 minutes longer. To keep the sauce from becoming too thick, add a little warm water as it cooks. Add the cooked sea bass and gently stir into the shrimp mixture.

Preheat the broiler. Brush the slices of bread with olive oil and broil 4 to 6 inches from the heat source until light golden on both sides.

Set a piece of toasted bread at the bottom of each soup bowl. Add 2 to 3 cups of the reserved broth to the fish mixture. Then ladle some into each bowl. Serve the delicately tomato-accented fish soup immediately.

GRAN FARRO

Bean and Farro Soup

Serves 6 to 8

Renata Marsili

Farro, or emmer, is an ancient wheat grain that Romans ate 2,000 years ago and that Tuscans who live around Lucca and the hills of the Garfagnana continue to eat today. The grain comes as a whole berry or crushed into fine pieces and, while both are delicious cooked in this soup, the whole grain is traditional. The people of Lucca buy farro at their *gastronomie*, delicatessens, or at special seed and grain shops where they find it in bulk. Wherever they get it, Lucchese women cook it into winter soups like this one, an emblematic dish of their city.

There are probably as many versions of gran farro as there are grandmothers in Lucca. Some have a bit of prosciutto and some have no meat at all. The flavor of this one, Renata Marsili's splendid version, is deepened by the rich note the ham hock gives to the soup in which the soft crunch of farro plays against the mellow mixture of beans and vegetables. It is a perfect dish to make ahead and serve a day or two later, although at that point you will need to add extra water because the soup thickens as it cools. If you can't find farro, use spelt or kamut, which must be soaked overnight or for 12 hours, or soft white winter wheat berries, which should be soaked for 2 hours.

> **About 2½ cups (1 pound) dried borlotti or cranberry beans
>   or 1½ (15-ounce) cans borlotti beans**
> 1 ham hock
> **2 cups (10 ounces) whole-grain farro**
> **¼ cup extra-virgin olive oil**
> 1 celery rib, finely chopped
> 1 large onion, finely chopped
> 1 small carrot, finely chopped
> 1 teaspoon minced garlic
> 5 leaves of fresh sage
> Several marjoram buds
> 1 (8-ounce) can Italian plum tomatoes, chopped
> 1 teaspoon sea salt
> Freshly ground black pepper
> Extra-virgin olive oil

Soak the borlotti beans for 12 hours or overnight in a large bowl with cold water to cover by 2 or 3 inches. Drain the beans, rinse, and put them in a large stockpot covered by 3 inches of unsalted cold water. Add the ham hock, cover, and simmer until the beans are tender, skimming off foam as necessary, 1 to 1½ hours.

Soak the farro with enough cold water to cover by 2 inches for 2 hours.

While the beans are simmering, pour the oil into a large, heavy sauté pan and sauté the celery, onion, carrot, garlic, sage, and marjoram over moderately low heat, stirring occasionally, only until the garlic and vegetables are soft but have not browned, 5 to 10 minutes. Add the tomatoes, stir to mix in well, and cook gently for 20 to 30 minutes.

When the beans are tender, drain them, reserving their cooking water. Cut the meat off the ham hock. Puree the beans and the meat from the ham hock with some of the cooking liquid by whirling them in a processor or blender. Grandmothers also press the beans through a sieve using a large spoon or spatula and chop the meat fine. Return them to the large stockpot with the remaining cooking water. Add the drained farro to the pot and cook over very low heat, stirring frequently so the mixture doesn't stick, until the farro is tender, 30 to 45 minutes, even an hour, according to Renata Marsili. Season with salt and pepper and serve with a thread of fruity extra-virgin olive oil drizzled over each portion.

The soup becomes very thick as it cools. If you plan to serve it later, you will need to add substantial water when you reheat it.

Farro, emmer, is a healthful barley-like grain of the *Triticum dicoccum* family with a nutty delicious taste. This ancient wheat was cooked by Romans two millennia ago and is still much used in the western parts of Tuscany and in the Abruzzo, where it appears in thick, hearty soups and salads. Farro is now available in this country both crushed and in whole grains—see the Source Guide to Ingredients—but if you can't find it, substitute spelt, barley, kamut, or soft white winter wheat berries, which must first be soaked and drained.

L'ULTIMA RIBOLLITA

The Ultimate Ribollita

—

Serves 12

*R*ibollita, a Florentine bean soup that is based on bread, is called *zuppa del cane* ("soup of the dog") in Tuscany because it's so elemental. "If this soup is for dogs," says Luisa Cappelli, "those dogs are extremely lucky."

Luisa was born in Tuscany, but she married a man from Genoa and lived in that city for decades, returning to Chianti from time to time to tend the vineyards from which she makes wine and Vin Santo. She learned to make ribollita from her mother-in-law, whose passion for cooking was all enveloping. Luisa discovered that, like her mother-in-law, the more she cooked, the more she loved it and the more she cared about every facet of being in the kitchen. Searching out the best ingredients, she began buying pepper from an old man at the port of Genoa. She bought some for herself, some for friends, and some to take to Chianti. Spending her extravagant energies by cooking many dishes day after day, she found herself returning to the old man for more and more pepper until on one visit he looked at her quizzically and quietly asked if she had a trattoria.

If you were truly following all her directions, you would start with the bone remaining from a prosciutto, being certain that the fat on the rind wasn't rancid. Three days before beginning to cook, you would put it in boiling water to clean it and make the rind softer, then you would change the water frequently until the rind was really soft. At that point you would cut it in pieces. Luisa swears that the soup has the most exquisite flavor when it is made on a wood or charcoal fire with the top of the pot covered with ashes. I can't imagine that it could taste any better than this ribollita that is more like a pudding than a soup.

To make a true ribollita—ribollita means "boiled again," so this is for the day after you have served the original soup—take a 12-inch cast-iron Dutch oven or deep casserole, add 3 or 4 tablespoons of extra-virgin olive oil and as much of the soup as the pot will hold. Heat it up over a low fire and serve.

(continued)

2½ cups (1 pound) dried cannellini beans

9 cups cold water

6 whole garlic cloves and 2 minced garlic cloves

14 leaves of fresh sage

1 tablespoon sea salt

8 tablespoons extra-virgin olive oil

Sea salt

2 carrots, minced

½ celery rib, minced

2 red onions, minced

10 ounces kale (about 1 bunch), thick ribs removed, finely sliced

2 zucchini, finely chopped

2 leeks, well cleaned, white and green portions sliced

2 Yellow Finn potatoes, peeled and diced

1 cup loosely packed leaves of fresh basil

2 tablespoons tomato paste dissolved in ¼ cup of the bean cooking water

1 teaspoon sea salt

Freshly ground black pepper

1 chicken bouillon cube or 1 cup chicken broth, preferably homemade

1 loaf (1 to 1½ pounds) country-style bread, sliced

Extra-virgin olive oil (optional), for drizzling

Soak the beans for 12 hours or overnight in a large bowl with cold water to cover by 2 or 3 inches.

The next day drain the beans, place them in a large, deep pot that holds at least 6 quarts and is preferably made of earthenware with a glazed interior. Cover with 9 cups of cold water, bring to a boil, and simmer very, very slowly, just "a veil of boiling" in Luisa's description. You must not put any salt in the water because it would peel away the skin of the beans, but do add the 6 whole garlic cloves and the fresh sage leaves. When the water begins to simmer, add 2 tablespoons of olive oil to soften the beans, cover the pot tightly, and let the beans cook 1½ hours. You may be tempted to peek, but don't give in. Just let the beans cook and when they are finished, you must toss in the 1 tablespoon salt at the exact minute that you turn off the heat and the boiling ends. If the beans sit for a few hours at this point, they get even better.

Luisa says to take all the vegetables imaginable and mince them very well and then go for a walk. Instead, take the remaining 6 tablespoons of olive oil and sauté the minced carrots, celery, onions, and 2 minced garlic cloves over very low heat for 20 minutes, stirring often, until they are golden.

Remove 1 cup of the cooked beans and set them aside. Remove 2¼ cups of the bean cooking liquid and set it aside. Separately, puree the rest of the beans; if the mixture is too dense, add more cooking water. Return the whole and pureed beans to the pot and add the sautéed vegetables, the kale, zucchini, leeks, potatoes, and basil leaves. Stir in the dissolved tomato paste and add 1 teaspoon salt, some freshly ground pepper, some reserved bean cooking water, and a chicken bouillon cube. Cover and cook very slowly for at least 2 hours. If the mixture is too dense, add some more bean cooking water or chicken broth. Make the soup a day ahead for the best flavor.

When you are ready to serve, warm a soup tureen by pouring very hot water into it and letting it sit for 5 to 10 minutes. Pour out the hot water and layer slices of stale country bread—it must not be toasted—in the tureen between layers of the vegetables. This ribollita should definitely not be thin or soupy. For the best flavor, let it sit for 12 hours or overnight at room temperature so that the bread can soak up the broth and taste even better. Drizzle with olive oil and serve.

TIP: Many nonne agree: never add salt to the soaking or cooking water of beans. It breaks the skin, splits the beans open, and toughens them.

FAGIOLI SECCHI: Dried beans are known in Italy as the meat of the poor, because they are so inexpensive and so full of protein (they actually have slightly more than an equivalent amount of meat). They are the basis of pasta e fagioli, of minestrone, and of purees of beans served on grilled bread with a thread of olive oil. Le nonne always soak their beans for 12 hours, or overnight, covered by 2 to 3 inches of cold water, water that in earlier decades was rainwater or water from the well. Next morning or whenever they are ready, they drain them and cover them with lots of fresh cold water, bring them to a boil, and cook the beans until they are tender. Beans are cooked by themselves or with a prosciutto bone or pancetta for flavor and, depending on which nonna is talking, they are usually cooked without salt because it toughens the beans and causes their skins to split. But there is no agreement on the subject. Some women salt the water because it flavors the beans as they cook. You can follow one of four nonna paths: add the salt at the beginning or near the very end of the cooking or immediately after the beans have finished cooking or after letting them sit for a few minutes.

Borlotti beans, pale pink and speckled, are like our cranberry beans. They are used in soups and stews. See the Source Guide to Ingredients. Some are now grown in California, then shipped to Italy, where they are cooked and canned and shipped back to the United States.

Cannellini beans, medium-size white kidney beans, are cooked throughout Italy and are the bean of choice in Tuscany. Faith Willinger, author of *Red, White, and Greens*, a book about the Italian way with vegetables, discovered that the tinier white toscanelli beans she eats in Florence are really Great Northern beans from the United States.

Chickpeas (*ceci*) are also known as garbanzo beans. Small, pale gold, and wrinkled, these nutty-tasting beans must be soaked in cold water, often with a pinch of baking soda, to soften their skins, before they are cooked over very low heat for several hours.

Lentils (*lenticchie*) are the only legumes that do not need to be soaked before cooking, but they should be washed well. Discard any that float to the surface along with any stones that may have crept into the lot. You can cook and keep them in their liquid for 1 to 2 days before you plan to finish a dish with them.

If you decide to use canned beans, drain and rinse the beans very well in cold water. Half a pound—2½ cups—of dried beans becomes 5 to 6 cups when cooked. A 15-ounce can equals 2 cups of cooked beans; a 19- or 20-ounce can, 2½ cups. Two cups of cooked beans produce 1½ cups of pureed beans.

A quick version for boiling beans, although not one that most Italian grandmothers would be familiar with: Put the beans in a large pot with fresh water to cover by at least 2 inches and bring to a boil. Turn off the heat, cover with a lid, and leave for 1 hour. Drain the hot water, rinse the beans, and cover once again with cold water and simmer until done, 30 to 45 minutes.

PANCOTTO PUGLIESE
CON RUCHETTA E PATATE

Bread Soup with Arugula and Potatoes

—

Serves 4

Angela Padrona, now sixty-five, has lived near Monopoli in Apulia all her life. She grew up in a family of nine children—eight girls and one boy—and they all worked on their small plot of land all day long. They collected fava beans, peas, and whatever wild greens there were, and harvested grain with a scythe. They made pecorino, provolone, and mozzarella from sheep's and cow's milk. Theirs was a complete country life, entire in what they ate from their land over the arc of the year. Remembering dishes from her childhood, Angela mentioned pancotto, a simple blend of the products of the land and the wonderful bread of Apulia. She described it with nostalgia in her voice and I've tried to reproduce this dish of her youth.

(continued)

About 5 (1¼ pounds) yellow-fleshed potatoes, such as Yellow Finn or
  Yukon Gold

6 cups water

About 5 cups (8 to 12 ounces) torn arugula leaves, measured with any
  large stems removed

4 garlic cloves, thinly sliced

About ⅛ teaspoon red pepper flakes

¾ to 1 teaspoon sea salt

About 3 slices of stale country-style bread, sliced

4 to 6 tablespoons extra-virgin olive oil

Peel the potatoes, cut them in wide slices, and cook in 6 cups of boiling salted water for about 10 minutes. Add the arugula and garlic cloves and continue cooking until the potatoes are tender, about 5 to 10 minutes more. Add red pepper flakes, salt, and the bread, and let stand off the heat until the bread is soft. Drizzle olive oil over the top. Taste for seasoning. Serve warm or at room temperature.

MINESTRA DI FUNGHI E PATATE

Mushroom and Potato Soup from Friuli

—

Serves 6

This big, full-flavored soup, made only of mushrooms and potatoes, is so thick that you could call it a stew without meat. A long, slow, almost dry simmer concentrates the earthy flavor of the mushrooms with powerful results, creating a perfect hearty dish for a cold winter's meal. The soup also makes a wonderful Sunday night supper.

The little bit of sour cream is a clear indication of the soup's Slavic influence, but finding sour cream in Friuli is so unlikely that Gianna Modotti instructed me to make my own. She mixes just enough strained lemon juice into heavy cream to make sour cream with the consistency of yogurt. Don't be surprised at the amount of salt in the soup; the potatoes absorb it thirstily.

1 ounce dried porcini mushrooms

2 or 3 tablespoons unsalted butter

1 tablespoon all-purpose flour

1 pound fresh mushrooms, preferably cremini (brown)

1 onion, minced

1 garlic clove, minced

¾ teaspoon minced fresh marjoram; substitute rosemary if you can't find
marjoram

1 to 1½ teaspoons sea salt

Freshly ground black pepper

3 large white potatoes (about 1½ pounds), peeled and diced

2 tablespoons sour cream

3 tablespoons freshly grated Parmigiano-Reggiano cheese

3 tablespoons minced flat-leaf parsley

Soak the porcini mushrooms in 1½ cups of warm water for at least 30 minutes. Drain in a sieve lined with cheesecloth or two layers of paper towels, reserving the liquid for another dish. Squeeze the porcini, letting any extra moisture fall into the water in which they soaked. Wash them in several changes of cold water and chop them roughly.

Melt the butter in a 3-quart heavy saucepan and when it foams, sift the flour directly into the butter, stirring it gently until it has thickened. Add both kinds of mushrooms, the onion, garlic, and marjoram and cook until all the moisture from the mushrooms has been absorbed and the mixture is dry. Cover and continue simmering over very low heat for 1 hour, bathing the contents with a little hot water every once in a while to prevent them from sticking. At the end of that time, add salt and pepper along with as much water as is necessary to make a soup, about 3 to 3½ cups. Add the potatoes to the pot, bring to a boil, and cook, bubbling lightly, over medium heat until they are tender when pierced with a fork, about 30 minutes. Just before serving, whisk in the sour cream, grated Parmigiano-Reggiano cheese, and parsley.

GREENS

Broccoflower or Roman Broccoli *(broccolo romano)*: Broccoflower looks like a pale green cauliflower, but has a more delicate flavor than its white counterpart.

Broccoli Rabe *(cima di rapa; rapini)*: Broccoli rabe could be a broccoli plant with many small flowering heads that produce yellow flowers, but its pungent, slightly bitter, and tantalizing edge means that it has more character than its milder-flavored relative. Choose firm thin, branches that are entirely green with few buds. Trim away any coarse stems. *Rapini*, the tender baby shoots of the plant, have an almost silky texture. All of them can be boiled, steamed, and braised like broccoli. Cook until the stems lose their crunch, anywhere from 3 to 10 minutes.

Cabbage: Savoy cabbage *(cavolo verza)* is used for stuffing (see *Involtini di Cavolo*, page 287) and for inclusion in soups and dishes like *Sacrao* (page 279). *Cavolo nero* is Tuscan kale, for which kale is a fine substitute (see below), and *cavolo cappuccio* is ordinary cabbage.

Kale: The closest we can come to *cavolo nero*, the famed Tuscan black cabbage, is kale. The most common types have a deep green frilly leaf or a bluish-green leaf with less-pronounced curl. They are excellent in soups and rustic savory torte.

Swiss Chard: This Italian green *(barbarbietole)* is mild yet earthy, sweet with just a hint of bitter undertones. Cut away any large ribs, but use the stems and stalks separately, after first pulling away the strings of the fibrous stems just as you would with celery. Cook the two parts separately.

CREMA DI ZUCCA E PATATE

Smooth Creamy Pumpkin and Potato Soup

—

Serves 4

*T*his is a truly elegant soup," said Luisa Cappelli, tantalizing me long before I actually got to taste it. "And since it is so easy to make, you can look like an expert without much exertion." Something we are all more than happy to go along with. Her wintertime soup relies on amber-colored pumpkin or butternut squash. In Tuscany, a big pumpkin is known as a *zuccone*, as is anyone who is a bit slow in school, being as thick as the rind of the pumpkin and just about as hard to get through to.

Although it's called a crema, there is no cream in the soup, only a tiny bit of milk that smooths and blends together the flavor of the squash and the depth of the potatoes. This is really a soup for all occasions, from the most elegant dinners to an informal Sunday night supper when it is happily paired with a salad and some good country bread.

Luisa is many people's idea of a perfect cook and nonna. She makes up nursery rhymes and songs for her grandchildren, but she certainly doesn't make up anything where her food is concerned. She is tenacious about truly authentic tastes and she works painstakingly so her recipes work and taste delicious without being complicated.

Scant 1½ pounds pumpkin or butternut squash, peeled, seeded, and cut
   into 1-inch-thick slices (3 cups)

2 medium potatoes (8 ounces each), peeled and cut in 1-inch slices

1½ tablespoons unsalted butter

2½ cups chicken broth

A pinch of coarse salt

½ to 1 chicken bouillon cube, well crumbled (optional)

⅓ cup milk

Tiny cubes of croutons (optional)

3 tablespoons finely chopped flat-leaf parsley

(continued)

Put the squash and potato slices in a large bowl with cold water to cover by 2 inches, and leave for 30 minutes to 1 hour. Drain them well and pat them dry.

Melt the butter in a large, heavy pot and sauté the squash and potato over very low heat for 10 to 15 minutes, until they are slightly soft and very slightly golden, stirring from time to time to be sure they don't stick to the bottom.

Bring the chicken broth to a slow boil and add it carefully to the pan with a pinch of coarse salt. Simmer the mixture, covered, for 20 minutes, stirring once in a while. Drain the vegetables and puree them in a food mill or whirl them in the processor. Return the puree to the pot with the liquid, add the bouillon cube (if you are using it), being sure it dissolves completely, and simmer for 5 to 7 minutes more over a very low fire, mixing well and tasting for seasoning. If the soup tastes a bit pallid, add the other half bouillon cube or a bit more salt. If the soup is too thin, slowly boil it down to the desired consistency. At the end, add the milk, stirring constantly, and just before serving, stir in the optional tiny croutons and sprinkle the parsley over the top.

TIP: Luisa Cappelli always cooks with coarse salt.

ZUPPA CON LE ZUCCHINE

Zucchini Soup with Ribbons of Sweet Basil

—

Serves 6

Zucchini today, zucchini tomorrow, and zucchini for days to come: the humble zucchini grows with such ferocity that it challenges cooks to keep up with its fertility. Annita di Fonzo Zannella has always lived in Campodimele, a tiny mountain town in Lazio, and while almost everything she cooks comes from the vegetables and fruits of her fields, her zucchini soup is truly a find! Take a little bit of everything from the garden—onions, tomatoes, potatoes, green beans, and the zucchini and their flowers—cook them all in good broth, and finish the soup with a handful of basil leaves and a dusting of good Parmesan cheese. Richer tasting and more satisfying than it sounds, this soup translates the unassuming zucchini into a glorious dish.

2 tablespoons extra-virgin olive oil

1 onion, chopped

1 tomato, peeled, seeded, and roughly chopped

3 large zucchini, diced

3 medium potatoes, peeled and diced

4 ounces green beans, ends trimmed, chopped into 2-inch lengths

A handful of zucchini flowers (optional)

6 cups chicken broth

1 cup roughly torn leaves of fresh basil

Salt

Freshly ground black pepper

6 slices of stale country-style bread

Freshly grated Parmigiano-Reggiano cheese

Warm the olive oil in a heavy 4-quart saucepan and sauté the onion and tomato over low heat for about 15 minutes, until the onion is limp and the tomato has wilted. Add the zucchini, potatoes, beans, and the flowers if you are using them; pour in the broth, bring to a boil, and cook over low heat for about 12 minutes. Add half the torn basil leaves, salt, and pepper and continue cooking for another 3 to 5 minutes, or until the beans and zucchini are tender when pierced by a fork.

While the soup is cooking, preheat the broiler. Set the slices of bread on a broiler pan 3 or 4 inches from the heat source and broil for about 4 minutes a side, until lightly crispy.

When the soup is ready, set each slice of bread in a soup bowl, pour the soup over it, add the remaining basil leaves, and serve with grated Parmigiano-Reggiano cheese.

ZUPPA VERA CONTADINA

A *True Country Soup*

—

Serves 6

I think of this nourishing bean and vegetable soup as the Italian country equivalent of Proust's madeleine because it inevitably brings back memories of childhood for countless Italians. It essentially asks you to empty the contents of the vegetable garden into a pot and let them cook together slowly, flavors melting and building one on the other. The soup is even better on the second day; just be sure to add extra stock or water when you warm it up because it will thicken as it sits at room temperature or is refrigerated.

The cooking time of dried beans depends on their age; older ones will take longer to soften and become tender. Giovanna Dolfi-Zenzi Lusignani uses fresh borlotti beans when they are in season, and if you have fresh cranberry beans, please follow her example. Use 1 pound (unshelled weight), shell them, and add them to the pot instead of the drained canned beans.

The signora is the wife of a baker, her sons are bakers, and she sells bread in the shop connected to their bakery in the tiny town of Pellegrino Parmense in a green valley between Parma and Piacenza. I watched her make an immense stockpot full of bean soup that is served layered with bread, for which she used sturdy slices cut from a loaf made in the bakery. It is a great restorative, which is why it was once ladled out for children who had been working in the fields since light first appeared in the sky. They must have been delighted when, at about eight or eight-thirty in the morning, women appeared carrying the soup in wicker baskets. They served it up, giving the hungry recipients a rest at mid-morning, as well as something delicious to eat.

1 cup (6½ ounces) dried borlotti or cranberry beans or 1½ (15-ounce)
    cans borlotti or cranberry beans, drained and rinsed well

2 ounces lardo, pancetta, or salt pork

2 garlic cloves

2 spring onions

⅓ cup loosely packed flat-leaf parsley leaves

2 large potatoes, peeled and diced

2 carrots, finely chopped

1 celery rib, finely chopped

1 onion, finely chopped

About 8 cups chicken broth, preferably homemade

2 teaspoons to 2 tablespoons fruity red wine, to taste

Salt and pepper

6 slices of country-style bread, slightly stale and lightly grilled

½ cup (2 ounces) freshly grated Parmigiano-Reggiano cheese

Extra-virgin olive oil for drizzling

If you are using dried beans, soak them for 12 hours or overnight in a large bowl with water to cover by 2 to 3 inches. Drain and rinse well.

Chop together the lardo (or pancetta or prosciutto), garlic, onions, and parsley; Signora Lusignani uses a mezzaluna, but a knife or food processor works well too. Put the mixture in a heavy-bottomed 4-quart pot, place it over low heat, and cook for about 5 minutes. Add the drained and rinsed dried beans, the potatoes, carrots, celery, onion, and 8 cups of broth, cover, and simmer for 2 to 2½ hours until the beans are tender. If you are using drained canned beans, add them after 1¾ hours. Check every once in a while to be sure there is still enough liquid; add more broth or water, if necessary. Add the red wine at the end, season with salt and pepper to taste, and cook for an extra 2 or 3 minutes. Although this is meant to be a thick soup, be sure to add enough liquid that it can be eaten with a spoon, not a fork.

You may toast a piece of bread and put it at the bottom of each bowl of soup or you may do as la nonna does and take a big bowl, put a layer of grilled bread in the bottom, cover with a layer of the bean mixture, sprinkle half the Parmigiano-Reggiano cheese over the top, and repeat until the bowl is full. Drizzle a little olive oil over each serving at table.

PANE E PIZZE

Bread and Pizza

SAVORY

PANE CASARECCIO
Homemade Country Bread

PIZZA ALLA NAPOLETANA
A Tuscan Fantasy of Neapolitan Pizza

SFINCIONE
Sicilian Focaccia

FOCACCIA DI PATATE ALLA GENOVESE
Potato Focaccia from Genoa

SCHIZZOTTO
Golden Milk Bread from Padua

BOCCONCELLO
Pecorino Cheese Bread

FILLED VEGETABLE TARTS AND PIES

CAPPELLO DI GENDARME
Gendarme's Cap, a Calzone from Lecce

TORTA DI PORRI E ZUCCA
Leek and Butternut Squash Tart

PIZZA DI CARCIOFI
Filled Artichoke Pie

PIZZA RUSTICA ALLA NAPOLETANA
Neapolitan Ricotta, Mortadella, and Salami Pie

SWEET

MARITOZZI FABRIANESI
Sweet Rolls Bursting with Raisins from Fabriano

PANE NOCIATO
Cinnamon- and Rum-Flavored Walnut Bread

PANINI DI PASQUA
Spicy Easter Rolls

BREAD

Bread has always been the Ur-food of the country, the primary nourishment upon which Italians depend. Bread, made simply of flour, water, yeasts from the air, and salt from the sea, feeds people and connects them to family, to land, to the greater powers of the cosmos. It begins with yeast, the soul of its being, a living product suspended in a dormant state, which returns to life once when it is dissolved in warm water or kneaded vigorously into the dough and again when the heat of the oven miraculously transforms four simple ingredients into loaves baked on the hearth. Women knead the anxieties and uncertainties of daily life into their dough and shape it into wheels as round as the sun.

FLOUR (*Farina*): There are two kinds of wheat in Italy: *grano tenero,* soft and hard wheat from *Triticum aestivum*; and *Triticum durum,* a much harder high-protein wheat from which the durum wheat and semolina for pasta are milled. Flour from *grano tenero* is graded in five categories; 00 is the most refined—all the husk and whole grain have been sifted away. Grade 0 has had most of its husk and germ extracted, leaving a light-beige tint from the remaining nutrients. Flours 1 and 2, rarely seen or used in Italy any more, have much more of the bran and endosperm; nothing has been extracted from whole wheat flour.

Although 00 Italian flour is as soft as talcum powder and is slightly lower in gluten than our unbleached all-purpose flour, I use the creamy American flour with excellent results when making Italian breads and pizze. For most dessert baking I use American all-purpose flour or a mixture of all-purpose and pastry flour. Do not use bread flour, with its extremely high gluten content; no Italian grandmother has such flour, and the recipes would not work correctly with it.

Although few Italian grandmothers measure their ingredients, other than by the handful or the pinch, every American should measure flour correctly. Pour your flour into a very large bowl. Stir it with a spoon several times to aerate it well. Scoop a metal measuring cup through the flour and then use a knife to level off the flour. That's all. Store any whole wheat flour in the refrigerator so that the oil in the germ doesn't become rancid.

PANE CASARECCIO

Homemade Country Bread

—

Makes 3 loaves

Flour, water, salt, and yeast: the breads of the Italian countryside combine four of the most basic ingredients on earth to create delicious country loaves with thick chewy crusts. Many years ago I learned to bake Italian country bread with Nella Galletti at her home in the Umbrian countryside and later discovered that Annita di Fonzo Zannella makes bread the same way. Nella made traditional saltless bread for which she kept her ingredients in a large *madia*, a deep wooden chest that held both flour and the natural yeast that came from keeping some dough of that week's baking and setting it aside to be used as leavening for the next week's bread. She mixed the starter with the flour and then began pouring scoops of water directly into the mixture, beating and mixing and kneading for at least 40 minutes. The amounts were immense! She kneaded so vigorously that the dough became like a huge blanket that she kept turning and pummeling and kneading some more until it was elastic and silky and very resilient. Her muscles had a definite workout. After she allowed the dough its initial rise, she shaped it into rounds, let them rise again on floured canvas she pleated between loaves so they wouldn't fuse, and set them on a board. When they were ready—doubled and full of air bubbles—she called a neighbor, who hoisted the board onto his shoulder and took its many loaves to the hot wood-burning oven. Nella swabbed the oven with rainwater that she had saved to create steam and then she slid in the rounds. An hour later, out came the crunchy crusted bread that would feed Nella, her family, and her neighbors for the week.

When I explained to Nella that Americans don't have such natural starter available to them, she suggested making a biga, a starter with almost no yeast at all, and letting it rise for two days. You don't have to do anything for the two days in which it sits at room temperature, but you must be sure to start your bread baking with enough time to allow the biga to ferment and develop its rich flavors.

BIGA (BREAD STARTER)

¼ teaspoon active dry yeast or ⅟₁₀ small cake fresh yeast

¼ cup warm water

¾ cup plus 2 tablespoons water, room temperature

2½ cups (about 11 ounces) unbleached all-purpose flour

DOUGH

1½ teaspoons active dry yeast or ½ cake (⅓ ounce) fresh yeast

¼ cup warm water, 105° to 115°F. for dry yeast, 95° to 105°F. for fresh

2⅓ cups water

1 cup (about 8 ounces) biga measured at room temperature

About 5½ to 5¾ cups (about 1¾ pounds) unbleached all-purpose flour

1 tablespoon sea salt

Cornmeal for the baking stone(s)

To make the biga: Stir the yeast into the warm water and let stand until creamy, about 10 minutes. Stir in the remaining water and then the flour, 1 cup at a time. If you are making the biga by hand, mix with a wooden spoon for about 4 minutes. If you are using a heavy-duty electric mixer, mix with the paddle at the lowest speed for about 2 minutes.

Rising: Place the sticky biga in a large lightly oiled bowl, cover with plastic wrap, and let rise at cool room temperature for 24 to 48 hours. The starter will triple in volume, then fall back upon itself. It will still be wet and sticky when you use it, so moisten your hands when you scoop some out to measure it. Cover and refrigerate after 48 hours. You may keep the biga refrigerated for up to 5 days.

To make the dough by hand: Stir the yeast into the warm water in a large mixing bowl; let it stand until creamy, about 10 minutes. Add the room temperature water and the biga. Squeeze the biga through your fingers to break it up and then stir it vigorously with a wooden spoon until the water is chalky white and the starter is well shredded. Begin stirring the flour mixed with the salt, 2 cups at a time, into the yeast mixture. Beat well with a wooden spoon until the dough comes together into a shaggy moist mass. Flour your work surface and your dough scraper and keep a mound of flour nearby for your hands. Turn the dough out onto the floured surface and, with the help of the dough scraper and as little extra flour as possible, turn and knead the dough until it gradually loses its stickiness, although it will remain wet.

By heavy-duty electric mixer: Stir the yeast into the warm water in a large mixing bowl; let it stand until creamy, about 10 minutes. Add the room temperature water and the biga. Squeeze the biga vigorously through your fingers to break it up until the water is chalky white and the starter is well shredded. Add the flour and salt and with the paddle attachment mix until the dough comes together. You may need to add up to 4 tablespoons more flour, but the dough will never come away from the sides and bottom of the bowl. Change to the dough hook and knead for 4 to 5 minutes at medium speed. You may finish kneading the sticky wet dough by hand on a well-floured work surface, sprinkling the top with up to 4 tablespoons more flour.

First rise: Place the dough in a lightly oiled bowl. If you have a straight-sided translucent plastic container, please use it so that you can mark exactly where the dough starts and measure its progress until it has tripled. Cover tightly with plastic wrap and let rise until tripled and full of air bubbles, about 3 hours.

Shaping and second rise: Turn the sticky dough out onto a well-floured work surface. Flour a dough scraper and have a mound of flour nearby for your hands. Pour the dough out of the bowl but *do not punch it down.* Lightly flour the top and cut into 3 equal pieces. You can moisten your hands in water if the dough seems very sticky; wet hands do not stick to wet dough. Flatten each piece and roll it up lengthwise, using your thumbs as a guide for how tight the rolls should be. Turn the dough 90 degrees, gently pat it flat, and roll it up again, still using your thumbs as a guide. Shape each piece into a ball by rolling the dough between your cupped hands, using the surface of your work table to generate tension and create a taut skin on the surface of the dough. Place the loaves on floured parchment paper, set them on baking sheets or pizza peels, cover with a heavy cloth, and let rise until doubled, about 1 hour.

At least 30 minutes before you plan to bake, heat the oven(s) to 450°F. with a baking stone(s) inside.

Baking: Just before baking, sprinkle the stones with cornmeal. Gently invert the loaves onto the stones—you may leave whatever parchment paper has stuck to the wet dough for 15 minutes or so and remove it once the dough has set. You may prefer to slide the loaves onto the baking stones without turning them over; you may also leave them on the baking sheets and set them directly on the stones. The bread will look deflated when you initially put it in, but it will puff up like a pillow in no time. Bake until golden brown and crusty, about 35 minutes, or until a tap on the bottom produces the hollow sound that indicates the loaf is baked. Cool on racks.

VARIATION: Use 1 scant cup (5 ounces) whole wheat flour, preferably stone-ground, and 4¾ cups (1⅓ pounds) unbleached all-purpose flour

Profile of *Annita di Fonzo Zannella*

Annita di Fonzo Zannella tried not to look surprised when I arrived on her doorstep one Sunday morning. I had come to meet her son, the mayor of Campodimele, a city that is much in the news because so many of its residents live into their eighties and nineties. Of the various theories attempting to explain their long healthy lives, several credit the food: some suggest that the people of Campodimele owe their good fortune to eating *cicherchia*, a white bean that grows locally, or to small snails from the fields cooked in a tasty tomato and onion sauce, or even to a daily ration of *scalogne in pinzimonio*, shallots dipped in olive oil. Everyone is waiting for Dr. Pietro Cugini at the Policlinico Hospital in Rome to finish his studies and explain why so many old people in Campodimele have the cholesterol count of infants.

These octogenarians and nonagenarians have really put the quiet, medieval, walled hill town—population 850—on the map. All summer long there are now celebrations—American bands, Russian ballerinas, even a large well-attended *sagra* in mid-August when *cicerchie* are the beans served in big bowls of *pasta e fagioli*. When the mayor was late, his architect-brother Pietro took me home to their mother, an extremely gracious woman who was short, stout, and gray-haired, the Italian country version of a Russian babushka. With only the briefest hesitation, she invited me into the living room, where she pulled the shutters closed to shield her very light-sensitive eyes. Within ten minutes her husband, visiting children, and grandchildren had all arrived to add to the conversation about childhood, family, and food in a town that may be 90 minutes from Rome but seems light-years away in terms of its way of life.

Annita has lived here all her life, staying with her mother after her father left to find work in America when she was young. Two of her three brothers followed and none ever returned. Yes, she agreed, people here live very long healthy lives—one of her uncles died at a hundred and three and a vigorous neighbor lives by himself at ninety-nine, working in the fields every day. Everyone has worked hard all their lives and lived on what the countryside provided. Often there wasn't much choice—beans and bean soups, homemade pasta, lots of potatoes, and many and various vegetables cooked in a multi-

Campodimele

plicity of ways. It turns out that the signora is rather a contrarian who doesn't go along with the talk about Campodimele as a paradise. Where people once grew all their own food, she says, now they eat some of what they grow and feed the rest to their animals, and buy whatever they want from the greengrocer. And they use fertilizer! There was no running water in Campodimele until 1963, no sewer until 1976. Women used to begin the day by lighting a fire, then walking down a long steep hill to the wells in the countryside below where they collected the water and returned with it balanced on their heads. Does she think that the famous *cicerchie*, small legumes as white as cannellini beans but tinier, the size and color of a baby's tooth, could be responsible for the great age of the population? A shrug of the shoulders. *Cicerchia* grow well in Campodimele, she acknowledges, but many people don't like them because they had to eat so many during World War II. She mentions *lumachine*, small snails from the fields, cooked with onions, tomato sauce, and mentuccia, a local wild mint. To get the tiny snails out of their shells, people once bent the outer tine of a fork and used it to spear them.

I accepted her offer of a tour of Campodimele, and as we walked over the cobbled streets of the city, past arbored entrances to immaculate homes and past the remaining slender stone towers that have been transformed into houses, I explained to the signora that I wanted to meet other women her age and to be in their kitchens to watch them cook. She found an excuse not to introduce me to any of the women we passed. She was dismissive—"Bianca! *Fuh! Niente!*"—but she was also full of stories about the old days in Campodimele, so when she invited me home for lunch, I accepted with alacrity. Much to her surprise, I followed her into the kitchen, thereby unnerving both her and her husband.

Prosperity may have come to Campodimele, but like most of the older people, the signora and her husband continue to work hard and grow much of what they eat. Hot red peppers were spread out to dry on the kitchen windowsill along with a variety of other herbs and garlic from their land just outside the town. They live in harmony with the rhythms of nature, getting up at dawn, going to bed early, and preserving food as the agricultural cycle provides. June is the month for putting up cherries and figs, she explained, August the time to make tomato sauce and jams because the fruit is ripest then, and December and January the time to pick olives and put them in brine. It may be that the fountain of youth lies in the fact that all the old people in Campodimele continue to work in their fields and their gardens and they live a life that has changed little in the last fifty years. The ubiquitous blue light of the television screen, seen through the windows of most homes in Italy, seems not to glow in their houses in the evenings.

By good fortune I arrived for the traditional *piatto unico*, the Italian two-for-one meal, which Signora Zannella makes by cooking pork sausage—hers are extremely lean with tiny pieces of potato and the taste of hot pepper—in a tomato sauce. The sauce came to table twice: once over homemade pasta for the first course and again with the sausage for the second. I noticed how easily she tossed onions, olive oil, and tomatoes in a small cold pan—she didn't warm the olive oil or sauté the onions first—she cooked them for a few minutes, then added the sausages, which were previously boiled to melt away any fat. She moved slowly and deliberately, without hurry or hesitation. A wooden spoon rested naturally in her hardworking hands. The state of the tomato determined when she added it. If it was meaty, she sautéed it with the olive oil and onion; if thin, she stirred it in with the sausage. When she put the sausage into the pan, she drizzled in a little more olive oil, a sprinkling of salt, some freshly chopped parsley, and a few basil leaves and kept one eye on the mixture until the tomatoes had the density of thick tomato juice.

Lunch was served in the spacious living and dining room, where reproductions of Manet and Renoir and abstract studies by the architect-mayor son, Paolo, hung on the walls. The now sizable house had grown from the original tiny rooms on one floor to an ample and gracious two-story residence, a conversion made possible when they incorporated the warehouse next door.

After pasta, Annita served a second course with fronds of broccoli rabe so tender they were practically prenatal and a mélange of ribbons of yellow, red, and green sweet peppers with skins so fine they didn't need to be peeled. We sat at table like almost every other Italian family on Sunday, with the television on, and we ate watching the news on RAI, the national broadcasting company.

Signora Zannella still makes the bread that is served at every meal and she bakes it in the large wood-burning oven next to their house. Her recipe: first you harvest the wheat, thresh it, take it to a miller to grind it, and then sift it to remove the largest pieces of bran. Use only *lievito naturale*, natural yeast, and set aside a piece and let it rise the day before you bake. Put the starter in the middle of the flour—which is kept in a deep wooden chest—and begin by putting salt in a scoop and then adding water very slowly at first to dissolve the salt; then continue adding but don't measure the water. Just let the flour determine how much it can absorb. Leave the dough to rise for 2 to 3 hours, depending on the temperature and on how warm your hands are. Shape ten loaves as 5-pound rounds, and set them one by one on floured canvas pleated between the individual loaves so they don't merge as they rise. Put them under a heavy cloth, although in winter they may rise inside the gas oven when it has just been lit.

I noticed that Annita didn't make the sign of the cross over the bread or the oven. "I don't hold much with that," she said, wrinkling her nose.

A contrarian even there, although she nodded favorably when we were stopped on our walk by an older woman and her husband on an outing from Rome. "This town is a dream, a dream, a piece of paradise, so peaceful, so perfect for a quiet weekend away from the noise of the city," the wife enthused. They had come to eat lunch in the local restaurant, aptly named La Longevità, and like everyone, they gravitated to the main piazza with its massive ancient tree shading the old men sitting on the bench below it. They took in the panoramic view over the valley below and noticed that the entire village with its many old people seemed to be out for the *passeggiata*. Being here made them think about life in this country village high on its hill. They were getting on, they said to each other; the people here live so long and were still productive. Yes, after a lunch of the local specialties, they might seriously consider spending time here, eating the famous *cicerchie* and living deep into old age in the cool fresh air of Campodimele.

PIZZA ALLA NAPOLETANA
A Tuscan Fantasy of Neapolitan Pizza
—

Makes 2 pizzas, to serve 2

*P*izza has been *the* food of Naples for about a century, but it didn't appear in other regions of Italy until after World War II. It certainly wasn't something that Tuscans ate routinely, so it seems particularly remarkable that Emma Grassi Bensi, who cooked for the Cappelli family just outside Florence, was making these during World War II. Despite the deprivations and dramatic scarcity of the time, Emma had at her fingertips a multitude of ingredients that grew on the land.

Emma Grassi Bensi

And when she made this pizza for Minnuccio, the son of her employers, he ate it in the barn by himself, savoring every taste, every drop of oil and sprinkle of cheese.

DOUGH

> 1¼ teaspoons (½ package) active dry yeast
>
> ¼ cup milk, warmed to 105° to 115°F.
>
> 1 egg
>
> 1 egg yolk
>
> 1 cup (5 ounces) unbleached all-purpose flour
>
> ¼ teaspoon sea salt

TOPPING

> Extra-virgin olive oil
>
> 1 cup roughly chopped ripe tomatoes, seeded, peeled, and squeezed so that
> no extra moisture remains
>
> A handful of fresh basil leaves, roughly torn
>
> Sprinkles of dried oregano
>
> Sprinkles of sea salt
>
> Freshly grated pecorino toscano or Parmigiano-Reggiano cheese
>
> Cornmeal for the baking stone

Sprinkle the yeast over the warmed milk in a large bowl or mixing bowl, whisk it in well, and let it stand until creamy, about 10 minutes. Whisk in the egg and egg yolk, then add the flour and salt with a wooden spoon or the paddle attachment of a heavy-duty electric mixer and mix well until a dough is formed. If you are making this by hand, place the dough on a lightly floured work surface and knead it until it is velvety and firm, 7 to 10 minutes. If you are making this by mixer, change to the dough hook and knead on low speed for 3 minutes. Although the dough is very slightly sticky to begin with, it loses its stickiness with a few sprinkles of flour and a brief kneading.

First rise: Transfer the dough to an oiled container, cover it tightly with plastic wrap, and let rise until doubled, about 1 hour to 1 hour and 10 minutes.

Shaping: Divide the dough in half. Using a rolling pin, roll each piece to a large circle that is about ¼ inch thick. The dough should be golden, tender, and easy to roll.

Baking: At least 30 minutes before you plan to bake, preheat the oven with a baking stone inside to 500°F. Just before baking, drizzle a thin wash of olive oil over the dough, then spread some of the tomato on top of each pizza, sprinkle it with basil, dried oregano, salt, and cheese. Sprinkle the stone with cornmeal and slide the two pizzas on top. Immediately lower the oven to 450°F. and bake for about 8 minutes, until the dough is golden brown and the cheese has melted.

Bread crumbs, *pan grattato*, are just grated bread. Let your country loaf go stale and grate it on the fine or medium holes of your grater, then toast the crumbs in the oven or in a pan on the stove to dry them fully. Italian grandmothers differentiate between using truly stale bread, which produces very fine crumbs, and fresher bread with the crust cut off, which, when processed to coarse crumbs and dried in the oven, produces softer fuller crumbs.

SFINCIONE

Sicilian Focaccia

—

Serves 6

*P*eople in Partinico love this *sfincione*, the Sicilian version of a fat focaccia in which a topping of cheese and crunchy bread crumbs plays against tangy anchovies and a sweet tomato sauce. It's spicy and filling, a treat for a picnic or a midday meal, the rustic Sicilian equivalent of a thick pizza with everything on top. You could even cut it in small squares to serve as part of an antipasto.

Giovanna
Passannanti

In making the sfincione, Giovanna Passannanti is careful to use soft bread crumbs made with bread from which the crust has been removed, not fine dry crumbs grated from stale bread. Serve the sfincione at room temperature.

SPONGE

    2½ teaspoons (1 package) active dry yeast or
        1 cake (⅔ ounce) fresh yeast

    ¾ cup warm water, 105° to 115°F. for dry yeast,
        95° to 105°F. for fresh yeast

    ¾ cup (3½ ounces) unbleached all-purpose flour

DOUGH

    ¾ cup milk, room temperature

    2 tablespoons extra-virgin olive oil or best-quality lard

    Sponge (see above)

    3 cups plus 1 tablespoon (14 ounces) unbleached all-purpose flour

    1½ teaspoons sea salt

TOPPING

    6 anchovy fillets under oil, drained and cut into small pieces; or 3 whole
        anchovies under salt, rinsed, filleted, and cut into small pieces

    1 cup (4 ounces) grated caciocavallo or shredded mozzarella cheese

    ½ cup soft fresh bread crumbs

Salsa di Pomodoro Siciliana (Tomato Sauce) (page 430)

2 medium onions, finely sliced

2 teaspoons dried oregano

¾ teaspoon sea salt

Freshly ground black pepper

3 to 4 tablespoons extra-virgin olive oil

To make the sponge: Sprinkle the yeast over the warm water in a mixing or mixer bowl and let stand until creamy, about 10 minutes. Whisk in the flour and stir with a wooden spoon until you have a batter-like dough. Cover tightly with plastic wrap and let rise until puffy and bubbly, 30 to 45 minutes.

To make the dough: Beat the milk and olive oil into the sponge with a wooden spoon or the paddle attachment of a heavy-duty electric mixer. Stir in the flour and the salt, mixing to make a dough. Knead by hand on a lightly floured work surface for 8 to 10 minutes, or change to the dough hook and knead in the mixer for 3 minutes until the dough is velvety and sticky.

First rise: Place the dough in a lightly oiled bowl, cover tightly with plastic wrap, and let rise until doubled, about 1 hour to 1 hour and 15 minutes.

Preheat the oven to 425°F. with a baking stone inside.

Second rise: Generously oil an 11 × 17-inch baking pan. Place the dough in the pan, press it as far toward the edges as it will go, and cover with a towel. After 10 minutes, stretch it again to the edges, cover, and let it rise for 20 more minutes.

Topping the sfincione: Sprinkle the anchovy pieces and the cheese over the dough, pressing them evenly over the surface. Sprinkle half the bread crumbs over them, then spoon on the tomato sauce and the onions. Sprinkle with the oregano, sea salt, and pepper to taste. Distribute the remaining bread crumbs over the top, then drizzle with the olive oil, being sure to bathe any exposed surfaces.

Baking: Set the baking pan directly on the baking stone and bake until the crust is crispy and crunchy, about 22 to 30 minutes.

TIP: Giovanna Passannanti washes salted anchovies and sardines with vinegar to rid them of their smell.

FOCACCIA DI PATATE ALLA GENOVESE

Potato Focaccia from Genoa

—

Serves 8 to 10

*D*on't judge this focaccia by others you have eaten because this particular one deserves a place all its own in the pantheon of fine breads. It comes from Luisa Cappelli, a resident of Genoa for decades, who knows that this focaccia's porous texture and delicate interior come from the fact that it is made with equal weights of potatoes and flour. Besides serving the focaccia at dinner or tea, Luisa cuts it into tiny triangles, fills them with butter and prosciutto, and adds them to the selection on an antipasto platter.

- 2 medium potatoes (1 scant pound) — *mashed.* *1½ cup mashed*
- 1 cup milk *less ¾*
- 2½ teaspoons (1 package) active dry yeast or
  1 cake (⅔ ounce) fresh yeast — *1 T + 2 t crumbled*
- 3 cups plus 1 tablespoon (14 ounces) unbleached all-purpose flour *350g*
- 2 teaspoons sea salt
- 10 to 12 leaves of fresh sage, finely chopped
- 6 tablespoons extra-virgin olive oil, plus 2 tablespoons for the pan
  and 1 or 2 tablespoons for drizzling over the top
- 1½ to 2 teaspoons coarse sea salt

Peel and slice the potatoes and boil in salted water until they are tender, about 20 minutes. Drain, then mash them immediately with a fork or potato ricer, being careful to eliminate any lumps. Cool to room temperature.

Warm the milk to 105° to 115°F., sprinkle the yeast over the top, and whisk it in. Let it stand until creamy, about 10 minutes.

By *hand:* Mix the flour, potatoes, 2 teaspoons sea salt, and finely chopped sage leaves together and put them on your work surface. Make a well in the center of the mixture, pour in some of the dissolved yeast, and begin to work in the flour mixture, alternating with the yeast and 6 tablespoons of the oil as you mix in the flour, until you have a roughly elastic mixture. Knead until you have a soft and elastic dough, 8 to 10 minutes. Roll into a ball.

By heavy-duty electric mixer: Whisk 6 tablespoons of the olive oil into the yeast mixture. Add the riced potatoes, flour, 2 teaspoons sea salt, and sage leaves and mix with the paddle attachment until a dough is formed. Change to the dough hook and knead on low speed for 2 to 3 minutes, until the dough is soft and slightly sticky. Finish kneading briefly on a lightly floured work surface.

First rise: Set the ball of dough in an oiled bowl, cover tightly with plastic wrap, and let rise until doubled, about 1 hour.

Shaping and second rise: Brush 2 tablespoons of olive oil on a 10½ × 15½-inch baking pan with 2-inch sides. Place the dough in the pan and press it out to the edges. With your hands moistened in oil, dimple the top, leaving small declivities for the oil. Sprinkle coarse salt crystals over the top, letting them fall into the holes. Cover with a kitchen cloth, set in a protected part of your kitchen where currents of air can't affect it, and let rise until half-doubled, about 30 minutes. Sprinkle a little more olive oil over the top.

Baking: At least 30 minutes before you plan to bake, preheat the oven, with a baking stone inside, to 400°F. Place the baking pan directly on the baking stone and bake until the top and the underside are golden, about 25 minutes. Serve warm or at room temperature.

SCHIZZOTTO

Golden Milk Bread from Padua

—

Makes 3 loaves

When Lucia Rossi Pavanello was growing up in the countryside outside Padua, women made this bread at home and baked it in a wood-burning oven. Most families made it with some water, but Lucia's family used all milk. What a difference! The soft fine-textured interior is so delicate and golden that it looks like a brioche dough made with butter and eggs. I have made a sponge to open the texture and deepen the taste a bit.

Lucia's mother tested the heat of the brick oven by sweeping the ashes away from a spot on the oven floor and then sprinkling a little bit of polenta. If the polenta burned, the oven was hot enough. When she put the bread in the oven, she set a metal sheet or plate over the top and covered it with hot embers, essentially making an oven that was hot from above and below. More than a half century later Lucia still makes this bread and her friends bring the prosciutto to eat with it. It also makes extraordinary toast.

SPONGE

> 1½ teaspoons (generous half package) active dry yeast or ½ cake
> (⅓ ounce) fresh yeast
>
> ¾ cup milk, warmed to 105° to 115°F. for dry yeast, 95° to 105°F. for
> fresh yeast
>
> 1 cup (scant 5 ounces) unbleached all-purpose flour

DOUGH

> ½ teaspoon active dry yeast or ⅙ small cake fresh yeast
>
> 2 cups plus 4 to 7 tablespoons milk, warmed to 105° to 115°F. for dry
> yeast, 95° to 105°F. for fresh yeast
>
> Sponge (see above)
>
> ⅓ cup olive oil
>
> 6¼ cups (1 pound, 14 ounces) unbleached all-purpose flour
>
> 4 teaspoons sea salt
>
> Cornmeal or coarse semolina, as needed

To make the sponge: Sprinkle the dry yeast or crumble the fresh yeast over the warmed milk in a medium-size bowl and whisk it in; let stand until creamy, about 10 minutes. Stir in the flour with a wooden spoon until the mixture is smooth. Cover with plastic wrap and let rise until doubled, 30 to 45 minutes. The sponge will be soupy.

To make the dough by hand: Sprinkle the dry yeast over the milk or crumble the fresh yeast into the milk in a large mixing bowl or mixer bowl and whisk it in well. Let stand until creamy, about 10 minutes. Stir in the sponge, then the oil, and mix well. Beat in the flour, 2 cups at a time, and continue stirring until the dough is thoroughly mixed, about 5 minutes. Stir in the salt in the last minutes. Turn the dough out onto a lightly floured work surface and knead until the dough is velvety, smooth, but slightly sticky, 10 to 15 minutes.

By heavy-duty electric mixer: Add the sponge and oil to the yeast mixture in the mixer bowl and mix with the paddle. Add the flour and salt and mix with the dough hook on medium speed (#4 on a Kitchen Aid) until the dough is velvety, smooth, but still slightly sticky, 3 to 4 minutes.

First rise: Place the dough in a lightly oiled large straight-sided container, cover tightly with plastic wrap, and let rise until the dough has risen to 2½ times its original volume, about 2 hours.

Shaping and second rise: Divide the dough into three equal pieces on a lightly floured work surface. Lightly stretch each into a rectangle, and transfer to parchment paper set on baking sheets or to wooden pizza peels sprinkled with cornmeal or coarse semolina, or to oiled baking sheets. Cover with kitchen towels and let rise until half-doubled with noticeable air bubbles under the skin, 30 to 45 minutes.

Baking: At least 30 minutes before baking, preheat the oven to 425°F. with a baking stone inside. Score each loaf with a razor or very sharp knife, cutting five slashes on top vertically and then horizontally, like an expanded tic-tac-toe pattern. If you are baking the loaves directly on the stone, sprinkle it with cornmeal just before sliding the loaves onto it. Bake until the top is golden and a solid tap on the bottom produces the hollow sound that indicates the loaves are done, 30 to 35 minutes.

BOCCONCELLO

Pecorino Cheese Bread

—

Makes 1 large ring to serve 8 to 10

*S*lice into this ring of cheese-flavored bread and you will taste the mid-morning meal that reinvigorated people as they threshed grain in the Umbrian countryside. Nella Galletti remembers everything about the long days spent in the fields—the hard work of slicing sheaves to the ground with a sickle, the hum and comfort of other people's company, the sweltering heat of midsummer, and the pleasure of stopping to eat, replenishing energy expended under the strong June sun.

Nella continually fed and kept alive a natural yeast starter that she used when making bread every week, but she agreed that making the biga, or starter, two days before you plan to bake the bread, would work well. Just mix the three ingredients together, leave them at room temperature the first day, and set them in a refrigerator for the second. You will have some leftover starter, and I hope it will encourage you to bake more breads. A starter adds complexity and depth to any dough.

Eat this bread with roast chicken, smoked meat, soups, green salad, and even fresh fruit.

Two days before you plan to bake, make a biga (page 104).

DOUGH

   1½ teaspoons active dry yeast or ½ scant cake fresh yeast

   1½ cups plus 1 tablespoon warm water, 105° to 115°F. for dry yeast, 95°
      to 105°F. for fresh yeast

   ½ cup (4 ounces) biga (page 104), measured at room temperature

   3 tablespoons extra-virgin olive oil or best-quality lard

   3¾ cups (18 ounces) unbleached all-purpose flour

   ⅔ cup (2 ounces) grated pecorino cheese

   1½ teaspoons sea salt

   A pinch of freshly ground black pepper

   ⅓ cup (2 ounces) tightly packed diced pecorino cheese

1 tablespoon olive oil

By hand: Sprinkle the yeast over the warm water in a large mixing bowl and whisk it in; let stand until creamy, about 10 minutes. Add the biga and vigorously squeeze it between your fingers to break it up. Stir in the olive oil. Mix the flour and the grated cheese with the salt and pepper and stir it into the yeast mixture. Knead on a lightly floured work surface, until the dough is sticky and slightly gritty, but elastic and responsive, about 8 to 10 minutes.

By heavy-duty electric mixer: Stir the yeast into the water in the mixer bowl; let stand until creamy, about 10 minutes. Using the paddle attachment, mix in the biga until it is well blended. Mix in the oil, then the flour, grated cheese, salt, and pepper and mix until the dough pulls entirely away from the sides. Change to the dough hook and knead at low speed for 3 minutes, until the dough is sticky, but elastic and responsive. The texture may be slightly gritty from the cheese.

First rise: Place the dough in a lightly oiled bowl, cover it tightly with plastic wrap, and let rise until doubled, about 1 hour and 15 minutes.

Shaping and second rise: Turn the dough out of the bowl onto a lightly floured work surface. Sprinkle the diced cheese over the surface of the dough, leaving a 1-inch margin all around; roll up, kneading in the cheese. Oil a large tube pan such as a ring mold or savarin pan. Roll and stretch the dough on your lightly floured work surface into a rope that is about 24 inches long. Place it in the oiled tube pan and pinch the edges together firmly to form a ring. Cover with a kitchen towel, and let rise until well doubled, 1 hour.

Baking: At least 30 minutes before you plan to bake, preheat the oven to 425°F. with a baking stone inside if you have one. Brush the surface of the bread with olive oil, slide the pan directly onto the hot stone, if you are using it, and bake until the top is golden, about 30 to 35 minutes. Cool briefly, then remove from the mold so the bottom crust doesn't steam and get soggy. Cool on a rack.

CAPPELLO DI GENDARME

Gendarme's Cap, a Calzone from Lecce

—

Makes 2 calzone, to serve 6 to 8

*T*his filled focaccia with its strange name first appeared when the Bourbons ruled the south of Italy. The bakers of Lecce deep in the region of Apulia must have been inspired by the hats the gendarmes wore—Napoleon's famous headgear had the very same shape—and decided to form their focaccia in homage.

DOUGH

2 teaspoons dry active yeast or ⅔ cake (½ ounce) fresh yeast

1⅓ cups warm water, 105° to 115°F. for the dry yeast, 95° to 105°F. for the fresh yeast

2 tablespoons extra-virgin olive oil, plus a little extra for brushing the tops

3¾ cups (18 ounces) unbleached all-purpose flour

1¼ teaspoons sea salt

Cornmeal or coarse semolina as needed

FILLING

3 tablespoons extra-virgin olive oil, plus extra for brushing the tops

1 onion, finely sliced

2 heads frisée (about 1⅓ pounds), well washed and chopped

6 meaty (about 8 ounces) cherry-size or Roma tomatoes or canned Italian-style tomatoes, drained, seeded and roughly chopped

1 tablespoon capers (preferably salt-cured), well drained and rinsed in cold water

2 tablespoons black olives in brine, drained and pitted

Sea salt

Freshly ground black pepper

By hand: Sprinkle the yeast over the warm water in a small bowl, whisk it in, and let stand until creamy, about 10 minutes. Stir in the olive oil. Mix the flour and salt, make a mound of it in a large bowl or on a well-floured work surface, and then make a large well in the center. Gradually pour the dissolved yeast mixture into the well, working the flour from the inside of the well into the liquid with your fingers. Continue until the flour is absorbed. Knead until silky, malleable, elastic, and very slightly moist, 10 to 15 minutes.

By heavy-duty electric mixer: Sprinkle the yeast over the warm water in a mixer bowl, whisk it in, and let stand until creamy, about 10 minutes. Mix in the olive oil with the paddle. Add the flour and salt and mix until the dough comes together. Change to the dough hook and knead at medium speed for 3 minutes, until the dough is silky, malleable, elastic, and very slightly moist.

Rising: Place the dough in a lightly oiled bowl, cover tightly with plastic wrap, and let rise until doubled, 1½ to 2 hours.

Preheat the oven to 425°F. with a baking stone inside, if you plan to use one.

To make the filling: Warm the olive oil in a large saucepan and sauté the onion until it is limp and the frisée until it has wilted. Add the tomatoes, capers, and olives and continue sautéing over medium-high heat, stirring every few minutes, until all the moisture evaporates, about 25 minutes. Add salt and pepper to taste and set aside to cool.

Shaping: Divide the dough in half and cover the piece you are not using. On a lightly floured work surface, roll the first piece of dough into a 10-inch circle and set half the filling in the center, leaving a 1-inch border all around. Fold the dough in half. Press the edges together tightly with your fingertips, then fold the edges over and crimp them with your fingertips. Arrange the dough to look like a Napoleonic hat with a high dome and slightly tapered sides. Repeat with the second piece of dough and filling. Brush the tops with olive oil.

Baking: Set them on an oiled baking sheet or on a pizza peel sprinkled with cornmeal or coarse semolina. If you are using a baking stone, sprinkle it with cornmeal or coarse semolina just before you plan to bake, set the 2 calzone on it, and bake until golden, about 20 minutes.

GREENS FROM THE WILD: *Radicchio, radici di campo, erbe,* and *cicoria* are general words indicating greens that grow spontaneously. What they describe can be anything from slightly bitter dandelion greens and arugula (rocket) to nutty *barba di cappuccino* (monk's beard with its spiky leaves) and *ortica,* nettles, which lose their prickles but not their flavor when rolled into pasta or cooked with greens. They are used for salads and ravioli fillings, eaten with hard-boiled eggs, and cooked into vegetable tarts. *Torte di erbe* were once made totally with *radici di campo,* but they are now cooked with cultivated spinach or Swiss chard.

TORTA DI PORRI E ZUCCA

Leek and Butternut Squash Tart

—

Serves 6

Rina Ramponi has lived all her life in Aulla in the Lunigiana region at the northwestern frontier of Tuscany near Carrara. She first went to the work for the Waterfield family at their fortress castle before World War II. "She knew everything about wild greens," swears Maria Chiodetti, a cook of great talent who, like Rina, has been like part of the family for decades. All these years later, the two widows still live on the property, sharing a handsome house.

What lives they had! They did the cooking and planting and much of the menu planning, and they also were part of the amazing adventures of their employers. They not only met a procession of literary figures such as Iris Origo and Freya Stark, but they knew Bernard Berenson well enough that Maria refers to him as BB. Signora Beevor, the Waterfields' daughter, and her dashing artist husband were married at I Tatti, Berenson's famous Renaissance art-filled villa just outside Florence.

Rina's vegetable tart is low and shallow, a sweet mixture of leeks and butternut squash enclosed in the envelope of a simple savory dough. Rina used to go into the fields and pick wild greens and radicchio. She tossed the leaves for a salad, or served them with hard-boiled eggs, or cooked them into a savory tart such as this one. As one more sign of the changing times, chard is now routinely sold already boiled and pressed into a round the size of a tennis ball, and that is what Rina uses today instead of the mixed greens she once collected.

Rina's tart is extremely versatile. Cut it in slices or wedges for a first course or appetizer, serve it as a main course for lunch, brunch, or supper, or use it as a vegetable side dish.

DOUGH

> 2 cups (10 ounces) unbleached all-purpose flour
>
> 1½ teaspoons sea salt
>
> ¼ cup extra-virgin olive oil, plus a little extra for the glaze
>
> 10 to 11 tablespoons ice-cold water

FILLING

> 3 tablespoons extra-virgin olive oil
>
> 4 medium (about 12 ounces) leeks, washed thoroughly,
>   green part cut in ½-inch-thick slices
>
> ¾ pound butternut squash, peeled, seeded,
>   and cut into ¾-inch cubes (about 2 cups), cooked in salted water
>   until tender, then roughly mashed
>
> 8 scant ounces Swiss chard, boiled, squeezed dry, and cooled
>
> ½ cup (2 ounces) freshly grated Parmigiano-Reggiano cheese
>
> ¼ teaspoon sea salt
>
> Freshly ground black pepper

By hand: Mix the flour and salt together in a large bowl. Stir in the olive oil and then slowly add the water; mix until smooth. If the dough is dry, mix in an extra tablespoon of water. Gather the dough into a ball, cover it with plastic wrap, and leave at room temperature for 30 minutes.

By heavy-duty electric mixer: Combine all the ingredients in the mixer bowl and stir with the paddle attachment until they come together as a dough. Cover with plastic wrap and leave at room temperature for 30 minutes.

To make the filling: Warm the olive oil in a large, heavy sauté pan and sauté the leeks until golden, about 10 minutes. Add the butternut squash and chard and cook for another 5 minutes. Set aside to cool. Stir in the Parmigiano-Reggiano cheese and salt and pepper.

Preheat the oven to 375°F.

Shaping: Divide the pastry dough into two pieces, one slightly larger than the other. Cover the one you are not using. Roll the larger piece on a lightly floured work surface to form a 13-inch circle, large enough to line the bottom and drape over the sides of a well-oiled 9-inch tart pan or springform with a removable rim. Lift the dough gently onto your rolling pin and lay it inside the pan. Cover with the vegetable mixture and smooth the top with a rubber spatula. Roll the remaining dough to form a circle about 9½ to 10½ inches in diameter and set it carefully over the filling. Trim the edges of the larger piece with a sharp knife, fold over the overhanging dough, and crimp the two together to seal the edges. Brush the surface with olive oil and pierce the crust with a fork in several places to allow steam to escape.

Baking: Bake for 40 minutes. Remove from the oven and very gently remove the pan sides or springform. Return the pan to the oven and cook for 15 more minutes, or until the pastry is uniformly golden. Slide the tart off the bottom of the pan, cool on a rack and serve warm or at room temperature.

PIZZA DI CARCIOFI

Filled Artichoke Pie

—

Serves 8

*L*iliana d'Ambrosio describes herself as a 150 percent Napolitana with a mother, grandmother, aunts, and even mother-in-law who are all Neapolitan. She is an impassioned cook so phenomenally focused that she can make dinner for 20 in no time at all. Organization is one of the keys to her success: she can make the pastry for this extremely versatile artichoke tart a day or two ahead and assemble the tart the day before she serves it. And then what does she do? She cuts it in small wedges as an appetizer or part of a buffet or serves it for lunch, brunch, or a light supper.

PASTRY

> 2 cups plus 2 tablespoons (10 ounces) unbleached all-purpose flour
> ½ tablespoon sea salt
> ½ cup olive or peanut oil
> ½ cup cold water

FILLING

> 8 medium artichokes
> 9 cups water
> 2 lemons, cut in half
> ½ cup olive oil
> 2 cloves garlic, lightly flattened
> Sea salt
> Freshly ground black pepper
> 6 eggs
> ½ cup (2 ounces) freshly grated pecorino cheese
> ½ cup (2 ounces) freshly grated Parmigiano-Reggiano cheese
> ½ cup (4 ounces) very finely diced pancetta,
>   coppa, and/or salami

GLAZE

> 1 egg yolk beaten with ¾ teaspoon corn or olive oil

To make the dough: Combine the flour and salt in a bowl. Make a well in the center and add the oil. Blend until the mixture resembles coarse meal. Sprinkle with the water and mix with a fork until the dough comes together. Cover with plastic wrap and leave at room temperature for 30 minutes.

To make the filling: Clean the artichokes by cutting them into quarters, then snapping away all the outer leaves until only pale green ones remain. Remove and discard the chokes and cut each quarter into 6 or 8 slices. Place them in 8 cups water with the juice and the squeezed halves of 2 lemons to keep them from discoloring. Drain and place them in a 3-quart pot with ½ cup olive oil, the garlic cloves, the remaining 1 cup water, salt, and pepper. Cover and cook, checking to see if more water is needed, until the slices are tender, and almost falling apart, 15 to 20 minutes.

Beat the eggs with the pecorino and Parmigiano cheeses, salt, and pepper. Add the pancetta, coppa, and/or salami and mix in well.

Preheat the oven to 375°F. Lightly oil a 9- or 10-inch springform pan or deep baking dish.

Divide the pastry in 2 pieces, one slightly larger than the other. Roll the larger piece out to form a 15-inch round; it should be as fine as the dough for thin pasta. Lift the dough on a rolling pin and lay it inside the prepared pan or baking dish so that it completely covers the bottom and drapes over the sides. Fill with the artichoke mixture and smooth the top with a rubber spatula. Roll the second piece of dough to form a 10-inch round and lay it over the filling. Trim the edges, and crimp them together well to seal the artichoke pizza. Brush the top with the glaze—the beaten egg yolk and oil—and pierce the crust with a fork to allow steam to escape.

Baking: Bake for about 60 minutes, until the top is golden brown. Liliana always makes this artichoke pie the day before she plans to serve it because she is convinced it tastes better that way. She covers and leaves it at room temperature until she serves it.

Pizza Rustica alla Napoletana

Neapolitan Ricotta, Mortadella, and Salami Pie

—

Serves 6

*L*iliana d'Ambrosio's pizza rustica is amazingly versatile. Cut it in small squares and serve it as an appetizer or part of a buffet. Make it the centerpiece of a brunch, a light lunch, or Sunday night supper. Liliana always bakes it the day before she plans to serve it and leaves it at room temperature. I've even seen her make calzoncini with this pastry, shaping tiny little envelopes of dough that enclose the same filling, frying them until they are golden, and then serving them with smoked mozzarella and fine strands of fresh basil.

Liliana entertains for 40 as if it were nothing. When she makes this pizza rustica as part of a buffet for such a group, her practiced hands put together the pastry for the crust in 10 minutes. She loves big family celebrations—the more people the better—and when her son comes home, she starts cooking three days before. Only one word of caution: be careful not to overbake the pizza rustica lest the filling become soggy.

PASTRY

2 cups (10 ounces) unbleached all-purpose flour

½ tablespoon sea salt

½ cup olive or peanut oil

½ cup cold water

FILLING

2½ cups (20 ounces) ricotta cheese, drained, if necessary

3 eggs

3 tablespoons grated aged pecorino romano cheese

3 tablespoons freshly grated Parmigiano-Reggiano cheese

A few gratings of nutmeg

Salt

Freshly ground pepper

1 cup (5 ounces) cubed mortadella

1 cup (5 ounces) cubed salami, preferably soppressata

GLAZE

1 egg yolk beaten with ¾ teaspoon corn or olive oil

To make the dough: Combine the flour and salt in a bowl. Make a well in the center and add the oil. Blend until the mixture resembles coarse meal. Sprinkle with the water and mix with a fork until the dough comes together. Cover with plastic wrap and leave at room temperature for 30 minutes.

To make the filling: Press the ricotta cheese through a sieve or whirl in a processor to aerate. Beat in the eggs. Stir in the grated cheeses and nutmeg, the salt and pepper, and then the mortadella and salami. Taste for salt and pepper; the mixture should be piquant.

Preheat the oven to 375°F. Lightly oil a 9- or 10-inch springform pan or a deep baking dish.

Divide the pastry in 2 pieces, one slightly larger than the other. Roll the larger piece out to form a 15-inch round; it should be as fine as the dough for thin pasta. Lift the dough on a rolling pin and lay it inside the prepared pan or baking dish so that it completely covers the bottom and sides. Fill with the cheese mixture and smooth the top with a rubber spatula. Roll the second piece of dough to form a 10-inch round and lay it over the filling. Trim the edges, and crimp them together well to seal the pizza rustica. Brush the top with the egg glaze and pierce the crust with a fork to allow steam to escape.

Baking: Bake for about 60 minutes, until the top is golden brown. Serve at room temperature.

Sweet Breads

MARITOZZI FABRIANESI
Sweet Rolls from Fabriano Bursting with Raisins
—

Makes 18 rolls

Who would guess that these plump sweet rolls are made specially for Lent, a time normally characterized by darkness and deprivation? It's true that no eggs find their way into the dough, but sweet raisins by the handful and orange zest more than make up for their absence. Franca Farinelli, who made watermarks in the famous hand-made paper of Fabriano for decades, is an enthusiastic baker of such traditional local fruit-filled sweets as *tortiglione*, strudel-like logs filled with apples, pears, dried figs, raisins, and nuts; wreath-shaped *ciambelle*; and these irresistible sweet *maritozzi*.

SPONGE

    1¼ cups (6½ ounces) raisins
    2 cups warm water

3¾ teaspoons (1½ packages) active dry yeast or 1⅔ small cakes (1 ounce) fresh yeast

¾ cup (3½ ounces) unbleached all-purpose flour

DOUGH

4 cups (20 ounces) unbleached all-purpose flour plus 2 to 3 tablespoons for the raisins

¾ cup (5 ounces) sugar

A pinch of salt

Sponge (see above)

¾ cup raisin water, reserved from above

Grated zest of 1 orange

2 teaspoons vanilla extract

3 tablespoons extra-virgin olive oil

GLAZE

1 egg white

1 tablespoon sugar

1½ teaspoons rum

To make the sponge: Cover the raisins with the warm water in a bowl and leave for 30 minutes. Drain, setting the raisins aside for later use and reserving all the water. Warm ¾ cup of the raisin water to 105°F., transfer to a medium-size bowl, sprinkle the yeast over the top, whisk it in, and let stand until foamy, about 10 minutes. Whisk in the flour and stir until smooth. Cover with plastic wrap and let rise until very frothy and bubbly, 20 to 30 minutes.

To make the dough by hand: Place the flour, sugar, and salt in a large mixing bowl. Stir in the sponge, reserved raisin water, orange zest, vanilla, and olive oil and stir gently, then more vigorously until the mixture forms a dough. Knead on a lightly floured surface until the dough is soft and smooth but no longer sticky, 8 to 10 minutes.

To make the dough by heavy-duty electric mixer: Place the sponge in a mixer bowl. Add the ¾ cup raisin water, flour, sugar, salt, orange zest, and vanilla and mix with the paddle until blended. Stir in the olive oil. Change to the dough hook and knead on medium speed for 3 to 4 minutes, until the dough is soft, smooth, and not sticky.

First rise: Place the dough in a well-oiled bowl, cover tightly with plastic wrap, and let rise until doubled, about 2 hours.

Shaping and second rise: Squeeze the reserved raisins dry and toss them with 2 to 3 tablespoons flour to coat them lightly. Spread the dough out on a lightly floured work surface and sprinkle the raisins over the top of the dough, leaving a 1-inch margin all around. Pat them into the surface of the dough, tuck in all four sides, and roll it up. Flatten the dough into a 12 × 7-inch rectangle and press it as much as you can. Cut into eighteen equal pieces and pinch the edges of each one closed to keep the raisins sealed inside. Roll each into a ball and then, with the palm of your hand, into a long oval shape, like the weaving bobbin they are said to resemble. Set on oiled baking sheets, cover well with towels, and let rise again until doubled, about 1 hour.

Baking: At least ½ hour before you plan to bake, preheat the oven to 400°F. Bake the maritozzi until golden on top, 18 to 20 minutes.

While the maritozzi are baking, make the glaze by beating the egg white until frothy, beating in the sugar and then the rum. Immediately brush the tops with the glaze.

PANE NOCIATO

Cinnamon- and Rum-Flavored Walnut Bread

—

Makes 2 loaves

*L*ucky Franca Farinelli. Whenever she and others in Le Marche make this extraordinary walnut bread, they can simply buy the amount of bread dough they need from the neighborhood baker. I have assumed that Americans must first make the dough, so the process turns out to be entirely different. I have cut back on the honey and added some sugar in its place, and I use rum or anisette instead of Mistrà, a traditional anise-flavored liqueur. Even with these changes, this is a sensational bread for breakfast or midday tea.

    2 teaspoons active dry yeast

    ½ cup warm water, 105° to 115°F.

    2 tablespoons sugar

    ¾ cup (3½ ounces) unbleached all-purpose flour

DOUGH

    2½ teaspoons (1 package) active dry yeast

    ¼ cup milk, warmed to 105° to 115°F.

    Sponge (see above)

    ½ cup warm water

    ¼ cup olive oil or best-quality lard, melted

    2 tablespoons honey

    3 tablespoons rum or Sambuca liqueur

    ¾ teaspoon cinnamon

    ½ cup (3½ ounces) sugar

    Grated zest of 1 lemon

    3¾ cups plus 2 to 3 tablespoons for the raisins (1 pound, 1½ ounces)

        unbleached all-purpose flour

    1 teaspoon sea salt

    2¼ cups walnuts, toasted in a 350° oven for 10 minutes

        and roughly chopped

    Cornmeal as needed

To make the sponge: Whisk the yeast into warm water in a small bowl, stir in the sugar, and let stand until foamy, 5 to 10 minutes. Whisk in the flour, cover tightly with plastic wrap, and leave until actively bubbling, 30 to 45 minutes.

To make the dough by hand: Sprinkle the yeast over the warmed milk in a large bowl, whisk it in, and let stand 5 to 10 minutes, until creamy. Add the sponge and mix until smooth. Stir in the warm water and olive oil, then continue stirring as you add the honey, rum, cinnamon, sugar, and lemon zest. Mix in the flour and the salt, 1 cup at a time, until the dough comes together well; it should be slightly sticky, but you may want to add 1 more tablespoon of flour. Knead on a lightly floured surface until the dough is firm, elastic, moist, and somewhat velvety, about 8 to 10 minutes.

To make the dough in a heavy-duty mixer: Sprinkle the yeast over the warmed milk, whisk it in, and let it stand 5 to 10 minutes, until creamy. With the paddle attachment, stir the yeast mixture into the sponge and then add the warm water and olive oil. Stir in the honey, rum, cinnamon, sugar, and lemon zest. Mix in the flour and the salt until the dough comes together well; it should be slightly sticky, but you may want to add 1 more tablespoon of flour. Change to the dough hook and knead for 3 to 4 minutes until the dough is firm, elastic, moist, and somewhat velvety. Finish by sprinkling a little flour on your work surface and kneading the dough briefly.

First rise: Place the dough in a lightly oiled straight-sided container, cover it tightly with plastic wrap, and let rise until doubled, about 2 to 2½ hours.

Shaping and second rise: Turn the dough out onto a lightly floured work surface and shape it into a 13 × 12-inch rectangle. Sprinkle the walnuts over the surface, leaving a 1-inch border all around. Turn in the edges on every side and roll up like a jelly roll. Pat and flatten it as well as you can to distribute the walnuts evenly inside. Cut the dough in half. Tuck in the cut ends to seal the edges and keep the walnuts inside, then pinch the edges closed. Pat the tops again to distribute the walnuts evenly, then flatten each piece, and roll it into a ball. Place the dough on the lightly floured pizza peels or oiled baking sheets covered with parchment paper. Cover them with a towel and let rise until doubled, about 2½ to 3 hours.

Baking: At least 30 minutes before you plan to bake, preheat the oven to 425°F. with a baking stone inside, if you have one. Sprinkle the stone with cornmeal just before sliding the loaf onto it. Bake for 5 minutes, lower the oven to 400°F. for 10 minutes, then turn the oven down to 375°F. and finish baking for 30 to 35 more minutes, until the bread is golden and sounds hollow when tapped on the bottom.

PANINI DI PASQUA

Spicy Easter Rolls

———

Makes 16 rolls

These spicy Easter rolls are like hot cross buns with a lot of character. They are eaten with a hard-boiled egg in Arezzo and surrounding areas on the day of Easter, but I would eat them all year round. The dough is essentially the bread of every day with the addition of such special ingredients as Vin Santo and saffron and a number of tantalizing spices that include cloves, cinnamon, coriander, and even juniper berries. Two millennia ago, Romans sprinkled flowers and powdered saffron on the emperors' routes and perhaps the golden saffron in these rolls is a sign of their ritual use for a special celebration.

SPONGE

> 1 tablespoon active dry yeast or 1⅓ cakes (½ ounce) fresh yeast
>
> ½ cup milk plus 2 tablespoons, warmed to 105° to 115°F. for active dry yeast, 95° to 105°F. for fresh yeast
>
> ¾ cup (3½ ounces) unbleached all-purpose flour

DOUGH

> 2 cups (10 ounces) raisins
>
> ⅔ cup plus 2 tablespoons water reserved from soaking the raisins
>
> Sponge (see above)
>
> 3 tablespoons extra-virgin olive oil
>
> 5 tablespoons Vin Santo
>
> ½ teaspoon ground cloves
>
> ¾ teaspoon ground coriander
>
> 1½ teaspoons cinnamon
>
> 3 juniper berries, flattened with the side of a cleaver
>
> A large pinch of saffron; if you are using threads, dissolve them in the Vin Santo
>
> 2¾ cups plus 1 tablespoon (14 ounces) unbleached all-purpose flour, plus 2 tablespoons for the raisins
>
> ½ teaspoon sea salt

GLAZE

> 1 egg white

To make the sponge: Sprinkle the yeast over the warmed milk in a mixing bowl and whisk it in; let stand until creamy, about 10 minutes. Stir in the flour until well blended. Cover with plastic wrap and let stand until bubbly, about 30 minutes.

To make the dough: While the sponge is rising, put the raisins in a bowl, cover them with warm water, and let them plump for 30 minutes. Drain, reserving the water and squeezing the raisins dry. Set the raisins aside.

Stir ⅔ cup plus 2 tablespoons of water reserved from soaking the raisins into the sponge. Add the olive oil and the Vin Santo and mix well using a wooden spoon or the paddle attachment of a heavy-duty mixer. Mix the spices, flour, and salt together and add to the bowl 1 cup at a time, mixing well until a dough is formed. Set the dough on a lightly floured work surface and knead for 8 to 10 minutes, until the dough is velvety and elastic. If you are using the mixer, change to the dough hook and knead for 2 to 3 minutes at medium speed until the dough is velvety and elastic.

First rise: Place the dough in a well-oiled bowl, cover tightly with plastic wrap, and let rise until doubled, about 1 hour.

Shaping and second rise: Pat the raisins dry and toss them with 2 tablespoons of flour to coat their surfaces. Turn the dough out on a lightly floured surface. Without punching it down, pat it flat and then roll it into a 10 × 16-inch rectangle. Sprinkle the raisins evenly over the surface, leaving a 1-inch margin all around. Turn in all four sides and roll up the dough. Flatten the top with your hand, patting it out as much as possible, cover, and let it rest for 10 minutes covered by a kitchen towel.

Divide dough into sixteen equal pieces. Begin shaping each roll by pinching closed the open sides of the dough. Then roll each one across your lightly floured work surface from one cupped hand to the other, using the surface to generate tension, and pull the dough taut across the top. Set on oiled baking sheets, cover with a towel, and let rise until very puffy, about 1 hour.

Baking: At least 30 minutes before you plan to bake, preheat the oven to 425°F. with a baking stone inside if you plan to use one. Bake the rolls on the baking sheet until deep golden, about 20 to 22 minutes.

6

PRIMI PIATTI

First Courses

Pasta, Polenta, e Risotti

(Pasta, Polenta, and Rice Dishes)

—

PASTA

PASTA AGLI SPINACI CON FEGATINI
Spinach Pasta with a Grappa-Splashed Chicken Liver Sauce

TAGLIARINI E FAGIOLINI VERDI
Tagliarini with Cubes of Fresh Tomatoes and a Swirl of Green Beans

MEZZE MANICHE AI FUNGHI GRATTATI
Rigatoni with a Thick Mushroom Sauce

FUSILLI CON SUGO DI AGNELLO
Spaghetti with Lamb Sauce

PENNE AL MARE
Penne with a Garlicky Shrimp and Calamari Sauce

PASTA CON LE MELANZANE
Rigatoni with Eggplant and Mozzarella

PANIGACCI
Ligurian Pasta Layered with Pesto and Parmigiano-Reggiano Cheese

ORECCHIETTE E BROCCOLI RAPE
Orecchiette Pasta with Tender Leaves of Broccoli Rabe

PISAREI E FASOI
Pasta and Beans from Piacenza

TRENETTE COL PESTO
Trenette with Pesto, Potatoes, and Green Beans

SPAGHETTI COL PESTO ALLA TRAPANESE
Pasta with Almond and Basil Pesto from Trapani

PIZZOCCHERI
Buckwheat Tagliatelle Layered with Potatoes, Cabbage, and Cheese

PASTA CON LA RUCOLA
Pasta with Arugula and Tomatoes

SPAGHETTI UN PO' "DIVERSI"
Spaghetti Just a Little Bit Different than Usual

PASTA ALLA PALOMBARA
Pasta with Tuna, Anchovies, Pine Nuts, and Currants

PENNE AL TONNO
Penne with Fresh Tuna, Capers, and Black Olives

CIALZONS ALLA FRUTTA
Prune- and Fig-Filled Ravioli with Cinnamon-Scented Butter

TORTELLI DI PATATE
Ravioli Filled with Nutmeg-Flavored Potatoes

Tortelli di Zucca
Tortelli with a Nutmeg-Scented Pumpkin Filling

Ravioli in Camicia
Naked Ravioli

POLENTA

Polenta Concia
Polenta Layered with Cheeses and Black Pepper

Variation:

Polenta Taragna Concia
Buckwheat Polenta Layered with Cheese and Black Pepper

Variation:

Pasticciata di Polenta
Polenta Layered with Tomato Sauce and Parmesan Cheese

Matuffi
Creamy Scoops of Polenta Layered with Tomato Sauce

Polenta Incatenata
Polenta and Beans

Polenta con Ragù Bianco
Polenta with a White Ragù of Pancetta, Sausage, and Ham

Toc' in Braide
Farmer's Sauce

RICE

RISO CON LE FAVE VERDI
Rice with Green Favas

PANISSA
Beans and Rice, Salami, and Vegetables from Vercelli

RISO, SEDANO, E SALSICCE
Rice, Celery, and Sausages

RISO E PISELLI
Creamy Rice and Peas

RISO E ZUCCA
Creamy Pumpkin or Butternut Squash–Flavored Rice

RISO DEL SAGRA
Rice with Chicken Livers

RISOTTO ALLA RUCOLA
Risotto with Arugula

Pasta

The shapes of pasta may be infinite in number, but the types of pasta number only two: dried pasta made from semolina flour and fresh egg pasta made from soft wheat flour. Though some women continue to make pasta by hand at home, everyone uses dried pasta at least some of the time. Industrially made pasta first appeared in Italy in the 1820s or 1830s, and many women who are now grandmothers remember when it first came into their households, a novel product indeed. These days everyone uses spaghetti, fusilli, penne, bucatini, lasagne, tiny pastine for soup, and dozens of other shapes.

Fresh egg pasta is much in evidence in northern Italy, home of a still buttery cuisine. It is as likely to be served as fettucine as to be stuffed with any number of vegetable or meat fillings and appear as ravioli, tortelli, tortellini, or cappelletti. The famous historian Piero Camporesi envisions pasta run wild in the culinary landscape of the Lombard-Veneto plain, "a mountain of cheese, rivers of broth running into a lake of soup and a pelago of puddles, a shore of fresh butter, sausages of veal, golden tomacelle, basins of pappardelle and lasagne, pots full of tortelli, tagliatelle and gnocchi." The older women of Apulia still take the time to make orecchiette, ear-shaped pasta, from a firm durum wheat dough; they make capunti and other tubular pastas as well, although their daughters and granddaughters are unlikely to continue the practice. These pastas are also made commercially and are widely available.

When making pasta for four people, Italian grandmothers bring a big pot filled with at least 4 quarts of water to a rolling boil and throw in a handful or two of coarse salt. They put the pasta in the water and, if the water stops boiling, may cover the pot until it comes back to the boil. They cook dried pasta until it is al dente, which simply means that it still has a bit of resistance when bitten into. They drain it, but not totally. They always let some of the cooking water cling to the pasta so it won't dry out, and save some of the water in case it is needed to moisten the sauce. Contrary to rumor, Italians never put oil in the pasta cooking water and they never rinse the pasta under cold water once it has cooked. Keep pasta in your larder and you'll never be without dinner.

Pasta agli Spinaci con Fegatini

Spinach Pasta with a Grappa-Splashed Chicken Liver Sauce

—

Serves 4 as a first course, 2 to 3 as a main course

*I*f you were traveling in Tuscany today, you might still find spinach pasta with a chicken liver sauce, but in the past and perhaps still in the best of all possible worlds, the pasta would be made with very finely chopped spinach and the sauce would have rabbit livers tossed with local grappa. When I asked Morena Spinelli for her advice in making the dish, she quoted an old saying, "*Baccalà, fegatina, e uova: più che cuoce, più che rassoda.*" Which is to say: "Salt cod, chicken livers, and eggs: the longer you cook them, the tougher they get." A cautionary instruction about the livers. Tuscans really know good food: the pasta *is* especially delicious when made with rabbit livers. Pass freshly grated Parmesan cheese at the table.

3 tablespoons extra-virgin olive oil

2 medium-size white onions, minced

5 ounces chicken or rabbit livers, preferably from organically raised free-
    range chickens, any greenish areas discarded, cut in eighths

10 leaves of fresh sage

½ cup grappa

4 to 5 quarts water

1½ tablespoons coarse salt

10 ounces spinach-flavored spaghetti

2 ripe tomatoes, peeled, seeded, and chopped

¾ teaspoon salt

Freshly ground black pepper

Warm the olive oil in a large, heavy sauté pan and sauté the onions over low-medium heat until soft, about 15 to 20 minutes. Add the livers and the sage leaves and sauté for 3 minutes over medium heat until the livers have lost their raw red color. Pour in the grappa and cook at high heat until it has evaporated, about 3 minutes.

(continued)

While the sauce is cooking, bring a large pot with 4 to 5 quarts of water to a boil, add the coarse salt, and cook the spaghetti according to the instructions on the package.

When the grappa in the sauce has evaporated, add the tomatoes, salt, and pepper and cook over low-medium heat for about 15 minutes until the sauce is smooth and concentrated. Drain the pasta, saving 3 to 4 tablespoons of the cooking water in case it is needed to moisten the pasta sauce, and toss it into the pan with the sauce until it is well mixed. Serve at once.

TAGLIARINI E FAGIOLINI VERDI

Tagliarini with Cubes of Fresh Tomatoes and a Swirl of Green Beans

—

Serves 4 to 6

*T*his stunning combination from Apulia is as delicious as it is beautiful. Toss diced juicy summer tomatoes with fresh egg tagliarini and then scatter brilliant green beans over the top in an elegant edible calligraphy. So simple. So appealing. So elemental, suggested Angela Padrona, a nonna who is known for her expertise in making the pastas of Puglia. Of course, she can immediately find the green beans called *fagiolini pinti* that grow only in her region. They are extremely long, like Chinese long beans, and brilliant green. Use Blue Lake or any fresh green beans. Serve with grated pecorino or Parmesan cheese.

> 3 tablespoons extra-virgin olive oil
> 6 medium-size juicy ripe tomatoes, peeled, seeded, and diced
> 9 leaves of fresh basil
> ¼ to ½ teaspoon sugar (optional)
> 4½ teaspoons coarse sea salt
> 10 ounces fresh green beans, trimmed
> 1 pound fresh egg tagliarini, tagliatelli, or fettuccine, store-bought or homemade (page 174)
> Salt
> Freshly ground black pepper

Warm the olive oil in a 10- or 12-inch heavy sauté pan, add the tomatoes, and cook over low heat until they have melted, about 10 minutes.

Tear the basil leaves roughly by hand, add to the tomatoes, and cook for a minute or two longer. Taste the tomatoes; if they are slightly acidic or lack sweetness, stir in the sugar. You may make this ahead and set it aside.

Bring two large pots, each with at least 4 quarts of water, to the boil. One is for the beans and the other for the pasta. Add 1½ teaspoons coarse sea salt to the boiling water in the first pot, toss in the green beans, and cook until they are tender, about 8 minutes. Drain and set aside very briefly.

Add the remaining tablespoon of coarse sea salt and the tagliarini to the boiling water in the second pot and cook until they are al dente, about 3 minutes. Drain, reserving a little of the cooking water to use in case the sauce is dry.

Warm the tomato sauce if you made it ahead, toss the tagliarini in the pan with it, season with salt and pepper. Scatter the green beans in a random pattern over the top, warm them together for a minute or two, and serve hot.

Mezze Maniche ai Funghi Grattati

Rigatoni with a Thick Mushroom Sauce

—

Serves 6

Andreina Pavani Calcagni dreamed up this pasta sauce and should be acclaimed! The secret lies in finding the right mushrooms. Be sure to get brown (not cultivated white button) mushrooms. They are known by various names: cremini, Italian mushrooms, golden mushrooms, or portobellos, which are simply brown mushrooms grown to maturity until their caps have opened to reveal chocolate brown gills. Grating the mushrooms concentrates their taste and brings out their intense, deeply woody flavor.

> 1 pound fresh mushrooms, preferably brown, cremini,
>   or portobello mushrooms
> 1 tablespoon unsalted butter
> 4 to 5 tablespoons extra-virgin olive oil
> 2 garlic cloves, cut in half
> ⅛ teaspoon red pepper flakes
> 1½ cups chicken broth
> ½ chicken bouillon cube
> 1½ tablespoons finely chopped flat-leaf parsley
> Salt (optional)
> At least 4 quarts water
> 1 tablespoon coarse sea salt
> 1 pound short tubular pasta, such as mezze maniche or rigatoni
> Freshly grated Parmigiano-Reggiano cheese for tossing

Clean the mushrooms with a moist paper towel or mushroom brush. Put the butter and oil in a large, heavy sauté pan and using the largest holes in the grater, grate the mushrooms directly into it. Add the garlic cloves and red pepper flakes and turn the heat to medium. Sauté until the mushroom liquid evaporates, about 10 minutes. Add the chicken broth and the bouillon cube, which intensifies flavor and may also eliminate the need for salt, and cook over high heat for 10 to 12 minutes. Remove from the heat, discard the garlic cloves, if you wish, add the parsley, and set aside while the pasta finishes cooking. Taste for salt.

While the sauce is cooking, bring a large pot with at least 4 quarts of water to a rolling boil and add the coarse sea salt and the pasta. Cook according to the manufacturer's instructions, until al dente. Drain the pasta well and toss it into the pan with the sauce. Mix the pasta and sauce together over medium heat for 1 to 2 minutes. Remove from the heat, stir well one final time, and finish by tossing with Parmigiano-Reggiano cheese. Serve immediately.

VARIATION: Make risotto (page 298) flavored with the mushroom sauce. Add the rice after the mushroom liquid evaporates; then add ⅔ cup dry white wine and when it has boiled away, start adding the boiling chicken broth. Proceed as directed.

BOUILLON CUBES *(Brodo di Dado)*: Bouillon cubes give a strong burst of flavor to soups, sauces, broth, stews, and braised meats. They come in four flavors in Italy: chicken, beef, mushroom, and vegetable. Most Italian cubes have animal fats and MSG, although a few, such as the Generoso brand, do not. Try to find bouillon cubes without any additives, but if you cannot, taste carefully for salt because the cubes can be extremely salty. Even so, many grandmothers' little trick of crumbling such a cube directly into many dishes gives an amazing boost to the flavor of sauces. Good homemade meat stock and chicken or vegetable broth are excellent substitutes.

Fusilli con Sugo di Agnello

Spaghetti with Lamb Sauce

—

Serves 6

*P*asta with a lamb sauce is nourishing, filling, unexpectedly satisfying—dinner in a single course. The only difficulty with re-creating this dish from Molise—besides the fact that Italian lamb is flavored by the aromatic grasses and herbs it feeds on—is that an entire lamb in Molise is likely to weigh about 15 pounds, while the leg—only the leg—of an American lamb can weigh 6 pounds or more. To approximate the taste of the Italian meat, use extremely lean boneless lamb cut from the shoulder.

Like many women in the centuries-old Albanian community of Ururi in Molise, Ausilia d'Arienzo makes her own pasta by rolling a cylinder of smooth dough around the rib of an umbrella and then, with a single tug, deftly extracts the rib, producing a rustic equivalent of spaghetti or bucatini. But she doesn't call it spaghetti; her name for the strands is fusilli, from the dialect word for the ribs of an umbrella.

There are two ways to serve the pasta. You can toss it with the sauce, then sprinkle on as many hot red pepper flakes as you want, and serve it with grated pecorino cheese. Signora d'Arienzo turns one course into two by carefully removing the pieces of lamb and some of the sauce. She tosses pasta with the lamb-flavored sauce and serves the lamb as a second-course stew with a green salad.

Tomato Sauce

1½ pounds ripe tomatoes, 2 cups drained canned tomato pulp or Italian
plum tomatoes, juices reserved, or 2 cups bottled organic tomato
puree. See Source Guide to Ingredients.

3 tablespoons extra-virgin olive oil

1 small onion, minced (optional)

2 small garlic cloves, minced (optional)

Salt

Pasta Sauce

3 to 4 tablespoons extra-virgin olive oil

1 small onion, finely minced

1 carrot, diced

2 tablespoons minced flat-leaf parsley

1 bay leaf, preferably fresh European variety

1½ pounds very lean lamb from the shoulder, organically raised,
     if possible

¾ cup dry white wine

Salt and freshly ground black pepper

At least 4 quarts water

1 to 1½ tablespoons coarse salt

1 pound spaghetti

¼ to ½ teaspoon red pepper flakes

3 to 4 tablespoons grated pecorino cheese

If you are making tomato sauce using fresh tomatoes, peel them by plunging them into boiling water for barely a minute; the skin will slide off easily. Press them or the canned plum tomatoes through a food mill or sieve to remove the seeds, but reserve the juices. Warm the olive oil in a large heavy pot, add the onion and garlic (if you are using them), and sauté only until the garlic barely begins to take color, about 4 minutes. Add the tomatoes and their juices and simmer over moderate heat for about 30 minutes.

To make the pasta sauce: Place a heavy, flameproof casserole, preferably terra-cotta or enameled metal, with the olive oil over very low heat. Once the oil is warm, add the onion and carrot and sauté over medium-low heat until the onion is soft and translucent, 10 to 12 minutes. Stir in the parsley and bay leaf. Remove and discard any fat from the lamb and cut it into bite-sized pieces. Push the onion and garlic to the edges of the pan (or remove and set them aside, returning them to the pan once the meat has browned). Add the meat and cook over medium-high heat until it is browned on all sides, about 10 to 15 minutes. Pour in the wine, raise the heat, and boil to cook away the wine, about 15 minutes. When the wine has almost entirely evaporated, stir in the tomato sauce, cover the pan, and simmer over low heat until the lamb is very tender, about 1 hour to 1 hour and 30 minutes, stirring from time to time. If the sauce seems to be drying out, add a little water or broth. Remove the bay leaf and season to taste with salt and pepper.

While the sauce is cooking, bring a large pot with at least 4 quarts of water to a rolling boil. Add the coarse salt and the pasta. Cook the pasta according to the directions on the package, drain, and toss in the pan with the sauce over low heat for a minute or two to mix thoroughly. Sprinkle with red pepper flakes and serve with grated pecorino cheese.

VARIATION: Substitute free-range chicken for the lamb, cooking only until the chicken is tender.

PENNE AL MARE

Penne with a Garlicky Shrimp and Calamari Sauce

—

Serves 6 to 8 as a first course, 4 to 6 as a main course

Renata Marsili is *una vera lucchese,* a true native of Lucca. She is also the matriarch of her family, much loved by the various members of the younger generation. We met through her grandson, Alberto Marsili, who works at the family's small and impeccable wine shop in Lucca. He described her as the prototypical nonna—informal, warm, loving, and full of energy, especially in the kitchen, her constant habitat—and he insisted that I had to meet her. A long and careful courtship followed: several phone calls between members of the family preceded my phone introduction and then our first meeting. I sat in a living room with the nonna and Tilde, one of her daughters; we talked for an hour and, having convinced the signora of my seriousness, I was invited back for a session in the kitchen. More phone calls. Another appointment. Finally the day arrived. She cooked and cooked and cooked—chopping on a small kitchen table and sautéing, simmering, and frying on a small old-fashioned four-burner stove. Then we sat down at the dining room table, three generations of her family and me, and we ate any number of traditional Lucchese dishes, among which this pasta was a star.

Signora Marsili lives mere steps from a wonderful fish market. She cooks her calamari with an immense amount of spring garlic, although you would never know it from the final taste, and she stirs in a little milk at the end of the cooking to thicken the sauce and bring it all together.

At least 4 quarts water

1 tablespoon coarse sea salt

¼ cup extra-virgin olive oil

¼ cup minced sweet spring garlic or 2 to 3 tablespoons minced older garlic

⅜ teaspoon red pepper flakes

12 ounces calamari, cleaned, cut into ½-inch strips

8 ounces shrimp, peeled and deveined, cut into ½-inch strips

½ cup dry white wine

5 tablespoons milk

⅓ cup chopped flat-leaf parsley

1¼ teaspoons sea salt

1 pound penne

Bring a large pot with at least 4 quarts of water to the boil. Add the coarse salt.

While the pasta water is coming to a boil, warm the olive oil in a 12-inch heavy skillet large enough to hold all the pasta. Add the garlic and red pepper flakes and cook over low-medium heat, stirring frequently, and being certain that the garlic remains pale and barely golden, 2 to 3 minutes.

Add the calamari and shrimp and sauté over medium-high heat until the shrimp are pink and the calamari tender, 4 to 5 minutes, being careful not to let the garlic brown. Pour in the white wine and after 3 or 4 minutes, when it has cooked down a bit, stir in the milk. Mix the sauce well and simmer for about 3 minutes until it thickens a bit. Toss in the parsley and taste for salt.

Meanwhile cook the penne and drain, but save some of the water in case the sauce needs moistening. Toss the drained pasta with the sauce in the pan and stir the two together over medium heat for a minute or two, adding a bit of the reserved cooking water. Serve immediately.

VARIATION: This sauce can also be stirred into risotto (page 303).

TIP: A word of caution. Spring garlic looks a bit like a big scallion, and is tender with a clear white skin. If you are using older garlic, use half as much and cut out any green shoot inside the clove.

TIP: Renata Marsili adds a little bit of milk to a seafood sauce or fish dish to amalgamate the flavors and make a suave, smooth sauce.

PASTA CON LE MELANZANE

Rigatoni with Eggplant and Mozzarella

—

Serves 6 as a first course, 4 as a main course

*L*iliana d'Ambrosio, a sensational Neapolitan cook, must know the entire culinary repertory of her remarkable city. Sometimes she makes a *sartù di riso*, Naples' richest and most elaborate dish, and other times she whips up this eggplant and pasta recipe in minutes. Don't bother to peel the eggplant and don't worry about bitter juices. Just cut the eggplant into dice, plunge them into water for 15 minutes, and never look back. This dish typifies the best of what Italy can offer: take four or five simple ingredients and make a pasta that sings with the freshness of tomato, the creaminess of eggplant, the piquant bite of pecorino, and the melting smoothness of mozzarella.

> 3 pounds fresh tomatoes or 2¼ cups bottled organic tomato puree
> (See Source Guide to Ingredients)
> 2 medium eggplants, firm and glossy
> 2¼ cups (9 ounces) grated pecorino romano cheese
> Olive or peanut oil
> At least 4 quarts water
> 1 tablespoon coarse salt
> 1 pound rigatoni
> 2 cups (8 ounces) cubed best-quality mozzarella (½-inch cubes)

Press the fresh tomatoes through a food mill directly into a deep, heavy pot and simmer for 30 minutes over a low fire. If you are using tomato puree, you need only warm it briefly.

Cut the eggplants into 1-inch dice and put into a bowl with salted water. Leave for 15 minutes, then drain and pat dry.

Put 1 cup of the pecorino cheese on each of two separate dinner plates. Pour olive or peanut oil into a large, deep frying pan to a depth of 1½ inches and heat to 375°F., or until a tiny piece of eggplant bubbles and dances in the oil. Because there are so many, you will need to fry the eggplant cubes in two batches until they are golden and soft, 2 to 3 minutes. After you remove each batch of eggplant with a slotted spoon, immediately toss it in one cup of pecorino cheese and mix well. Add the still hot eggplant cubes to the tomato sauce and simmer the mixture for 5 to 10 minutes.

While the eggplant is cooking, bring a large, heavy pot with at least 4 quarts of water to the boil, add the coarse salt, and cook the rigatoni according to the directions on the package until they are al dente. Drain the pasta and immediately toss with the sauce in the pan, add the remaining ¼ cup pecorino romano, put the pot back on the heat, and add the mozzarella. Stir until the cheese has melted. Serve immediately.

PANIGACCI

Ligurian Pasta Layered with Pesto and Parmigiano-Reggiano Cheese

Serves 8 as a first course or appetizer, 4 as a main course

Vittoria Genovese, a wonderful cook from the Lunigiana region of Liguria, was amazed that I'd never heard of panigacci. To correct the gap in my pasta experience, she whipped up a thin batter in a flash and then spooned it onto a hot griddle, essentially making crepes. She stacked them in layers, painting a wash of pesto and sprinkles of grated Parmigiano-Reggiano cheese between each one and the next, and served up the simplest and most delicious pasta torte in a matter of minutes.

The batter should be as thin as crepe batter; keep thinning it until you get it right. Vittoria suggested using a nonstick pan instead of the *testo*, a large flat griddle of fireproof terra-cotta clay or iron, but she told me I must oil it the traditional way: cut a potato in half, dip it into olive oil, and use it to spread oil over the surface of the pan. Although most people make panigacci and serve them immediately, Vittoria has been known to make ten or twelve about half an hour before it is time to eat. She sets them in a deep bowl over a pot of boiling water and covers them with a kitchen towel. When people are ready at table, she dips each one for a second in the boiling water, puts it on a plate, spreads a thin layer of pesto over the top, and repeats the process until all the panigacci are used up. At the end, she sprinkles grated Parmigiano-Reggiano cheese and drizzles olive oil over the top of what looks like a cake. To serve, she just cuts a wedge for everyone and passes a little extra cheese. Serve it with a wash of pesto (page 157) with olive oil and salt, or with tomato sauce. You can also cut the panigacci into ribbons, like fettuccine or tagliarini, and toss them with sauce.

> 2 scant cups (9 ounces) unbleached all-purpose flour
>
> ¾ teaspoon sea salt
>
> 2⅓ cups water
>
> 1 potato
>
> ¼ to ⅓ cup extra-virgin olive oil
>
> 1 cup pesto (page 157)
>
> ½ cup (2 ounces) freshly grated Parmigiano-Reggiano cheese

Make a smooth crepe-like batter by putting the flour and salt into a large bowl and mixing in the water, whisking at the beginning to prevent lumps from forming, then stirring with a wooden spoon. You can also mix the ingredients in a blender until smooth. Keep thinning until you get the fluid consistency of crepe batter.

Cut the potato in half and dip one half into the olive oil. Heat an 8- or 9-inch Teflon pan until it is hot, almost smoking. Impale the oiled potato half on a fork and use it to spread the oil over the surface of the pan. Fill a ladle half full of the batter and pour it in to coat the bottom of the pan in a very thin circle. Use the bottom and side of the ladle to pat the batter down and flatten it as much as possible. Let it cook for 2 to 3 minutes and when it begins to pull away from the bottom of the pan, turn it over and cook briefly on the other side. Bubbles will appear in the dough. When they are cooked, both sides should look speckled and lightly brown, but you may need to turn them twice to achieve this effect. You will probably have to throw away the first crepe before you get it right. Lightly re-oil the pan for each crepe.

You may keep them for half an hour as Vittoria does or serve immediately with a thin wash of pesto sauce and sprinklings of Parmigiano-Reggiano cheese between each layer. You may also cut them into strips, toss with pesto, olive oil, and salt, and serve with grated Parmigiano-Reggiano cheese.

Orecchiette e Broccoli Rape

Orecchiette Pasta and Tender Leaves of Broccoli Rabe

—

Serves 4 as a first course, 2 or 3 as a main course

This dish is in the repertoire of every grandmother in Apulia. Maria Andriani's may be the tastiest one I have eaten. Maria makes her own orecchiette pasta, which gets its name from the ear it resembles, by combining equal amounts of wheat and durum flours with warm water and salt, but it isn't necessary to follow suit. Dried orecchiette are now available from many pasta makers. If you can't find broccoli rabe, substitute dandelion greens, if you like their bite, or broccoli, if you prefer a subtler taste.

1 to 1½ pounds broccoli rabe

At least 4 quarts water

1 tablespoon coarse sea salt

1 pound orecchiette

3 tablespoons extra-virgin olive oil

3 large garlic cloves, minced

6 anchovy fillets under oil, drained and minced; or 2 to 3 anchovies under
    salt, rinsed and minced

¼ teaspoon red pepper flakes or 1 fresh hot red pepper, minced

Salt

3 to 4 tablespoons best-quality extra-virgin olive oil

2 to 3 ounces ricotta salata cheese

Wash the broccoli rabe well. Discard any thick stalks, peel the thinner stems and cut into 2-inch pieces. Roughly chop the tender sprouts and leaves of the broccoli rabe.

Bring a large pot with at least 4 quarts water to a rolling boil. Add coarse salt first, then the pasta. Orecchiette can take anywhere from 10 to 18 minutes to cook; check your package for cooking times. Add the broccoli rabe when 6 to 7 minutes remain so that the two cook together in the same water until both are tender.

Meanwhile, warm the olive oil over low-medium heat in a medium sauté pan, add the garlic and anchovies, mash them with a wooden spoon to a paste, and cook for about 4 to 5 minutes, until the garlic is barely softened and beginning to turn golden. Add the red pepper flakes and continue cooking briefly. Taste for salt. Drain the pasta and broccoli rabe, toss them into the pan with the anchovies and garlic, and mix together well.

Transfer to a heated serving platter, toss with the best-quality extra-virgin olive oil, grate the ricotta salata cheese over the top, and serve immediately.

PISAREI E FASOI

Pasta and Beans from Piacenza

—

Serves 6 as a first course, 4 as a main course; recipe doubles easily

*P*iacenza's best-known dish starts with *pisarei*, chewy pasta shaped like large grains of wheat. They are a legacy of times of extreme poverty when everything had to be used up, even the last remaining bread crumbs. Usually the pisarei—so called because they bear a certain resemblance to little boys' penises (in Italian, *pisellino*)—were eaten with *faso*, or beans, a combination of cereals and legumes that

Pia Zoli Maestri

was a substitute for the proteins they couldn't get from meat, which was far too expensive. The bread crumbs give a provocative crunch to the homemade pasta in this classic dish that is fast disappearing from the tables of Piacenza.

Pia Zoli Maestri warned me not to add salt to the cooking water because it toughens the skin of the beans and causes them to split open. Nutritious and filling, pisarei e fasoi is such a filling pasta dish that it is usually served as a one-dish meal. Although its preparation takes some time, it can easily be made ahead in steps and assembled when you are ready to serve it. It keeps well and can be reheated. Pass the Parmigiano-Reggiano cheese at the table.

BEAN SAUCE

> **2 cups (1 pound) dried borlotti or cranberry beans or 1 (19-ounce) can Italian borlotti or cranberry beans, undrained**
>
> **10 cups water**

4 tablespoons unsalted butter

1 small white onion, sliced extremely fine

⅓ cup (2 ounces) minced pancetta, salt pork, or bacon

1 cup meat broth or 1 meat bouillon cube dissolved in 1 cup hot water;
    if you use the cube, beware its saltiness

2 teaspoons tomato paste, just enough to add color

8 leaves of fresh basil

2 European bay leaves, preferably fresh; use only 1 bay leaf if you are
    using dried California bay leaves

Substantial grindings of fresh black pepper

PISAREI PASTA

½ scant cup fine dry bread crumbs

About ¾ cup very hot water

2 cups (10 ounces) unbleached all-purpose flour

1 egg

At least 4 quarts water

2 teaspoons salt

To make the bean sauce: If you are using dried beans, 12 hours before you plan to start cooking, soak them in a large bowl covered with water to cover by 2 to 3 inches. Drain and rinse well in cold water. Put the drained beans in a 4- or 5-quart heavy-bottomed pot, cover with 10 cups water, and cook at a slow simmer for 2 hours, or until they are tender. Drain, reserving the cooking water. Begin here if you are using canned beans. Drain them, reserving the liquid.

Melt the butter in a large, heavy pot, preferably nonstick, and add the onion; cook over low heat until the onion is pale and limp, about 15 minutes. Add the pancetta and cook for another 5 to 6 minutes. Add the beans and 1½ cups of the cooking water, the meat broth, the tomato paste, basil leaves, bay leaves or leaf, and lots of pepper. Cook over medium heat for 4 to 5 minutes. If the sauce is too thick, add more cooking water or broth. Remove and discard the bay leaves.

While the beans are cooking, make the pasta. Place the bread crumbs in a bowl and add enough hot water to soften them, stirring it in well. Put all but 2 tablespoons of the flour in a large bowl; make a hole in the center and set the moistened bread crumbs in it. Mix, adding the egg, and then using the very hot water to make a firm but elastic dough. Continue working the dough and then kneading it on a lightly floured work surface for about 10 to 12 minutes, adding sprinkles of flour as necessary. The pasta dough will be firm and silky. You can also mix the dough in a heavy-duty electric mixer for about 5 minutes. Cover and let the dough rest 30 minutes to 1 hour.

Divide the dough into 14 pieces. Cover the pieces you are not using. Cut each piece in half and using your palms roll each into a log as long and thin as a pencil, about ⅜ inch in diameter. Cut off tiny pieces, each about ½ inch long. Press each one firmly against the work surface with your thumb to make what look like little gnocchi. Each one should be very fine and about the size of the borlotti beans you are cooking to serve with the pasta. You may put these on a baking sheet lined with parchment paper, sprinkle them with semolina or a granulated flour like Wondra, cover, and keep in the refrigerator until you are ready to use them later that day.

To cook the pasta, bring a large pot with at least 4 quarts of water to the boil, add salt, and boil the little pisarei for about 7 to 15 minutes, depending on how fresh they are, until they are tender. Drain and serve tossed with the borlotti bean sauce. (You can make the sauce 2 days ahead and store it in the refrigerator. The pasta can be made and shaped 1 day in advance. Reheat the sauce and beans about 30 minutes before cooking the pasta. You can reheat any leftovers without problems.)

TRENETTE COL PESTO

Trenette with Pesto, Potatoes, and Green Beans

—

Serves 4 to 6 as a first course, 3 or 4 as a main course

*M*any years ago when we lived in a small village in Liguria, Iva Spagnoli cooked for us from time to time. Iva, a perpetually good-natured woman, lived by herself; her son worked in a bank nearby. She grew her own vegetables, fruits, and herbs, had a passel of rabbits, and made olive oil from the olives on her tree. She was living evidence that thrifty Ligurians rely on the ingredients they can coax from the rocky hillsides and mountainous landscape of their region, which wraps around the Mediterranean from just beyond Nice to the northern tip of Tuscany.

Pesto may be one of Italy's best-known exports, but Iva taught me the true way that Ligurians make and eat the brilliant green sauce. She started with sweetly pungent aromatic basil that she picked in her garden and she pounded it in a mortar with garlic, pine nuts or walnuts from her tree, sea salt, and cheese, then slowly added delicate oil from Ligurian olives. She tossed it with trenette, slender pasta that is only slightly wider than linguine, and with the potatoes and tender green beans with which they had been cooked. She always finished the dish with a nut-sized piece of sweet butter.

Pesto freezes well, but leave out the cheese and add it only when you are ready to use the pesto. Transfer the sauce to a freezer container, film the top with ⅛-inch olive oil, cover with a tight-fitting lid, and store in the refrigerator or freezer for up to 4 months. If you can't find Sardinian pecorino, use all Parmigiano-Reggiano cheese. Pass freshly grated pecorino or Parmigiano-Reggiano cheese at the table.

PESTO

    1½ teaspoons minced garlic

    ¼ cup pine nuts or walnuts, toasted briefly in a 350°F. oven

    1 cup tightly packed leaves of fresh basil, cleaned

    ¼ teaspoon sea salt

    6 tablespoons grated Sardinian pecorino cheese and 6 tablespoons grated Parmigiano-Reggiano cheese or ¾ cup grated Parmigiano-Reggiano cheese

    ½ cup extra-virgin Ligurian olive oil

PASTA AND SAUCE

    5 quarts water

    1 tablespoon coarse sea salt

    2 medium (about ½-pound) new potatoes, peeled

    4 ounces tender young green beans, trimmed

    1 pound trenette, linguine, or tagliatelle

    1 to 2 tablespoons unsalted butter, room temperature

    Salt

    Freshly grated pecorino or Parmigiano-Reggiano cheese for sprinkling

You may puree all the ingredients for pesto in a blender or in a food processor fitted with the steel blade. To be authentic, pound together the garlic and pine nuts or walnuts in a marble mortar with a pestle. Add the basil and salt—use coarse sea salt when making the pesto in a mortar—and grind them, crushing to a coarse paste. Add the cheeses. Transfer to a bowl and whisk in the best Ligurian olive oil drop by drop, as if you were making mayonnaise, until you have a creamy sauce. If the sauce is too thick, slowly add more oil and taste for seasoning.

Bring a large pot with 5 quarts of water to a rolling boil and add 1 tablespoon coarse sea salt. Add the potatoes and green beans and cook until both are truly al dente, 5 to 7 minutes. If one is done before the other, remove it first. Drain, cool slightly, and slice the potatoes. Bring the water back to a boil, add the pasta, and cook until it is still slightly al dente. Reserve about ⅓ cup of the cooking water.

Using a slotted spoon or strainer, toss the pasta, potatoes, and green beans on a warmed serving platter. Whisk 2 tablespoons of the pesto into a small ladle full of the cooking water, add the butter, and toss with the pasta. Add the rest of the pesto, taste for salt, sprinkle with pecorino cheese, and serve immediately.

VARIATION: Use fresh trenette or any other fresh egg pasta cut in narrow strips. Cook the vegetables in the boiling water until they are about 3 minutes from being done. Add the pasta and cook until it is al dente. Drain the pasta and vegetables, reserving a ladle of the cooking water, and proceed as above.

SPAGHETTI COL PESTO ALLA TRAPANESE

Pasta with Almond and Basil Pesto from Trapani

—

Serves 6 as a first course, 4 as a main course

America has long since fallen in love with the basil pesto of Genoa, but wait until people discover this spicy pesto sauce from Trapani. Dazzling to taste, incredibly simple to prepare, it is a sensational Sicilian alternative to the winning northern combination.

Antonietta de Blasi Rocca, the grandmother who gave me this recipe, insisted that it must be made in a mortar to get the right texture. That may make a difference, but I've made it several times in a blender and a food processor and it is delicious. Make it a few hours ahead so that the flavors can mingle well. Serve it on spaghetti and pass lots of grated pecorino or Parmigiano-Reggiano cheese at the table. Have enough on hand for the seconds that your guests will inevitably demand.

> ¾ cup (3½ ounces) blanched almonds
> 1 teaspoon sea salt
> 4 medium garlic cloves, roughly chopped
> 1 cup or 50 large leaves of fresh basil
> 5 sprigs of flat-leaf parsley
> ⅛ teaspoon red pepper flakes
> 6 small (about 1½ pounds) tomatoes, peeled, seeded, and roughly chopped
> ½ cup extra-virgin olive oil
> At least 5 quarts water
> 1½ tablespoons coarse sea salt
> 1¼ pounds spaghetti

If you are making this in a food processor, set the almonds and sea salt in the bowl fitted with the steel blade. Grind together until they are so fine they are almost a coarse flour. Add the rest of the ingredients except for the water, coarse salt, and spaghetti and process until they are a creamy sauce.

If you are making this in a marble mortar, pound the almonds with a pestle. Add the salt, garlic cloves, basil, parsley, and red pepper flakes and crush them well. The salt will help you crush the other ingredients. Transfer to a bowl, mix in the tomatoes, and amalgamate the mixture with the oil. You can keep this pesto for 2 or 3 days in the refrigerator or freeze and keep it for 2 or 3 months.

Bring a large pot with at least 5 quarts of water to a rolling boil, add 1½ table-spoons coarse sea salt, and cook the pasta until al dente. Drain and toss with the pesto on a warmed serving platter. Serve immediately.

TIP: If a garlic clove is old, it may have sprouted a small green interior shoot. Remove it, says Luisa Cappelli; it is sharp and bitter.

———

Tall, thin, and stylishly dressed in flowered silk and high-heeled black shoes with a single strap, Antonietta deBlasi Rocca was so upbeat, so full of smiles and soft giggles and enthusiasm, that the word *allegra* seemed invented to describe her. Her mouth curled up in merriment, lighting up her long, narrow face. She lives with her daughter's family in a very large beautiful house in the city of Alcamo in Sicily, where she was born and has lived all her eighty-three years.

Mother of three and grandmother of four, she seems to have lived an enchanted life. When she was growing up, every Sunday was a celebration; the long dining table always held a big group—there were four sisters, one brother, and both parents, just to begin with. Her mother would make tiny rice balls or minute meatballs floating in allspice-flavored broth, and *biancomangiare*—blancmange—a simple milk pudding. The family often went to the country where their sheep and cows gave the milk for cheeses and desserts. They never needed to go shopping: fishermen arrived at the door with their catch still dripping, and the butcher appeared with choice cuts of meat.

Before the war the family, by now extended, made the journey to the seaside on muleback every summer to spend two months at her sister's husband's family house. It sat on a high bluff overlooking the sea, but only men and children were allowed to go to the beach, leaving the women at home to cook lunch with the help of the maid each family brought along. Women weren't allowed to bathe because it was generally agreed that water depleted energy. To replenish it, the men had to eat hard-boiled eggs, which is why Antonietta has an amazing repetoire of eggs cooked in various tantalizing ways. After a while, the men took to passing the days wearing only their pajama bottoms with elasticized waists, allowing them to eat to their heart's content. Family members weren't even required to bestir themselves to go out for Sunday mass; they had a church at home where mass was said. "We were always in company, always in a group. When water hadn't yet come into houses, we all went to the well together. When there wasn't any light, we stayed together all day and then lit the fireplaces at night."

Alcamo was fortunate during World War II because,

unlike Palermo and Trapani, it wasn't bombed, but the family went to the country anyway. Every week they, like others, held an open house. Whole groups of friends moved between various houses and then, in the evening, there were dances at the men's club and also at public places where entrance fees were charged.

Given the strictness with which girls were guarded in those days, it is astonishing that Antonietta met her husband at the movies. Her father was against the match from the beginning and put a lock on her window so she couldn't go out on the balcony. Ultimately he changed his mind but the couple couldn't be married until her older sister found a husband. Once that came to pass, Antonietta's wedding took place at her newly married sister's house where everyone danced on the terrace all night long. At the time there were only two cars in all of Alcamo. Her brother owned one, a very snappy convertible, and when Mussolini came to the city, he borrowed it to parade up and down the main street.

When her own children were little, Antonietta went to her mother's house every evening and, much to her husband's consternation, always stayed late. (Girls traditionally went to their mothers and men to their club.) But while the family was still in Alcamo during the war there were blackouts, and her husband and her sisters' husbands used to wait outside while the women continued gossiping inside, the men getting angrier and angrier as they stood holding the flashlights with which to light the way home.

Antonietta has dedicated an immense part of her life to cooking and even at eighty-three is frequently in the large, light-flooded white-tiled kitchen. There's plenty of room for her daughter to cook in one area while she's at work in another. "She's a great temptress," said Michèla, her daughter-in-law, who can't resist her almond tart. Michèla's husband, Mimmo, can't resist anything his mother makes that has sugar in it. He doesn't have to. She seems to be in the kitchen regularly baking for him and other family members.

Antonietta still makes dishes she learned from her mother. A specialty from early in her marriage: broccoli parboiled in the water into which she then put the pasta to cook. In the past she would drain the broccoli and sauté it before tossing it with the pasta, but now she first sautés fennel-flavored sausage with the broccoli and pronounces it a great success. And, in a turnabout of generations, she makes spicy *pesto alla trapanese*—an uncooked tomato, basil, and almond pesto made only in Trapani—a collaboration between mother- and daughter-in-law. The dish is what Italians call a *squisitezza*—so tantalizing and so simple—one more triumph made with ingredients that grow in the strong heat of the Sicilian sun.

PIZZOCCHERI

Buckwheat Tagliatelle Layered with Potatoes, Cabbage, and Cheese

—

Serves 6 to 8 as a first course, 4 to 6 as a main course

*P*izzoccheri are dark and dappled slightly nutty-tasting tagliatelle made of buckwheat in the Valtellina, the mountainous area of Lombardy that arcs across a broad valley just above the northern end of Lake Como. When Lina Vitali was growing up in the tiny town of Montagna in the 1920s, she made pizzoccheri daily with her grandmother; and Esther Saini, now a white-haired grandmother, could already turn them out alone when she was twelve. Lina introduced me to Esther and this is her recipe, unmodified by the passage of time. Layered with chunks of potato and cabbage leaves and tossed with melted cheeses and garlic-flavored browned butter, the buckwheat pasta is part of a robust country dish.

The Valtellina is at such a high altitude that the cuisine has always been conditioned by the availability of ingredients. Corn, rye, and buckwheat were staples, but the potato, the newcomer ingredient in this recipe, did not arrive in the Valtellina until the end of the eighteenth century, when it remained a curiosity for a while.

For some years eating buckwheat was a bitter reminder of times of poverty and deprivation in the Valtellina. But time has passed, rustic food has become chic, and buckwheat has reappeared in the dishes that people eat enthusiastically at home and in trattorie. You can make your own pizzoccheri, as Esther Saini still does, but if you buy them packaged, you need not spend much time putting the dish together.

PASTA

    1 pound dried pizzoccheri pasta imported from Italy
       (See Source Guide to Ingredients)

    OR

    1 cup (about 7 ounces) unbleached all-purpose flour

    2 cups (10 ounces) buckwheat flour

    1 egg

    Salt

    ⅔ cup water; you may need 2 or 3 more tablespoons

At least 4 quarts water

1 tablespoon coarse salt

8 ounces waxy boiling potatoes, peeled and cut in walnut-sized chunks

8 ounces savoy cabbage, leaves separated and cut into long thin strips

Salt (optional)

SAUCE

1¾ sticks (7 ounces) best-quality unsalted butter

About 6 to 8 garlic cloves, slivered

A few leaves of fresh sage, torn into pieces (optional)

2 cups (8 ounces) diced young bitto, Montasio, or fontina cheese

1 cup (4 ounces) freshly grated Parmigiano-Reggiano cheese

Freshly ground black pepper

If you are making the pasta, sift the two flours together on your work surface and add the salt. Make a well in the center. Combine the egg and water and pour into the well. Start mixing the flour to form a dough; you may need more or less water, depending on the flour and the humidity of the day. The dough will be rough and scrappy at first, but as you mix and knead, about 15 minutes if you are doing this by hand, you will produce a smooth dough, as for tagliatelle. Roll it out to be very slightly thicker than usual, about ⅛ inch thick. You may also run it through a pasta machine, taking it down to the third-to-last notch. Cut into fettuccine-width ribbons about ¼ inch wide and then cut each of those to be about 4 inches long.

If you are using dried pasta, begin the recipe at this point. Bring a large pot with at least 4 quarts of water to a rolling boil, add 1 tablespoon coarse salt, and drop in the potatoes. Cook over medium-high heat until they are barely tender when pierced by the tip of a knife, 2 to 3 minutes. Next add the cabbage leaves and cook over high heat just until they are no longer crunchy, no more than 5 minutes. Now toss in the pizzoc-cheri noodles and cook them over the same medium-high heat, skimming off any foam, until the pasta is al dente, about 4 to 5 minutes if you are using fresh pasta, 8 minutes for the dried. Drain all the ingredients well.

While the pasta is cooking, make the sauce: Melt the butter with the garlic cloves over medium-high heat in a small sauté pan, but do not let the garlic burn. Add the optional sage leaves and cook until the butter is the color of chestnuts.

To make the finished dish, put a large layer of the pasta on the bottom of a buttered heatproof baking dish, cover with a few of the cooked cabbage leaves, sprinkle some potatoes over them, and then a good-sized handful of the diced bitto cheese. Top with a handful of grated Parmigiano-Reggiano cheese and more pizzoccheri. There are many more pizzoccheri noodles than anything else so be prepared to use them with a free hand as you assemble the dish. Finish with freshly ground black pepper. Pour the sauce over the top of the pizzoccheri and serve immediately.

Pasta con la Rucola

Pasta with Arugula and Tomatoes

—

Serves 4 as a first course, 3 as a main course

*A*rugula grows wild in many regions of Italy, where its leaves can be as fine as baby spinach or as large as dandelion greens with stems as thick as watercress. Some arugula is spicy, some strong and pungent; fine tender leaves work best in this dish. It's no surprise that arugula often appears in salad, but grandmothers in Apulia have another trick up their collective sleeve. They stir it into a pasta sauce just long enough for the peppery green to wilt and be warmed. The result, as Italians say: *eccessionale*. All you need is some arugula, juicy ripe tomatoes, fruity green olive oil, pasta, and about 15 minutes.

Serve the arugula and tomato sauce with cavatelli, short homemade pasta that looks a bit like small gnocchi or seashells. Colavita and Il Pastaio make dried cavatelli—see the Source Guide to Ingredients—but you can also use fusilli or gnocchetti.

4 tablespoons extra-virgin olive oil

2 medium garlic cloves, crushed

3 large (1 pound) firm ripe plum tomatoes, peeled, seeded, and chopped,
    or 1 (16-ounce) can Italian plum tomatoes, drained

¾ teaspoon fine sea salt

Freshly ground black pepper

About 2 cups arugula leaves

4 quarts water

1 tablespoon coarse sea salt

1 pound short pasta, such as cavatelli, fusilli, or gnocchetti

Abundant freshly grated pecorino or half Parmigiano-Reggiano
    and half pecorino cheese

Heat the oil with the garlic in a large, heavy skillet or saucepan over low heat until the garlic is limp but not brown, about 3 or 4 minutes. Add the tomatoes, fine sea salt, and pepper and simmer over medium heat for 15 minutes to concentrate the sauce. If you are using canned tomatoes, flatten them with the back of a wooden spoon, and press them through a sieve before adding them to the pan.

Wash the arugula well to remove any dirt clinging to the leaves.

While the sauce is cooking, bring a large pot with 4 quarts of water to the boil, add the coarse sea salt, and then the pasta and cook until it is tender but still al dente. Drain the pasta, add it to the sauce, then toss in the arugula and mix it with the pasta and sauce for a minute or two so the arugula just wilts. Transfer to a warmed serving platter, toss again, and sprinkle abundant grated cheese over the top.

Spaghetti un Po' "Diversi"

Spaghetti Just a Little Bit Different than Usual

—

Serves 6

*L*uisa Cappelli tells me so many of her culinary secrets. Always cut a garlic clove in half and remove any green vein; it's what makes garlic taste bitter. Wash basil leaves very gently, essentially wiping them with a moist paper towel, and then pat them dry—never wring them out—before cutting them in fine ribbons with a very sharp knife.

The most important part of this very simple recipe is mixing the ingredients together well, so they "marry" and are equal, no one taste overwhelming the other.

6 to 8 tablespoons extra-virgin olive oil
3 garlic cloves, cut in half
4 slices of country-style bread, saltless Tuscan if possible,
    at least 2 days old
⅛ teaspoon red pepper flakes
Salt
¾ teaspoon dried oregano
5 quarts water
1 tablespoon coarse sea salt
1 pound vermicelli or spaghetti
½ cup (2 ounces) freshly grated Parmigiano-Reggiano cheese
About 10 or 11 leaves of fresh basil

Warm 2 to 3 tablespoons of the olive oil in a large sauté pan and sauté the two halves of one garlic clove and the slices of bread over medium heat until the garlic is pale golden and the bread barely toasted. Let the bread cool until you can handle it easily and then tear or crumble the slices into small pieces. Discard the garlic.

Heat 2 to 3 tablespoons of olive oil in a large nonstick pan, add another two halves of one garlic clove and sauté over the lowest possible heat until the garlic just begins to turn golden. Crush the clove to release its fragrance in the oil and then discard it. Stir in the crumbled bread, add the red pepper flakes and salt, mix, and sauté over very low heat until the bread crumbs are crisp and crunchy, 12 to 15 minutes.

In a separate small sauté pan, heat 1 to 1½ tablespoons more oil with the remaining split clove of garlic and the dried oregano and stir them over very low heat for 10 to 15 minutes. Discard the garlic clove.

Meanwhile, bring a large stockpot with 5 quarts of water to a rolling boil, add the coarse sea salt, slide in the pasta, and cook according to directions on the package until it is al dente. Drain, saving a bit of the pasta water in case the pasta seems a bit dry. Add the pasta to the pan with the bread crumbs. Pour in the oregano and garlic-flavored oil, stir in the freshly grated Parmigiano-Reggiano cheese, sprinkle the fresh basil leaves cut into thin ribbons over the top, and mix all the ingredients together well. If the pasta seems a bit dry, stir in some of the reserved pasta water, and serve immediately.

TIP: Many Italian grandmothers, Luisa Cappelli among them, always save some pasta cooking water to add to the sauce.

Pasta alla Palombara

Pasta with Tuna, Anchovies, Pine Nuts, and Currants

—

Serves 6 as a first course, 4 as a main course

*T*his recipe comes from Antonina LoNardo, a grandmother from Palermo whom I met when she was visiting her daughter and son-in-law in the little town of Valledolmo deep in the center of Sicily. Her family were *palombari*, deep-sea divers, who went to sea for 9 months every year. They caught and preserved tuna and when they returned, their preserved tuna became the basis of many of their favorite dishes. They serve this dish with a frilly pasta they call margherita, which looks like narrow lasagne with its ruffled edge.

1 garlic clove, crushed in 1 piece

1 small onion, finely chopped

3 tablespoons extra-virgin olive oil plus 1 to 2 tablespoons (optional)

6 anchovy fillets under oil, drained and mashed; or 3 whole anchovies under salt, well rinsed, filleted, and mashed

3 tablespoons finely minced flat-leaf parsley

1 cup peeled, seeded, and chopped fresh tomatoes, or 1 cup canned Italian plum tomatoes, drained and pressed through a food mill or sieve to remove the seeds

2 tablespoons pine nuts

2 tablespoons currants

Salt

Freshly ground black pepper

4 quarts water

1 tablespoon coarse sea salt

1 pound thin frilly-edged dried pasta, such as fettucelle, lasagnette ricce, pappardelle, or tagliatelle

12 ounces (2 cans) albacore tuna packed in olive oil, drained

½ cup toasted bread crumbs

In a large, heavy skillet, sauté the garlic clove and the onion in the olive oil over medium-low heat until they are pale golden, about 10 to 12 minutes. Remove the garlic clove. Add the mashed anchovies and, stirring with a wooden spoon, let them melt over the heat, dissolving in the oil. Stir in the parsley, tomatoes, pine nuts, currants, salt, and pepper and cook over medium heat for 7 to 10 minutes. Set this mixture aside.

Bring a large pot with 4 quarts of water to the boil, add the sea salt, and cook the thin, frilly pasta until it is al dente. Drain the pasta but reserve some of the pasta cooking water in case you need to add it to the sauce.

Flake the tuna with a fork, add it to the anchovy-tomato sauce, and mix it in well. Toss the pasta with most of this sauce, add 1 to 2 tablespoons of extra-virgin olive oil, if needed, put the remainder of the sauce over the top, and serve immediately sprinkled with the toasted bread crumbs.

ANCHOVIES *(Acciughe)*: Some grandmothers from southern Italy use anchovies in place of salt, for these tiny fish carry the flavor of the sea and can be scooped out of nearby waters or bought at the markets at almost no cost. They are used in two ways: as a replacement for salt and as fish in their own right. Buy them packed in salt, if you can, which allows them to taste as close as possible to fresh anchovies. When you are ready to use them, rinse them under cold running water to remove the salt clinging to their skins. Scrape away the skin with a knife, and slit them open down the back. Remove the spine and take care to feel for and remove any tiny remaining bones. If anchovies in salt are not available, find anchovies packed in olive oil inside glass jars that allow you to see how meaty and firm the contents are.

PENNE CON TONNO

Penne with Fresh Tuna, Capers, and Black Olives

—

Serves 8 as a first course, 4 to 6 as a main course

This is such a quick recipe, says Laura Mansi Salom, that the most time-consuming step is going to the market to buy the fish. Be sure to use the best tuna you can find. Choose brined black olives such as small Ligurian or Niçoise olives; but don't use Gaetas or kalamatas, because they are very salty—and please stay away from tasteless California black olives. The simplest way to pit the olives is to set them on a cutting board and press down on them firmly with the side of a cleaver. That loosens the flesh and makes it easy to pull out the pit.

> 2 pounds (about 4) large ripe tomatoes or 1 (28-ounce) can Italian plum
>   tomatoes, drained
> 2½ to 3 tablespoons extra-virgin olive oil
> ⅛ to ¼ teaspoon minced fresh hot red pepper or red pepper flakes
> ¾ teaspoon finely chopped fresh sage
> 1 teaspoon finely chopped fresh rosemary
> ¾ teaspoon finely chopped fresh marjoram
> ¼ cup capers, preferably salt-cured, well rinsed and well drained
> ⅓ cup drained black olives in brine, pitted
> ½ pound fresh tuna fillet, cut in bite-size chunks
> At least 4 quarts water
> 1 tablespoon coarse sea salt
> 1 pound imported penne or rigatoni pasta
> 2 tablespoons finely chopped flat-leaf parsley
> 10 leaves of fresh basil, roughly torn

Peel and chop the tomatoes roughly and put them and the olive oil in a large sauté pan. Warm briefly over medium heat. Add the minced pepper, sage, rosemary, marjoram, and capers and cook for about 15 to 20 minutes. The sauce can be made ahead to this point. Add the olives and raw tuna and simmer just until the tuna is cooked through, about 4 to 5 minutes.

Meanwhile bring a large pot with at least 4 quarts of water to the boil, add the coarse salt and the penne, and cook according to the pasta maker's instructions. Drain, reserving some of the cooking water in case the pasta seems dry.

Spread the penne on a warmed serving platter. Pour the sauce over the top, mix it in, add pasta cooking water if necessary, and finish with the finely chopped parsley and the torn basil on top.

CAPERS (*Capperi*): Capers are the small unripe buds of a plant that grows wild around the Mediterranean basin, climbing into tiny clefts and minute openings in stone walls and cliffs. Capers come in two sizes: tiny non-pareils, which are usually bottled in a vinegar brine, and a much fatter variety that is often preserved under salt. The finest capers are collected on the islands of Sicily, such as Pantelleria, and kept under salt. They must be soaked in cold water for 15 minutes and then rinsed before they are used, but they truly taste of caper and add immeasurably to a dish, while the brined variety may taste strongly of the vinegar in which they are preserved. Keep salt-preserved capers in the refrigerator and you will have them for up to 2 years.

CIALZONS ALLA FRUTTA

Prune- and Fig-Filled Ravioli with Cinnamon-Scented Butter

—

Serves 6 to 8

*C*ialzons are common in Friuli, the magically beautiful region in the north-eastern part of Italy, but the fillings are so personal that they vary not from village to village, but from family to family. Some cialzons have more than forty ingredients that may include everything from chocolate and cinnamon to dried figs and raisins. These cialzons come from Gianna Modotti's family, and she says that while even the dimensions of cialzons change with astonishing frequency, the one thing that remains constant is the filling's sweet flavor. The taste comes from the time when spice merchants called Cramars brought spices from Venice across the Carnia mountains as they made their way to Austria and Germany. The people of the area were much too poor to afford expensive spices, but they could exchange their panoply of homemade cheeses and prosciutti for some of those spices, and then invent pastas as enticing as these.

This is definitely a first course, not a main course, pasta, although adventurous eaters might want to serve the sweet fruit-filled cialzons for dessert, using very little smoked cheese. You may have some filling left over. These are often prepared for Christmas Eve.

FILLING

    3 or 4 (2 ounces) prunes, pitted

    3 or 4 (2 ounces) dried figs

    ⅓ cup red wine

    ¼ teaspoon cinnamon

    1⅓ cups (10 ounces) fresh ricotta cheese, drained

PASTA

    1 pound egg pasta dough, homemade (page 174) or store-bought

    At least 5 quarts water

    1½ tablespoons coarse sea salt

    4 tablespoons unsalted butter

    2 teaspoons sugar

    ½ teaspoon ground cinnamon

    3 to 4 tablespoons grated smoked ricotta or smoked mozzarella cheese

Place the prunes and figs in a small saucepan and half cover them with the red wine. Add the cinnamon and warm over low-medium heat for 10 to 15 minutes, stirring every once in a while, until they are no longer hard or dry. Drain and dice them and set them aside to cool. Press the ricotta through a sieve and mix it with the cooled figs and prunes.

If you buy pasta dough, buy it in wide strips. Brush off any flour or semolina that coats the exterior to prevent the sheets from sticking. Cover the dough that you are not using. Cut each piece into 4-inch-wide strips and run each through your pasta machine, starting at the widest setting and gradually rolling to the next-to-thinnest setting. You may need to stop and cut each piece in half as you roll it thinner and thinner.

Lay the thin strips on a lightly floured work surface. Using a 2½-inch cookie cutter, cut out the cialzons. Brush the circumference of one pasta circle with water, put a teaspoon of filling in the center, cover it with a second circle. With your fingertips, delicately press around the edges of each filled portion to fill the air pockets with stuffing. Pinch the edges firmly so no filling escapes as the pasta cooks, then use the back of a fork to close even more firmly and to give a charming pattern to the cialzons. Repeat with the rest of the pasta. You may reroll and reuse the dough scraps at the end.

Bring a large pot with at least 5 quarts of water to the boil. Add 1½ tablespoons of coarse sea salt and carefully lower a few of the cialzons into the pot. Cook until they float to the top, 1 or 2 minutes. Place in a warmed baking dish, cover well, and keep warm while you cook the rest of the pasta. Repeat with the rest of the cialzons.

Make the topping by melting the butter in a small sauté pan. Stir in the sugar and cinnamon. Pour over the cooked cialzons, toss with the grated smoked cheese, and serve immediately.

TORTELLI DI PATATE

Ravioli Filled with Nutmeg-Flavored Potatoes

—

Serves 6 to 8 as a first course, 4 to 6 as a main course

*S*ignora Lusignani's ravioli have the best of all worlds—silky nutmeg-flavored potatoes inside and funghi porcini outside. You can make the sauce up to 4 days ahead. Store it covered in the refrigerator. You can make the ravioli a few hours ahead, set them on a parchment paper–lined baking sheet or a baking sheet sprinkled with semolina flour, cover them with a kitchen towel, and leave them in a cool place until you are ready to cook them. You will have a bit of filling left over.

SUGO DI FUNGHI E POMODORI (WILD MUSHROOM AND TOMATO SAUCE)

> 1½ ounces dried porcini mushrooms
>
> 2 medium onions, minced
>
> 8 tablespoons (1 stick) unsalted butter
>
> 1 (20-ounce) can Italian plum tomatoes or bottled organic tomato puree
>
> Salt and freshly ground black pepper

PASTA

> 2½ cups (12½ ounces) unbleached all-purpose flour
>
> A pinch of salt
>
> 4 eggs
>
> 1 to 2 tablespoons milk (optional)

FILLING

> 3 medium potatoes (about 1 pound), boiled in their skins, then drained, peeled, and riced
>
> A large pinch of freshly grated nutmeg
>
> 7 tablespoons grated (1¾ ounces) freshly grated Parmigiano-Reggiano cheese
>
> 3½ tablespoons unsalted butter
>
> 1 egg
>
> 1 egg yolk
>
> Salt

Freshly ground black pepper
Milk
At least 5 quarts water
1½ tablespoons coarse sea salt

Cover the dried porcini mushrooms with warm water and leave to plump for 30 minutes. Squeeze the porcini, letting any extra moisture fall into the water in which they soaked. Drain through a sieve lined with paper towels or cheesecloth. Save the soaking liquid. Rinse the porcini well and slice them fine.

Sauté the onions in the melted butter over medium heat until translucent. Add the drained porcini mushrooms and cook for about 5 minutes. Stir in the tomatoes and cook over low-medium heat until the sauce comes together, 8 to 10 minutes. Season with salt and pepper. The sauce may be made ahead to this point and set aside, but you may need to thin it with some of the porcini soaking water or chicken broth before serving. When you are ready to serve, bring it to a gentle bubble in a pot large enough to accommodate the pasta.

Pasta by hand: To make the dough by hand, combine the flour and salt and set in a mound on a work surface. Make a well in the center, beat the eggs together, and pour into the well. Work the flour into the eggs from the sides of the well with a fork and knead until you have a soft dough.

By processor: Set the flour and salt in a processor fitted with the dough or steel blade and pulse several times to mix. With the motor running, pour the eggs down the feed tube and mix only until the dough has come together loosely around the blade. If the dough is too stiff, add a little milk. Remove from the bowl and knead on a lightly floured work surface for about 3 minutes.

Gather the dough into a ball, cover with plastic wrap, and leave at room temperature for 15 to 30 minutes.

While the dough is resting, prepare the filling. Combine the riced potatoes, nutmeg, Parmigiano cheese, and butter in a bowl; beat in the egg, egg yolk, salt, and pepper; and mix until well combined. Cover the bowl and set aside while you roll out the pasta dough. Divide the dough into four pieces and roll each into a thin sheet. If you are using the pasta machine, roll to second-to-last thinness.

Filling the dough: Working with one sheet at a time, cover the sheets you are not using. Lay a sheet on a lightly floured work surface and distribute teaspoon-sized portions of the filling at least 1½ inches apart. Use your fingertip or a brush to moisten the edges of the pasta sheet with milk. Carefully place a second sheet of the pasta dough on top of the first and press with your fingertips to separate the rows of filling. With a ravioli cutter, cut along straight lines on the vertical and horizontal to form each raviolo square. Press the edges closed with your fingertips to seal well.

Bring a pot with at least 5 quarts of water to a rolling boil, add 1½ tablespoons of coarse salt, carefully drop in the ravioli, and cook for about 5 to 6 minutes. When done, drain and put immediately into the pot with the warm funghi sauce and serve.

TIP: This sauce is outstanding when served with polenta.

TORTELLI DI ZUCCA

Tortelli with a Nutmeg-Scented Butternut Squash or Pumpkin Filling

—

Serves 4 to 6 as a first course, 3 to 4 as a main course

*A*lthough she has lived in Chianti all her married life, Anna Marezza comes from near Parma in Emilia-Romagna. As a little girl she would come running whenever her mother called out, *"Vieni, si fa i tortelli—*Come, we're going to make tortelli." There was something magical about the experience for her. All her problems seemed to shrink away as she became involved in making these delicious tortelli.

Anna has immense feeling for the region where she grew up and still brings her butter back from Parma when she's been home for a visit. Ask her at any time; she always has a freezer full of it.

FILLING
> 5 ounces butternut squash or pumpkin, peeled and seeded
> 2 tablespoons unsalted butter
> Substantial gratings of fresh nutmeg
> Salt
> 2½ tablespoons freshly grated Parmigiano-Reggiano cheese

PASTA
> ¾ pound egg pasta, cut into 3-inch-wide strips (page 174)

   3 tablespoons unsalted butter

   1 ripe tomato, peeled, seeded, and diced

FOR THE PASTA

   At least 5 quarts water

   1½ to 2 tablespoons coarse sea salt

   Freshly grated Parmigiano-Reggiano cheese

Grate the butternut squash or pumpkin. Sauté it in the butter over very low heat, prefer-ably in a nonstick pan, being careful that it never burns but gives up its own water as a medium to cook in, about 15 to 20 minutes. It should break down into a smooth mass. The mixture must be cooked until it is quite thick; if it were soft, it would ruin the inside of the pasta. Off the heat stir in the nutmeg, salt, and Parmigiano-Reggiano. The filling may be made ahead to this point and set in the refrigerator, wrapped in plastic wrap, for up to 2 days.

   You may make the egg pasta as grandmothers did for centuries, or you may save time and buy it. If you buy sheets of good-quality fresh egg pasta, brush off the flour or semolina used to keep the sheets from sticking to each other. Cut the pasta into 3- or 4-inch-wide strips and cover the ones you are not using so they won't dry out. Use your pasta machine to roll each strip to the next-to-last setting; the pasta will be thin but not transparent. Lay each strip on a work surface and cut out circles with a 2½-inch cookie cutter. Brush a little water around the circumference of a circle and set a tea-spoon of filling in the center. Brush the circumference of a second pasta circle with water and set it on top of the circle with the filling. Press the edges together with your fingertips, so no filling will escape, then use the tines of a fork to press them together even more firmly and to create a decorative edge.

   Make the topping by melting the butter over low heat in a small sauté pan. Add the tomato and cook for a minute or two.

   When you plan to cook the pasta, bring a large pot with at least 5 quarts of water to a rolling boil, add 1½ tablespoons of coarse salt, and cook the pasta only until the water returns to the boil and the tortelli float to the surface, 2 to 4 minutes. Drain and serve immediately topped with the warm butter and tomato. Pass freshly grated cheese.

Ravioli in Camicia

Naked Ravioli

—

Serves 6 as a first course, 4 as a main course

*S*ome Italians call these *ignudi* ("naked ravioli") and others call them *ravioli in camicia* ("ravioli in their undershirts," very loosely translated) because they are just the filling, without the pasta dough, shaped like dumplings and then poached. This recipe from Andreina Pavani Calcagni is very simple—there's no pasta to deal with, after all—so you can just mix, shape, and cook until these tasty dumplings rise to the top of the bubbling water. Use the best-quality ricotta and the freshest spinach you can find.

PASTA

> 1 pound fresh spinach, weighed after cleaning and stemming
>
> 2 teaspoons unsalted butter
>
> 1 teaspoon sea salt
>
> 1⅔ cups (12 ounces) best-quality ricotta cheese
>
> 1½ cups (6 ounces) freshly grated Parmigiano-Reggiano cheese
>
> Substantial gratings of fresh nutmeg
>
> 1 egg yolk
>
> 2 tablespoons all-purpose flour for the ravioli and extra for coating the ignudi
>
> 6 quarts water
>
> 1½ tablespoons coarse salt

SAUCE

> 4 tablespoons unsalted butter melted with 10 leaves of fresh sage
>
> ¼ cup (1 ounce) freshly grated Parmigiano-Reggiano cheese

Remove any tough stems from the spinach, then wash the leaves well in three changes of cold water to remove all traces of sand and dirt. Drain and place the spinach and all the water clinging to the leaves in a 4-quart pot. Cook over medium heat until the spinach wilts and is tender, 4 to 5 minutes. Drain well in a colander. To get all the water out, place the spinach in a potato ricer and press just hard enough to squeeze out any remaining moisture. You should have 1⅓ cups of spinach.

Warm the butter over medium heat in a 10-inch sauté pan, add the spinach and salt, and cook until there is almost no water left. Chop the leaves very fine, place in a large bowl, and set aside to cool briefly. Stir in the ricotta and Parmigiano-Reggiano cheeses, the nutmeg, egg yolk, and 2 tablespoons of flour and mix well. If the mixture seems too moist to shape, you should set it in the refrigerator for 2 hours. Shape a couple of test ravioli into walnut-sized balls. Sift some flour onto a plate.

Bring a large pot with 6 quarts of water to the boil and add 1½ tablespoons coarse salt. Test a sample ravioli by rolling it very lightly in the flour, then lowering it into the water in a slotted spoon and poaching for 2 to 3 minutes, just long enough to rise to the top. If the pasta holds its shape, finish shaping the rest of the ignudi, lightly rolling them in flour and poaching them a few at a time. If you have a long-handled colander, you can set it in the boiling water and lower the ravioli into it. Just remove and drain them when they are poached. If the test ravioli don't hold their shape, add a little more flour to the mixture and test again.

Preheat the oven to 375°F. Place the poached ignudi in a baking dish, drizzle with the butter melted with the fresh sage leaves, and sprinkle with the grated cheese. Bake for about 10 minutes, until the cheese is lightly browned.

Polenta

Polenta today is both rustic and chic, a dish appearing in restaurants all over northern and central Italy topped with everything from a wreath of quail to wild mushroom ragù. It is only recently that many women would think of making polenta voluntarily. So many years of scarcity had cast it as the food of deprivation and every bite was overlaid with memories of sadness and hard times. Earlier in this century, people ate polenta because they had no choice. They ate it two or three times a day, perhaps cooked in a little milk or broth, perhaps with a bit of salami, cabbage, cicoria, or green beans. In many families the big dome of polenta was poured onto a board in the center of the table and everyone sat around—no plates required—scooping out a space for sauce or flavoring and spooning up the polenta right in front of them. For holidays and very special days in the lives of the poor, the glowing golden circle of polenta was turned out onto a wooden board and a single herring was slapped against each person's piece, the rare moment in the countryside when the taste of meat or fish came to table.

The implements of cooking polenta are almost sacred. When the fascist government decreed that metal and iron be collected to serve the country during the war, people didn't want to give up their pots and pans for patriotic use. Women's first small resistance to the war came when they held on to their copper pots. How, they asked themselves, could they possibly give away the *paiolo* in which polenta had always been cooked? They represented the connection of one generation to the next—"this one was Mother's, this one Grandmother's." Confronted with an almost universal refusal, the prefects from the National Institute relented and announced that *paioli* didn't need to be given up. At which point so many countrywomen decided that if *paioli* didn't need to be handed over, surely they could also hold on to their *testi*, the terra-cotta or cast-iron disks that were heated in the embers and used for cooking.

Polenta can be creamy, as it is in Lucca, where Renata Marsili makes matuffi, soft scoops of polenta topped with a layer of tomato sauce; or it can be as firm as it is in Friuli, where it is cut with a taut piece of wire or string. Some families in Piedmont serve polenta with a garlic and anchovy sauce—not the famous, more elaborate bagna cauda—and others with a mixture of anchovies and greens. Tuscans and Ligurians beat polenta right into their minestrones and vegetable soups, making a thick rib-sticking meal in a bowl called *intruglia* or *polenta incatenata*. Many people eat polenta with whatever greens they can gather—wild asparagus, rucola, cicoria—with crayfish from the stream, with snails from the fields, or with the bounty of hunters—small birds such as thrush (in Bergamo they are placed in a hollow on top of the polenta and the dish is known as *polenta e osei*) or quail, partridge, pheasant, and guinea hen. Families eat *polenta concia* sprinkled with cheese and black pepper, *polenta pasticciata* layered with a wash of tomato sauce and blizzards of grated grana, *polenta incatenata* with greens cooked in the pot right along with the cornmeal, or *polenta in furla*, cooked in cream and served with grated cheese.

POLENTA CONCIA

Polenta Layered with Cheeses and Black Pepper

—

Serves 8 to 10 as a first course, 4 to 6 as a main course

Polenta is to the arc of land that runs from Friuli through Lombardy and the Veneto what pasta is to Emilia Romagna and what bread is to Tuscany: a delicious base for flavorings that are limited only by the imagination of the cook and the ingredients on hand. Polenta can be seasoned with beans, favas, fish, sausages, cheeses, or meat; it can be compact, high, soft, or dense. Entire cookbooks have been devoted to polenta. Lina Vitali makes polenta concia, a simple dish from the mountainous Valtellina, where impressive quantities of cow's milk cheeses are produced. This version of polenta is cooked and then layered with the local cheese called bitto—Italian fontina with its nutty flavor most approximates its taste—handfuls of grated Parmesan cheese, and lots of freshly grated black pepper.

6 cups water
2½ teaspoons coarse sea salt
1⅔ cups (8 ounces) medium-grind cornmeal
½ pound bitto or fontina cheese
4 to 6 tablespoons freshly grated Parmigiano-Reggiano cheese
Substantial gratings of black pepper
4 tablespoons unsalted butter
2 garlic cloves, lightly smashed with the side of a large knife
Leaves of fresh sage (optional)

Bring 6 cups water and 2½ teaspoons coarse salt to a vigorous boil in a very large pot. If you have a *paiolo,* an unlined copper pot with a slightly concave bottom, by all means use it, but a heavy-bottomed copper or stainless steel saucepan will be fine. Reduce the heat to medium-low. Let the cornmeal fall into the pot from your left hand in a slow steady stream while using a whisk in your right hand to keep lumps from forming. Continue stirring sporadically with a long-handled wooden spoon, being very careful to eliminate any lumps by crushing them against the sides of the pot. Keep the water at a steady simmer and stir from the bottom of the pot toward the top, almost as if you were folding egg whites into a batter. The polenta will thicken, bubble, and hiss as it cooks. When it comes away from the sides of the pot, after 30 to 45 minutes, the polenta is ready. Be sure to taste for salt.

Pour the polenta out onto a marble slab or onto a wooden board covered with a kitchen towel and let cool.

Preheat the oven to 350°F. Butter a shallow 3-quart baking dish.

Cut the polenta into ½-inch-thick slices. Italian grandmothers cut slices of polenta using a wire or thick cotton string; if you use a knife, dip it in hot water so it won't stick to the polenta. Place one layer of polenta slices in the dish, cover with a layer of finely sliced fontina or bitto cheese and a large dusting of grated Parmigiano-Reggiano cheese and black pepper, and keep layering the polenta, cheeses, and pepper, finishing with a layer of cheese. Brown the butter with the garlic and (if you are using it) the sage, discard the garlic, and pour over the top. Bake in the oven for 30 minutes, or until the layers of polenta are very hot.

VARIATIONS:

> **POLENTA TARAGNA CONCIA** (Buckwheat Polenta Layered with Cheese and Black Pepper): Use buckwheat polenta. Sauté 2 minced onions in the butter and layer them in the pan with the polenta, bitto or fontina, and Parmigiano-Reggiano cheese.
>
> **PASTICCIATA DI POLENTA** (Polenta Layered with Tomato Sauce and Parmesan Cheese): Layer the polenta with Sugo finto—"fake" tomato sauce (page 428)—and Parmigiano-Reggiano cheese.

Profile of *Lina Vitali*

—

Lina Vitali has definitely been in the kitchen. When she walks down the long garden pathway to greet me, she is wrapped in a full-length pinafore-style apron sprinkled with flowers. She whisks me through the gates, past a garden full of herbs, tomatoes, and trees laden with quince, and into the house, whose walls are lined with art and extraordinary frescoes. On the way I meet Franco, her husband of forty-five years, who transported her from a mountain village to Morbegno, where he grew up and where they have lived ever since. Then I am in the kitchen, a space no more than four feet across and perhaps eight long that permits two people to work together, if they know each other's rhythms and habits intimately. Lina learned to cook from her mother and grandmother in the small village of Montagna where she grew up above Sondrio, high in the mountains of the Valtellina in Lombardy. It is only about an hour from where she lives now, but light-years distant in terms of a way of life.

"Come quickly," she says, anxious to return to her gnocchi. "My grandmother used to make *gnocchetti* using milk from a cow when it had just given birth. Imagine how delicious they were!" Lina makes hers by cooking red-skinned potatoes without peeling them and then ricing them when they are cool enough to handle. She makes a very soft dough and uses a wet teaspoon to scoop little balls from it, then drops them into salted boiling water. They are done when they rise to the top, and she immediately scoops them with a slotted spoon into individual bowls, putting the browned butter and sage leaf sauce over them at table because they stay hotter that way.

When Lina changes her clothes after lunch, the sparrow-sized woman with a quiet manner is suddenly transformed into a self-assured, well-dressed woman in a handsomely tailored suit. As we make the ten-minute walk into the center of town, she greets half the people we pass by name, and it is clear that she is both well known and well respected. Lina has been a grammar and secondary school teacher in Morbegno as well as principal of the middle school for a number of years, and we are on our way to a fair and conference on the subject of the foods of the Valtellina.

Morbegno

"It was perfect serendipity that you arrived this weekend. The conference means we can see and taste a lot of local products that I couldn't ever have assembled by myself. But, since my thesis topic was about the culture of these mountains, peasant culture, and culinary roots, I can tell you that the food of the Valtellina is really hearty because it was meant to fill up workers so they could go back to their heavy labors. In the nineteenth century there used to be about the same number of cows and contadini; the cows are still there, but the country people are fast disappearing."

Life was hard for most people. They lived on polenta. They ate polenta boiled with goat's milk in the morning. They ate polenta with butter and salami, or polenta with a salad of cicoria for their other meal. I lost track of how many ways polenta could be made in Valtellina. There was polenta *santa*, polenta made with milk from Valchiavenna; polenta *concia*, slices of polenta layered with cheese and butter and lots of freshly ground pepper; polenta in *furla*, cooked in cream and served with cheese; polenta *crupa*, buckwheat polenta with potato and cheese stirred in at the end. This tiny list doesn't even begin to reckon with the ingenuity of the cooks who used all the flora and fauna as ingredients, mixing potatoes, beans, even *tartufi* into polenta. And then they enriched it with the extraordinary butter and cheeses that are unique to the area. The most famous cheese, bitto, is made only in limited quantities of cow's milk from two valleys and has a deep flavor that is somewhat reminiscent of really fine fontina.

The cooking of Valtellina is the original slow food, the opposite of the fast eating that has now made great inroads in Italian cities. Country people and shepherds had one pot—it might have been bronze or copper or natural stone called *pietra ollare*—and one implement for stirring called a *bastone*, which was as long as an oar and as flat as a paddle. They used it for cooking everything from the ubiquitous polenta to long, slow stews and meats, even the bread soup called pancotto.

Lina and Franco have both saved their mothers' recipe notebooks. Lina's is huge, crammed full of extra pages that have been stuck inside in random clumps, while Franco's is slenderer but clearly every bit as absorbing to its owner. It holds treasured recipes that recall his youth and as he reads them, memories of his childhood, not just the food but people and events, come tumbling back. "Here's *paradel*," he exclaims, like an explorer come upon a land he knew would be there. Lina once won first prize when she made the bread pudding–like dessert that uses only stale bread, milk, apples, sugar, lemon zest, and walnuts, all products any local housewife would have at hand. "And *torta della zucca*! Here," he says, showing me the page with a recipe for a pumpkin tart made with crumbled amaretti, apples, and cocoa. Franco has kept these recipes carefully and Lina has always made them so that the food of his childhood was part of the lives of their children and grandchildren. Their two daughters are doctors, one a gynecologist, the other a geriatrician, and they come for frequent visits with their families. Franco and Lina reminisce as we talk about their food and eat wonderful bread made by his brother, a baker. Every few minutes Lina disappears to the cellar and brings forth yet another delicious berry jam or a jar of what she calls *marmellata di mele cotogne*, quince preserves, that are very reminiscent of applesauce if it had been made with quince.

"I grew up making *pizzoccheri* almost every day at my grandmother's, but I'm going to take you to Esther Saini, who is a real expert," Lina announced. And so off we drove, winding our way high into the mountains beyond Sondrio, passing hundreds of apple trees and multiple plots of land divided into tiny fractions, indications of how many times a single piece of earth had been divided among heirs as generation followed generation. Wheat will not grow in these high mountains. Instead, rye is sown and when it has been harvested, it is followed by a crop of buckwheat that grows to maturity very rapidly. Lina sighed. "People no longer cultivate buckwheat because the economy is richer. We all still love to eat *pizzoccheri* cooked with potatoes and cabbage and served with browned butter and garlic, only now the buckwheat is imported from Tunisia and Turkey."

When the simpler world of the earlier half of this century still existed, people ate and used only local products. Franco's mother's recipe for *costine al laveggio*, pork chops cooked with herbs and wine over very low heat until the meat falls away from the bones, depends on being cooked very slowly in a pot, or *laveggio*, made from pietra ollare, a smooth local stone that needs no oil, no butter, no fat of any kind so that a dish tastes purely of its ingredients. Once all parts of life were interwoven and connected and endured from generation to generation. "Now," says Lina, rolling her eyes very slightly, "it's like doing archaeological research."

Still, when we arrive in the tiny village where Esther Saini lives, she has all the local ingredients on hand: buckwheat flour, eggs from her son's chickens, an outrageous amount of delicious fresh butter, and unforgettable local cheeses. She makes *pizzoccheri* by combining the wheat and buckwheat flours on her big marble table, then breaking the eggs right into the center and working them into a rough dough. She kneads it for quite a while before rolling it out thin and cutting it into tagliatelle-sized ribbons. She cooks the pasta in the same water with the potatoes and cabbage and serves them layered with an outrageous amount of butter (2 ounces per portion!) and substantial slivers and gratings of cheese. Clearly a dish to stoke a hardworking laborer!

She learned to cook this robust food from her mother many years ago—she is now a white-haired grandmother of twelve—and cooks only the dishes of the small area where she lives. She makes *sciatt*, buckwheat dumplings with bitto cheese that melts inside them, and she still uses lard to fry them for the crunchiness it adds. With the sciatt comes a salad of wild greens called *raperonzolo*, whose wonderful clean taste had just the right lightness to follow the filling *sciatt*, and *brazadei*, large rounds of rye that look like big flat doughnuts. They are made once a year and hung on long strings in the attics of people's houses; when first baked they are as soft as regular rye, but they dry out as time passes and after a while must be dipped into red wine to soften them enough for eating.

After lunch we are so full that we wander off lazily into the sunny afternoon, strolling up and down the tiny lanes of San Rocco. Lina picks flowers from the astensio plant which grows on the stone walls high in these mountains and thinks about making a liqueur with them. Franco takes me to see a field where the red-stemmed, red-flowered buckwheat grow. Valtellina, an alpine valley which is only an hour from Lake Como, has a great patrimony of foods that are undiscovered by most of Italy. It may be in the same region as Milan, but it is as far from that modern city as the shepherds who are still making cheeses are from Milanese businessmen in their Mercedes-Benzes.

CORNMEAL (Polenta): Polenta, which is simply the Italian word for cornmeal, comes in a variety of grinds. Look for medium-grind cornmeals with a granular texture, which become fairly creamy polentas, and coarser stone-ground whole cornmeals, which cook to a firmer consistency. Always buy the freshest cornmeal you can. Polenta with the hull and germ of the corn removed will keep at room temperature; others must be kept in the refrigerator to prevent the germ from becoming rancid. *Polenta taragna,* dappled beige buckwheat polenta, is used in the Valtellina, while white cornmeal is cooked in the Veneto, where its creamy consistency goes well with vegetable and fish dishes. Quick polenta—precooked, dried, and boxed—needs only 5 or 6 minutes from start to finish to be ready. Stay away from powdery fine cornmeal and please don't be tempted by the precooked tubes of polenta; they look easy to deal with but lack at least one critical ingredient: taste.

Matuffi

Creamy Scoops of Polenta with Tomato Sauce

—

Serves 4 to 6

When Renata Marsili wants to eat polenta, she makes matuffi, the traditional creamy soft polenta of Lucca and Versilia, the region that borders the Mediterranean Sea. Use a big ladle or serving spoon to scoop the polenta into a warmed serving dish, top it with a layer of sauce, and repeat, finishing with the sauce. Sprinkle a blizzard of grated Parmigiano-Reggiano over the top and let the feasting begin!

POLENTA
  Salt
  6¼ cups water
  1⅔ cups (8 ounces) organic stone-ground polenta

SAUCE
  ***Pommarola* (page 429) or *Sugo finto* (page 428)**
  Freshly grated Parmigiano-Reggiano cheese

Bring the salted water to a vigorous boil in a very large pot. If you have a *paiolo*, an unlined copper pot with a slightly concave bottom, by all means use it, but a heavy-bottomed copper or stainless steel saucepan will be fine. Reduce the heat to medium-low. Let the cornmeal fall into the pot from your left hand in a slow steady stream while you use a whisk in your right hand to keep lumps from forming. Continue stirring sporadically with a long-handled wooden spoon, being very careful to eliminate any lumps by crushing them against the sides of the pot. Keep the water at a steady simmer and stir from the bottom of the pot toward the top. The polenta will thicken, bubble, and hiss as it cooks. When it comes away from the sides of the pot, but is still creamy and soft, after 30 to 45 minutes, the polenta is ready. Be sure to taste for salt.

Use a big serving spoon to scoop the polenta in oval scoops and set into a large, warmed serving bowl. Top with a layer of sauce, and repeat, ending with the sauce and cheese. Serve immediately.

POLENTA INCATENATA

Polenta and Beans

—

Serves 8 to 10

Wﬁat do you get when you cross bean soup and polenta? A
meal in a bowl, a favorite of people in the Lunigiana area, where this
substantial and filling dish fills stomachs and soothes souls on a cold
winter's day. A perfect after-ski meal to eat sitting around the fireplace, *polenta incatenata*, or "polenta unleashed," is made with
polenta cooking right in the pot in which the beans and kale are
slowly bubbling. They all simmer together into a lovely creamy mixture.

Vittoria Genovese

The recipe is a favorite of Vittoria Genovese, who strongly recommends that you
put any leftovers on a board, cut them into strips or diamonds, and fry them until they
are crunchy and crisp. Her sotto voce advice: it's even better that way.

> 2⅔ cups (1 pound) dried borlotti or cranberry beans
>
> 11 cups cold water
>
> 1 celery rib
>
> 2 pounds Tuscan kale or regular kale, thick stems removed, sliced very fine
>
> 2 cups (10 ounces) medium-grind cornmeal or polenta, preferably
> stone-ground
>
> 3 tablespoons extra-virgin olive oil, plus extra for drizzling
>
> 1 tablespoon sea salt
>
> Freshly ground black pepper
>
> Freshly grated Parmigiano-Reggiano cheese

Soak the beans overnight or for 12 hours in a large bowl with cold water to cover by 2 to
3 inches. When you are ready to make the dish, drain and rinse the beans under two
changes of cold water. Pour 11 cups of water into a large, heavy kettle or stockpot, add
the celery rib, and bring to a boil. Add the beans and simmer over low heat for about 20
minutes. At this point, stir in the kale and continue cooking for about 15 minutes longer,
until the kale is softened but not yet tender. With a ladle remove about one quarter of the

beans, kale, and their cooking liquid, and set them aside. Discard the celery rib.

Bring the contents of the pot back to a boil. Start adding the cornmeal in a slow constant stream, always mixing with a wooden spoon to be sure that no lumps form. When the cornmeal has all been incorporated, lower the heat and, stirring sporadically to prevent the cornmeal from sticking, let the mixture simmer for about 20 minutes. At that point, add the 3 tablespoons of the olive oil and salt and return the reserved beans, kale, and bean cooking liquid to the pot. Continue cooking for another 30 to 40 minutes, stirring from time to time with the spoon, until the beans are tender and the mixture is creamy. The polenta must remain very soft, and Vittoria is adamant that you must not add more water.

Top with freshly ground black pepper and grated Parmigiano-Reggiano cheese, drizzle with olive oil, and serve.

POLENTA CON RAGÙ BIANCO

Polenta with a White Ragù of Pancetta, Sausage, and Ham

—

Serves 4 to 6

*V*anda Grannini in Corinaldo, a beautiful small town in Le Marche, has several secrets for making her tasty polenta. First, she doesn't bring the water to a full boil, but just gets it hot; next she stirs in a chicken bouillon cube to add flavor, and only then does she begin to sprinkle in the cornmeal. Why is the sauce called a white ragù? Because there isn't a single tomato in it. Make the ragù earlier in the day or the day before you plan to serve it, refrigerate, and skim off the fat that comes to the surface.

Vanda Grannini

RAGÙ Bianco

> 3 tablespoons extra-virgin olive oil
>
> 1 onion, chopped
>
> ¼ cup (2 ounces) diced pancetta
>
> 2 mild sausages, removed from their casings and crumbled
>
> Scant ½ cup (2 ounces) cubed ham (½-inch cubes)
>
> 3 cups meat broth, preferably homemade
>
> Grindings of black pepper or a pinch of red pepper flakes
>
> Salt (optional)

POLENTA

> 5 cups water
>
> 1 chicken bouillon cube
>
> 1⅔ cups (9 ounces) regular- or medium-grind polenta
>
> Salt (optional if the chicken bouillon cube is used)

To make the ragù bianco: Warm the olive oil in a large sauté pan and sauté the onion over low-medium heat until soft and translucent, 10 to 15 minutes. Add the pancetta, sausage meat, and ham, and cook until the sausages have lost all their pink color, about

10 minutes. Start adding the meat broth ½ cup at a time, keeping the mixture slowly bubbling until the broth has been well reduced. Pour in another ½ cup of the broth and repeat every 10 minutes for 1 hour, until all the broth has been added and the sauce is rich and thick. Add black pepper and taste for salt, although it is unlikely that you will need it. Let stand at room temperature or in the refrigerator to skim off the fat that comes to the surface. Reheat it at a slow bubble.

To make the polenta: Heat the water in a 4- or 5-quart heavy-bottomed pot until it is hot. Stir in the chicken bouillon cube and let it dissolve. Slowly sprinkle in the cornmeal in a thin stream, first whisking it in, then stirring constantly with a wooden spoon, being careful to eliminate any lumps by crushing them against the sides of the pot. Keep the water at a steady simmer and stir frequently, but not all the time. The polenta will thicken, bubble, and hiss as it cooks. It is ready when it pulls away from sides of pot, after about 30 to 40 minutes. Taste for salt.

Pour the hot polenta onto a large platter, spread the ragù on top, and serve immediately.

TIP: Efresina Rosichini and Vanda Grannini have a startling polenta secret: start drizzling in the polenta when the bubbles have just begun to appear in the water. Do not wait until it is boiling. That way you don't have to worry about lumps forming as you stir in the polenta. The necessity for boiling water turns out to be an old wives' tale that has not been questioned for centuries.

Toc' in Braide

Farmer's Sauce

—

Serves 2

*W*omen in the Carnia mountains of Friuli used to make very firm polenta, which they cut with a string and then wrapped in their husbands' colored cotton handkerchiefs as a meal for the men while they were cutting wood in the forest. They made the polenta in a big copper cauldron with a round bottom, called a *paiolo*, and stirred it with a round-handled flat stick as long as a rolling pin.

Although polenta in the Carnia mountains is as firm as Venetian polenta is soft—especially when it is meant to be carried all day—I have followed other Friulani cooks and made this polenta as creamy as scrambled eggs. No one can ever get enough of it. Serve it soft, like this, or firmer, if you prefer, with the *Frico Cotto con Patate e Cipolla* (page 292).

1 tablespoon unsalted butter
1 garlic clove, minced
½ cup diced onion
1 cup plus 2 tablespoons salted water
¼ cup cornmeal or polenta (preferaby stone-ground)
⅔ cup milk, plus additional if needed
Salt
Freshly ground black pepper
Freshly grated Parmigiano-Reggiano cheese

Melt the butter in a small sauté pan, add the garlic clove and onion, and cook over very low heat until they are pale and golden, 10 to 12 minutes.

Meanwhile, bring the salted water to a boil in a large, heavy pot and sprinkle in the cornmeal in a steady fine stream, stirring frequently with a wooden spoon always in the same direction to get rid of any lumps. When the garlic and onions are ready, add them to the pot along with the milk, salt, and pepper and mix well. Cook over very low heat for 1 hour or until the polenta comes away from the sides of the pot. You may need to add a little extra milk as you cook to keep the polenta mixture soft and creamy.

Rice

Rice is grown in the humid swath of land stretching from Piedmont and Lombardy through the Veneto, where grandmothers often specify exactly which type of short-grain rice to use in a dish, especially in risotto, in which the grains swell to a creamy plumpness as they cook and absorb the liquid. And what a difference a grain makes! Carnaroli, Vialone Nano, Baldo, and Arborio are the preferred types for risotto, although many nonne tout the virtues of the first two with especial fervor. Baldo is a new arrival on the scene. Nonne specifically urge using originario, a very short round rice, for puddings. Never use long-grain American rice for risotto.

RISO CON LE FAVE VERDI

Rice with Green Favas

Serves 6

Fava beans, *fave*, also known as broad beans, are grown and eaten all over central and southern Italy. I saw several generations of Sicilian families sitting together on their front steps in Vallelunga, talking and shelling peas and fava beans. Some they used for recipes like this one, and others they saved by stuffing them into freezer bags. In some cases the women collect the favas when they have dried on the plant, shell them, and leave them to dry longer. If they shell fresh favas, they may eat them fresh, cook them, or freeze them with their interior skins still on and peel them when they are ready to use them.

All but the youngest fava beans must be shelled and peeled before they are cooked. To ease this arduous task, bring a pot of water to the boil, plunge in the favas and leave them very briefly, then drain, and the fava skins should slip off easily.

(continued)

5¼ cups chicken broth, plus extra if needed
2⅔ cups (2 pounds) shelled and peeled fresh fava beans
⅓ cup finely chopped fennel tops
1 teaspoon fennel seeds, crushed and chopped
2 cups Arborio rice
Freshly ground black pepper
½ cup (2 ounces) freshly grated Parmigiano-Reggiano cheese
1 tablespoon extra-virgin olive oil
Sea salt

Bring the broth to a boil in a 2-quart pot. Add the fava beans, fennel, and fennel seeds, turn down the heat, and simmer for 5 to 7 minutes. Now you are ready to add the rice and simmer, adding a little extra broth if necessary, until the rice is tender, 22 to 25 minutes. Once the rice is cooked, add the pepper, cheese, olive oil, taste for salt, and serve.

PANISSA

Beans and Rice, Salami, and Vegetables from Vercelli

—

Serves 6 to 8

Rice, beans, salami, and vegetables: panissa is the rich and robust dish with which the city of Vercelli identifies itself. Served on Sunday as a blessing and acknowledgment of well-being, it has been considered simple country food in Piedmont for more than two centuries, although families of every background eat it with pleasure.

Rice, first planted in Piedmont in the fifteenth or sixteenth century, is to the Piedmontese what bread is to other regions of Italy: a basic ingredient on which much of the cuisine is based. Ornella Reneglio, whose recipe this is, insists on getting the rice with which she makes her traditional bean and rice panissa from a miller in Vercelli who raises it organically. "Did you ever see the movie *Bitter Rice?*" she asked me. "It was all about poor young women from Piedmont but also from Brescia, Cremona, and Mantua, who came on trains and stayed in dormitories on the rice farms. They worked very long hours standing in the waters of the rice fields, cleaning away weeds and underwater grasses and stones from the plants and then picking the rice." Now the owners of those farms are the sons and grandsons of the owners of that time, they all have agricultural degrees, and they use advanced equipment such as lasers to be sure that the water covers the rice seedlings to just the right extent. They no longer need the women to do the picking.

In the part of Piedmont where Vercelli is located, the *battuto*, the initial sauté of onion, garlic, and pancetta, is called a *doté*. Ornella says that the appearance of cloves is evidence of the strong French influence in the region—they share a border, after all—and that cloves stuck into onions are common in Piedmont. The dish calls for *salame della duja*, small fresh pork salami made with garlic and red wine, dried for 10 days, covered with snowy white fat, and kept for anywhere from a few weeks to a whole year. You can substitute a fairly mild and soft salami, such as soppressata. Borlotti beans take the place of silky-skinned Saluggia beans. Even with all these substitutions, the panissa is captivating, with its subtle, deep flavors.

This is a very hearty first course or a perfect one-dish winter supper. Serve it with a red Piedmont wine, preferably a Ghemme or Gattinara.

(continued)

1¼ cups (8 ounces) dried borlotti beans or cranberry beans

10 cups cold water

4 ounces mild and relatively soft salami, such as soppressata, cut in ½-inch-thick slices

3 tablespoons unsalted butter

1 small onion, with 2 or 3 whole cloves stuck into it and then quartered

1 garlic clove, finely minced

Scant ½ cup (3½ ounces) finely ground pancetta, lardo, or salt pork, made into a creamy paste in a pestle or food processor

1 small carrot, diced

1 celery rib, diced

3 tablespoons finely minced flat-leaf parsley

1½ cups Vialone Nano, Carnaroli, or Arborio rice

2 cups full-bodied red wine

1 tablespoon tomato paste

2 cups chicken broth (optional)

Salt

Freshly ground black pepper

Soak the beans for 12 hours or overnight in a large bowl with water to cover by 2 to 3 inches. Drain the beans, cover them with 10 cups of fresh cold water, add the salami, and slowly bring to a boil. Simmer until the beans are tender, 1¼ to 2 hours, depending on how fresh they are. Drain and reserve the cooking liquid; you should have about 3 cups, but do not worry if you have less. Remove the salami slices. Crumble them, if they are soft enough, or whirl them in the processor fitted with the steel blade.

Warm the butter in a heavy 4-quart pot or deep, heavy casserole, add the clove-studded onion, garlic, and pancetta, and sauté over moderate heat until the onion and garlic are pale and golden, about 8 to 10 minutes. Add the carrot, celery, parsley, and crumbled salami and sauté for several minutes longer. Turn the heat to low, add the rice, and stir it in for about 2 minutes, coating the grains well. Add the cooked beans to the pot, pour in the wine, stir in the tomato paste, and boil for about 2 minutes. Then begin adding the reserved bean cooking liquid, about ½ cup at a time, over moderate heat. The process is the same as for risotto: cook until the rice has absorbed all the liquid, stirring occasionally, then add another ½ cup of the bean liquid and continue cooking and stirring, using all the bean liquid and, should you need it, some or all of the broth, until the rice is tender, if still very slightly al dente. Discard the cloves, taste for salt, and serve with a sprinkling of freshly ground black pepper.

RISO, SEDANO, E SALSICCE

Rice, Celery, and Sausages

—

Serves 4

*V*anna Corbellani Camerlenghi grew up in Mantua, where she learned to make this traditional dish by watching her grandmother cook it. Like most Italian women, Vanna doesn't really measure, she just scoops up a handful of rice for each person; she gauges the quantity of water instinctively, crumbles a bouillon cube for just the right balance of flavor and saltiness. This dish used to be flavored with lesser cuts of pork, but it is rare now to find it prepared at all. It is fast becoming a memory. Vanna recommends Vialone Nano rice as best for this dish.

*Vanna Corbellani
Camerlenghi*

The sausage that Mantuans use is called *luganega*. It is simply a long, thin pork sausage seasoned only with salt and pepper.

> 2 tablespoons extra-virgin olive oil
>
> 2 tablespoons unsalted butter
>
> 2 cups finely chopped white or yellow onions
>
> 1¼ cups finely chopped celery
>
> Salt
>
> Freshly ground black pepper
>
> 2 pork sausages (about ½ pound), casings removed, crumbled
>
> 1 cup plus 6 tablespoons chicken or meat broth or 1 chicken or meat
>   bouillon cube dissolved in 1⅓ cups hot water, plus extra if needed
>
> ⅓ cup tomato, peeled, seeded, and chopped
>
> ½ cup Vialone Nano, Arborio, or Carnaroli rice
>
> Freshly grated Parmigiano-Reggiano cheese

Warm the oil and butter in a 3-quart heavy pot over medium heat, add the onions, celery, salt, and pepper and sauté until they are limp and golden, 7 to 10 minutes. Add the crumbled sausage, broth, and tomato, and simmer for 10 minutes. Now stir in the rice, cover, and simmer for about 25 minutes, until the rice is tender and has absorbed all the liquid. Add a little extra broth if necessary and mix from time to time so the rice doesn't stick to the bottom of the pot. Serve with lots of grated cheese.

RISO E PISELLI

Creamy Rice and Peas

—

Serves 6

*A*s creamy as the finest risotto and as fresh as springtime, this risotto from Vicenza stirs peas, onions, strands of fresh basil, and Parmigiano-Reggiano cheese into homemade broth. If you can't find fresh peas, thaw tiny frozen ones instead. The fresh spring peas that Gianna Magri Bari uses come from the kitchen gardens of the Venetian lagoon and are so sweet and so revered that they are stirred into *risi e bisi*, the dish celebrating the feast day of St. Mark, patron saint of Venice.

> 3 tablespoons unsalted butter
>
> 2 onions, diced
>
> 2 garlic cloves, minced
>
> 1 pound fresh peas (when shelled they should measure 2 cups)
>   or 1 (10-ounce) package tiny peas, thawed
>
> 5½ to 6 cups chicken or meat broth, preferably homemade
>
> 1⅛ teaspoons sea salt
>
> 2 tablespoons olive oil
>
> 1½ cups Arborio or Vialone Nano rice
>
> 1 ripe firm, small tomato, peeled, seeded, and diced
>
> ⅓ cup freshly grated Parmigiano-Reggiano cheese

Warm 1½ tablespoons of butter in a large sauté pan over medium-low heat and sauté half the onions until golden brown; add the garlic and sauté only until it is soft and pale gold, 2 to 3 minutes. Add the fresh peas now, if you are using them, with about ½ cup of broth, and a pinch of salt, and cook over medium-low heat until the peas are tender, 20 to 25 minutes. You may need to add about 2 tablespoons additional water or chicken broth during the cooking. Set aside.

Heat the remaining chicken broth to a continuous simmer in a 3-quart pot.

Warm the remaining butter and the olive oil over medium heat, add the remaining diced onion, and sauté until it is soft and golden, about 12 minutes. Add the rice, stirring quickly and thoroughly, and sauté until all the grains are translucent and well coated, 2 to 3 minutes. Begin making the risotto by stirring in ⅓ cup of simmering broth at a time, being sure the rice absorbs each ladleful before adding the next. When the rice has cooked for about 18 minutes, add the previously cooked peas or the thawed peas and the diced tomato. Continue cooking until the rice is tender and creamy and the peas are soft. Season with the remainder of the salt and add the cheese, stirring it in well, and serve immediately before the rice absorbs the liquid.

RISO E ZUCCA

Creamy Pumpkin or Butternut Squash–Flavored Rice

—

Serves 4 to 6

I've seen golden pumpkin-like squashes with thick bumpy rinds and immense oval pumpkins that must weigh 100 pounds. I've seen cylindrical pumpkins, pale green pumpkins, pumpkins so flattened I thought someone had sat on them, and pumpkins that have grown to be 6 feet long. No wonder there are so many recipes in northern Italy for rice flavored with pumpkin! If you don't have a pumpkin, butternut squash is an excellent alternative.

This winter dish looks like a risotto and tastes like a risotto, but it doesn't take any of the constant attention and stirring of a risotto. Beat butter and cheese into the mixture at the end and serve Vanna Corbellani Camerlenghi's irresistible golden risotto straight from the Mantuan countryside.

3 cups (1 pound) peeled, seeded, and diced pumpkin or butternut squash
3½ cups chicken broth or 3 chicken bouillon cubes dissolved in 3 cups of
    water
1½ cups Carnaroli, Vialone Nano, or Arborio rice
Salt
Freshly ground black pepper
2 tablespoons finely chopped flat-leaf parsley
4 tablespoons unsalted butter, room temperature
½ cup (2 ounces) freshly grated Parmigiano-Reggiano or grana cheese   *(continued)*

Cook the diced pumpkin in barely simmering broth in a covered 3-quart pot for 8 or 9 minutes. Add the rice, cover, bring the broth back to a boil, and continue cooking at a simmer, stirring from time to time with a wooden spoon, until the rice has absorbed the broth, about 15 to 18 minutes. Remove from the heat, add salt and pepper to taste, stir in the parsley, butter, and cheese, and serve immediately.

RISO DEL SAGRA

Rice with Chicken Livers

—

Serves 6 as a first course, 4 as a main course

*T*his is simple food from the farm—a chicken or two could provide the egg, the livers, and the basis of the broth. At festivals in the Mantuan countryside the rice took the place of elegant *agnolini*, round circles of pasta stuffed with much more expensive ingredients. Vanna Corbellani Camerlenghi remembers its deep rich flavors from the many years ago when rivers and canals that etched the landscape washed over expanses of rice fields. Now, she says nostalgically, you are very unlikely to find it anywhere, and if you did, you would know that it celebrates the past glory of plentiful harvests. How does it taste? In Vanna's words: *Ottimo!*

Many Americans choose not to eat chicken livers, but Mantuans know that using a tiny amount of the livers from free-range, organically raised chickens gives a wonderful flavor to this delicious rice, with its nutmeg and Parmesan accents.

3 tablespoons unsalted butter
½ cup diced white onion
2 cups Arborio, Vialone Nano, or Carnaroli
5½ cups chicken or meat broth
2 or 3 chicken livers, very preferably from free-range, organically raised
    chickens, trimmed of green areas and connective tissue, and cut in
    tiny pieces
1 egg

3 tablespoons freshly grated Parmigiano-Reggiano cheese
¼ teaspoon salt
Freshly ground black pepper
Freshly grated nutmeg

Melt the butter in a large, heavy pot and sauté the onion until it is limp. Add the rice and sauté it for 1 or 2 minutes over medium heat, stirring to coat all the grains with butter until they are opaque. Bring the broth to a simmer in a separate 3- or 4-quart pot. Add one ladleful of broth and a few of the chicken liver pieces. Continue, adding broth and tiny pieces of chicken livers while the rice cooks until it has absorbed all but 4 tablespoons of the broth, about 16 to 18 minutes.

While the rice is cooking, beat the egg with the Parmigiano-Reggiano cheese, salt, freshly ground pepper, and freshly grated nutmeg in a small bowl.

When the rice has cooked, take a little broth and add it to the beaten egg mixture. Repeat, incorporating a bit of the broth as insurance against curdling. Then slowly pour the egg into the rice mixture and serve immediately.

RISOTTO ALLA RUCOLA

Risotto with Arugula

—

Serves 6 as a first course, 4 as a main course

*T*he haunting edge of pureed arugula gives creamy risotto a startling depth and intensity and marbles its whiteness with deep green as well. If your arugula seems particularly bitter, reserve a bit and taste the rice before you add the final tablespoons. You may not need to add them. Nonna Lucia Rossi Pavanello, provider of many simple and arrestingly delicious recipes, triumphs again.

> **6 cups chicken broth plus 1 or 2 tablespoons for pureeing the arugula**
> **2½ to 3 cups tightly packed arugula leaves, to make 1 cup when pureed**
> **2 to 3 tablespoons unsalted butter**
> **1 celery rib, finely chopped**
> **1 onion, finely chopped**
> **1½ cups Italian rice, such as Arborio, Carnaroli, or Vialone Nano**
> **⅓ cup freshly grated Parmigiano-Reggiano cheese**
> **Salt**

Bring the 6 cups broth to a boil in a 2-quart saucepan and keep it at a simmer.

Puree the arugula leaves in a processor or blender with a tablespoon or two of chicken broth.

Heat the butter in a large, heavy saucepan. Add the celery and onion and sauté over medium heat until the onion is translucent, about 5 to 8 minutes. Add the rice and cook just long enough to coat the grains thoroughly with the butter, about 2 minutes. Pour in ⅓ cup of the broth and cook, stirring, until the liquid has been absorbed. Add all but 2 tablespoons of the pureed arugula leaves and continue adding the broth, ⅓ cup at a time, stirring constantly over medium heat. When 1 cup of broth is left, taste first and decide if you want to add the final 2 tablespoons of arugula puree. Continue adding the broth until you have used it all; the rice will be somewhat soupy. Add the cheese at the end and season with salt. Serve immediately.

Profile of *Lucia Rossi Pavanello*

Lucia Rossi Pavanello has four great-grandchildren, ten grandchildren, and six grown children—three daughters and three sons, one of whom calls from Piedmont every morning at 7:30 as her personal alarm clock. Many of their friends call her Nonna Lucia—she's grandmother to numerous self-adopted adults, undoubtedly because she's so down-to-earth, so friendly and forthright and easy to confide in.

She wears soft pink blouses, has a rosy complexion that is set off by her luminous white hair and pearl earrings, sets the table with a pink tablecloth on which she puts deep pink roses, and has fingernails beautifully manicured with pink polish. She lights up when I ask about her children, but even without any prompting, many of her sentences begin, "My children love . . ." and there follows a wonderful-sounding dish that may be as simple as *sugoli*, a thick, almost candylike *gelatina* made from red grapes, or as complicated as a three-layered and -colored dessert filled with coffee-flavored pastry cream.

Twelve years ago, after her husband died, Nonna Lucia moved to San Remo to be near one of her daughters. She lives in a spacious apartment with greenery all around, and a balcony overlooking an allée of palm trees and the calm expanse of the Mediterranean sea. She has every convenience now, but when she was growing up on a large farm in the countryside outside Padua, life was much sparer. It began with a breakfast of caffè latte and crunchy, biscotti-like twice-baked slices of bread kept in the handsome wooden chest that now sits in her hallway. She walked five kilometers to and from school each day and she grew up eating whatever they raised, along with the peacocks, rabbits, and partridges that were part of everyday meals.

Of course they had no refrigeration then or later in 1936, when she married her husband, who was truly the boy next door, for he came from the family whose immense farm abutted theirs. They relied on the iceman who slid big blocks of ice inside the icebox two or three times a week. They cooked in a wood-burning oven, on the hearth, and on the grill-like burner of their wood-fired stove. Hot water existed only in one place. Before electric light arrived in the 1940s, the family had only gaslight, carried in tubes that needed constant cleaning, but they were enough to allow her to embroider every night.

In the days when her family was growing up, there were nine at table for every meal—Nonna Lucia's much-loved mother-in-law lived with them for thirty years—and everything she cooked, then as now, came from her mother and mother-in-law's recipes. When I visited she swept me into her kitchen, saying, "*Questo è il mio regno*—This is my kingdom," and pointing to an amazing lineup of machinery: an electric mixer, a food processor, a prosciutto cutter, a pasta machine, a microwave, a big Minigel for making ice cream, and an instant hot water kettle. She has a revolving spice holder in the cabinet with an electric motor that turns it, making it easy to find the jar she's after. The kitchen is spotless. When I ask if she uses any cookbooks, she just laughs. "*Tutto qui*—all here," she says, pointing to her head.

When she went to visit her daughter who lives in Los Angeles —the first time to meet her nephew's fiancée, next for the wedding, and then for the birth of first grand-child—she went immediately into the kitchen. No jet lag, no indecision. She knew exactly where she wanted to be. Whenever she goes anywhere in the family, they clamor for her gnocchi in four colors: with pesto, with tomato sauce, with butter and sage, and, improbably, with sugar, cinnamon, and butter. I watched her make pasta, some rolled very thin for sliding into the depths of soup and some a bit thicker and wider to be served tossed with butter and grated Parmigiano-Reggiano cheese. Her soup broth is so simple that she calls it *brodo matto*, crazy broth. With a smile that said "Watch this," she poured hot water into a pot, added two bouillon cubes and two stalks of celery, leaves included, and simmered for 20 minutes. That's it; that's all. Next she tossed a handful of crystals of coarse sea salt into a nonstick pan, got them sizzling hot, and cooked our veal in a flash, just until it was tender and juicy.

When Nonna Lucia was growing up, most of the family slept in four double beds; she and her sister in one, her parents in one, her grandfather and brother in one, and her brother-in-law and brother in another. The remaining two brothers each had a single bed. Her mother did the wash two times a year with the help of four women who came early in the morning and began the day with bread soup flavored with Parmesan cheese and drizzled with olive oil, with a glass of red wine and coffee. They went into the river and beat those sheets vigorously and then poured water into a huge cauldron, scented it with bay leaves, and brought it to a rolling boil with a fire underneath. Once it was boiling, they added ashes collected from the vines and mulberry branches they had burned in the indoor fireplace. The mixture boiled for a half hour and then, to check if it was ready, her mother stuck her finger inside and touched it to her tongue to taste, as if it were pepper. They dried the sheets by hanging them over an immensely long cord, but ironing them was out of the question. Instead, she said, pantomiming the parts of two women, one at each end of the sheet, she pretended to beat and snap it in the air again and again, then, like them, hit it against her knees and snapped it again even harder until it looked completely wrinkle-free. The sheets were folded and kept in a huge chest. She smiles, "I can still remember the wonderful clean aroma of the ashes."

Nonna Lucia goes to mass every morning, has tea and a *dolce* and watches the American soap opera *Beautiful* every afternoon, plays cards, and exchanges visits and meals with her numerous friends. When I went to see her, she had had several terrible blows. Her remaining brother died at 97; her closest friend, a neighbor, and a cousin to whom she was very close, all died in the space of a month. All but the first were entirely unexpected, yet she was completely open about these deaths, talked about them, and then passed on to other things.

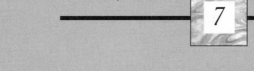

SECONDI PIATTI

Second Courses

Pollame, Pesce, e Carne

Courtyard Animals, Fish, and Meat

—

**COURTYARD ANIMALS OF ALL PERSUASIONS:
CHICKEN, RABBIT, TURKEY, AND GOOSE**

POLLO CON LE OLIVE
Roast Chicken Stuffed with Black Olives

POLLO E POMODORI
Chicken with Tomatoes and Allspice

POLPETTE DI POLLO
Crispy Chicken Croquettes

'NCIP 'NCIAP
A Scramble of Leftover Chicken, Red Onions, and Eggs

POLLO ALLA CONTADINA
Chicken, Country Style

Variation:
CONIGLIO ALLA CONTADINA
Rabbit, Country Style

CONIGLIO IN PORCHETTA
Rabbit Cooked Like Suckling Pig

CONIGLIO DI NONNA REGINA
Rabbit with Salami Sauce

INSALATA DI CONIGLIO
Rabbit Salad

FAGIANO O FARAONA ALLA SENESE
Pheasant or Guinea Hen with Black Olives

OCA ARROSTO
Roast Goose Flavored with Fennel, Garlic, and Rosemary

TACCHINO FARCITO
Turkey Breast Stuffed with a Garlic and Parsley Frittata

SALSICCIA DI TACCHINO
Pistachio and Mortadella-Studded Turkey Loaf

FISH

BACCALÀ ALLA VICENTINA
Creamy Baccalà as They Cook It in Vicenza

STOCCAFISSO DELLA CANTINA SOCIALE DI VALDINEVOLA
Gratin of Cod, Potatoes, and Tomatoes

PESCE AL FORNO
Baked Sea Bass with Green Sauce

SAN PIETRO IN SALSA
John Dory in a Balsamic Vinegar Sauce

Variation:
LUCCIO ALLA RIVALTESE
Pike or John Dory as Cooked in a Tiny Village near Mantua

INSALATA DI POLPO
Octopus Salad

PESCE IN ACQUA PAZZA
Fish Cooked in "Crazy Water"

ORATA ALLA GRIGLIA
Grilled White Fish with Garlic and Parsley

SEPPIE IN ZIMINO
Squid with Swiss Chard

MEAT

PEPOSO
Peppery Beef Stew

BAGIANA
Beef Stew with Fresh Favas, Green Peas, and Tiny Artichokes

BRASATO E PATATE IN UMIDO
Beef Braised in Red Wine with Potatoes

LA GENOVESE
Neapolitan Pot Roast and a Creamy Pasta Sauce

CARNE ALLA PIZZAIOLA
Beef the Pizza Maker's Way

SPEZZATINO ALLA LUCCHESE
Veal Stew with Eggplant, Sweet Peppers, and Tomatoes

Variation:
SPEZZATINO ALLA LUCCHESE
Beef Stew with Eggplant, Sweet Peppers, and Tomatoes

BISTECCA DI VITELLO AL SALE
Veal Steak Cooked with Salt

Osso Buco
Braised Veal Shanks with Anchovy-Spiked Gremolata

Coscia d'Agnello Arrosto
Roast Leg of Lamb Studded with Prosciutto and Rosemary

Agnellino Spezzatino
Young Lamb Braised with Garlic, Sage, Rosemary, and Marjoram

Agnello in Umido
Braised Lamb with Green Olives

Variation:
Agnello agli Spinaci
Lamb Braised with Spinach

Braciole di Maiale Contadine
Pork Chops Smothered in Creamy Onions

Costine di Maiale Cotte nel Brodo di Polenta
Pork Chops Cooked in the Broth of Polenta

Arrosto di Maiale al Latte
Pork Loin Roasted in Milk

Pizza di Carne
Pizza Made with Meat Instead of Dough

Sacrao
Cabbage and Sausages from Emilia

Lenticchie alla Paesana
Lentils and Pork Sausage, Country Style

Salsicce e Broccolleti di Rapa
Pork Sausages with Broccoli Rabe and Crushed Coriander Seeds

Chicken, Rabbit, Turkey, and Goose

Rabbits, courtyard animals often raised by grandmothers, are fed on the grasses and herbs of the hills and grow to be no larger than 2¼ to 2¾ pounds. People who can't imagine eating rabbit should substitute free-range chicken, although they will never know what they are missing. Grandmothers routinely begin cooking a rabbit or hare by putting it in a pan without any oils or liquid and turning the heat to high. The process draws off the water, which is known as the "wild element," and it is always thrown away.

Chickens, like rabbits, are courtyard animals. They are often fed corn, which makes their flesh firm and causes the yolks of their eggs, called *rossi* or "reds," to become a brilliant orange color. Free-range chickens, *pollo ruspante*, are easily found in Tuscany, but elsewhere grandmothers bemoan the loss of these tasty traditional chickens with their firm flesh. Free-range chickens in America have been raised on a nonmedicated diet, making them healthier as well as better tasting.

Goose, the poor man's pig, is used with the same frugality and inclusiveness as pork. The feathers become down and the meat is roasted, braised, or conserved as salame, sausages, or the Italian equivalent of confit packed in snowy white goose fat. The traditional menu on the day that the wheat was threshed in Tuscany found goose being served in numerous ways: as a homemade sausage studded with carrots and pistachio nuts; as a ragù for fettuccine; and as a main course in which it was braised with mushrooms. Lina Vitali in Morbegno in the Valtellina wanted to have enough meat during wartime, so she bought geese and learned how to raise them by reading a book. It turned out to be a great deal harder and noisier than she had expected.

POLLO CON LE OLIVE

Roast Chicken Stuffed with Black Olives

——

Serves 4 to 6

*T*his is a roast chicken for real lovers of olives and olive oil. It is as delicious as it is simple, although I am hard-pressed to explain why a mere handful of olives inside the cavity of a chicken can make such a difference. Call it a miracle from Adele Rondini in Le Marche. Serve the chicken with boiled or roasted potatoes.

> 1 (5-pound) roasting chicken, preferably free-range and organically raised, room temperature
> ½ teaspoon sea salt
> Freshly ground black pepper
> 4 medium garlic cloves, unpeeled
> 2 cups (12 ounces) black olives in brine, preferably Niçoise type, pitted
> 1 lemon
> 2 tablespoons extra-virgin olive oil
> 3 sprigs flat-leaf parsley

Preheat the oven to 425°F.

Remove the giblets and excess fat from the cavity of the chicken. Rinse the chicken inside and out under cold running water. Dry it thoroughly. Sprinkle salt and pepper inside the cavity, then fill it with the garlic and black olives. Squeeze the juice of half a lemon over the skin, then rub it with the extra-virgin olive oil. Put both halves of the lemon and the three parsley sprigs inside the cavity. Truss it closed.

Place the chicken, breast side down, on a roasting rack in a heavy roasting pan or heavy ovenproof skillet. Roast for 30 minutes, then turn the chicken over to brown the breast for 20 to 30 minutes longer. To test for doneness, insert an instant thermometer under the leg or at the thickest part of the thigh to see if the internal temperature is 170°F. (be careful not to pierce the cavity), or insert a knife in the same place and see if the juices run slightly rosy. They should not be red, which indicates that the chicken is not ready; nor should they be or clear, which indicates that it is overcooked. Remove the chicken from the oven and allow it to rest at room temperature for 15 minutes before carving and serving with the olives. You may mash the roasted garlic with juices from the roast, warm them together, taste for salt and pepper, and pass at table.

POLLO E POMODORI

Chicken with Tomatoes and Allspice

—

Serves 4

Whenever the Passannanti family were in the Sicilian countryside for the harvest and crushing of the grapes, they ate this dish of chicken and tomatoes flavored with allspice. So simple to make. So appealing to eat. Use any leftover sauce for pasta.

1 (2½- to 3-pound) free-range chicken, preferably organically raised, quartered

Coarse salt

1 lemon

3 to 4 tablespoons extra-virgin olive oil

¼ cup water

6 medium (about 2 pounds) tomatoes or 1 (28-ounce) can Italian plum tomatoes, cut in half and pressed through a strainer or sieve to remove skin and seeds, juices reserved

5 allspice seeds, 4 whole and 1 crushed

Salt and freshly ground black pepper

Sugar (optional)

Wash the chicken well and remove any fat. Scrub the chicken with coarse salt, then place in a bowl of cold water with the juice of a lemon squeezed into it for anywhere from a few minutes to overnight. If overnight, cover and refrigerate. Drain, rinse, and dry it well.

Drizzle the oil in a 10- or 12-inch sauté pan and sauté the chicken over medium-high heat until it is golden all over, about 15 minutes. Remove the chicken from the pan and pour off the excess fat. Deglaze the pan with ¼ cup of water, boiling the pan juices and scraping up any little bits stuck to the bottom.

If you are using fresh tomatoes, plunge them into boiling water for 1 minute to loosen the skin and then peel it off easily. Cut the tomatoes in half and squeeze the juices and seeds into a sieve or strainer set over a bowl. Discard the seeds, chop the tomatoes, and add to the juices in the bowl. Return the chicken to the pan and add the tomatoes, allspice, salt, and pepper. Simmer, covered, for about 35 to 40 minutes, until the chicken is tender. Transfer the chicken to a serving bowl and cover it well while you boil the sauce over high heat until it has reduced by half, about 5 to 8 minutes. Taste for seasoning. Signora Passannanti sometimes mixes in a bit of sugar if the tomatoes seem to need it. Serve the chicken with the sauce while it is warm.

TIP: Giovanna Passannanti always scrubs free-range chickens with coarse salt, then washes them in water with lemon juice and rinses them well.

POLPETTE DI POLLO

Crispy Chicken Croquettes

—

Serves 3 to 4 as the main course, 6 as an appetizer

*I*talian ingenuity with leftovers must come in the DNA. I'm very partial to Rosa Vigna's croquettes that begin with leftover chicken and are given a new crunchy existence for an entirely different meal. Just dip the little ovals in fresh bread crumbs so they will be crunchy on the outside, soft inside once you've fried them. Rosa Vigna may have grown up in Sardinia, but she has lived in Tuscany so long that she has absorbed local culinary tradition. This is her version of a speciality in Chianti.

> 2 cups finely ground or minced boiled or roasted chicken, any fat, skin,
>   and bones removed
> 1 egg
> 1 egg yolk
> ¼ cup finely minced flat-leaf parsley
> 2 medium garlic cloves, minced
> Substantial gratings of nutmeg
> 1 teaspoon salt
> Freshly ground black pepper
> 1 cup dry bread crumbs, the more homemade and rustic, the better
> Olive oil for frying
> Lemon wedges

Mix together the chicken, egg, yolk, parsley, garlic, nutmeg, and salt and pepper in a large bowl until they are thoroughly blended. Shape the mixture by rolling it first with your palms, then forming rounds or ovals the size of a large egg. Rosa Vigna's are as long as lozenges and fluffy like pillows. Fill a dinner plate with the bread crumbs and roll each polpetta to completely cover the exterior. Repeat until all the mixture is used up.

Heat 1 to 1½ inches of olive oil in a deep cast-iron skillet. When it is really hot and bubbling well, slide in a test piece of the mixture; it must bubble and sizzle and take color quickly when a few bread crumbs are dropped in it. Use a slotted spoon to slide the polpette into the hot oil and cook until they are golden brown all over. It doesn't take long, since the meat is already cooked and you only need to brown the outside. Drain on absorbent paper towels and serve immediately, sprinkled with salt and garnished with lemon wedges.

TIP: Frying should be done with oil hot enough (350°, 375°, even 390°F.) that the food is instantly sealed, allowing little oil to be absorbed. No Italian grandmother has a frying thermometer, but every one has a secret trick or way to know when it's time to fry. Test the oil with a drop of batter or bread crumbs; if it sizzles immediately, it's time to fry.

VARIATION FROM EMMA GRASSI BENSI IN PANZANO: Add 1 large boiling potato, boiled, drained, peeled, and riced. Set it aside to cool to room temperature before adding to the mixture. Then stir in 2 to 3 tablespoons freshly grated Parmigiano-Reggiano cheese and proceed.

VARIATION: Instead of the potato, use 4 slices of bread, crusts removed, soaked in 1 cup cold milk for 10 minutes. Squeeze the milk out of the bread. Crumble the bread and add to the bowl with the meat. Mix in well. Discard the milk.

'Ncip 'Nciap

A Scramble of Leftover Chicken, Red Onions, and Eggs

—

Serves 6 to 8

*P*ronounced n-cheep, n-chop, this wonderful dish probably gets its name from the sound of the knife chopping up the chicken. It is a brilliant way to use leftovers. Morena Spinelli, who grew up in a family of ten, takes whatever she has on hand—some meat, a poached chicken, even some of both—and turns them into a dish that disappears in a flash. Do the same for an inspired and easy Sunday night supper or an informal family dinner.

> 1 medium chicken, fryer, or stewing hen, boiled and boned, or an
>   equivalent amount of leftover boiled meat
> 1 tablespoon unsalted butter
> 2 tablespoons extra-virgin olive oil
> 4 red onions, finely chopped
> ⅓ to ½ cup chicken broth, preferably homemade
> 9 eggs
> ½ teaspoon sea salt

Remove the skin of the chicken and cut the meat in small chunks. Warm the butter and oil in a large, heavy sauté pan or skillet, add the red onions, and sauté over low heat until the onions are soft and translucent, 20 to 30 minutes. Do not let them brown. Add the chicken chunks and cook briefly, just long enough to heat them, then pour in the broth, and cook over low-medium heat for 2 to 3 minutes.

Beat the eggs and salt in a bowl with a fork, then pour them over the top of the onion and chicken mixture, and cook over high heat. Keep turning the mixture with a fork, as you are essentially making a frittata that goes on top of the onion mixture. Cook only until the eggs are set but still creamy. Serve immediately.

Tip: To poach or boil chicken or meat, first bring the water to a boil in a deep pot, then put in the meat and/or chicken and any vegetables you are using for flavor.

POLLO ALLA CONTADINA

Chicken, Country Style

—

Serves 4 to 6

*M*any people in the Tuscan countryside have raised chickens, ducks, and rabbits and cooked them interchangeably in recipes like this one. Duck and rabbit may be harder to find and cost more than chicken in America, but tell that to a Tuscan contadina and you'll get a look of surprise. If you use rabbit, cook it an extra 15 or 20 minutes, but otherwise all instructions are exactly the same. Emma Grassi Bensi's addition of nutmeg and grated lemon zest gives the sauce an elegance beyond its rustic beginnings. Be sure to serve it with lots of bread. This dish is delicious the next day.

1 chicken, about 3 to 3½ pounds, cut into 8 pieces
½ lemon
6 tablespoons extra-virgin olive oil
1 red onion, finely sliced
2 garlic cloves, minced
1 carrot, finely chopped
1 celery rib, finely chopped
2 tablespoons chopped flat-leaf parsley
2 teaspoons finely chopped fresh rosemary
Finely grated zest of 1½ lemons
½ cup red wine, preferably from Chianti
3 small ripe tomatoes, peeled, seeded, and chopped
¼ cup boiling chicken broth or 1 chicken bouillon cube dissolved in ¼ cup
    boiling water
Salt
Freshly ground black pepper
About ⅛ teaspoon freshly grated nutmeg

Rub the pieces of chicken with the juice of ½ lemon.

Warm 4 tablespoons of the olive oil in a 10- or 12-inch heavy skillet or sauté pan and sauté the onion, garlic, carrot, celery, parsley, rosemary, and one third of the lemon zest over low-medium heat for 15 minutes, until the onions are soft but not yet golden.

Use a second heavy sauté pan to warm remaining 2 tablespoons of olive oil; add the chicken pieces and sauté over medium-high heat until they are golden brown, about 15 minutes, turning frequently to brown them evenly. At the end turn the heat to high, pour in the red wine, and let it boil briskly until it evaporates. Transfer the onion mixture to the pan with the chicken pieces, stir in the tomatoes and stock, turn the heat to low, cover, and cook slowly for 25 to 30 minutes, or until the chicken is tender when pierced with the tip of a knife. Once the meat is tender, uncover and cook for another 10 minutes, or until the sauce thickens. Taste for salt and pepper.

Transfer the chicken to a serving platter. Press the sauce through a wire-mesh sieve or puree it in a food processor or blender, adding the gratings of nutmeg and the remaining grated zest of lemon. If the sauce is too dense, add a little more broth. You will have about 1½ cups of sauce. Pour the sauce over and around the chicken and serve immediately.

VARIATION:

> CONIGLIO ALLA CONTADINA (Rabbit, Country Style): This dish can also be cooked with a 2¼- to 3-pound rabbit.

TIP: Renata Marsili tenderizes rabbit or chicken by macerating it in lemon juice and water and leaving it in the refrigerator for 1 to 3 hours before frying.

CONIGLIO IN PORCHETTA

Rabbit Cooked Like Suckling Pig

—

Serves 4

*A*ll over central Italy milk-fed pigs are stuffed with a filling of wild fennel, garlic, and rosemary, roasted on a spit, and served at great dinners and at festivals. Someone with vision and taste saw the virtue of using the same stuffing in rabbits and this dish has long been a favorite in Le Marche.

Luciana Codiluppi Frigio was one of six women I met in Le Marche, sitting around a table talking about the recipes of their favorite foods. All six spoke nonstop for at least an hour, barely pausing for breath, much less for listening to a neighbor. One woman retired from the fray after 20 minutes and while the others stayed, at the end it was clear that Luciana was the victor, a woman who knew more traditional recipes than anyone else and who had a deep conviction about their great taste. If this rabbit is any example, she is certainly right.

1 rabbit (about 2½ pounds)
1 (750 ml) bottle dry white wine

STUFFING

3 or 4 garlic cloves
⅛ teaspoon red pepper flakes
1 teaspoon chopped fresh marjoram
1 branch of fresh rosemary, needles chopped
2 tablespoons extra-virgin olive oil
8 ounces Italian sausage—either plain or fennel-flavored—
    skinned and crumbled
1 rabbit liver, chopped
Salt and freshly ground black pepper
5 tablespoons chopped fennel leaves
¼ teaspoon fennel seeds, crushed
1 egg

3 tablespoons olive oil
¼ cup dry white wine
½ cup chicken or meat broth
3 garlic cloves, smashed
1 branch of rosemary

Wash the rabbit with cold water inside and out. Cover the rabbit with the white wine and leave it in the refrigerator for 2 or 3 hours. Remove the rabbit from the marinade and pat it dry inside and out. Discard the marinade.

In the meantime, make the stuffing: Begin by chopping the garlic and red pepper flakes together, then add the marjoram and rosemary, and chop them all into a fine mixture. Warm the olive oil in a large, heavy sauté pan and sauté over medium heat only until the garlic is pale golden. Add the sausage, liver, salt, and pepper and sauté only until the sausage is soft and no longer pink, 6 to 8 minutes. Add the tender leaves of fennel and the fennel seeds and when the leaves have wilted, remove the mixture from the heat, transfer to a bowl, and set aside. Use a wooden spoon to incorporate the egg and bring the mixture together. Let it cool and then spoon the filling into the cavity of the rabbit. Close the cavity with skewers and string or with a needle and thread.

Choose a heavy pot such as a Dutch oven that will comfortably accommodate the rabbit. Warm 3 tablespoons of olive oil over medium-low heat, add the rabbit and brown over medium heat, turning to be sure it browns evenly all over, about 15 to 20 minutes. Set the rabbit aside while you pour off the oil, then return the rabbit to the pot. Add the white wine, chicken or meat broth, the garlic cloves, and a branch of rosemary, reduce the heat to low, cover, and finish cooking on top of the stove. Baste every 10 minutes with the liquid in the pot, until a fork pierces the meat easily, about 1 hour and 10 minutes.

Cut the rabbit into serving pieces. Place on a serving platter and serve surrounded with spoonfuls of the stuffing.

CONIGLIO DI NONNA REGINA

Rabbit with Salami Sauce

—

Serves 4

*G*ianna Modotti grew up living with her grandparents in the Alps of Carnia, the stunning and dramatic mountainous area in northeastern Friuli. Like most families there, they kept rabbits, and, like most families, they cooked the rabbit over the *fogolar furlan*, the Friulan hearth where families gather for warmth, conversation, and the good smells and tantalizing flavors of the food being prepared in their midst. This particular dish, with its Slavic influence, comes from the *pianura*, the flat plains of Friuli.

2 cups red wine

2 cups water

1 onion, quartered

1 garlic clove, peeled and cut in half

Several sprigs of fresh rosemary

Several leaves of fresh sage

Juice of ½ lemon

RABBIT

1 rabbit, about 3½ pounds, cleaned and cut in 8 pieces, liver reserved

1½ tablespoons extra-virgin olive oil

1½ tablespoons unsalted butter

¼ cup very finely diced pancetta

2 tablespoons finely minced fresh sage

1 tablespoon finely minced fresh rosemary

1 large onion, diced

3 tablespoons finely minced flat-leaf parsley

2 or 3 garlic cloves, minced

Salt

Freshly ground black pepper

½ cup dry white wine

SAUCE

4 garlic cloves

2 to 3 tablespoons extra-virgin olive oil

Reserved rabbit liver

1 chicken liver

1 large slice of soft salami, such as soppressata

Salt

Freshly ground black pepper

½ to ¾ cup dry white wine

¼ teaspoon lemon juice

(continued)

Combine the wine, water, onion, halved garlic, herbs, and lemon juice in a large bowl, immerse the rabbit pieces, refrigerate, and leave for 24 hours. Drain and pat thoroughly dry. Discard the marinade.

Sauté the rabbit pieces over a medium-low fire in a large, heavy, nonreactive skillet or nonstick sauté pan without any oil or butter for about 10 minutes to draw off any water. Remove the rabbit pieces to a platter, discard any water that has accumulated, and wash the pan.

Warm the 1½ tablespoons olive oil and butter in the heavy skillet, and sauté a combination of the pancetta, sage, and rosemary over medium heat until lightly browned. Add the onion, parsley, and garlic and sauté over medium-low heat until the onion and garlic are limp but not browned, about 10 to 15 minutes. At that point remove the above mixture to a platter, return the rabbit pieces to the pan, and sauté very slowly over medium-low heat until lightly browned, about 15 minutes. Season with salt and pepper, return the sautéed vegetable and herb mixture to the pan, and begin bathing with the white wine over a very low fire, adding more wine whenever the last portion has been absorbed. Cook for about 20 minutes, until the rabbit is tender when pierced by the tip of a knife.

While the rabbit is cooking, make the sauce. Warm the garlic in abundant oil in a small heavy pan; once the cloves are pale and soft, discard them. Mince the livers and salami together to a paste in a food processor or blender. Add the paste to the oil, sprinkle it with a little salt and pepper, and cook over high heat until the mixture loses its raw red color. Bathe it with the wine and the spritz of lemon juice. Stir, cover, and cook over low heat for 40 minutes. Serve the rabbit with its herbs and vegetables on a warmed platter and pass the sauce.

Profile of *Gianna Modotti*

"*Sono una montanara*," ("I am a woman of the mountains,") was Gianna Modotti's improbable description of herself. Delicate, urbane, dressed with great style and restraint, she seems the quintessential opposite of a mountain person. With her precise manner of speaking and quiet well-modulated voice, Gianna Modotti is the essence of *gentilezza*. It is hard to imagine her trudging around the mountains but not at all surprising to hear that she went to schools run by nuns or that she is a graduate of the Scuola Istituto di Economia Domestica, an institute that taught all the courses required for a regular university degree as well as gastronomy, etiquette, and all the domestic arts and skills, including the now forgotten decorum associated with paying calls and receiving them.

Gianna Modotti was born and spent all her childhood in the rustic Carnia mountains of Friuli, the lovely region of Italy tucked into the foothills of the Alps between Venice and Trieste. She lived with her parents and grandparents in the house of her nonna. "When I woke up in the morning, I always smelled the aromas floating up from the kitchen right into my bedroom window. We had a huge table in the kitchen and my aunt and my nonna always cooked on the *fogolar*," the special grill-like fireplace of the region in which the flame burns under an onion-shaped hood that carries the smoke up into a chimney.

Her grandparents lived in great measure from what the land provided. "My grandfather had a passion; he didn't go hunting, but he had a place where he got little birds, *uccellini*. It's prohibited now, but then he would come home and go into the kitchen with feathers flying all around in the air. He threaded the birds on wooden skewers like this: first a bird, then a sage leaf, then a piece of lardo, and so on. He didn't put them on a spit but in a glazed earthenware pot, and they cooked very, very slowly so the little birds braised in the fat as it melted. My grandfather served the uccellini with very soft polenta and, when there weren't any uccellini, he made *uccellini scappati*, which means little birds that have flown away. He substituted cubes of veal marbled with fat and threaded the skewers the same way. When the meat was all cooked, some melted lard remained and the sage leaves had become transparent."

Then there were the frogs. Her white-mustachioed grandfather and his assistant went frog hunting at night. As they approached a pond, the assistant held a glass lantern in one hand and a big iron fork in the other, which he used to impale the frogs. Next morning when Gianna came down to the kitchen, she found the frogs, now skinned, but they moved and trembled anyway! She was terrified! The frogs were tiny, no more than 4 inches long, and they were dipped into eggs and bread crumbs and then fried. All fear and squeamishness fled. "*Erano squisiti*," she remembers. "They were incredibly delicious."

Although she is delicate and refined, Gianna Modotti is as interested in the food of the poor as she is in the culinary imprint of the cuisine of Emperor Franz Joseph, who established his court in the eastern part of Friuli near Gorizia. Everyone in Friuli had cows and cheesemaking was so common that cheese was considered poor people's food. During the summer when men went out to work, the women stayed home to feed everyone, but they needed to go to the mountain fields to cut hay for the cows. Just before setting off, they often lit a fire in the kitchen and put potatoes and onions and the crust left from making cheese into a black pan. They covered it and put it near, not on, the flame. When they returned home, the crust had melted and the *frico*, soft potatoes and onions cooked with cheese, was ready.

She still makes that Friulian frico, a dish like soft hash-brown potatoes with slices of cheese that melt over the top. In her family it was always served with one of two side dishes: *uova all'aceto*, eggs scrambled to an amazing creaminess and enriched with a drop or two of vinegar, or *toc' in braide*, garlic-flavored polenta cooked in milk. She is quick to explain that the golden polenta of the mountains of Friuli is entirely different from the creamy white polenta of nearby Venice. "Ours is always hard enough to be cut into pieces with a string or wire; that way it keeps longer. Men who were working in the forest used to wrap slices of the hard polenta in their colored cotton handkerchiefs and take them to eat at work, which is why the dish came to be known as *polenta da mendo*, from *mendare*, the verb to take."

Gianna Modotti is so small that when she makes polenta in the *caldaio*, a deep, round-bottomed pot, she almost has to stand on her tiptoes to reach into the bottom as she stirs. She uses a wooden stick as long as a rolling pin and as flat as a board and stirs as if she were folding egg whites into a batter. She doesn't stir all the time, but she certainly keeps her eye on the bubbling mass during the hour that the cooking requires. That's traditional.

It is no wonder such practices have stayed with her. Food was an intimate part of the fabric of her family life, of the immensely varied countryside, and of the familiar mountainous landscape of childhood. She lived those early years intensely and can still remember the smells, the tastes, the look of the kitchen, and her aunt and grandmother's special touch with ingredients and the dishes they made. She has lived most of her adult life in Udine, the largest city in Friuli, but has never lost the emotional connection to or taste for the food of her beginnings.

She has been fascinated by the rich culinary heritage of the region for decades. There were no written recipes in Friuli before 1800 for the simple reason that most women didn't know how to write. The first recipes came from noble houses and were the result of exchanges between the cooks at such houses. Gianna Modotti wanted to teach people about the food of Friuli, but her husband wouldn't hear of it. She didn't question his judgment but waited until her three children were grown. Then she went back to the sisters' school and taught gastronomy and the rules of the household until the school closed.

Now she gives cooking classes at her house in Udine with the recipes of Friuli. Her preparation, precise organization, and deep knowledge convince students that they are in the hands of an expert. Whether she is teaching the food of the Renaissance through the preparation of an elaborate banquet or the rustic recipes of the Carnia mountains, she quietly and confidently demonstrates the individuality of each recipe. Friuli may be bound by Venetian culture, but numerous conquerors—Austrians, Slavs, and other Middle Europeans—have traversed this crossroads and left their culinary stamp everywhere. History can be tasted in the dishes she teaches: *kock di pane con salsa di pere*, bread pudding with pear sauce, is inflected with its Austrian beginnings, mushroom and potato soup is clearly Middle European (the tip-off is the sour cream, an ingredient unknown in Italy), while *baccalà* comes from Venice. Her own children cook, but not the way she does. One son helps his wife at home with the cooking and the three children; but the architect doesn't have much time, and the artist, the most critical, has very refined tastes and likes to invent new flavor combinations.

Gianna Modotti, on the other hand, is always collecting traditional recipes and cares deeply about documenting authentic dishes. She was once in the countryside of Friuli in a tiny village near the seaside town of Grado, where she saw two women talking. One stood outside the house and the other slightly inside—the kitchen was like those in Naples in that you need only open the window and you're in the kitchen. Woman number one asked her friend what she was going to make for dinner and the answer of woman number two sounded so delicious that when the conversation was over Signora Modotti went up to the woman and asked if she could please have the recipe. "Of course," the cook answered, "I'd be delighted," and she proceeded to enumerate all the ingredients, which included a newspaper. She told Signora Modotti exactly what to do, but when she was finished, the signora asked in her typically polite way, "Excuse me, but what do I do with the newspaper?" "Oh," replied the other woman, "I always put it down on the floor because otherwise it gets oil spots from the frying and this floor is so hard to clean!"

A cautionary tale from a woman who cares deeply about the authentic dishes of Friuli.

INSALATA DI CONIGLIO

Rabbit Salad

—

Serves 4 as a main course, 6 as a first course

*O*nce you've eaten rabbit salad, you'll wonder what you ever saw in its chicken equivalent. It is richer than chicken salad and more festive, but every bit as easy to prepare. Calogera Federico in Valledolmo, Sicily, serves it when her husband comes home from hunting. She cooks a hare and you should too, if you have access to one; otherwise, rabbit makes a delicious substitute. The more vegetables you put in the broth, the better it will be. If you are lucky enough to find fresh European bay leaves at your local farmer's market, I strongly recommend using them. Otherwise use dried European bay leaves. The California bay leaves packaged by many spice companies have a much stronger taste than their Italian or French equivalent. If they are all you have, use only two of them.

Calogera Federico

While the rabbit is cooking, she cooks short-grain rice in water, drains and serves it in the broth from the rabbit. I prefer making risotto with the rabbit broth.

1 medium hare or rabbit (2¼ to 2¾ pounds)

1 lemon, cut in half

2 or 3 bay leaves, preferably fresh European variety

1 celery rib, chopped

2 onions, preferably long red bulb spring onions, chopped

2 carrots, chopped

1 medium potato, cut in quarters

⅓ cup coarsely chopped flat-leaf parsley

3 tomatoes, roughly chopped

2 teaspoons coarse salt

A pinch of red pepper flakes

¼ to ⅓ cup extra-virgin olive oil

⅓ cup minced flat-leaf parsley for sprinkling

Put the rabbit in a large pot, cover it with cold water, add the lemon and fresh bay leaves, and bring to a boil. Immediately pour off the water and set the rabbit aside. Wash the pot with cold water to rid it of any scum. Return the rabbit to the pot with fresh cold water to cover by 2 inches. Add the celery, onions, carrots, potato, coarsely chopped flat-leaf parsley, and tomatoes, partially cover, and cook at a slow simmer, turning the rabbit once or twice, until the meat flakes with a fork, about 1 hour.

Drain, saving the broth. Press the vegetables through a sieve or through a food mill and return them to the broth. You should have about 8 cups. Use for making rice or risotto, if you wish.

Let the rabbit cool just until it is easy to flake the meat. Whisk together the salt, red pepper flakes, and olive oil and toss with the rabbit meat. Serve with sprinklings of minced parsley decorating the top.

Fagiano o Faraona alla Senese

Pheasant or Guinea Hen with Black Olives

Serves 4 to 6

*W*hat could be more festive than an autumnal dinner of pheasant served with a steaming mound of polenta? Italians are amazed to hear Americans talk about pheasant as if it were exotic and rare and are even more surprised that it isn't readily available, but I have discovered that many poultry purveyors will order it with no problem. This recipe comes from Siena via Luisa Cappelli. Its sausage and black olive sauce is perfect with polenta; should you decide to serve polenta, you can increase the amount of tomato liquid in the sauce to 3⅓ cups. The black dry-cured olives plump up during the slow cooking and are fat and succulent when they come to table. Luisa sometimes substitutes guinea hen for the pheasant.

> 2 pheasants (3 to 3½ pounds), quartered
>
> 3 tablespoons extra-virgin olive oil
>
> 3 garlic cloves, finely sliced
>
> 6 Italian pork sausages, seasoned only with salt and pepper
>
> 1¼ cups (7 ounces) dry-cured black olives, such as French, Italian, or Moroccan
>
> 1⅓ cups high-quality dry white wine
>
> 2½ cups liquid from canned Italian plum tomatoes; use 3⅓ cups if you are serving polenta
>
> Salt
>
> Freshly ground black pepper
>
> Polenta (optional, page 182)

Wash the pheasant quarters and pat them dry. Put them in a high-sided 10- or 12-inch casserole or sauté pan, "one next to the other, like fiancés" says Luisa. You will probably need to sauté them in two separate batches. Sprinkle the olive oil over the pheasant pieces and then distribute the garlic slices over them. Remove the sausages from their casings and crumble them to cover the pheasant pieces well. Turn the heat to very low and cook slowly, turning often, to brown them evenly all over, being careful that the sausage doesn't dry out, about 15 to 20 minutes. Add the olives and stir them around for 1 minute. Pour the white wine over the top, turn the heat to high, and cook until most of the wine has evaporated, leaving only a thick concentrate.

Drain the tomatoes through a colander into a large bowl. Pour the liquid into the pan with the pheasant; save the tomatoes for another use. Cover the top of the pan with parchment or waxed paper or a very tight-fitting lid and cook over low heat for about 1 hour to 1 hour and 15 minutes until tender. Taste for salt and pepper after 10 minutes.

Turn the polenta, if you have made it, onto a large platter or wooden board. Serve the pheasant on top of the polenta.

OCA ARROSTO

Roast Goose Flavored with Fennel, Garlic, and Rosemary

—

Serves 6 to 8

*N*ella Galletti remembers the intense work and long days of the wheat harvest, when 300 or 400 people worked threshing the wheat with their scythes. They cut the sheaves and tied them together. There were 20 or 30 alone on the *aia*, the great open terrace, where they beat the sheaves to release the wheat from the chaff. Dust rose and swirled, thickening the air the workers breathed, while the hot sun beat down on them. Ten, fifteen, even twenty geese like these were served at the end of a day to celebrate the days of intense labor that crowned a year of work in the fields.

Geese are known to be fatty animals, so the addition of pancetta to an under-the-skin stuffing seems improbable. The many incisions in the goose skin allow the fat to drain easily and bathe the skin, helping it to brown.

1 large goose, innards set aside
Salt
2 tablespoons olive oil

BATTUTINO: MIXTURE FOR UNDER THE SKIN
1½ tablespoons (1½ ounces) pounded or pestled pancetta or salt pork
¼ cup roughly chopped wild fennel or roughly chopped fennel leaves and
    ½ teaspoon fennel seeds, slightly crushed
1 teaspoon finely chopped fresh rosemary
1 large garlic clove, minced
Salt and freshly ground black pepper

STUFFING
2 large garlic cloves, roughly chopped
2 tablespoons chopped fresh rosemary

½ cup finely chopped wild fennel or roughly chopped fennel leaves

1 teaspoon fennel seeds

6 tablespoons olive oil

Preheat the oven to 425°F.

Wash the goose and dry it well. Pull away any fat from the cavity and discard it or set it aside for use another day. Salt the interior. Chop the goose kidney and liver finely. Warm the olive oil and sauté the minced innards until they are lightly browned. Set aside to cool.

Make the mixture for pressing under the goose skin: Nella pounds the pancetta to a creamy mass in a pestle, then chops it together with the fennel, rosemary, and garlic. I find that chopping the pancetta first, processing it, then pulsing the other ingredients in the food processor works very well. Transfer to a bowl, add the sautéed kidney and liver, and season with salt and pepper.

To make the stuffing: Mix together the garlic, rosemary, and fennel and spoon inside the cavity of the goose. Use skewers and string to truss the goose and pull it closed. Use string to tie the wings close to the body.

Using a middle-sized knife cut 1- or 1½-inch-long incisions in the flesh of the goose and put a little of the battutino inside each one. The more you can get in, the better, says Nella. Be sure to make three or four such cuts in the thighs.

Place the stuffed goose on a rack in an oiled baking pan. Salt it top and bottom. Heat the 6 tablespoons of olive oil to very hot and very carefully pour it all over the goose, covering both legs as well as the body. Bake for 20 minutes at 425°F., lower the temperature to 350°F., cover the goose with aluminum foil, and continue baking until the goose is tender, 2 hours to 2 hours and 10 minutes. Test by piercing the thigh with a pointed knife. The juices that run out should not be pink. Remove the foil for the last 20 to 30 minutes of the cooking so that the skin can brown and crisp well.

TACCHINO FARCITO

Turkey Breast Stuffed with a Garlic and Parsley Frittata

—

Makes 8 involtini, serves 4 to 6

*T*hin slices of turkey enclose an arabesque of mortadella inside a golden center with tiny sprinkles of parsley. Spoon some of the cooking juices over the top and serve these for lunch or dinner or for buffets and lunches on hot days. Amelia Innocenti, cuoca extraordinaria in Florence, knows how to take simple ingredients—a homemade frittata, a little mortadella, and slices of turkey breast—and turn them into an astonishing dish fit to be the centerpiece for a dinner or an elegant lunch.

FRITTATA

> 1 tablespoon unsalted butter
>
> 1 tablespoon olive oil
>
> 2 large cloves garlic, finely chopped
>
> ⅓ cup finely chopped flat-leaf parsley
>
> 6 eggs, lightly beaten
>
> ¼ teaspoon sea salt
>
> Freshly ground black pepper

> About 8 pieces (1⅓ pounds) turkey breast, cut ¼ inch thick and flattened
>
> 2 slices best-quality mortadella
>
> 1½ tablespoons unsalted butter
>
> 1½ tablespoons extra-virgin olive oil
>
> 2 cups milk

To make the frittata: Melt the butter and oil in a 10-inch sauté pan, preferably nonstick, and add the garlic and parsley, cooking very slowly over low heat until the garlic is pale and soft. Pour the beaten eggs, salt, and pepper over the top and cook over the lowest possible heat for 16 to 18 minutes, until the top is set. Using a plate larger than the circumference of the pan, carefully invert the frittata and then slide it back into the sauté pan. Allow it to cook only until the bottom is set, about 2 minutes. Set aside to cool.

Pat the pieces of turkey breast dry on paper towels and lay them on a flat surface. Cut the frittata and the mortadella into as many pieces as you have turkey slices. Set a piece of frittata and a mortadella slice on each piece of turkey breast and trim them to leave a 1-inch margin, being careful that nothing extends beyond the meat. Roll each piece up and tie it with two pieces of string.

Warm the butter and oil in a 3-quart saucepan, preferably nonstick, and sauté the turkey until it is golden on all sides, about 10 minutes. Add the milk, covering the turkey rolls by slightly more than half, and simmer for about 45 minutes, until the meat is tender when pierced by the point of a knife. Turn the turkey rolls every 10 minutes and baste frequently with the milk. Strain the pan juices and reserve them. If they seem too liquid, boil down to concentrate them.

Serve the turkey at room temperature. Cut each roll into 1-inch slices with their beautiful parsley-flecked golden centers. Serve the pan juices as a sauce over the top or on the side.

SALSICCIA DI TACCHINO

Pistachio- and Mortadella-Studded Turkey Loaf

—

Serves 10 to 12

There are two ways to make this dish, one for ceremonial occasions and the other for every day. For elegant events, Nella Galletti bones the turkey, carefully saves the skin, and stuffs the filling back into it, making a galantine. But for eating on an everyday basis, she mixes all the ingredients together, rolls them into the form of a sausage, and then bakes it. Serve warm or at room temperature as a delicious main dish. This can also make an excellent antipasto when cut in thin slices and served with cornichons, black olives, and lightly pickled vegetables preserved under oil (page 426).

(continued)

1 medium onion, diced

2 medium garlic cloves, minced

2 tablespoons extra-virgin olive oil

3 pounds ground turkey

4 ounces ground pork

7 ounces ground veal

1 scant cup (4 ounces) freshly grated Parmigiano-Reggiano cheese

3 eggs, well beaten

2 tablespoons finely chopped flat-leaf parsley

Grated zest of 1½ lemons

1 small carrot, diced

50 pistachio nuts, shelled and toasted for 5 minutes in a 350°F. oven

4 ounces best-quality mortadella, cut in ¼-inch-thick slices and diced

2 teaspoons sea salt

Freshly ground black pepper

¾ teaspoon freshly grated nutmeg

Preheat the oven to 375°F.

Sauté the onion and garlic in the olive oil in a small sauté pan over low-medium heat until soft and pale, about 5 minutes; be very careful not to let the garlic burn. Set aside to cool. Mix or grind together the ground turkey, pork, and veal and place in a large bowl. Stir in the Parmigiano-Reggiano cheese and the eggs. Add the onion and garlic mixture, parsley, lemon zest, carrot, pistachios, mortadella, salt, pepper, and nutmeg and vigorously beat them into the meat mixture with a wooden spoon.

To form the mixture into a long sausage, set it on a sheet of aluminum foil that is at least 2 feet long. Pat the meat into a rectangle that is about 3 inches thick. Starting at the long end, use the foil to help you roll up the meat into a log, like a large, long sausage. Fold under both ends of the foil and press them and the seam firmly to seal the package well. Place it, seam side down, in a lightly oiled baking pan.

Bake the sausage for 45 minutes, until the internal temperature is 140°F. and the juices run clear. Let it rest for 10 to 15 minutes so it can set before serving. You can make the sausage a few hours ahead on the day that you plan to serve it and let it rest, covered, in a cool place. The sausage keeps well, refrigerated, for 2 or 3 days. Be sure to bring it out of the refrigerator at least 1 hour before you plan to serve it so that it can be at room temperature.

Fish

—

Almost every region of Italy has a coastline and most also have inland lakes and rivers. Since many days of eating a meatless diet were part of Church requirements for centuries, it is hardly surprising that fish have played an important part in Italian cooking and eating. Some fish, such as eel, pike, and carp, come from local rivers, lakes, and streams. Others, such as sea bass, grouper, tuna, and red mullet, are from the Mediterranean and Adriatic seas. Still others, such as baccalà and stockfish, arrive from the north already preserved by salting or drying.

Tiny steely blue fish, *pesce azzurro*, include small inexpensive fish such as anchovies, sardines, and herring that are eaten in antipasti and sauces, marinated, baked with wine or bread crumbs, or fried. Anchovies are used as the flavor of salt in dishes; it often takes asking a clever cook what makes the special flavor of a dish to elicit the presence of anchovies. These tiny flavorful fish are remarkably versatile.

The internal water system in the plain of Padua and Lombardy is made up of rivers, lakes, canals, rice fields, and still pools in which frogs, known as "the siren of the canals," thrived, small birds fed, and a paradise of small fish lived. An entire repertory of dishes—*risotto con le rane*, risotto with frogs' legs; *rane in guazzetto*, frogs' legs stewed in a tomato sauce; and *brodo di rane*, frog broth—came just from these internal waterways. Over the past thirty years, as herbicides have been used to kill the weeds, almost none of the animal life remains, so dishes that were common in the time of the nonne now depend on imported items or can't be made at all.

White fish that are common in Italy, such as the orata, gilthead bream, dentice, sea bream, and *cernia*, grouper, are either unknown or extremely hard to find here, but firm white-fleshed fish such as John Dory (*pesce san pietro*), sea bass (*spigola*), or turbot (*rombo*) can be substituted in some cases. Recipes using a popular fish such as *ricciola*, or amberjack, can be made with pompano. Excellent swordfish and tuna, two staples of southern Italian cooking, are widely available.

In Italy mollusks, such as squid, come in multiple forms and sizes. In a single market in Lucca, I found calamari with long legs, white seppie with long tentacles, *totani*, which have a long narrow body but no tentacles, and cuttlefish. Several types of octopus sat next to them on their beds of ice.

Shellfish are equally various. Mussels—*mittili*, *cozze*, and *muscoli*—come in differing sizes; clams range from long narrow tubes called *cannolicchi* to a version as tiny as a baby's fingernail; shrimp can be *cannocchie* or *cicala* (small), *gamberetti* (tiny), *gamberi* (prawns), and *mazzancolle* (giant mantle shrimp).

Baccalà is codfish that has been dried in the wind of the cold and icy north and then preserved under salt. Confusingly, *stoccafisso*, stockfish, which is also cod, is called baccalà in Vicenza, although it is dried by being exposed to the sun. Both must be soaked in multiple changes of water over a period of 2 to 3 days, but baccalà is much easier to work with than *stoccafisso*, which looks like a stick ideally suited to disciplinary purposes. I like to buy boxes of ivory-colored baccalà fillets which are all the same size and thickness. Of course, you can also use fresh cod for the recipes asking for baccalà. Only people whose childhood memories are suffused with the rituals and flavors of baccalà would object.

BACCALÀ ALLA VICENTINA
Creamy Baccalà as They Cook It in Vicenza

Serves 6

Gianna Magri Bari, grandmother and grand cook who lives just outside Vicenza, is an expert on cooking *baccalà alla vicentina*, the traditional dish and glory of the city. This is her recipe. No matter how great her expertise, she wouldn't let me leave without visiting Virgilio Scapin, who is the official head of the Stockfish (Baccalà) Confraternity in Vicenza as well as being a novelist and the owner of a wonderful bookstore.

Strange as it may seem, Italy, a country surrounded by the sea on three sides, loves both *baccalà*, cod preserved in salt, and *stoccafisso*, stockfish dried in the sun and the wind. Both came to Italy from North Sea countries and were once an inexpensive source of fish. They are no longer cheap, but baccalà and stockfish remain favorites of the Italians, who consume greater amounts of them than any other fish save anchovies. Vicenza has always been in the dominion of Venice, and centuries ago, when Venetian traders went to

Norway, they began bringing back stockfish. Venice, with its location on the Adriatic, had no need of dried fish, but smaller inland cities, such as Vicenza, were happy to take it. Signor Scapin surmises that Vicenza's cooks prepared this dish when the Council of Trent met in Vincenza in 1545, a time when the Church was calling for abstinence and for many meatless days. A perfect choice: no meat but lots of flavor.

The first written information about *baccalà alla vicentina* comes at the end of the eighteenth and beginning of the nineteenth century in minutely detailed recipes in cookbooks of aristocratic and middle-class families. Popular as baccalà or stockfish was in trattorie, home cooks didn't know how to cook it and they didn't much care for the smell. The preparations always start with the fish that's as stiff as a stick. Stockfish is inedible in its dried form and must be beaten with a wooden hammer; before World War II there were specialists who went to special *botteghe* to beat it, then put it into water for 2 or 3 days, and pulled out the bones before it could be cooked.

Confusingly enough, stockfish is called *baccalà* in Venice and nearby Vicenza where all dishes, like this one, are made with stockfish. Nevertheless, I choose to use *baccalà* because it is easier to find and much easier to deal with. *Baccalà alla vicentina* is best made 12 to 24 hours before you plan to serve it. Reheat it very carefully until it is almost steaming hot and serve it with slices of soft and creamy polenta. It is also delicious the next day.

1¼ to 1½ pounds baccalà, preferably in fillets that are all the same size
2 small white onions, sliced
1 garlic clove, finely minced
1 tablespoon unsalted butter
1 tablespoon plus ½ cup extra-virgin olive oil
2 to 3 tablespoons all-purpose flour
1 tablespoon plus 1 teaspoon freshly grated Parmigiano-Reggiano cheese
2½ cups milk
Salt
Freshly ground black pepper
1 anchovy under salt, rinsed and filleted; or 2 anchovies under oil, well
rinsed and dried

At least 24 hours before you plan to cook, wash the baccalà well to remove its saltiness and to soften it. Set the baccalà fillets in a bowl and cover them with cold water. Change the water twice on the next two days.

(continued)

Sauté the onions and garlic in the butter and 1 tablespoon olive oil over medium-low heat until pale, about 8 to 10 minutes. Cut the baccalà into pieces no more than 2 inches wide. Toss the pieces in flour to coat them and place one next to the other in a lightly oiled 10- or 12-inch heavy-bottomed sauté pan, preferably one that is nonstick. Signora Bari recommends terra-cotta or aluminum but not stainless steel. Sprinkle the onion and garlic evenly over the top, sprinkle with the Parmgiano-Reggiano, and pour the remaining oil and all the milk over the baccalà, being sure the pieces are covered with at least ½ inch of the liquid. Place the pan on a very low fire; you may want to use a flame tamer. Be extremely careful to maintain a simmer and never allow the baccalà to boil. Boiling will toughen and ruin the fish. Be careful also that it doesn't stick; if it does and gets a crust, change pans immediately. The real secret is the slowness of the cooking, which leaves the fish soft and white as a dog's tooth, she says! Simmer very, very slowly—just enough to see a mere veil of bubbles in the liquid— for about 3 to 3½ hours until all the milk has been absorbed.

Once the milk has been absorbed, the dish is finished and you can take it off the heat. There will be a fair amount of oil left, but you can pour that off and you'll be left with tender tasty fish. The baccalà is best made ahead and refrigerated for 12 to 24 hours.

Stoccafisso della Cantina Sociale di Valdinevola

Gratin of Cod, Potatoes, and Tomatoes

—

Serves 4 to 6

*I*lario Taus was once the mayor of Corinaldo, a lovely walled town in the green depths of Le Marche, and he took very seriously my search for grandmothers who cooked local food. When he suddenly remembered a spectacular celebration at the local wine cooperative for which two older women made immense pans full of baccalà layered with potatoes and tomatoes, we leaped in his car and went for a visit. There they were, Marinella Rugini and Gina Baccolini, hard at work on the bottling line, and it took a lot of persuasion to convince them to divulge the recipe and its secrets.

They use stockfish, but they also use baccalà, dried cod, which they soak in cold water for 3 days, changing the water at least twice each day until it is tender and not salty when tasted. (See page 239 for instructions.) Baccalà used to be simple peasant food and cost almost nothing, but now it is every bit as expensive as many fresh fish. Dried salted cod may be the most popular and omnipresent fish in Italy, but fresh cod with its delicious flavor is hardly available at all. Baccalà, once soaked and desalted, tastes just like the fresh fish. When I explained to the two women that fresh cod is much easier to find in America and makes a subtler version of some Italian cod dishes, they agreed with my decision to use fillets of fresh cod for this dish. The preparation is simple and especially delicious because the potatoes, tomatoes, parsley, and bread crumbs combine so smoothly with the fish. Serve with rectangles of fried polenta.

> 1½ pounds fresh cod fillets, cut 1 inch thick, or other firm-fleshed fresh
>   white fillets such as halibut, or 12 ounces baccalà, soaked for 3 days
> 2 large ripe tomatoes (1 pound), peeled, seeded, and cut in half
> 3 small baking potatoes (1 pound), peeled and sliced
> Salt
> Freshly ground black pepper
> 2 garlic cloves, minced
> ⅓ cup minced flat-leaf parsley
> ½ cup dry bread crumbs, preferably freshly made
> ⅓ cup dry white wine
> 1 to 2 tablespoons water
> 3 tablespoons extra-virgin olive oil
> Very little milk

Preheat the oven to 350°F.

Cut the fish fillets in half. Lightly oil the bottom and sides of a baking dish large enough to hold half of the fish in one layer.

Spread one-third of the tomato in the bottom of the dish, cover them with half the fish, and then half the potatoes. Lightly season each layer with salt and pepper. Repeat, using one third of the tomatoes, the rest of the fish, the remaining potatoes, and end with the last of the tomatoes.

Mix the minced garlic, parsley, and bread crumbs, and strew them evenly over the top. Season with salt and pepper. Finish by mixing the wine, water, and olive oil and pouring over the top so the liquid moistens the mixture very well.

Cover the baking dish with aluminum foil and bake for 1 hour and 20 minutes, then remove the cover. Add a little bit of milk to the remaining liquid to bring the sauce together and bake for another 10 minutes until the fish is tender.

PESCE AL FORNO

Baked Sea Bass with Green Sauce

—

Serves 4

Many fish from the Mediterranean never find their way to the shores of America or they arrive at one coast but not the other. When Liliana d'Ambrosio bakes this fish, she uses *orata*, gilthead bream, a fish that is rarely available here. Substitute any whole firm-fleshed white fish, such as sea bass or red snapper. The fish is beautiful with its pointillist covering of green olives and the brilliant green sauce that is served on the side.

Liliana d'Ambrosio

> 1 whole sea bass (about 3 pounds), cleaned, or 3 pounds fillet
> 3 garlic cloves
> ½ cup flat-leaf parsley leaves
> Sea salt
> Freshly ground black pepper
> 1 slice of lemon
> ½ cup extra-virgin olive oil
> 2 teaspoons dried oregano
> ½ cup (3 ounces) drained green olives in brine, pitted and cut in half
> 1 tablespoon capers, preferably salt-cured, very well rinsed
> 3 tablespoons dry white wine
> 1 to 1½ tablespoons white wine vinegar

GREEN SAUCE (SALSA VERDE)

1½ cups tightly packed flat-leaf parsley, washed and stemmed

½ garlic clove, roughly chopped

2 tablespoons capers, preferably salt-cured, very well rinsed

About 7 green olives in brine, rinsed and pitted

Sea salt

Freshly ground black pepper

⅓ cup extra-virgin olive oil

1 tablespoon balsamic vinegar

Clean and wash the fish well inside and out. Dry it well.

Chop the garlic and parsley together until they are fine and mixed.

Cut a number of small incisions in the flesh of the fish on each side and press the garlic and parsley mixture into them. Season the stomach with salt and pepper, and place 1 lemon slice inside it.

Coat the bottom of a baking dish with olive oil. Rub both sides of the exterior of the fish with olive oil and dried oregano. Cover the top of the fish with the halved green olives, sprinkle with capers, and drizzle the white wine over the top. Leave for ½ hour. Season with salt.

Heat the oven to 350°F.

Bake the fish for about 30 to 35 minutes. After 10 minutes spritz the top with the vinegar. Check for doneness by sliding a knife along the backbone; the fish is ready when the flesh pulls away from the bone.

While the fish is baking, make the green sauce. Place the parsley, garlic, capers, green olives, salt, pepper, olive oil, and balsamic vinegar in a blender or food processor and process until you have a smooth puree. Serve the fish and pass the sauce separately.

SAN PIETRO IN SALSA

John Dory in a Balsamic Vinegar Sauce

—

Serves 4

*P*ike is the fish traditionally used in this dish when it is made in the countryside around Mantua, but Vanna Corbellani Camerlenghi assures me that when city-dwelling Mantuans can't get pike, they use delicate white-fleshed San Pietro, John Dory, instead. And a good thing too. Pike are full of tiny bones and are extremely difficult to scale. If John Dory, a saltwater fish, should prove difficult to track down, substitute cod, haddock, or scrod. I've even used trout with very happy results.

The use of balsamic vinegar in this tantalizing sauce locates its origins in a small section of northern Italy. Mantua in Lombardy is so close to Modena in Emilia Romagna that the two cities share a number of food traditions, including the use of balsamic vinegar. Balsamic vinegar was, until recently, used only by families in the area who produced it or knew someone who did. Now the secret is out and you'll find that its deep intense flavor permeates dishes all over the country.

FOR THE FISH

> 2 pounds John Dory fillets or fillets of cod, haddock, scrod, petrale,
>   or whole trout

COURT BOUILLON

> Leafy tops of 2 celery ribs
> 1 celery rib, roughly chopped
> 1 onion, quartered
> 1 carrot, roughly chopped
> 2 slices of lemon
> ½ teaspoon salt
> 5 black peppercorns
> 2 bay leaves
> 4 cups water

1 cup finely chopped flat-leaf parsley

4 garlic cloves, peeled

1 cup extra-virgin olive oil

Sea salt

Freshly ground black pepper

8 anchovy fillets under oil, drained and well rinsed and cleaned

6 tablespoons balsamic vinegar

Clean the fish well.

Set the celery tops, celery ribs, onion, carrot, lemon slices, salt, peppercorns, and bay leaves in a fish poacher, pour in 4 cups of water, bring to a boil, and simmer for 15 minutes to concentrate the court bouillon. Add the fish in a single layer. Be sure there is enough water to cover the fillets. Cook over medium-low heat, about 4 to 5 minutes, until the flesh is opaque and flakes when pierced with a knife point; turn the fish over, if it is not done after 5 minutes, and cook until the flesh flakes and is tender. Remove the fish and cut into 2-inch pieces. Discard the court bouillon.

Meanwhile make the sauce: Chop together the parsley and garlic. Set them in a small sauté pan with the olive oil, salt, and pepper and cook over low heat until they are soft and melting, about 5 minutes. Add the anchovy fillets, mash them into the garlic and parsley mixture, and let them cook over high heat for no more than 2 minutes. Add the balsamic vinegar and mix well for 1 to 2 minutes, cooking over low heat.

Choose a 12 × 7 × 2-inch ceramic or heatproof glass pan in which you can serve the fish. Spread a layer of sauce in the serving dish, place the fish on it, and then finish with the rest of the sauce, which should almost cover the fish. Refrigerate the dish overnight so the flavors meld. Serve at room temperature. This keeps for 1 week and the sauce only gets better as time passes.

VARIATION:

LUCCIO ALLA RIVALTESE (Pike or John Dory as Cooked in a Tiny Nearby Village): The fish is cooked in exactly the same court bouillon, but it is served with:

1 cup extra-virgin olive oil

Salt and freshly ground black pepper

Juice of 2 lemons

⅓ cup freshly grated grana or Parmigiano-Reggiano cheese
    or ⅓ cup finely chopped flat-leaf parsley

(continued)

Combine the oil, salt, and pepper in a bowl, whisk in the lemon juice, and beat the mixture well until all the ingredients are well amalgamated. Pour over the cooked fish. Then sprinkle the cheese over the fish. If the combination of fish and cheese seems strange or unlikely, I can assure you that it tastes delicious.

TIP: Fish that are cooked whole must be started in cold water so the skin won't break, allowing the fish to fall apart. Fish fillets, on the other hand, must be started in a liquid that is already boiling because the hot liquid seals the exposed flesh and keeps in the juices.

BALSAMIC VINEGAR (*Aceto Balsamico*) was originally produced only in Modena, Reggio Emilia, and the nearby countryside in Emilia Romagna and it was used only by the family, saved as part of a dowry, or given as a major tribute to someone as important as a pope or a titled noble. Traditional balsamic vinegar is made of the must of white grapes boiled down into a thick rich syrup. This syrup, with its deep sweet undertones, is aged for at least 10 years in a succession of barrels, each smaller than the last and each made of a different wood. No wonder a tiny bottle of a really good aged balsamic vinegar, which has the depth and smoothness of a great cognac, can easily cost $100. Balsamic vinegar has a much deeper, more intense flavor than any other vinegar and is used as a condiment to bring out the flavor of ingredients or a dish.

Most of the balsamic vinegars sold in this country are made commercially and are meant to be blended into dishes, rather than drizzled over them in minute quantities. These inexpensive versions are a mixture of wine vinegar, reduced grape must, and perhaps some young balsamic vinegar and they often get their color and sweetness from the addition of caramelized sugar. Because there is so much variation between them, it is important to taste balsamic vinegars. Choose those from Reggio or Modena with the richest, roundest flavor; Fini, Giuseppe Giusti, and Elena Monari Federzoni are good reliable brands. To bring out the flavor of the vinegar, you can boil it down a bit to concentrate the richness. If you can, use a very little aged balsamic vinegar along with some of the less-expensive type.

Profile of *Gisa Sotis*

—

Oaks, olives, and vines march over Gisa Sotis's hilly property with its stupendous view of Ischia and the bay of Naples in the distance and the medieval city of Minturno on the closest hill. Everywhere you look, something is growing. Four hundred grapevines produce very nice wine and her olives become more than 600 quarts of olive oil and brined olives. She has fruit trees, a kitchen garden from which she picks vegetables and herbs, even a very old carob tree with pods hanging in profusion. The carob was once used for flavoring alcohol and the pods were fed to the animals. Now Gisa's cats and dogs eat the short pasta made especially for pets that is dropped into their separate bowls at the exact same moment so they won't squabble. Her grandchildren—Nicoletta, affectionate and strong-willed at twenty-one months, and Danièle, a sweet, thoughtful boy of eight—are often at her side, for three generations live together in her very large and handsomely furnished house. She is the last of her generation, and she knows that she is the last to live the way her own mother and grandmother did. Gisa's daughter, Grazia, has a Ph.D. in Italian and Comparative Literature and teaches in Rome, a two-hour commute; Grazia's husband, Aldo Maiettini, works for a large Swedish telecommunications company and travels frequently.

Gisa Sotis might be more sophisticated than her mother, a countrywoman who worked in the fields all her life, but like her mother, she still cultivates the earth. "I can't let it go," she says, although her impressively straight posture, her styled wavy dark hair, and her well-tailored dress belie the fact. Gisa is still thin and strong in her middle seventies and can easily pass for ten years younger. She lives in Minturno di Tufo in southern Lazio, not far from Gaeta, where she raised her family with her late husband, and she moves at the fast pace of a modern woman.

The family often collects in the kitchen. Gisa is a wonderful cook who can make a lunch or dinner in about half an hour. "It doesn't make sense to spend a lot of time cooking. I love doing it, but not all the time," she says, filling the cavity of a fish with garlic and parsley and a single slice of lemon with such speed that my eyes can barely track her movements. "I love doing this. It's easy. I don't like sleeping. I do things with

Minturno di Tufo

speed," she says, her strong hands reaching for an onion and slicing it in seconds.

Gisa learned to cook watching her grandmother, who came from Gaeta on the nearby Mediterranean coast, just as Nicoletta, at less than two, intently watches her grandmother and follows her movements thoughtfully. Whenever Danièle set the table, carefully putting out napkins and plates, Nicoletta refused to move and lose her view of Gisa. Gisa talked to her in an adult voice—no baby talk or special cadences—and was so soothing that the baby relaxed as Gisa turned on water to clean the clams and fill a big pot for the pasta.

Gisa is particularly masterly at cooking fish. She and Grazia have a long-standing relationship with the man from whom they buy at the outdoor fish market in nearby Formia, and he gives her only the freshest and the best fish. His selection is astonishing: turbot and amberjack; giant mantis shrimp and smaller gamberi, which he tossed into a cone of paper; gilthead bream and a silvery bream known as marmora, squid that has an internal bone and ink sac; and calamari, which has neither. She buys the sea bass her late husband especially loved and cooks it the way he preferred, simmered in water flavored with parsley, garlic, and salt with a slice of lemon added at the end. The cooking liquid makes a delicate and extremely light soup. It is very like the *pesce in acqua pazza* she makes with its additional vegetables in the broth.

Whatever she cooks is simple, not "*sofisticato*," a word she pronounces with disdain. To Gisa, sophisticated food is tarted up and so full of sauces that you can't taste the original ingredients. And weren't those what it was all about? "*Come odori, uso quello che c'è sul terreno, che si trova: aglio, cipolla, prezzemolo, basilico*—For flavoring I use whatever the earth provides: garlic, onions, parsley, basil. It's easy to cook well here," she says. "We have everything good to eat within a few miles." Naples is almost within view and so are dairies that make mozzarella, farms on which tomatoes grow to great sweetness, and the Mediterranean, whose fish give the flavor of the sea. Gisa wants all things in their season and couldn't imagine why anyone would even try to find basil or tomatoes in the winter. She always makes tomato sauce in the summer and then, "When you use it, it will taste like summer in a bottle." Fish have always been as seasonal as herbs and vegetables, and Gisa is disturbed by the new phenomenon of farming fish. It distresses her that sea bass, mussels, and *vongole veraci*, tiny sweet-tasting clams, are now available all year round. Fishermen from Gaeta and Formia, the two nearby large cities on the sea, do their fishing in big trawlers on the high seas, while small boats leave from Minturno with small nets, not the huge ones that inadvertently catch and harm fish that they didn't mean to capture. The smaller fish brought home on the small boats from Minturno are really good, Gisa says with assurance, and it is those fish that she often cooks.

Gisa's husband, Antineo Sotis, came from the inland village of Itri, but he adored the sea and ended up building a small wharf for pleasure boats in Minturno di Tufo. Fishermen from the area use it in wintertime; from May to September it is for sport fishermen and lovers of the sea. Many of the fishermen remember Gisa's husband with affection and pride and bring or give her fish they have just caught.

Gisa Sotis may preserve the old ways, but she is also up-to-date. Her large freezer is amazingly well stocked with everything from homemade lasagne to cubes of veal. She loves fresh octopus and when she discovered that putting an octopus in the freezer for a day softens the meat and tenderizes the flesh, she said farewell to old onerous methods of beating it with a mallet. Open the freezer and you'll always find an octopus on ice.

Tradition goes by the wayside when necessity requires it. One day Gisa was with a young Italian friend who had come to visit and neither had a car. How to get to the fish market in Formia? "No problem," said Gisa, who waved over the first person driving by. Of course she knew the driver—she knows everyone in Minturno di Tufo. But she's unselfconscious and self-possessed; she does what she wants. One night she made a three-course dinner in an hour from beginning to end, we ate it with pleasure, and she bid us good night. The next morning she was up and out of the house at four for a pilgrimage to the enormous sanctuary of Padre Pio.

INSALATA DI POLPO

Octopus Salad

Serves 4 to 6

*G*isa Sotis used to tenderize octopus by beating it with a meat tenderizer until she discovered that leaving it overnight in a freezer did the same thing. Just let it thaw and put it in the pot to cook. Other cooks toss a wine cork into the water in which the octopus is cooking because, they say, the enzymes in the cork automatically tenderize the octopus. Choose your method of nonna wisdom and plunge forward. If you find cooked octopus in the fish department of Asian markets, just slice it and toss with the dressing.

1½ pounds cleaned octopus
1 wine cork (optional)
1 onion, cut in half
1 celery rib, sliced
¼ cup finely chopped flat-leaf parsley
⅓ cup extra-virgin olive oil
Sea salt
Freshly grated black pepper
2 tablespoons lemon juice

Tenderize an octopus as Gisa Sotis does by putting it in the freezer overnight—my preference—but if you forget or are in a hurry, cook it with a wine cork in the water. Bring a large pot of water—enough to cover the octopus—to a boil. Add a wine cork, if you are using one, the onion, celery, and octopus and bring to a rolling boil. Reduce the heat and keep the water at a constant bubble for about 45 to 50 minutes, or until tender, but very slightly al dente. Turn off the heat and leave the octopus in the cooling water for 20 minutes. Remove and drain the octopus.

Slice the octopus into thin pieces, and toss with the parsley, olive oil, salt, pepper, and lemon juice. Serve hot or at room temperature.

VARIATION: Giuseppina Peppino De Lorenzi, a splendid cook from Lequile, deep in southern Apulia, adds yellow-fleshed potatoes, such as Yellow Finns, to the water halfway through the cooking. She slices both the octopus and the potatoes and serves them at room temperature with the same dressing.

PESCE IN ACQUA PAZZA

Fish Cooked in Crazy Water

—

Serves 4

*F*ish cooked in crazy water? Local lore has it that fishermen used to make it with sea-water and a single rock collected from the depths of the harbor that was thickly encrusted with mollusks and algae. What makes it crazy? Carola Francesconi, the greatest authority on Neapolitan food, says the name is used for any dish in which seawater is the major ingredient. The local fishermen who named the dish may or may not have tossed into the pot a few fish from their catch to provide a bit of flavor. These days people use garlic, tomatoes, red pepper flakes, and salt to flavor the "crazy water" in which they poach sea bass or whatever white fish is at hand and they always serve it with slices of grilled bread at the bottom of the bowl. Drizzle with olive oil and eat with abandon.

When Gisa Sotis took me to the fish market at Formia, not far from Gaeta, she stopped to talk to the fish vendor from whom she has bought fish for years. We looked at his amazing variety of fish and then I listened as the two of them and the fisherman's wife had a long conversation about how local families have made this dish for generations. Here's how Gisa makes hers.

4 tablespoons extra-virgin olive oil

4½ cups water

½ cup finely chopped flat-leaf parsley

2 medium garlic cloves, finely chopped

2 medium (1 pound) meaty ripe tomatoes, peeled and diced

¼ teaspoon red pepper flakes or ½ small fresh hot red pepper, minced

1 teaspoon sea salt

1 whole sea bass (approximately 2 pounds), cleaned,
    or 2 pounds sea bass fillets

4 slices of country-style bread

Choose a 2-inch-deep fish pan or poacher that will hold the fish comfortably. Pour in a mixture of 2 tablespoons olive oil, 4½ cups water, parsley, garlic, tomatoes, red pepper flakes, and salt, cover with a top, and simmer for about 20 minutes. Set the cleaned whole fish or the fish fillets inside the pan, cover, and cook in the hot mixture, the crazy water, until the sharp tip of a knife easily pierces the thickest part of the flesh. Always keep the liquid at a simmer, being especially careful not to let it boil vigorously.

While the fish is simmering, grill, toast, or broil the bread on both sides 3 to 4 inches from the source of heat.

Remove the fish from the water and fillet it, if it is whole. Serve each portion of fish in a bowl on a slice of grilled bread and pour over the crazy water. Drizzle a little extra olive oil over the top.

ORATA ALLA GRIGLIA

Grilled White Fish with Garlic and Parsley

—

Serves 4

*W*atching Gisa Sotis at work was an endless pleasure. She went to the fish market, bought a few fish, and knew exactly what she wanted to do with them. Nothing took more than a very few minutes or a very few ingredients and what she produced was stupendous: simple, easy, and completely genuine. The skin got crispy and the meat stayed juicy.

For this she grilled *ricciola* or amberjack, a fish very much like pompano, and flavored it with three ingredients she picked right on her property: garlic, lemon, and parsley. Simple and delicious! If you can't find pompano, use any firm-textured whole small white fish, such as red snapper, striped bass, trout, or sea trout.

4 whole pompano (about 1 to 1½ pounds) or any small firm-fleshed white
    fish (see headnote), cleaned
10 garlic cloves, roughly chopped
1 cup loosely packed roughly torn flat-leaf parsley, stems removed
Juice and pulp of 2 lemons
Salt
Freshly ground black pepper
½ cup extra-virgin olive oil

Wash the fish well under running cold water. Dry and set on a platter. Place 2 cloves of garlic and 2 or 3 tablespoons of roughly torn parsley inside the cavity of each fish. Divide the remaining garlic and parsley into equal portions and set them inside the opening just under the mouth. Finally, put half the juice and pulp of the lemons inside the cavities of the fish and spread the remainder over the top. Sprinkle with salt and pepper and rub with olive oil.

There are several ways to cook the fish. You may build up a fire using good hardwood or hardwood charcoal for your grill. Let it flame and then die down until you have a nice bed of hot embers. You may also broil the fish using the same principles. The main difference is that the heat will come from above so that the smoky flavor will be missing.

When you are ready to cook, brush a little olive oil on the cooking surface and set the grill or broiling pan 4 to 6 inches from the source of heat. If your fish are small, you may want to use a special grid or basket made for fish; otherwise, place the fish directly on the grill and cook 3 to 5 minutes a side, turning once. Test for doneness by inserting a sharp knife next to the bone; the fish is ready when the flesh is firm and opaque and pulls away from the bone. Transfer immediately to a warmed platter.

To make the fish on a stove top, heat a heavy griddle or ridged cast-iron skillet over high heat. Brush it with a little olive oil and arrange the fish on it. Reduce the heat to medium and cook 3 to 4 minutes on one side, 2 to 3 minutes on the other. Check for doneness as above.

TIP: Many Italian grandmothers use trimmings from whatever trees they may have because a wood fire gives its own flavor while charcoal does not, although it does provide a constant temperature.

SEPPIE IN ZIMINO

Squid with Swiss Chard

—

Serves 4 to 6

Amelia Innocenti cooks all the classic Florentine dishes, but ask her to name her favorites, and she immediately mentions this one. The squid cooks with the chard, tomatoes, garlic, and wine, until it is silky. It's a rich and filling dish, the centerpiece for a nourishing meal, and it even pleases people who usually flinch at the mention of squid.

Most fish markets now sell cleaned squid, so it's unlikely you'll have to tackle that chore yourself.

> 2 pounds Swiss chard
> ¼ cup extra-virgin olive oil
> 1½ medium-sized white onions, sliced extremely fine
> 2 garlic cloves, minced
> 1½ pounds cleaned squid, washed and patted dry; bodies cut into rings ½ inch thick, tentacles cut into small pieces
> 2½ tablespoons dry white wine
> ⅔ cup tomato sauce or 3 ripe tomatoes, peeled, seeded, and chopped
> 1 to 1½ teaspoons sea salt
> 1 small dried hot red pepper, minced, or about ⅛ to ¼ teaspoon red pepper flakes

Wash the Swiss chard leaves well. Remove any thick ribs. Chop the leaves roughly into strips. Set them aside.

Meanwhile warm the olive oil in a large 4-quart pot and sauté the onions and garlic over low heat until they are pale golden, about 5 to 10 minutes. Add the squid and sauté for 2 to 3 more minutes over a very low heat, turning constantly. Pour in the wine and boil down until it has almost evaporated. Add the tomato sauce, the chard, sea salt, and red pepper, bring to a boil, cover, lower heat, and cook over low heat for about 25 to 30 more minutes, until the squid is silky and the greens well cooked. You may need to remove the cover, raise the heat, and cook away any excess liquid. Taste for salt and serve. Serve with grilled or toasted bread.

VARIATION: You can use spinach instead of Swiss chard.

PEPOSO

Peppery Beef Stew

Serves 4 to 6

*W*hat could be easier? Toss five ingredients into a pot and cook for about 3 hours. Just be sure that you use beef cut from the shank and that you cook it in a terra-cotta or heavy enameled casserole so that the meat can cook slowly and steadily. If you don't have such a casserole, lower the oven temperature to 350°F. or even 325°F. If you have a wood-burning oven, all the better. Although the amounts of both garlic and pepper seem immense, they mellow during the long, slow cooking and melt into the glaze of meat at the end.

The spicy Tuscan dish, which comes from Impruneta just outside Florence, gets its name from the word for pepper, which is present in copious amounts, along with equally vigorous quantities of garlic and red wine. Why all the pepper? Perhaps because it encourages everyone to drink lots of local Chianti. Serve the peposo with whole boiled potatoes, as some local nonne do, or with slices of grilled country bread.

> 3 pounds boneless beef cut from the shank, in 2-inch cubes
> 10 garlic cloves, peeled
> 1 teaspoon sea salt
> 1 scant tablespoon black peppercorns: do not grind but chop coarsely in a mortar, a nut grinder, or a wooden bowl
> 1 bottle (750 ml) Chianti wine; a hearty red, such as a Zinfandel or Sangiovese, would be a good substitute

Preheat the oven to 375°F.

Put the meat, garlic, salt, and pepper in a heavy 4-quart ovenproof pot, preferably one of terra-cotta, and pour in the red wine so it just covers the meat. Cover the pot with a lid, and cook for about 3 hours, until the meat is soft and the sauce almost creamy. If a lot of liquid remains, reduce the sauce over low heat or in the oven until it is thick and creamy, about 35 minutes. The dish reheats in a 300°F. oven, although you will need to add extra broth.

VARIATION: Make the same dish with veal stewing meat cut from the shank.

BAGIANA

Beef Stew with Fresh Favas, Green Peas, and Tiny Artichokes

—

Serves 4

*T*his recipe for *bagiana*, a mysterious word that appears in no dictionaries, comes from Rimini on the Adriatic coast of Emilia Romagna, where the Agricultural Secretary underwrote a project collecting recipes from old people as a way of documenting an important part of the culture. I imagine that the men and women who shared their recipes and their memories must have been deeply touched as they recalled the smells and tastes of their now distant childhoods. Some of the dishes would be very familiar even to Americans, while others, like this singular stew, are clearly local. I had never even heard of a stew with fresh favas, peas, and artichokes, but it took only one bite to know a wonderful combination when I tasted it. You can make this stew ahead through the addition of the artichokes and tomato paste.

When you buy fava beans, be sure to choose beans with bright green pods and a firm structure. If you can't find the silky young fava beans of springtime, you will need to remove the skins covering the beans. To skin the beans, bring a large pot of water to the boil, plunge the beans into it, and let them cook for 2 to 3 minutes. Drain and immediately immerse them in cold water. When you are ready, you should have no problem popping the beans right out of their skins. A time-saving alternative: you can buy dried favas already skinned from Middle Eastern markets. See Source Guide to Ingredients.

½ cup minced white onion

⅓ cup (2½ ounces) diced pancetta

3 tablespoons extra-virgin olive oil

1 pound lean beef, cut into 1-inch cubes

¼ teaspoon sea salt

Freshly ground black pepper

10 baby artichokes

1 lemon

1 teaspoon tomato paste dissolved in ½ cup warm water

2 pounds fresh young fava beans, shelled

2 pounds fresh peas, shelled

Sauté the onion and pancetta in the olive oil in a 4-quart pan or a Dutch oven over medium heat until the onion is limp and pale golden, 10 to 15 minutes. Add the meat, salt, and pepper and cook over very low heat for 1 hour. It's important to keep an eye on the meat to be sure that it doesn't dry out and to keep the heat low enough so the meat doesn't need additional liquid.

While the meat is cooking, trim the artichokes by breaking off all their tough outer leaves. Next, snap off each leaf by bending it backward with a sharp snapping motion to remove the stringy upper portion. Continue snapping off the tough tops until you reach the pale green leaves of the inner cone. Cut off the top portion of the leaves of the cone. Immediately rub the exposed parts with a lemon half and squeeze both halves of the lemon in a large bowl of water. Immerse the trimmed artichokes in the acidulated water.

Drain the artichokes. Add them and the tomato paste dissolved in water, cover the pot, and cook for 10 minutes. Stir in the shelled fava beans and the peas and continue cooking for 5 to 10 minutes longer, or until the vegetables are tender.

Brasato e Patate in Umido

Beef Braised in Red Wine with Potatoes

—

Serves 6

*T*his secret recipe comes from Ornella Reneglio, via her grandmother's maid, who was with the family until she was eighty-four years old. She, in turn, got the recipe from her friend and contemporary, the cook in a great Piedmontese house.

The taste of this remarkable braised beef depends on using the very finest ingredients available. You must start with a really nice piece of meat—were you in Piedmont, you would opt for the most prized of all Piedmontese beef from Carrù. Then you must marinate it in vintage Piedmontese wine. Ornella's family set twelve bottles of good Barbera aside until they had aged for 20 to 25 years and used them over a period of time to make this dish. Piedmontese grandmothers once made this in glazed earthenware casseroles, which they covered with a top that sealed it almost hermetically, and they cooked it over a very low flame in a long slow braise of wine and aromatic herbs. At the end, the vegetables are pureed to a cream and served with the meat.

> 5 or 6 garlic cloves, peeled and threaded on a bamboo skewer
>
> 2½ pounds boneless beef in one piece, such as point of the rump, bottom round, or best possible pot roast
>
> 1 bottle (750 ml) aged Barbera, Barolo, or Cabernet Sauvignon (see Note)

FOR BRAISING

> 1½ tablespoons unsalted butter
>
> 1½ tablespoons extra-virgin olive oil
>
> Salt
>
> Freshly ground black pepper
>
> 10 leaves of fresh sage
>
> 1 carrot, roughly chopped
>
> 1 onion, roughly chopped
>
> 1 celery rib, roughly chopped
>
> 1½ pounds potatoes, peeled and cut in half

At least 12 hours before you plan to cook, stick the skewer with the garlic cloves into the meat, and put the meat in a large glass bowl. Cover with as good a bottle of old Barbera or Barolo as you are willing to use. If you don't have such fine wine, see the note below. Turn the meat several times at night and again in the morning to immerse it evenly. The meat becomes almost black with the wine.

In the morning remove the meat, reserving the marinade, and dry it thoroughly.

Warm the butter and oil in a large, deep, heavy-bottomed casserole or pot, add the meat, and brown it evenly over high heat to seal the juices, 10 to 15 minutes, season it with salt and pepper, then transfer it to a platter and set it aside.

Add the 10 sage leaves, carrot, onion, garlic, and celery to the casserole and cook over medium heat until they are tender, about 5 to 8 minutes. Pour in the reserved wine from the marinade, bring it to a boil, and scrape up any little crisp bits left from the previous cooking. Return the meat to the casserole, reduce the heat to medium low, and bring the liquid to a simmer. Cover the meat first with foil and then with a tight-fitting top, and keep at a simmer, stirring and turning the meat several times to allow it to braise evenly for about 2 to 2½ hours. Adjust the liquid by adding extra wine if the wine begins to boil away. Add the potatoes and continue cooking for another 30 minutes, or until both the potatoes and the beef are tender when pierced by a knife. If the potatoes are done first, remove them and leave the beef simmering until it is tender. Strain out the vegetables and puree them to a cream in a processor or blender. Taste for salt and pepper. Serve the puree with the meat and the potatoes. You can make this dish a day ahead, cover, and refrigerate. Reheat it gently when you are ready to serve it. It is delicious the next day as well.

NOTE: If you don't have old wine, marinate the meat 12 to 24 hours before with:

> 10 leaves of fresh sage
> 1 carrot, roughly chopped
> 1 onion, roughly chopped
> 1 celery rib, roughly chopped
> 1 bottle full-bodied red wine, such as Cabernet Sauvignon or Barbera

VARIATION: Brasato is made in nearby Lombardy with a full-bodied white wine, such as any of those from Oltrepò Pavese.

LA GENOVESE

Neapolitan Pot Roast and Creamy Pasta Sauce

—

Serves 4 to 6

*T*his dish is real home cooking, something that you would never find in a restaurant. It was once *the* sauce made by poor people in Naples for Sundays and holidays before it was supplanted by the now famous ragù. It uses the same principle as ragù—the vegetables cook for a long time with a piece of meat that benefits from long cooking. Of the three women who gave me their recipes for la Genovese, two purposefully omit tomatoes and carrots, even though their mothers and aunts always used them. I am following Liliana d'Ambrosio, who uses both and cooks the sauce to bring back the tastes of her childhood, the food of Neapolitan families for generations. When Gisa Sotis cooks Genovese, she uses red onions; Ines Pernarella puts the sauce through a food mill at the end to make a puree as soft as butter.

Perhaps there are a few Neapolitans who ponder the mystery of why this purely Neapolitan dish is called Genovese when not a hint of it exists in the cooking of Genoa, but certainly there are thousands more who just plunge their forks into what is for them the food of home. All it takes is masses of onions cooked slowly with the beef and a few vegetables to produce an irresistible sauce in which the onions almost melt to a sweet creamy mass. The grandmothers' tradition is to serve half the creamy sauce as a first course with pasta that is somewhere in size between ziti and perciatelli and then serve the rest with the meat, which may follow immediately or appear the next day. You could, of course, serve most of the sauce with the meat and save any leftover sauce for pasta later.

When I persisted in asking why a dish from the area around Naples was called Genovese, none of the nonne could give me an answer. Domenico Manzon, an expert on the food of Naples, says that this method of cooking is definitely a Neapolitan invention which has nothing at all to do with Genoa. Its heritage is probably from the Angevins, who used rich thick sauces made with meat, vegetables, and onions.

⅔ cup extra-virgin olive oil

7 tablespoons (3½ ounces) diced pancetta

3 pounds finest pot roast in one piece, such as point of the rump, or bottom round

8 large (about 4 pounds) white onions, finely sliced

2 to 3 carrots, chopped

½ celery rib, finely chopped

⅓ cup finely chopped flat-leaf parsley

3 tablespoons finely chopped fresh basil

1 teaspoon finely chopped fresh marjoram

1 meat bouillon cube

⅓ cup dry white or red wine

2 medium tomatoes, peeled, seeded, and chopped,
   or 1 tablespoon tomato concentrate or tomato paste

PASTA

4 quarts water

1½ tablespoons coarse salt

1 pound ziti or perciatelli, or substitute a fresh egg pasta
   such as fettuccine or tagliatelle

Warm the olive oil and pancetta in a deep, heavy casserole or a 12-inch heavy sauté pan large enough to hold the meat and all the onions comfortably. Add the meat and cook it over high heat until it is golden brown, turning often so it doesn't stick, about 15 minutes. Once it is browned, remove the meat to a plate. Add the onions, carrots, celery, parsley, basil, and marjoram to the pot and cover. Cook over the lowest possible heat until the onions are soft and limp but have taken on no color, at least 25 to 30 minutes. The onions are plentiful and must cook very slowly; they are almost the entire liquid for the sauce. Return the meat to the pot and cook over the lowest possible heat for about 20 minutes, turning the meat several times. Add the meat bouillon cube, cover, and cook slowly over very low heat, adding wine and tomato or tomato paste a little at a time and scraping the bottom of the pot to be sure the meat doesn't stick. Cook until the onions are soft and melting like a cream, another 2 to 2½, even 3 hours. The onions become a thick mass and the meat is ready when it can be easily pierced with a knife. Ines Pernarella, one of my sources, told me that she put the onions in the food processor at the very end to make a true cream of the sauce.

Bring 4 quarts of water to a boil in a large pot, add 1½ tablespoons of coarse salt, and cook the pasta until it is al dente. If you are being as traditional as a Neapolitan nonna, serve a bit more than half of the sauce over the pasta and the rest over the sliced meat.

CARNE ALLA PIZZAIOLA

Beef the Pizza Maker's Way

—

Serves 4

*I*nes Pernarella, who is now in her late eighties, grew up in the medieval hill town of Monte San Biagio on the border between Lazio and Campania. Earlier in the century it was very common for southern Italians to go to America, sometimes just long enough to earn money and sometimes to immigrate. Ines's mother ran a trattoria, and whenever any relatives returned home or sent American friends for a visit, this is what she served. She was sure that Americans would want to eat beef, and this is how it is cooked in her part of Italy.

Ines Pernarella

This dish is a great choice when people want just a little red meat. It's fast and easy to make—20 minutes from start to finish—and it has the unmistakable flavor of its Italian origins.

Choose a cut of beef that is full of flavor and cooks quickly, such as London broil. Ask your butcher to trim away all the fat and to cut and pound the pieces to a ¼-inch thickness. If such an accommodating person doesn't exist in your life, use a mallet and do it yourself. The real challenge to making this dish taste authentic lies in finding wild oregano. Unless you are remarkably lucky and come upon some, I recommend using a fine imported Italian or Greek dried oregano, such as Peloponnese.

6 to 8 pieces of beef, in ¼- to ⅜-inch-thick slices

6 tablespoons extra-virgin olive oil

3 garlic cloves, crushed

4 large ripe tomatoes (about 2 pounds), peeled, seeded, and cut in strips

1 teaspoon sea salt

Freshly ground black pepper

3 tablespoons finely torn fresh basil leaves

1½ to 2 teaspoons fresh wild oregano or 1 teaspoon dried Italian or Greek oregano

Trim any fat or gristle from the meat and flatten the slices to a ¼-inch thickness—or better yet, have your butcher do so—by pounding them as thin as possible.

Pour the olive oil into a sauté pan large enough to hold all the meat in one layer without crowding, add the garlic, and sauté over low-medium heat for about 3 minutes, being careful not to let the garlic burn. Remove the garlic, add the beef, and brown very quickly over high heat, 1 to 2 minutes a side. Sprinkle the garlic over the beef slices on the bottom, cover with the tomatoes, sea salt and pepper, the torn basil leaves, and the oregano. Cover the pan and cook over low heat for about 12 to 20 minutes, depending on the cut of meat, until the tomatoes have made a fairly thick sauce. You may need to add a little hot water during the cooking to thin it.

When the meat is tender, serve it on heated plates with some of the sauce spooned over the top.

SPEZZATINO ALLA LUCCHESE

Veal Stew with Eggplant, Sweet Peppers, and Tomatoes

—

Serves 4

When I went to see Laura Mansi Salom, knowing that she had grown up in the immense house in Lucca that has since become the city museum, I was certain I'd find an aristocratic woman with a taste for elegance. And I did. But I hadn't guessed that she would also be extremely lively, entirely engaged in the contemporary world, or that she would love to entertain frequently, sometimes in large garden parties and other times with homey food that can easily be made ahead.

This stew is luxuriously full of the flavors of eggplant, sweet peppers, tomatoes, and potatoes that enfold the subtle taste of the tender cubes of veal. It is a perfect dish for a chilly evening. I have substituted oregano and mint to create a taste as close as possible to Tuscan nepitella, a wild mint that grows profusely in the region. Be sure there is lots of sauce and serve it with creamy polenta or with leftover polenta cut in triangles and grilled or fried.

(continued)

This whole dish may be made 1 day ahead. You can roast the peppers 2 or 3 days in advance and refrigerate them.

> 1 very large eggplant, firm and glossy
> Salt
> 3 large sweet peppers: 1 red, 1 yellow, 1 sweet green
> 1¼ pounds lean veal stew, cut in 2-inch cubes
> ¼ cup all-purpose flour
> 1½ to 2 tablespoons unsalted butter
> 4½ to 5 tablespoons extra-virgin olive oil
> ⅓ cup dry white wine
> 3 pounds tomatoes, peeled and chopped, juices reserved
> ¼ teaspoon finely chopped hot red pepper or red pepper flakes
> 1½ teaspoons finely chopped fresh oregano
> ¾ teaspoon finely chopped leaves of fresh mint
> 2 potatoes, peeled and sliced in rounds
> Freshly ground black pepper

Peel and cut the eggplant into cubes, set them in a colander, sprinkle with salt, and leave to drain the bitter juices, about 1 hour.

Roast the peppers over a direct flame or under the broiler. Turn them so they char evenly, and then transfer them to a bowl or paper bag, cover or close up tightly, and leave for about 30 minutes, or until they are cool enough to handle. The skin will peel off easily; remove the seeds, cores, and ribs, and slice them into thin strips.

Meanwhile, toss the meat with enough flour to coat the pieces lightly. Warm the butter and 1½ to 2 tablespoons extra-virgin olive oil in a large, heavy sauté pan or flameproof casserole, preferably terra-cotta, add the meat, and sauté until the meat is evenly browned on all sides. Pour in the white wine and cook it down over high heat until it has evaporated. Add the tomatoes and hot red pepper, cover, and cook for 1 hour and 45 minutes to 2 hours, or until the meat is very tender.

While the meat is cooking, warm the remaining extra-virgin olive oil, add the sliced peppers, marjoram, and mint and cook over medium-high heat for 10 minutes.

Pat dry the eggplant cubes, add them, cook for 10 more minutes, and finally add the potatoes and cook until they almost crumble, 15 to 20 minutes. If the mixture seems dry at any point, begin by ladling a cup of the liquid from the tomatoes that are cooking with the meat. Cover and simmer for 30 to 35 minutes, adding more liquid from the tomatoes as needed. Stir frequently, being sure to keep the vegetables moist.

When the meat is tender, stir the vegetables into the meat mixture, taste for salt and pepper, mix them together well, and serve. The stew can be made a day ahead and reheated at a low temperature.

VARIATION: Make the spezzatino with beef stewing meat.

Profile of *Laura Mansi Salom*

Laura Mansi Salom's elegant profile looks straight out of a Renaissance portrait. Lean, lithe, and stunning, with fine high cheekbones and jet-black hair drawn back on her neck, Laura looks incontrovertibly aristocratic, although she has no interest in resting on old family laurels. Yes, she is seventy, but she could be in her fifties, a tireless and voluble woman who is entirely up-to-date.

Laura has just started teaching cooking to Italians, using only recipes that can be done quickly and without fuss. Her approach is everything that her growing up was not. She spent her childhood at Palazzo Mansi, the great house in Lucca, with three chefs, one for each course, plus a pastry cook. The family ate a major five-course meal twice a day with four or five wines, to say nothing of an elaborate tea in the afternoon, but Laura is convinced that people must have just tasted, not eaten with vigor, because no one was fat. *"La vera mangiata si fa più ora"* ("People really eat more now"), even if there aren't all the various courses and the food is much simpler.

"We lived with all kinds of waiters and cooks, but World War II brought about the big changes. My grandparents tried to keep up the same life after the war was over. When I went back to eat with them, I felt I had entered another world. I had gotten used to the much more dynamic modern life and they seemed terribly old-fashioned and boring to me. I have lived in these two worlds that are so varied and so different; I don't know what to regret. I'm happy to have lived the other life, but I don't have the spirit or

Lucca

desire to relive it. I prefer the life of today—it's so much more easygoing, more dynamic. It was beautiful to see both worlds and to watch them meet, but I leave the old ways behind without regrets."

Her own house in Segrominio in Monte with its collection of fine porcelains, antique furniture, large well-kept gardens and a spectacular view over the plain of Lucca still speaks of the way of life in which she grew up. Even the enormous kitchen, with its numerous cabinets bursting with immense platters and bowls, which she uses for all her parties, is on the scale of an earlier time. The room easily accommodates all the Italian women who come to watch her demonstrate her new recipes—*spezzatino alla lucchese,* veal stew with sweet peppers, *torta di verdure,* two layers of Parmesan-flavored mashed potatoes enclosing a filling of spinach—and to eat the day's lesson as well. Laura often settles here for meals with her grandchildren, not in the adjacent formal dining room with its cabinets full of porcelains and antique treasures.

"It used to be that we went into the salon after a meal and were offered a glass of Malvasia or Marsala, or a waiter passed a tall iced carafe of lemonade. Sometimes he had punch and *mandarino,* a mandarin orange liqueur which was very chic, or *nocino,* a strong walnut liqueur which we still make ourselves, but no one ever thought of offering a *digestivo,* in those words, as they do now." Very déclassé, is the subtext.

"I love life now—I'm really attracted to the new. I'm so curious." When her children ask her to do something, she tells them that she'll do it when she's old, but then they look at this dynamic and elegant woman who is full of projects and ask, a bit plaintively, when will that be. "*Sono una nonnina diversa:* I'm not your typical grandmother—no crocheting for me.

"I'm much happier in this life. I think of my grandparents' life as a time when husbands went off from their towered castles and left their wives behind in chastity belts." Laura Salom has clearly not been left behind. Yes, she remembers the spectacular and complicated food that appeared at her grandmother's table and sometimes she will even serve a *pasticcio di riso,* risotto layered with meat, tiny fresh peas, and mozzarella; or a *pasticcio di maccheroni,* an extravagant timbale of pasta and meats enclosed in a sweetened pastry crust. The dish was perfectly described by Lampedusa in *The Leopard,* where it is served at a dinner in Palermo, prompting the thought that the geographical and cultural distances between nineteenth-century Tuscany and Sicily may have been enormous, but not, perhaps, in the elegantly constructed dishes created in the kitchens of the aristocracy:

"Good manners apart, though, the appearance of those monumental dishes of macaroni was worthy of the quivers of admiration they received. The burnished gold of the crusts, the fragrance of sugar and cinnamon they exuded, were but preludes to the delights released from the interior when the knife broke the crust; first came a smoke laden with aromas, then chicken livers, hard-boiled eggs, sliced ham, chicken, and truffles in masses of piping-hot, glistening macaroni, to which the meat juice gave an exquisite hue of suede."

Laura knows that past, but "the truth is that I try to simplify everything. I love giving cocktail parties and buffets, parties with fifty or sixty people, and I love working my way around talking to them all. So exciting! So much energy!"

BISTECCA DI VITELLO AL SALE
Veal Steak Cooked with Salt

—

Serves 4 to 6

*N*onna Lucia Rossi Pavanello astounded me with this amazingly simple way of cooking meat. The salt keeps the meat soft—the exterior never gets tough as it does when browned in oil—and draws off all the fat. Most surprising of all, the meat doesn't taste salty, just well seasoned. Be sure that the meat fits easily in one layer. If you have more than fits comfortably, use a second pan. Using the same salt twice concentrates its taste and makes the meat much too salty.

> 3 veal sirloin steaks (about 2 to 2½ pounds), cut ½ inch thick; they will have a tiny bit of bone
> 2 to 3 tablespoons coarse sea salt
> Extra-virgin olive oil

Pat the veal steaks dry with a paper towel.

Toss a handful of coarse sea salt into a large nonstick sauté pan and heat the pan well. Add the veal steaks and brown them over high heat for about 4 minutes each side; they will only be lightly browned when tender. Serve with a thread of extra-virgin olive oil.

Osso Buco

Braised Veal Shanks with Anchovy-Spiked Gremolata

—

Serves 4

What's unusual about this recipe for osso buco? Look at the gremolata that is sprinkled on top. Instead of mixing garlic with the lemon zest and parsley, Ornella Reneglio follows her mother and grandmother by mashing in anchovies to create a provocatively subtle flavor. Ornella serves the veal shanks with risotto made with the addition of the fresh marrow from three beef bones, not from the osso buco itself, and a substantial sprinkling of saffron. She mixes in some extra gremolata and serves the osso buco arranged on top.

Osso Buco

> 4 tablespoons (2 ounces) unsalted butter
> 1 large onion, cut into chunks
> About 3 pounds large veal shank bones, cut 2 to 2½ inches thick
> About ¼ cup all-purpose flour
> Salt
> Freshly ground black pepper
> ½ cup dry white wine
> 1 cup chicken broth
> 1 tablespoon tomato paste dissolved in 2 tablespoons warm water

Gremolata Topping

> Finely grated zest of 1 lemon
> ⅓ cup finely chopped flat-leaf parsley
> 2 whole anchovies under salt, boned, rinsed, filleted,
>   and mashed; or 4 anchovy fillets under oil, rinsed and mashed

In a large, heavy, and deep casserole, such as an enameled one or Dutch oven, melt the butter, add the onion, and sauté over medium-low heat until it is pale and barely beginning to take on color, about 10 minutes. Remove the onion with a slotted spoon and set it aside.

Dry the veal shanks with paper towels. Flour them lightly and brown them over medium-high heat in the onion-flavored butter. Salt and pepper them as you turn them on every side until they are golden brown all over, 6 to 7 minutes. Pour in the wine and cook over medium heat until only 2 to 3 tablespoons are left. Arrange the veal pieces in the pan so they are standing upright with their large marrow openings on top. Return the onion to the pan; add the chicken broth and dissolved tomato paste. Cover and cook over very low heat for about 1½ hours, until the veal is tender when a fork pierces the meat.

While the veal is cooking, make the gremolata by chopping together the lemon zest, parsley, and anchovies. Five minutes before serving, drizzle a little over the top of each osso buco and finish cooking with the flavors of the topping infusing the dish.

Coscia d'Agnello Arrosto

Roast Leg of Lamb Studded with Prosciutto and Rosemary

—

Serves 4 to 6

Lambs in Italy are frequently so young and tiny that it is not at all unusual to find a 3-pound leg of lamb. Were we in Italy, the leg in this recipe would weigh no more than 4 pounds, and I urge you to try to find one that weighs no more than 5 pounds. Each pound takes 20 minutes to cook, so if your lamb is larger, plan accordingly. Italians like lamb well done; the taste and texture of this leg of lamb depends on being cooked the full amount of the time.

> 2 teaspoons chopped fresh rosemary or ½ teaspoon dried rosemary
> Scant ½ cup (2 ounces) chopped prosciutto
> Salt
> Freshly ground black pepper
> 1 (5-pound) leg of lamb
> 4 to 5 tablespoons best-quality lard or olive oil
> ⅓ cup red wine
> 3 medium russet potatoes, peeled, cut into small dice, and set in a bowl of cold water

(continued)

Preheat the oven to 450°F.

Combine the chopped rosemary and prosciutto in a small bowl. Make many incisions about ½ inch deep in the leg of lamb and fill them with the mixture. Salt and pepper the meat. Massage 2 tablespoons of the lard or olive oil into all sides of the leg of lamb.

Place the meat in a heavy roasting pan with the remainder of the lard and turn the leg to coat it. Roast for about 20 minutes. Lower the oven temperature to 375°F. and roast another hour and 15 minutes, occasionally basting with the wine and pan juices.

Forty-five minutes to 1 hour before the lamb is done, drain and pat dry the diced potatoes. Add them to the pan. When the lamb is done, transfer it to a cutting board and let it rest for 10 to 15 minutes. Tilt the roasting pan to remove as much fat as possible, then remove the rest by straining the juices. Slice the meat, arrange it on a warmed serving platter, spoon some of the juices over the meat, and serve hot with the potatoes.

AGNELLINO SPEZZATINO

Young Lamb Braised with Garlic, Sage, Rosemary, and Marjoram

———

Serves 4

*I*talian abbacchio or agnellino is baby milk-fed lamb that is no more than 40 days old. It is much smaller and tenderer than American lamb and has a delicate sweet flavor. Use organically raised lamb between the ages of 6 months and 1 year, if you can find it; if not, regular lamb will work fine. Cut it into cubes that are the size of an espresso cup or a little smaller, says Teresa Stoppoloni, from the little town of Cingoli in Le Marche. Teresa and her husband collect old cooking implements; terra-cotta amphorae that once held olives curing in brine line their marble staircase, and rolling pins, meat pounders, and terra-cotta cookware with the patina of age decorate shelves and walls. Teresa cooks guided by her intuition and knowledge passed down from generation to generation in her family. She wouldn't think of measuring her herbs; she just rubs the buds off a branch of fresh marjoram, tears up several fresh sage leaves, and strips the needles from the fresh rosemary. As for the olive oil: it's all done by eye, of course. In Italy the young lamb is cooked without any extra liquid until it gets a spritz of vinegar at the end, but our larger lamb needs to be treated a bit differently.

Teresa serves the lamb with roast potatoes and a little salad of wild greens.

4 to 5 tablespoons extra-virgin olive oil

3 or 4 garlic cloves, flattened

Several leaves of fresh sage, torn into large pieces

About 1 teaspoon chopped fresh marjoram

About 1 teaspoon chopped fresh rosemary

2 bay leaves, preferably fresh European variety; or 1 dry bay leaf

2½ pounds boneless lamb shoulder, trimmed of all fat
    and cut into 1½-inch pieces

½ cup dry red wine

Salt

Freshly ground black pepper

1 tablespoon red wine vinegar

Warm the olive oil in a heavy flameproof casserole—an earthenware pot that goes directly on the heat is ideal—add the garlic, sage, marjoram, rosemary, bay leaves, and lamb, and brown the pieces well over medium heat, being careful not to burn the garlic. You will probably need to do this in two batches. Once the lamb has browned, remove it from the pan, pour in the wine, add salt and freshly ground black pepper, and boil the wine until it is about half its original volume, 15 to 20 minutes. Return the meat to the pot; the lamb juices will mix with the remaining wine to provide enough moisture for the final cooking. Cover tightly, and cook until the lamb is almost tender, about 45 minutes, stirring and checking from time to time that there is enough liquid. Add water, if necessary, so that you have some sauce at the end. Remove and discard the bay leaves. Sprinkle the vinegar over the top of the meat, raise the heat, and stir, cooking the vinegar a bit. Taste for seasoning and serve.

VARIATION: I once spent a lazy afternoon with a group of women in their seventies and eighties at their seamstress's workshop in a tiny village outside Todi in Umbria. As the seamstress hemmed their skirts and altered their dresses, steadily working the pedal of a very old Singer, we talked about the food they cooked, and two of the women mentioned this very dish, but both of them added 2 teaspoons of grated lemon zest at the end.

AGNELLO IN UMIDO

Lamb Braised with Green Olives

—

Serves 4 to 6

Renata Marsili of Lucca, a cook with a glorious repertoire of dishes, assures me that this recipe works equally well with rabbit, chicken, or game. Whenever I think about trying one of the options, I can never renounce the lamb, so perhaps I'll never know. Pouring in the wine, Signora Marsili used a Lucchese expression to explain that the wine gives "*il sapore di rigno*" ("a somewhat wild taste"). Easy to prepare but unusual, this becomes a spectacular dish with the delicate accent of the green olives. The lamb is especially delicious served with polenta.

¼ cup extra-virgin olive oil

2 garlic cloves, minced

2 sprigs of fresh rosemary, needles minced

Full ⅛ teaspoon red pepper flakes

3 pounds boneless shoulder of lamb or boneless meat cut from the shank end of the leg of lamb, all fat trimmed away, cut into 2-inch cubes

1 cup dry white wine

½ chicken bouillon cube or ½ cup chicken broth

1 large (about 12 ounces) ripe tomato, peeled, seeded, and chopped

¾ cup (3½ ounces) green olives in brine, drained, rinsed, and pitted

Salt

Freshly ground black pepper

Warm the olive oil in a 10- or 12-inch heavy skillet or Dutch oven, and sauté the garlic, rosemary, and red pepper flakes over low-medium heat for 4 or 5 minutes, just until the garlic begins to turn golden. Add enough lamb to fit comfortably in the pan without crowding, and sauté, turning the cubes several times, until they are evenly browned. You may need to do this in two batches. Transfer all the lamb to a platter and set aside. Add the white wine and the bouillon cube and cook over medium-high heat until the liquid has reduced by about half. Return the lamb to the pan, add the tomato, cover, and cook over very low heat for about 1¾ hours, until the lamb is easily pierced with the tip of a knife.

You could serve the lamb now, but it is much better if you let it sit in the refrigerator for a few hours or overnight and reheat it when you are ready to eat. Skim off any fat and then cover and heat at a simmer for ½ hour. Stir in the olives during the last 5 to 10 minutes, taste for salt and pepper, and serve.

VARIATIONS:

AGNELLO CON GLI SPINACI (Lamb Braised with Spinach): When she makes this lamb, Renata Marsili always uses Tuscan peperoncini, tiny hot red peppers, instead of ground black pepper and says that a *dado*, a cube of chicken bouillon, gives it an extra-strong burst of flavor.

3 pounds fresh spinach, washed in several changes of cold water

Cook the lamb as above. Remove any thick spinach stems. Plunge the well-washed spinach leaves into a pot with only the water still clinging to the leaves and cook over medium-high heat for 2 to 3 minutes, just until the leaves have wilted. Drain them well. Add to the lamb during the last minute or two of cooking. Serves 4 to 6.

BRACIOLE DI MAIALE CONTADINE

Pork Chops Smothered in Creamy Onions

—

Serves 4 to 6

*E*mma Grassi Bensi is deep in her eighties, stands about 5 feet tall, has red hair cut in a pixie style, wears huge rose-colored glasses, and reads *Gente*, the *People* magazine of Italy. She has a deep throaty chuckle and lively appreciation of life, among whose pleasures she counts cooking the best Tuscan country dishes, like these pork chops in a sauce of onions that almost melt as they cook. Women from all over Italy cook onions so slowly that they become a creamy sauce, which is then used as a sauce for meat. The technique is common; the results are superb.

3 onions, sliced very fine
4 to 5 tablespoons extra-virgin olive oil
1 to 2 tablespoons water
Salt
Freshly ground black pepper
6 pork chops (about 2¾ pounds)
All-purpose flour with salt and pepper for dredging
½ cup dry red wine
1 to 2 tablespoons unsalted butter

Put the onions in a large, heavy skillet with 2 tablespoons of the olive oil, a tablespoon or two of water, salt, and pepper. Cover and cook them at the lowest simmer over the lowest possible heat—use a flame tamer if you need to—for 45 minutes to 1 hour, stirring occasionally. At the end the onions will be soft and creamy.

Dredge the pork chops in seasoned flour so they won't stick while cooking. Drizzle the remaining oil into a heavy sauté pan large enough to hold the chops comfortably without crowding, add the pork chops, and brown them, turning so they cook evenly. When they have browned, 2 to 3 minutes a side, pour in the red wine and boil until it evaporates. Put the cooked onions on top of the pork chops, cover, and cook together briefly on top of the stove so the flavors meld, turning the chops several times. The onions cook into a really thick sauce; at the end puree them in a processor or blender, adding a little water or a tablespoon or two of butter.

COSTINE DI MAIALE COTTE NEL BRODO DI POLENTA

Pork Chops Cooked in the Broth of Polenta

—

Serves 4 to 6

*C*ooking meat and polenta together without any stirring at all: what a revolutionary and delicious idea! Once the pork chops are browned, the polenta cooks with them in the oven in combined milk, broth, and pork juices. No time-consuming watch at the stove and no arduous stirring are required.

Gianna Modotti grew up in the Carnia mountains of Friuli and remembers the dishes cooked by her grandmother as if she ate them yesterday. The polenta of Friuli, the beautiful and unexplored region in the northeasternmost corner of Italy, appears in numerous dishes because the rigorous cold climate of the mountains calls out for food as warm and nourishing as this. I have dreams of introducing everyone to polenta in this easy way. I can't imagine who could resist, especially after eating a few spoonfuls of the soft creamy polenta that comes with the pork chops.

7 tablespoons unsalted butter

6 pork chops (about 2¾ pounds), trimmed of any fat

2 large garlic cloves, minced

3 leaves of fresh sage, torn; do not used dried sage
    if fresh sage is not available

1 bay leaf

1 sprig of fresh rosemary

½ cup dry white wine

1 cup milk

1 cup meat broth, plus extra if needed

½ cup plus 2 tablespoons coarse-grind polenta or cornmeal

Salt

Freshly ground black pepper

(continued)

Preheat the oven to 300°F.

Melt the butter in a 12-inch flameproof or enameled casserole that will go in the oven. Add the chops and sauté them over medium-high heat, turning to brown on both sides, about 8 to 10 minutes. Sprinkle the garlic, sage, bay leaf, and rosemary needles stripped away from the sprig. Bathe them with the white wine and cook over medium-high heat, turning frequently until the wine has evaporated, 10 to 15 minutes.

Meanwhile, mix together the milk, broth, and polenta. After a few minutes, add them to the pan, lifting each pork chop and pouring some of the mixture underneath so that most of the polenta is below the meat. Stir well to incorporate the liquid polenta mixture with the pan juices, then sprinkle salt and pepper over the top.

Put the entire mixture in the oven for 30 to 40 minutes, covered, adding slightly more warm broth if necessary, and cook until the polenta has thickened but is still soft and creamy. Remove and discard the bay leaf. Serve immediately.

ARROSTO DI MAIALE AL LATTE

Pork Loin Roasted in Milk

—

Serves 6

*G*ina Albano grew up in Liguria but she only learned to cook when she married in 1928 and moved to her husband's home in Bari. It was quite a transition. She wasn't allowed to go shopping—only men did that—and she wasn't familiar with much of the produce, but she had a good teacher in her husband, a real gourmet.

This delicious recipe, however, comes neither from her old home nor from the one which became hers on her marriage. A close friend from Naples gave it to her decades ago, and Signora Albano says that it is just one of several such dishes that show the definite affinity of the food of Naples and Bari, the two great ports of southern Italy. The dish takes almost no work: the pork poaches quietly in the milk until all that remains of the liquid is thick hazelnut-brown clusters of cream. Slice the pork and serve the creamy sauce on the side. Should you have any left over, it is delicious served at room temperature the next day.

2½ pounds boneless loin of pork, tied
6 tablespoons (3 ounces) finely diced pancetta or salt pork
1 carrot, diced
½ celery rib, diced
1 onion, diced
4 cups milk
⅓ cup dry white wine or water
Salt
Freshly ground black pepper

Pat the meat dry with paper towels.

Put the pancetta, carrot, celery, and onion with the pork in a heavy enameled casserole or Dutch oven just large enough to hold the meat. Pour in the milk, let it come to a slow boil, partially cover the pot, and cook over medium heat with the milk at a steady bubble, turning the meat from time to time, until the pork is tender when pierced with a fork and the milk has been reduced to nut-sized clumps, about 1½ hours.

When the meat is cooked, remove it from the sauce and keep it warm, covered with aluminum foil. Raise the heat and cook down the sauce until almost all the milk has been reduced to a thick collection of light brown clusters. Off the heat set the sauce in a sieve just to strain away any remaining milk and fat. Add ⅓ cup white wine to the cooking pot and boil it over high heat, scraping up any loose cooking residues from the pot with a wooden spoon. Taste for salt and pepper.

Cut the roast in ⅜-inch slices and serve with the pot juices over the roast and the sauce on the side.

PIZZA DI CARNE

Pizza Made with Meat Instead of Dough

—

Serves 2 as an informal main course, 4 as an appetizer

*I*t may sound like a contemporary fantasy to take a piece of meat, pretend that it is the dough for pizza, and then pile all the usual condiments on top, but Amelia Innocenti assures me that this is an old recipe she has known for decades. Tiny, nimble, and extremely clever in the kitchen, Signora Innocenti grew up in Florence and has been a cook in private houses much of her life, making traditional Florentine dishes for her fortunate employers. Although she never suggested it, this faux pizza would also be delicious made with ground turkey meat or ground beef.

> 10 ounces ground pork
> 2 tablespoons fine dry bread crumbs
> 2 tablespoons plus 1 teaspoon milk
> 2 pinches of sea salt
> 1/8 teaspoon freshly ground black pepper
> 1 teaspoon extra-virgin olive oil
> 2 anchovy fillets under oil, mashed
> 1 1/2 teaspoons capers, well rinsed and roughly chopped
> 1 medium tomato, peeled, seeded, and finely chopped
> 1 tablespoon lightly pickled vegetables, such as salsa di verdure (page 426), rinsed and chopped
> 1 tablespoon freshly grated Parmigiano-Reggiano cheese
> 1 tablespoon shredded fontina cheese
> 1 1/2 tablespoons finely chopped flat-leaf parsley

Mix together the pork, bread crumbs, milk, salt and pepper and let stand for 1 hour.

Brush the bottom of a heavy 12-inch skillet with the olive oil and then spread the meat over the bottom so it is about 1/2 inch thick. Treat it as if it were a pizza and sprinkle the anchovies, capers, tomato pieces, pickled vegetables, and grated cheeses over the top.

Place the pan over medium heat and cook until you hear the meat sizzling. Immediately cover, and cook over very low heat for 7 to 10 minutes, or until the meat is no longer pink. Use a spoon or baster to remove any extra fat.

Remove the cover, slide the "pizza" onto a serving platter, sprinkle the parsley over the top, and serve immediately.

SACRAO

Cabbage and Sausages from Emilia

—

Serves 4 to 6

*F*resh sausages in Emilia are spiced with a combination of coriander seeds, cinnamon, caraway, cloves, nutmeg, and star anise. Since it isn't possible to find such sausages here, I make a small mixture of the spices and let it bubble briefly in the butter before adding the sausages and cabbage for their final cooking. Giovanna Dolfi-Zenzi Lusignani assures me this dish is so local to her tiny town of Pellegrino Parmense that I'd never find it even 10 miles away.

> 6 fresh mild Italian sausages made without fennel
> 1 savoy cabbage (about 2 pounds), cut as fine as tagliatelle
> 3 tablespoons unsalted butter
> 2 coriander seeds
> Pinch of cinnamon
> Pinch of caraway seeds
> Pinch of ground cloves
> Pinch of freshly grated nutmeg
> 1 star anise
> 1 tablespoon red wine vinegar
> Salt

(continued)

Prick the sausages, cover them with water, and cook at a steady slow boil for 10 minutes. Remove them from the water and cut into 1½-inch pieces. Return the sausages to the pot, add the finely chopped cabbage, and simmer for 10 more minutes, reserving the water.

In a separate large, heavy sauté pan, warm the butter, add the spices, and let them melt briefly into the butter. Scoop up the sausages and cabbage with a slotted spoon, drain them well, and sauté them briefly in the butter, no more than 5 minutes. Add the wine vinegar, then the reserved water from the initial cooking, and cook for a little while longer, until the flavors have blended. Taste for salt.

VARIATION: For a delicious variation, use chard instead of cabbage.

LENTICCHIE ALLA PAESANA

Lentils and Sausage, Country Style

—

Serves 6 as a main course and 8 as a side dish

The day I drove from Iesi, with its beautiful wheat-colored stone buildings, over green hillsides to Cingoli, I was reminded once again of the beauty of the unexplored region of Le Marche. I was on my way to the small mountain town with its staggering views over the countryside to see Enea Angelucci and his wife, Teresa Stoppoloni, who both are passionate about truly local food. Lucky indeed are the workers who arrive daily at the couple's Hotel-Ristorante Miramonti to have a midday meal at the restaurant. They might sit down to a plate of these lentils, a nutritious and filling dish for almost any menu.

Be sure to chop the carrot and celery in big chunks so you can remove them.

2¾ cups (1 pound) dried lentils
3 garlic cloves: 2 whole, 1 finely minced
Salt
1 celery rib, cut into large chunks

1 carrot, cut into large chunks

1 bay leaf

2 small (about 5 ounces) mild pork sausages

2½ tablespoons extra-virgin olive oil

1 medium onion, finely chopped

1 small green or pale red tomato, peeled and chopped

¼ chicken or beef bouillon cube or ¼ cup beef or chicken broth

Spread the lentils on a flat surface and remove any stones and grit. Wash them well in a deep bowl of cold water and discard any that rise to the surface. Drain.

In a 4- or 5-quart heavy saucepan, combine the lentils, 2 whole garlic cloves, salt, celery, carrot, bay leaf, and enough water to cover them all generously. Bring to a boil, turn the heat down to a steady simmer, and cook until the lentils are tender but still intact, about 25 to 30 minutes. Add extra water, if necessary, to keep the lentils covered. Drain, reserving the cooking water; discard the garlic, celery, carrot, and bay leaf.

Remove the sausages from their casings, place the meat in a medium-size bowl, and mash it well with a wooden spoon until it is a single creamy mass. Warm the olive oil in a heavy-bottomed 3- or 4-quart saucepan and sauté the onion over low heat until it is soft and pale, about 10 minutes. Add the minced garlic clove and sausage meat and sauté only until the sausage is no longer pink, being careful not to overcook it. Add the lentils with about a cup of their cooking water, the chopped tomato, and the small bit of bouillon cube and cook for about 15 minutes, adding any extra lentil cooking water that is needed to keep the mixture moist. Taste for seasoning and serve.

SALSICCE E BROCCOLLETI DI RAPA

Broccoli Rabe and Pork with Crushed Coriander Seeds

—

Serves 4

*I*n the course of visiting grandmothers in the very southern portion of Lazio, I twice came across coriander-flavored sausages. The sausages in Monte San Biagio, called *petartella*, are extremely lean. The pork seems almost cut by hand; it is threaded with tiny pieces of potato and seasoned with coriander seeds. I told Ines Pernarella, an octagenarian native, that we didn't have such a sausage in America and wondered if I could add coriander seeds as flavoring to lean pork sausages. She wasn't crazy about the idea, but I just didn't want to give up the combination of flavors in the sausages and greens.

The other critical part of the dish is broccoli rabe, one of the tart leafy greens that Italians are so fond of. Find the youngest, most tender and delicate you can, preferably before the yellow flowers have developed. They are the perfect foil for the sweetness of the sausage. Serve this with something that's yet another foil, such as mashed potatoes or polenta.

> 4 lean sweet Italian pork sausages, preferably made with coriander seeds
> 3 tablespoons water, if needed
> 1 pound broccoli rabe
> 2 large garlic cloves, crushed
> 3 to 4 tablespoons extra-virgin olive oil
> ¼ teaspoon red pepper flakes or 1 small dried hot red pepper,
>   finely chopped
> ¼ teaspoon sea salt
> ⅓ cup dry white wine (optional)
> ¼ teaspoon coriander seeds, lightly crushed

Prick the sausages with a fork to allow the fat to drain out. Cook the sausages over medium heat in a skillet with 1 inch of boiling water for 15 to 20 minutes, turning them several times, until the water has evaporated and the sausage fat remains. During this period you may need to add about 3 tablespoons of water for extra moisture. Gently brown the sausages in the remaining fat, then drain and set them aside.

Wash the broccoli rabe; if they are as young and the shoots as tender as they should be, you won't need to trim or discard thick stalks. Sauté the garlic in the olive oil in a heavy sauté pan for about 2 minutes, being careful that it doesn't brown or burn. Add the broccoli rabe, the pepper flakes, and the salt, cover, and cook over very low heat until tender, about 10 minutes. While it is cooking, add the wine (if desired), a little at a time. Once the greens are tender, add the sausages to the pan, add the crushed coriander seeds, and heat just enough to warm the sausages through without browning, then serve.

Peperoncini are small red chile peppers. Their seeds are used often instead of black pepper in Tuscany (where they are confusingly called *zenzero,* "ginger"), Rome, Lazio, and points farther south. In Abruzzo these red pepper seeds are always in a big shaker on the table, and everyone sprinkles them on the food when it arrives. Elsewhere they are mixed with olive oil or with salt and olive oil and used as a condiment. A word to the wise: handle these peppers with care. Use rubber gloves because the volatile oils in the seeds can sting mercilessly if you have an open cut and can be devastating if you wear contact lenses and touch your eyes after touching the peppers.

8

PIATTI UNICI

One-Dish Meals

INVOLTINI DI CAVOLO
Stuffed Cabbage Leaves

CROSTATA DI FAGIANO
Pheasant Pie

FRICO COTTO CON PATATE E CIPOLLA
Cheese Cooked with Potatoes and Onions

SOUFFLÉ DI PORRI
Leek Flan with a Creamy Sweet Pepper Sauce

PASTICCIO DI RISO
Risotto Filled with Meat, Tiny Fresh Peas, and Mozzarella

TIELLA
Mussel, Potato, and Rice Cooked in a Terra-Cotta Casserole

TIMBALLO DI RISO
Layered Rice Timbale

PASTICCIO DI MACCHERONI
Laura Mansi Salom's Timbale of Pasta and Meats Enclosed in a Pastry Crust

INVOLTINI DI CAVOLO

Stuffed Cabbage Leaves

—

Serves 4 to 6

I've spent my whole life at the stove," says Vittoria Genovese, who lives in the tiny village of Nicola, population 120. "I'm so used to being in the kitchen that I don't think it's tiring—anyway, all my grandchildren come and keep me company." She started cooking in summer visitors' colonies when she was fifteen and for a while cooked at one restaurant in tiny Nicola at lunch and a different one at dinner. But once the family bought the trattoria Cervia in 1982, she and her daughter Sonia settled down in that kitchen.

Vittoria learned to cook first from her Nicolese mother-in-law and then from the entire little village. Mostly the family ate rustic food—polenta, panigacci, frittelle. "There wasn't much choice. We ate what there was. We always had a garden," a kind of wild woods from which they could pick greens and herbs, and olive trees from which they made delicate oil.

It still surprises Vittoria that a certain part of the Italian public knows the exotic and creative dishes of many cooks, but doesn't know the genuine tastes of local tradition. Her specialties, such as this stuffed cabbage, are all authentic dishes of the villages of Liguria and the Lunigiana. Once a year she makes celery with the same filling for the festa of the local saint, but otherwise, she rolls the delicate filling inside individual cabbage leaves and serves it to friends, family, and lucky visitors to the tiny town of Nicola.

(continued)

CABBAGE

>   1 large head (about 2 pounds) savoy cabbage
>   4 quarts water
>   Salt

TOMATO SAUCE

>   2 pounds fresh ripe tomatoes or 2 cups cut-up canned Italian plum
>   tomatoes, juices reserved
>   3 tablespoons extra-virgin olive oil
>   2 onions, minced
>   1 garlic clove, lightly crushed
>   Salt
>   Freshly ground black pepper

FILLING

>   ¾ cup milk
>   2 slices of country-style bread, torn in chunks
>   4 ounces finest-quality mortadella or prosciutto
>   4 ounces ground lean veal
>   2 ounces best-quality prosciutto
>   2 eggs
>   ¼ cup finely chopped flat-leaf parsley
>   1 teaspoon minced garlic
>   1/16 to 1/8 teaspoon freshly grated nutmeg
>   Sea salt
>   Freshly ground black pepper
>   ¼ cup (1 ounce) freshly grated Parmigiano-Reggiano cheese, plus ¼ cup
>   for sprinkling

Cut the cabbage leaves at their base, then pull them away gently. Be careful not to tear any of the leaves. Wash and dry them well.

Bring 4 quarts of water to a rolling boil, add salt, and when the water comes back to a boil, drop in the cabbage leaves. Cook just long enough to allow them to become limp, about 2 minutes. Remove them with a slotted spoon and place them over the sides and in the well of a colander to drain.

To make the tomato sauce: Peel the tomatoes, cutting them in half and squeezing out their seeds over a sieve. Discard the seeds, chop the tomatoes roughly, and reserve the juices.

Heat the oil in a large, heavy nonaluminum sauté pan and sauté the onions over low heat until soft and transparent, about 15 to 20 minutes. Mix in the tomatoes, crushing them with the back of a wooden spoon, then add the tomato juices, garlic, salt, and pepper and simmer, uncovered, over low heat for 30 to 45 minutes.

To make the filling: Warm the milk in a small saucepan, add the slices of bread, and simmer for 10 to 15 minutes, stirring occasionally, until the mixture is creamy. Set aside to cool.

Grind the mortadella, veal, and prosciutto in a meat grinder, a food processor, or a blender.

In a medium-size mixing bowl, beat together the eggs, parsley, garlic, nutmeg, salt and pepper, and ¼ cup Parmigiano-Reggiano cheese. Stir in the ground meats and the reserved milk and bread to make a creamy mixture.

Preheat the oven to 350°F. Lightly oil an ovenproof baking dish.

To stuff the leaves: Place a cabbage leaf on your work surface. Cut the central rib out of any large leaves. Divide the filling into as many portions as you have leaves. Shape each into an oval and place each oval at the end of a leaf, then roll each one up, tucking in the edges as you go. Clasp each one in the palm of your hand and squeeze it to release any liquid. Secure it with string or a toothpick.

Spoon a thin layer of tomato sauce over the bottom, and cover with a layer of stuffed cabbage leaves. Repeat with a second layer of tomato sauce and filled cabbage leaves. Finish by sprinkling with the remaining grated Parmigiano-Reggiano cheese.

Bake for about 30 minutes, until the cheese has browned on top. Serve hot or at room temperature.

CROSTATA DI FAGIANO

Pheasant Pie

—

Serves 8

A spectacular dish, served for centuries in great houses of Lucca, this savory pie is stuffed with pheasant, porcini mushrooms, pancetta, even some polenta and Parmigiano-Reggiano cheese. Although it is a lot of work, this *piatto unico*, or one-dish meal, is an extravaganza that can be made ahead and frozen. Laura Mansi Salom makes it for buffet dinners because it is easy to serve to a group.

PASTRY

1½ scant cups (7 ounces) all-purpose or unbleached all-purpose flour

½ teaspoon salt

10 tablespoons (5 ounces) unsalted butter

1 egg, lightly beaten

FILLING

1½ ounces dried porcini mushrooms

2 cups warm water

3 cups water

Salt

1½ cups (7 ounces) fine-grind polenta

1 cup half-and-half

1 scant cup (3½ ounces) freshly grated Parmigiano-Reggiano cheese

Freshly ground black pepper

7 tablespoons (3½ ounces) diced pancetta

1 tablespoon extra-virgin olive oil

1 small pheasant (about 1¾ to 2 pounds), quartered

½ onion, finely chopped

7 tablespoons (3½ ounces) unsalted butter

1 teaspoon minced fresh thyme

9 juniper berries, crushed flat with the side of a knife

1 teaspoon minced fresh marjoram

1½ teaspoons chopped fresh leaves of sage

⅓ cup dry white wine

GLAZE

1 egg yolk beaten with a little warm water

To make the pastry: Combine the flour and salt in a mixing bowl and mix well. Cut the butter into 10 or 12 pieces and rub them into the flour mixture with your fingers until it is the consistency of coarse cornmeal. You may also do this in a heavy-duty standing electric mixer using the paddle attachment or in the food processor, pulsing in the butter. Mix the egg into the butter-and-flour mixture and continue stirring until a dough is formed. Set the dough on a lightly floured work surface and knead it briefly until it is smooth. Form it into a thick disk and wrap in plastic wrap. Chill it in the refrigerator for at least 1 hour. It will keep up to 3 days.

Preheat the oven to 350°F. Butter a 10-inch springform pan, preferably one with a nonstick finish.

Divide the dough into two pieces, one twice as large as the other, and return the smaller part to the refrigerator. Set the larger piece on a lightly floured work surface and roll it out into a 16-inch circle.

Very carefully roll the dough up on your rolling pin and fit it into the bottom of the prepared pan, letting it drape up the sides. Line the bottom and sides with aluminum foil and weight it with pie weights or beans. Bake it for about 10 minutes, or just until the dough is set. Remove the foil and weights, prick the crust with a fork, and bake for 3 to 5 minutes longer until no moist glossy spots remain. Cool.

To make the filling: Cover the dried porcini mushrooms with 2 cups of warm water and leave for 30 to 45 minutes. Tenderly rinse the mushrooms, drain, and dry them. Chop them coarsely. Reserve the porcini liquid by straining it through a sieve lined with cheesecloth or paper towels. You will need ¾ to 1 cup of it later in the recipe.

Bring 3 cups of salted water to a vigorous boil in a large, deep pot. Reduce the heat to medium-low and slowly sprinkle in the polenta in a steady stream, first whisking it in, then stirring almost constantly with a wooden spoon. Keep the water at a steady simmer and stir frequently. The polenta will thicken and bubble as it cooks. At the end, when it comes away from the sides of the pot, after 25 to 35 minutes, stir in the half and half. Add half the cheese and salt and pepper. Spread the polenta on a lightly oiled sheet pan and set aside.

Preheat the oven to 375°F.

(continued)

Warm the pancetta and oil in a heavy 12-inch sauté pan, add the pheasant, and sauté over high heat until golden on all sides. Remove the pheasant. Add the chopped onion, butter, the mushrooms, all the herbs, and some salt and pepper and sauté briefly. Add the wine and boil over high heat until it has evaporated. Add ⅓ cup of the reserved porcini water, return the pheasant to the pan, cover, and cook the pheasant over medium heat until tender, about 10 to 15 minutes. Set the pheasant aside until it is cool. With your fingers, remove the meat from the bones.

Mix the pheasant meat, polenta, mushroom mixture, salt, and pepper and the remaining Parmigiano-Reggiano cheese. Fill the crust with this mixture.

Roll out the remaining piece of dough on a lightly floured work surface into an 11-inch circle. Brush the visible part of the baked pastry crust with the beaten egg. Lay the circle of newly rolled dough over the top of the filling and roll the small border over to form a crimped rim. Gently press it to the edges of the baked dough. Brush the top with the beaten egg yolk.

Set the springform pan on the middle rack of the oven. Bake for about 1 hour, until the top is golden brown, brushing the top every once in a while with a little more of the egg yolk glaze. Serve hot.

Frico Cotto con Patate e Cipolla

Cheese Cooked with Potatoes and Onions

—

Serves 4

This is real mountain food, a dish made only in the family of Gianna Modotti in the high recesses of the Carnia Alps. It is not the famous crunchy frico of Friuli, the cheese equivalent of potato chips, but hearty and stirring winter fare, which resembles soft hash brown potatoes until the cheese is introduced. This dish was born in the mountains and was always made by cooking the potatoes in a covered black pot that was set next to, but not on, the fire on the hearth. Now it is cooked directly on the stove, but in both cases the potatoes should not brown or become crispy; they must stay soft as they cook very slowly.

In Gianna Modotti's family this frico is served only with soft scrambled eggs (*Uova all'Aceto*, page 312) and/or the polenta of the area (*Toc' in Braide*, page 192).

2 to 3 tablespoons extra-virgin olive oil or 1 to 1½ ounces lard

2 medium potatoes (about 1 pound), peeled and diced

2 cups (10 ounces) diced onions

1 to 12 tablespoons water (optional)

½ teaspoon salt

About 4 cups (1 pound) finely sliced Montasio cheese, half semi-aged and the rest aged at least 1 year, or fontina cheese

Warm the olive oil in a 10- or 12-inch sauté pan, very preferably nonstick. Add the potatoes and onions and cook them over low-medium heat until they are soft and tender, but they must never brown. You may need to add up to 12 tablespoons of water, a little at a time, until the potatoes are completely cooked, 40 to 45 minutes. Stir and turn frequently to prevent them from sticking or browning, and season them with the salt. At the very last minute, spread the cheese over the top like frosting and mix until the cheese is completely incorporated. The heat will melt the cheese. Serve immediately.

SOUFFLÉ DI PORRI

Leek Flan with a Creamy Sweet Pepper Sauce

—

Serves 6

What Vittorina Seghesio calls a soufflé is really a pale green flan that never rises but remains soft and creamy like a custard. Serve this delicate dish with its wash of brilliant red pepper sauce for the centerpiece of a lunch or brunch. You can make the flan ahead and reheat it in a 200°F. oven for 20 minutes; warm the sauce separately. Depending on the season, you can also use 2½ cups of pureed celery, spinach, or asparagus to make the flan.

FLAN

 6 large leeks, white part only, well cleaned and sliced

 Salt

 2 tablespoons unsalted butter for buttering the molds

BESCIAMELLA (WHITE SAUCE)

 3 tablespoons unsalted butter

 1½ tablespoons all-purpose flour

 1½ cups boiling milk

 2 eggs, room temperature, beaten

 Freshly ground black pepper

 ⅛ teaspoon or more freshly grated nutmeg

CREMA DI PEPERONI (SWEET PEPPER SAUCE)

 3 to 4 large sweet red peppers, roasted, peeled, and seeded

 1 tablespoon unsalted butter

 1 garlic clove, minced

 ½ to 1 teaspoon anchovy paste

 ½ to 1 teaspoon extra-virgin olive oil

 1 tablespoon heavy cream (optional)

To make the leek flan: Boil the leeks in salted water to cover for 20 minutes, drain, squeeze dry, and puree in a food mill or processor. Set aside to cool.

Preheat the oven to 210°F. Butter very well a 1½-quart soufflé dish or six ½-cup molds or ramekins.

To make the besciamella sauce: In a heavy saucepan melt the 3 tablespoons of butter, whisk in the flour a little at a time, and cook over medium heat until all the lumps disappear and the mixture is well blended. Whisk in the boiling milk, stirring until the mixture is thick and smooth, and continue to cook for about 5 to 7 minutes. Remove from the heat to cool briefly. Whisk the beaten eggs, salt, freshly ground pepper, and nutmeg into the sauce and taste for seasoning. Stir in the pureed leeks.

Ladle the mixture into the prepared soufflé dish or the molds. Set in the oven and bake for 30 minutes, then raise the heat to 250°F. for 20 minutes more for the ramekins and 40 to 50 minutes more for the soufflé dish, until a knife inserted in the center comes out clean. The flan must never rise like a soufflé, but must remain like a custard. Leave the soufflé dish, but not the small molds, in the oven with the door ajar for 10 minutes, then let the flan or flans rest briefly.

To make the sweet pepper sauce: While the flans are baking, puree the roasted peppers in a food mill or a processor to make a cream. In a small pan, melt the butter, then add the garlic, anchovy paste, olive oil, and pureed peppers and cook slowly over low-medium heat for about 10 minutes, until the sauce is well amalgamated. Be very careful not to burn the garlic. At the end, stir in the optional cream.

To serve the individual ramekins, smooth a wash of sweet pepper sauce on each plate, unmold the leek flans, and set them in the center of the sauce. To serve the larger flan, center a platter over the soufflé dish and invert it. Spoon the wash of red pepper sauce around it. Pass the extra sauce.

Vittorina Seghesio is eighty-seven and cooks the traditional food of Piedmont side by side with her twenty-five-year-old grandson, Pierpaolo Rinaldi, who has a degree in political science as well as one from the hotel school in Mondovi. The two of them get into some magnificent fights. She prefers to scoop up ingredients in pinches, fistfuls, and bunches and never weighs anything. He fervently believes in scales. "Once upon a time there were no scales," she says with a sly smile, as if she'd just laid down a couple of aces, trumping his dedication to liters, grams, and weighed ingredients. A high-speed talker and mover, she never tastes anything either. The grandson insists that you have to taste to see if it's done, if it needs seasoning, if the texture is right. "Nonsense," she replies briskly. "Touch with your fingers, your hands. You'll know when it's right. Just look."

This tiny woman with devilish eyes and an irrepressible laugh is up at five-thirty each morning. By six, she has unlocked the front door of the family establishment—a small hotel and restaurant in the town of Monforte d'Alba in Piedmont—to serve coffee and grappa to the busloads of workers who arrive in the city square after a long night's work. Then she goes back to sleep—a nap, she insists—and gets up to do the cooking for both lunch and dinner in the family trattoria. In her free time, she launders all the sheets for the hotel and does the mending as well.

A nonstop talker, Vittorina sometimes pauses briefly when her grandson stops her from lapsing into dialect, gives him a benignly tolerant smile, and then leaps back into the verbal fray with plentiful dialect. The word for her is undaunted.

Vittorina has taken to traveling to watch what other people are cooking. She went to Perugia in 1995 for a convention of cooks and was the oldest and most celebrated one in attendance. When she cooked in Zurich the year before, she took them by storm with her food, although she didn't understand one word that was spoken. "That doesn't matter," she said, smiling broadly and shrugging an eloquent shoulder. "They loved what I made." Well they might have. She made them a leek soufflé with a wash of red pepper sauce—"it's not really a soufflé," she cautioned, "more a pale green flan that

Monforte
d'Albu

always stays creamy." And quail in a nest made of pureed potatoes. And tableaux of tagliarini with a porcini sauce.

Some years ago fifteen people came for a two-week stint at an experimental station in Monforte. Those same fifteen people arrived to eat every day, always ordering her potato gnocchi, which are soft as clouds. Clouds served with a tiny bit of tomato sauce spooned over the top.

Vittorina Seghesio was born in Monforte and never moved. Her father died very young, her mother was a tenant farmer, and her two sisters and brother were out on their own by the time she was fourteen. Left at home by herself, she took up cooking. She experimented and cooked and cooked some more and seventy-three years later is still thrilled to be in the kitchen. She was twenty-three when she got married; she and her husband lived in the countryside near Monforte with their four children. ("They all married well and the grandchildren are doing law and medicine," she says proudly.) In 1955 she and her husband bought an old house and restaurant and did an enormous remodeling. "The debts! You can't imagine." It didn't take long to fill up. All autumn long people come fair distances to eat in the rolling countryside of the Langhe and to drink the Barolos and Barbarescos and other phenomenal local wines, and to take home all the amazing products of this part of Piedmont—the white truffles, the wild mushrooms, and the special cookies and cakes. And they come to taste the food of the area that Vittorina cooks with the passion that has never left her heart or her hands.

She inspires allegiance in some: at a recent reunion of Alpine climbers, one of the younger men said to her, "If only we'd met you sooner, we'd never have let you go." And ribaldry in others: Twelve Scotsmen came for a wedding in Torino and she invited all forty-five members of the party to Monforte for a big bridal banquet. The Scotsmen appeared in their kilts and she asked one to show her his hairy legs. He pulled up his skirt a bit and she smiled broadly, and then he pulled it a bit higher. "That's okay with me," she said approvingly. "You can just keep on going."

Vittorina Seghesio stands no more than four feet ten inches high and has the energy of a bullet train. She'll joke about everything, but she's serious about food. She is teaching her grandson la cucina della nonna and she is determined that he get it right. For in the future after she has died, it will be he, like so many male chefs in trattorie and small restaurants all over Italy, who will carry on the tradition of making the food of home. She is adamant about using small white potatoes for gnocchi and she never peels them so they don't crack and let water in. When she makes bagna cauda, the famous Piedmontese "hot bath," she doesn't cut the garlic with a knife; she just dips five or six heads briefly in boiling water until they are "as soft as a straw." She lifts them out, peels and flattens them, and then puts the garlic pulp in a mixture of milk and olive oil with two large salted anchovies that have been cleaned and boned, and cooks them for a bit. At the end she puts in a "nut" of butter to make the bagna cauda richer and grinds in a dash of pepper. Meanwhile she roasts sweet peppers in the oven, peels and cuts them into big chunks, and serves them steaming hot with a spoonful of bagna cauda over the top. Last but not least: she serves almost anything with white truffles shaved over the top when they are in season.

Many people are delighted to meet a woman with such energy and such a passion for food. Recently a man who came for dinner was amazed when he learned her age. "Signora," he said, "I'm so moved. May I give you a kiss?" Surveying him carefully, Vittorina replied, "You're so handsome, you can give me two."

PASTICCIO DI RISO

Risotto Filled with Meat, Tiny Fresh Peas, and Mozzarella

—

Serves 8 to 10

*L*aura Mansi Salom offers another extravaganza from the aristocracy of Lucca. Optional, although highly recommended, is the addition of mozzarella that is diced and mixed into the meat mixture just before baking. Then, at the end, it is all soft and pulls into strings. The baking should not take longer than 30 minutes; it is only meant to heat the dish since all the component parts are already cooked.

RISOTTO

> 4 to 5 cups chicken broth, preferably homemade
>
> 2 to 3 tablespoons unsalted butter
>
> 1 white onion, diced
>
> 2 cups Arborio rice
>
> 1⅓ cups dry white wine, room temperature
>
> 20 threads of saffron or a large pinch of powdered saffron dissolved in
>   warm broth

RAGÙ AND FILLING

3 to 4 tablespoons extra-virgin olive oil

1 carrot, diced

1 celery rib, diced

1 onion, diced

2½ tablespoons minced flat-leaf parsley

8 ounces ground lean beef

3½ ounces chicken livers, chopped

3½ ounces ham, chopped

Salt

Freshly ground black pepper

⅔ cup dry white wine

½ cup chicken broth

1 white onion, diced

1 tablespoon unsalted butter

10 ounces fresh tiny peas, weighed after shelling
    or 1 (10-ounce) package frozen peas, thawed

2 cups (about 8 ounces) diced best-quality mozzarella cheese (optional)

FOR THE BAKING DISH

3 to 4 tablespoons unsalted butter

¼ cup fine dry bread crumbs

Place the chicken broth in a 2-quart saucepan, bring it to a simmer, and keep it at a constant low simmer.

Meanwhile, melt the butter in a 2-quart heavy-bottomed saucepan. Add the onion and sauté until it is soft and translucent but not colored, about 5 minutes. Add the rice, and stir until all the grains are thoroughly coated, about 2 minutes. Begin making the risotto by adding about ⅓ cup of the wine, and cook at a steady lively simmer, stirring, until the wine has all been absorbed. Continue by adding the simmering broth, ⅓ cup at a time, until it has all been absorbed and the rice is tender and creamy, about 16 to 18 minutes. While the rice is cooking, dissolve the saffron in a small bit of the broth and add it about halfway through the cooking. Set the risotto aside.

Preheat the oven to 350°F.

(continued)

Warm 2 to 3 tablespoons of the olive oil in a 10- or 12-inch heavy sauté pan over low-medium heat and sauté the carrot, celery, onion, and parsley until the onion is pale and limp, 10 to 12 minutes. Add the beef, chicken livers, and ham, turn the heat to medium-high, and cook just until they lose their pinkness, 5 to 7 minutes. Season with salt and pepper. Pour in the white wine and cook over high heat until it is about half its original volume, about 7 minutes. Add the broth and cook for another 5 minutes, until the mixture is quite concentrated.

Sauté the onion in the remaining tablespoon of oil and the butter until pale and limp. Add the peas and cook just until they are tender. Cool them briefly and then add to the meat mixture. If you are using the mozzarella, add it to the meat mixture.

To assemble, thoroughly butter the sides and bottom of a deep baking dish, such as a 9½- or 10-inch soufflé dish or charlotte mold, and sprinkle with the bread crumbs so they coat the interior well. Gently tap away any excess.

Spread half of the risotto on the bottom of the dish, cover it with the meat and pea combination, and then top it with the remaining risotto.

Bake for 30 minutes until all layers of the timbale are hot.

TIELLA

Mussel, Potato, and Rice Cooked in a Terra-Cotta Casserole

—

Serves 8 to 10

Every nonna I met in Apulia offered me a recipe for her tiella, a dish named for the terra-cotta casserole in which it is baked, but after tasting and testing many, I chose Maria Andriani's. When she makes the dish, she, like most people in Apulia, opens the mussels without cooking them, then strains and saves whatever liquid the mussels exude, and leaves the mussels on the half shell before sliding them into the interior of the layers. Since opening a mussel shell that hasn't been cooked is extremely difficult, I chose to cook the mussels just until they open, save the cooking liquid, remove the mussels from their shells, and set them, plumped up from the cooking, inside the layered mixture. The potatoes absorb the flavor of the mussels; the very slight crunch of the rice on top gives it a wonderful texture. Serve the tiella warm or at room temperature for almost any occasion. It's a perfect centerpiece for an elegant dinner or an informal lunch, for Sunday brunch or an alfresco meal.

> 1 pound mussels
> 6 tablespoons extra-virgin olive oil
> 1 pound Yellow Finn or Yukon Gold potatoes, peeled and thinly sliced
> Salt
> Freshly ground black pepper
> 1 onion, diced
> 2 cups ripe tomatoes, peeled, seeded, and diced
> 1 clove garlic, minced
> ¾ cup finely chopped flat-leaf parsley
> 1 bay leaf
> ½ cup (2 ounces) freshly grated Parmigiano-Reggiano cheese
> ½ cup Arborio rice

Preheat the oven to 350°F.

Wash and scrub the mussels thoroughly, pulling away their beards. Put the mussels in a wide pan with ½ inch of water in the bottom and cook, covered, over very high heat just until they open, about 3 to 4 minutes. Remove and strain the mussel liquid through cheesecloth or paper towels and reserve all of it, about 2 cups. Remove the mussels from their shells, discarding any that haven't opened, set them in a bowl, and cover until you are ready to use them. Discard the shells.

Use 2 tablespoons of the olive oil to oil a 9½ × 13 × 2-inch baking dish or 3-quart casserole, preferably of terra-cotta.

Start constructing layers by covering the bottom of the dish with half the potatoes. Sprinkle with salt and pepper.

Cover with a layer of all the onion, tomatoes, and garlic and 1 tablespoon of finely chopped parsley. Sprinkle with additional salt and pepper, drizzle with 2 tablespoons olive oil, and set a bay leaf on top.

Cover with a layer of half the Parmigiano-Reggiano and half the remaining chopped parsley. Over it goes a layer of all the mussels and the remaining Parmigiano-Reggiano and chopped parsley. Cover these layers with the remaining potatoes, additional salt and pepper, and drizzle the remaining 2 tablespoons olive oil over the top. Sprinkle the rice over the top. Finish by pouring ¾ cup of the mussel liquid over everything.

Cook in the preheated oven, basting every 10 minutes with the liquid in the bottom of the dish. Make sure to bathe the rice and help it cook.

Bake until the potatoes are tender and the rice is almost cooked, about 1 hour and 10 minutes. Add 4 tablespoons of simmering mussel liquid to moisten the rice, cover tightly with aluminum foil, and continue to bake another 15 to 20 minutes or until the rice is no longer crunchy.

Remove from the oven and leave, still covered, at room temperature for about 15 minutes to allow the steam to continue to bathe the rice. Let the dish rest about ½ hour. Serve warm or at room temperature. To reheat, sprinkle the top with some of the remaining mussel liquid and warm in a 350°F. oven. You can make the dish about 6 hours before you plan to serve it.

TIMBALLO DI RISO

Layered Rice Timbale

—

Serves 8 to 10

Amelia Innocenti's complicated but delicious timballo di riso is a dish from another time. Needless to say, this is a piatto unico. It stands alone: you don't serve anything else with it or after it, not even a vegetable, except maybe a salad.

4 tablespoons fine dry bread crumbs for sprinkling baking dish
6 to 7 tablespoons (3 to 3½ ounces) unsalted butter
2 to 3 tablespoons extra-virgin olive oil
8 ounces pork sausage, cut into tiny dice
8 ounces chicken, cut into tiny dice
8 ounces veal, cut into tiny dice
8 ounces lean pork, cut into tiny dice

Pommarola Sauce (page 429)

1 small red onion, diced

2 cups Arborio, Vialone Nano, or Carnaroli rice

¼ cup dry white wine

5 to 5½ cups chicken broth, preferably homemade

Freshly grated Parmigiano-Reggiano cheese

Freshly grated nutmeg

Salt

Freshly ground black pepper

Preheat the oven to 350°F. Generously butter a 13½ × 8¾-inch baking dish and sprinkle the bottom and sides with half the bread crumbs. Shake out the excess crumbs.

Warm 1 teaspoon of butter and 2 teaspoons of oil in a sauté pan over medium heat and sauté the sausage until it is lightly golden brown. Drain with a slotted spoon and place on absorbent paper towels.

Warm 1 teaspoon of butter and 2 teaspoons of olive oil over medium heat and sauté the chicken meat until it is lightly golden brown. Repeat with the veal and pork in the same sauté pan. Combine the Pomarola sauce with the meats.

To make the risotto: Warm 3 tablespoons of butter in a deep pot over medium heat. When the butter has melted, add the onion and sauté until it is translucent, about 5 minutes. Add the rice and stir for 2 to 3 minutes until every grain is coated with the butter. Pour in the wine and let it bubble away. Meanwhile, bring the broth to a simmer in a 3-quart pot. Start adding hot broth to the rice ½ cup at a time, waiting for the liquid to be absorbed by the rice before you add the next ½ cup, until the rice has absorbed all the liquid and is tender, 16 to 18 minutes. Add the grated Parmigiano-Reggiano cheese, freshly grated nutmeg, salt, pepper, and remaining butter.

Cover the bottom of the prepared baking dish with half of the rice mixture, spread the meats over it, and cover with the remaining rice. Top with the remaining bread crumbs.

Bake for 20 to 30 minutes until the crust is golden brown and the timbale is warmed through completely. Let the timbale rest for 5 minutes so the flavors can blend.

Pasticcio di Maccheroni

Laura Mansi Salom's Timbale of Pasta and Meats
Enclosed in a Pastry Crust

—

Serves 12

A Renaissance extravaganza, this rich pasta and meat dish with its slightly sweet pastry crust probably comes from the days of sumptuary laws when Tuscans were enjoined from eating more than three courses two times a day. Wily bon vivants dreamed up a delicious way to bypass such strictures by incorporating the ingredients of several courses into one dish and wrapping them all inside a single pastry crust.

Although this is definitely a complicated dish, its various sauces and the pastry itself can be made the day before and the finished product assembled on the day that you plan to serve it. The pastry crust is very fragile, but it can be pieced together and patched, even re-refrigerated, without any problem. The sweetness in the crust is a special taste and some people may choose to reduce the amount of sugar to as little as 2 tablespoons. The dish is every bit as glorious to look at as it is to eat. Expect your guests to be rapturous.

Pasta Frolla (Pastry Dough)

    1 stick plus 2 tablespoons (5 ounces) unsalted butter
    ½ cup (3½ ounces) sugar
    1 lemon
    1 egg
    1 egg yolk
    2¼ cups (11 ounces) unbleached all-purpose or all-purpose flour
    A pinch of salt

Ragù di Carne (Meat Sauce)

    2 scant ounces dried porcini mushrooms
    2 cups warm water
    2 to 3 tablespoons extra-virgin olive oil
    1 carrot, finely chopped

1 celery rib, finely chopped

1 onion, finely chopped

11 ounces ground beef

3½ ounces finely diced ham

7 ounces chicken livers, finely chopped

⅔ cup dry white wine

¼ cup chicken broth

¼ cup reserved porcini mushroom liquid

½ chicken breast, boned and cut in small dice

1 teaspoon all-purpose flour

1½ teaspoons unsalted butter

Salt

BESCIAMELLA (WHITE SAUCE)

3½ tablespoons unsalted butter

¼ cup (1 ounce) unbleached all-purpose flour

3½ cups milk

Salt

Freshly ground black pepper

6 to 8 gratings of fresh nutmeg

PASTA

4 quarts water

1 tablespoon coarse sea salt

1 pound (or a little more) short pasta such as penne or rigatoni

EGG WASH

1 egg yolk beaten with 1 teaspoon water

To make the pastry dough in a heavy-duty electric mixer: Cream the butter and sugar with the paddle attachment. Grate the zest of the lemon directly over the top of the mixture. Stir in the egg and egg yolk and mix well. Sift in the flour and salt and mix until the dough comes together well. You may want to knead it briefly on a lightly floured work surface. Shape into a disk, cover with plastic wrap, and set in the refrigerator for at least 1 hour.

By hand: You can make this by hand by putting the flour, sugar, and salt in a medium bowl, grating the lemon zest directly over the top, and then rubbing in the butter until the mixture has the texture of coarse cornmeal. Make a well in the center of the mixture, beat the egg and egg yolk together, and add them slowly to the flour mixture, mixing slowly until a dough forms. Shape into a disk, cover with plastic wrap, and set in the refrigerator for at least 1 hour.

While the pastry dough is chilling, make the meat sauce. Soak the dried mushrooms in 2 cups of warm water to cover for 30 minutes. Scoop up the porcini and squeeze them over the soaking liquid to get rid of any water. Strain the soaking liquid through a sieve lined with cheesecloth or a double layer of paper towels. Set it aside. Wash the mushrooms under cold water, drain, pat dry, and chop them coarsely.

Warm the olive oil in a large heavy skillet, add the chopped vegetables and sauté over medium heat until the onion is pale and golden, 5 to 7 minutes. Add the ham, ground meat, and chicken livers, and mushrooms and cook for 5 to 7 minutes longer, until the meats are no longer pink. Pour in the white wine and boil until it has evaporated, then add the chicken broth and porcini liquid, making certain that the mixture remains soft and not dry.

Meanwhile, dip the diced chicken meat in the flour and sauté briefly in the butter in a separate pan. Add the sautéed chicken to the meat sauce. Cook the mixture until most of the liquid has evaporated, 5 to 7 more minutes. Season with salt and set aside to cool.

To make the besciamella sauce: Melt the butter in a 2-quart pot. Off the heat, whisk in the flour and beat well to be sure you have no lumps. Whisk in the milk and cook over medium heat until the sauce has thickened, about 5 minutes. Strain to remove any lumps. Season with salt, pepper, and nutmeg. This must be a liquid besciamella sauce. Add the besciamella to the meat and chicken mixture and leave to cool to room temperature.

Meanwhile, bring a large pot with 4 quarts of water to the boil, add coarse sea salt, and cook the pasta until it is still very al dente; the pasta will cook further in the oven.

Mix the pasta well with the combined chicken, meat, and besciamella mixture. Season with salt and pepper. Set aside to cool briefly.

Preheat the oven to 350°F. Generously butter and lightly flour a high-sided 9½-inch nonstick springform or ceramic baking dish.

To make the pastry shell, divide the dough into 2 unequal pieces, one 3 times the size of the other. On a floured work surface, roll the larger piece into a 15-inch circle. It must be no more than ¼ inch thick or the dough won't be thin enough when cooked. Be sure to flour both the work surface and the dough. Put your rolling pin in the center of the dough and roll from the center in both directions. Give the dough a quarter turn and roll as above; continue, using flour as necessary and continually using your dough scraper to loosen the dough so it doesn't stick. When you have rolled it to a 15-inch circle, sprinkle a little flour over the surface and very carefully fold the piece in half and then in half again. Set it in the prepared pan and open the dough so that the segments line the entire springform and slightly overlap the tops of the sides. Press it against the sides and bottom of the pan. Spread the entire meat and pasta mixture over the dough; it will fill the interior right to the top.

Roll out the smaller piece of dough into a 10-inch circle and set it on top of the filling. Trim the dough where it overlaps, press the edges of the doughs together well, and crimp them. Brush with the egg wash. Poke holes with a fork in the top crust to allow steam to escape.

Bake for 35 but no more than 55 minutes, until the dough is golden. If the top browns too quickly, cover it with foil, and continue baking. Remember that every ingredient in the dish has already been cooked ahead, so this step is for cooking the pastry dough. Remove from the oven and cool. Loosen the sides with a knife and serve on a platter.

9

UOVA

Eggs

CIPOLLATA
Onion Frittata

UOVA ALL'ACETO
Eggs Scrambled with a Drop of Vinegar

UOVA IN PORCHETTA
Eggs Poached in a Fennel-Flavored Tomato Sauce

FRITTATA ALLE PATATE
Potato and Pancetta Frittata

FRITTATA CON CIPOLLE BIANCHE
Frittata with White Spring Onions

UOVA CON LA PEPERONATA
Hard-Boiled Eggs with Sweet Pepper Sauce

UOVA SODE CON SALSETTA
Fried Hard-Boiled Eggs in a Saffron Onion Sauce

CIPOLLATA

Onion Frittata

—

Serves 4

*E*ggs from the chickens, olives from the trees, and onions from the earth: a classic dinner in the Tuscan and Umbrian countryside is made with three ingredients that are almost always on hand. The onions are sautéed slowly in oil until they have lost all their pungency and become sweet and creamy. You may serve this immediately or let it cool to room temperature and make the frittata portable—it's perfect picnic food—by folding it inside two slices of bread.

> 2 to 3 tablespoons extra-virgin olive oil
> 2 medium-size red onions, cut into tiny dice
> 6 eggs
> Salt
> Freshly ground black pepper

Warm the olive oil over low heat in a 9-inch sauté pan, preferably nonstick, add the onions, and cook until they are soft and melting, at least 20 to 30 minutes.

Break the eggs into a medium bowl, add the salt and pepper, and beat them lightly with a fork only to blend. Pour the eggs over the top of the onions and continue cooking over the lowest possible heat, occasionally lifting the edge of the egg mixture with a wooden spoon to encourage any of the egg mixture to run to the edge, until the top is set, about 16 to 18 minutes.

Place a dinner plate over the sauté pan, and holding firmly with one hand, very gently invert the frittata onto the plate. Slide the frittata, cooked side up, back into the pan, and continue cooking very briefly, just long enough to set the bottom. Slide the frittata onto a platter and serve hot or at room temperature.

Uova all'Aceto

Eggs Scrambled with a Drop of Vinegar

—

Serves 2

*W*ho would have believed that a little wine vinegar could make the best scrambled eggs imaginable? Serve them with *Frico Cotto con Patate e Cipolla* (page 292) as Gianna Modotti always does, or double the recipe and eat them by themselves for an unparalleled treat.

2 eggs
½ to ¾ teaspoon sea salt
½ teaspoon red wine vinegar
5 grindings of black pepper
2 tablespoons unsalted butter

Beat the eggs with the salt, vinegar, and pepper. Warm the butter in an 8-inch sauté pan, preferably nonstick, and cook until it has browned. Remove from the heat and pour in the egg mixture. Scramble the eggs over the lowest possible heat just until they are soft and set.

UOVA IN PORCHETTA

Eggs Poached in a Fennel-Flavored Tomato Sauce

—

Serves 2

Eggs poached in tomato sauce are also known as *uova in purgatorio*, "eggs in purgatory," perhaps because the red of the tomato sauce is reminiscent of the flames of hell, a potential final destination, or perhaps because eggs in purgatory aren't as hot as *uova al diavolo*, "eggs the devil's way," which are made with the bite of hot peppers. Regardless of your theological leanings, this is an extremely easy dish to prepare when you look in the cupboard and find it is bare.

Adele Rondini, the source of the dish, didn't suggest any such niceties as peeling or seeding the tomatoes, but you may want to do so. You may also want to add a few extra fennel seeds to spice up the eggs.

> 2 tablespoons extra-virgin olive oil
> 1 garlic clove, finely minced
> 3 cups chopped, drained canned Italian tomatoes or bottled organic tomato puree (see Source Guide to Ingredients)
> 2 to 3 fennel seeds
> Sea salt
> Freshly ground black pepper
> 4 eggs
> 4 slices of country-style bread, toasted

Warm the olive oil in a large, wide sauté pan, add the garlic, and cook over low-medium heat just until the garlic is soft and begins to color, about 3 minutes. Add the tomatoes and the fennel seeds to the pan and simmer for 20 to 30 minutes, until the sauce is smooth but not thick. Season with salt and pepper.

Carefully break the eggs into the simmering sauce, cover the pan, and simmer on low heat without stirring just until the eggs are poached, about 6 minutes.

Place a slice of toasted country bread on the bottom of a large platter or in soup bowls, spoon a bit of sauce over each, spoon the eggs onto the toast, and cover them with the rest of the sauce. Serve steaming hot.

Frittata alle Patate

Potato and Pancetta Frittata

—

Serves 4 to 6

*C*ould there be anything simpler or more appealing than this potato frittata dappled with pancetta and sprinklings of parsley? As Anna Marezza makes it in Chianti, this flat Italian omelet is really the essence of Tuscan cooking: five ingredients combined with amazing simplicity and transformed into a versatile main-course dish.

Two of Anna's secrets: beat the eggs with a fork just enough to blend the whites and yolks. Use a very well-seasoned cast iron pan or nonstick pan, if you have one, and cook over the lowest possible heat so the frittata cooks very, very slowly and always remains moist. If inverting the frittata onto a plate makes you nervous, just slide the pan under a broiler to brown the top surface lightly.

> 2 to 3 tablespoons extra-virgin olive oil or unsalted butter,
>   plus 1 tablespoon if needed
> 3 tablespoons diced pancetta or salt pork
> 1 large potato or 2 medium potatoes, boiled or roasted, peeled, and diced
> 4 eggs
> Salt
> Freshly ground black pepper
> 2 tablespoons finely chopped flat-leaf parsley

Warm the olive oil over moderate heat in a 9-inch sauté pan, preferably nonstick, and sauté the pancetta until the fat begins to become crisp, 7 to 8 minutes. Add the diced potatoes and cook over moderate heat until they are soft and golden. Remove them from the skillet and set aside to cool briefly.

Break the eggs into a medium bowl and beat them with the salt and pepper only until they are blended. Add the pancetta and potatoes, return them to the sauté pan, with an extra tablespoon of olive oil or butter if needed, and cook over the lowest possible heat until the top is set, occasionally lifting the edge of the egg mixture with a wooden spoon, about 15 to 18 minutes.

Place a dinner plate over the sauté pan and, holding firmly with one hand, very gently invert the frittata onto the plate. Slide the frittata, cooked side up, back into the pan, and continue cooking very briefly, just long enough to set the bottom. Slide the frittata onto a platter, sprinkle with the finely chopped parsley, and serve hot or at room temperature.

Profile of *Anna Marezza*

Four generations of one family live together in a big Tuscan farmhouse in an open valley south of Greve in Chianti. For many years Anna Marezza, who became a grandmother at forty-seven, her husband Giuliano, and their parents were *mezzadri*, sharecroppers, essentially indentured farm workers living in the country. Scarcity shaped their lives. They worked extremely hard and had nothing. To this day both husband and wife are spare with their words and their gestures. They remember the time they call *la miseria nera*, "the black misery."

In those days eleven people lived in the house. They cooked in the fireplace on a stove that used charcoal as the heating source. If you opened what looked like "ovens" under the stove top, they were actually chambers where the charcoal was burned to heat the surface on top. They ate beans, beans, and more beans flavored with whatever herbs and greens they picked in the countryside. They ate quantities of bread and a little *companatico*, something to go with it. For dinner they cooked one potato and one onion. They made pasta with flour and water and drizzled a little oil over the top for flavor. If they had an egg, Anna said, with wonder in her voice, "it seemed a delicacy." With real sadness she explained, "For many years we feared we'd never eat one again."

Anna and Giuliano bought and restored their gray stone farmhouse ten years ago and installed heat. Even so, it is still cold and drafty enough that they keep a chair permanently at the interior of the enormous fireplace where everyone takes turns sitting to get warm.

Their lives have always revolved around family and farm, her domain being house and kitchen, his the fields and crops, woods and vineyards. They have learned how to make almost anything from the barest possibilities. She picks wild greens that find their way into salads and soups, knows which wild herbs will flavor their meals. He hunts birds and small animals, has a talent for finding enormous porcini mushrooms (the champion weighed over 2 pounds), makes wine and Vin Santo with their grapes. Both are serious and cautious.

Anna had to be prodded to give some examples of how they ate in dark times:

A big pan was set on the table full of dozens of tomatoes that were sieved to make a sauce; one egg was mixed into the center and remained liquid. They dipped in bread to scoop it up.

Farinata was made with boiling water, a drop of olive oil, and 2 to 3 tablespoons of flour in a coffee cup. Beaten together with a little salt, it became as smooth as cream. People still make farinata using chicken broth instead of water, but Anna hates it. "It sticks in your stomach," she says, "making you feel full for three days."

La pappina coi cavallucci used cavallucci, Sienese cookies, that were dipped into a little goat's milk, if there was some; if not, into water mixed with a little pig's blood, and then fried and sprinkled with sugar on each side.

When I saw Anna, she was forty-nine and had been married for thirty-two years. I would have guessed her to be at least ten years older than she was. She was sturdy and solid in the indeterminate wool sweater and skirt worn by middle-aged and older Tuscan farm women. The years had etched her dark eyes with surrounding lines. For the first time, she had stopped working as a cook at the local trattoria so she could stay home to take care of her grandchild while her daughter worked.

Through all their many years of misery, her husband kept saying to himself, "One day this house will be ours. I'll have my piece of land and I'll plant all the crops, trees, and vines that I want." The property belonged to the landlord for whom they worked it until 1961. At that point, when the sharecropping system was outlawed, Anna and Giuliano were not turned off the land, but began to work at the proprietor's trattoria in nearby Panzano. She cooked during the day for sixteen years while her husband was working the land. She could remember some of the dishes of her childhood, but this was her first opportunity to make traditional Tuscan food with a panoply of delicious local ingredients that were always available—porcini mushrooms, sheep's milk ricotta and fresh creamy pecorino cheese, eggs from hens kept on the property, fruity olive oil pressed from olives grown on the nearby hills of Chianti, the prosciutto and pancetta that flavor so many Tuscan dishes, rabbits and free-range chickens, vine-ripened tomatoes, squashes and cabbages, wheels of saltless Tuscan bread, aged Parmigiano-

Reggiano cheese for grating, pears and figs and juicy red grapes. When Anna went home at night, Giuliano went to the trattoria, earning money as a waiter. They were paid and also given a share of the profits. Giuliano, with his dream of buying the farm, saved nine million lire. He went to the landlord and offered it all. The landlord wanted fifty million. By the next year when he had saved more, it was still not enough. Finally, in 1985, he and Anna succeeded in buying their farmhouse.

They had lived in it for such a long time before it was theirs. It was often freezing cold. There were no windows in the house, leaving the interior exposed as the wind roared through it. They had no indoor bathroom and the outdoor one was a single hole dug in the ground. In those day landlords did nothing. When Anna was pregnant and her water broke, she was too embarrassed to go to the hospital. She went outside to wash herself in the primitive bath and then was in hard labor with no heat at all for ten hours. The room had no heat and was literally iced. To which Anna's husband said, "It makes you strong."

Thoughtfully Anna told me, "Watching my children grow like this, I realize that I have really *lived* a life." Her daughter is a schoolteacher with a government grant and she is married to the local doctor. "Now everything's done for you," Anna said. "No one has the hunger of a wolf."

FRITTATA CON CIPOLLE BIANCHE

Frittata with White Spring Onions

—

Serves 2 to 4

*V*anna Corbellani Camerlenghi's Mantuan frittata is richer than the usual Italian flat omelet because she adds a few drops of milk, a handful of bread crumbs, and an impressive amount of Parmesan cheese. If you can possibly find them, use small white spring onions because their sweetness is so enticing. This frittata makes a wonderful centerpiece for brunch or Sunday supper, but you can also cut it into small wedges and serve it as an antipasto or take it along on a picnic.

> 1 to 2 tablespoons extra-virgin olive oil, plus extra for the pan, if needed
> 6 round white spring onions, finely sliced
> Salt
> Freshly ground black pepper
> 4 eggs
> ¾ cup (3 ounces) freshly grated Parmigiano-Reggiano cheese
> 1 to 2 tablespoons fresh bread crumbs
> 1 teaspoon milk

Warm the olive oil over low heat in a 9-inch well-seasoned cast-iron skillet or sauté pan, preferably nonstick, add the onions, and cook over very low heat until they are soft and limp but never change color, about 12 to 15 minutes. Remove the onions from the skillet with a slotted spoon, season with salt and pepper, and set aside to cool briefly.

Break the eggs into a medium bowl and beat them lightly with a fork, then blend in the cheese and additional salt and pepper. Stir in the onions, the bread crumbs, and the milk. Add a little more oil to the pan, if necessary, and pour the egg mixture into it, cooking over the lowest possible heat, occasionally lifting the edge of the egg mixture with a wooden spoon and letting the creamy mixture run to the edge, until the top is set, about 13 to 15 minutes.

Place a dinner plate, or a large flat pot lid, as Vanna does, over the sauté pan, and holding firmly with one hand, very gently invert the frittata onto it. Slide the frittata, cooked side up, back into the pan, and continue cooking very briefly, just long enough to set the bottom. Slide the frittata onto a platter and serve hot or at room temperature.

UOVA CON LA PEPERONATA

Hard-Boiled Eggs with Sweet Pepper Sauce

—

Serves 4 to 6

Signora Lusignani cuts sweet red and yellow peppers into strips as thin as tagliatelle and cooks them with onions, a big handful of basil, and a few whole cloves for their fragrance. There are two ways she likes to serve the sauce. In one she cuts hard-boiled eggs in half, serves them on a bed of sweet pepper sauce, and spoons the rest of the sauce over them. In the other, she serves the sauce with *pollo alla*  *Giovanna Lusignani* *griglia*, grilled chicken. Perhaps Signora Lusignani doesn't need to decide which came first, the chicken or the egg, since she is willing to grant them both primacy where sweet peppers are concerned.

This sauce is so versatile that I use it with grilled fish or stir it into risotto at the end of the cooking.

> 4 large sweet peppers: 2 red and 2 yellow
> 3 tablespoons unsalted butter
> 1 onion, diced
> ½ cup chopped fresh basil leaves
> 3 whole cloves
> 1 tablespoon white wine
> Salt
> 6 hard-boiled eggs

(continued)

Peel the peppers with a vegetable peeler, remove their ribs, discard the seeds. Cut the peppers into strips no more than ½ inch wide and then cut those strips into small dice.

Melt the butter in a large, heavy sauté pan, add the peppers, onion, basil leaves, and cloves and cook over medium heat for 10 to 15 minutes, until the onions and peppers are soft. Just before serving, remove the cloves, drizzle the peppers with white wine, cook briefly, and taste for salt.

Cut the hard-boiled eggs in half, serve them on a bed of sweet pepper sauce, and spoon the rest over the eggs.

UOVA SODE CON SALSETTA

Fried Hard-Boiled Eggs in a Saffron Onion Sauce

—

Serves 6

Antonietta deBlasi is eighty-three now. She grew up in Alcamo, Sicily, and every summer in the decade before the war came, her entire family left the city by mule on a long and arduous trip to her sister's husband's family house overlooking the sea. During their 2-month stay, only the men and children went to the beach every day, while the women stayed home and cooked lunch. Women weren't allowed to bathe because it was generally thought that immersion in the water would deplete their energy. Men and boys could swim, but the only way they could replenish what energy was lost was to eat hard-boiled eggs. It can't be a surprise that Antonietta's family has lots of wonderful recipes for that life-restoring food.

Later, when Antonietta went to the beach with her own children, she sat on the sand with ropes tied to them. There was no tradition of women going to the sea and no tradition of teaching anyone how to swim. They just put children in the water with the ropes around their waists and hoped that in time they would learn to keep themselves afloat.

The egg is the star in this trompe l'oeil dish in which the hard-boiled eggs are fried until they are crispy and golden on the bottom and smooth and white on the top. Serve them with the golden saffron sauce spooned over the top.

6 eggs
2 onions, finely diced
A large pinch of saffron threads or powder dissolved in ¼ cup warm water
¼ cup extra-virgin olive oil
About ¼ cup all-purpose flour
Salt
Freshly ground black pepper
Olive oil for frying

Bring a large pot of water to the boil, place the eggs in it, reduce the heat, and simmer them for 13 minutes. Immediately pour off the hot water and replace it with cold running water until the eggs are bathed in cold water. Set them aside to cool. You can wait to peel them until you are ready to proceed.

Place the onions in a medium sauté pan with the saffron dissolved in warm water. Add the olive oil and simmer over the lowest possible heat, adding as much as ⅓ cup of warm water to keep the onions moist. Cook until they are soft and limp and the sauce is lightly concentrated, about 30 minutes. The recipe can be made ahead to this point.

Pour the flour into a shallow bowl and season it with salt and pepper. Heat 1 to 1¼ inches of oil in a medium-size sauté pan or deep fryer to 375°F. It should sizzle when a pinch of flour is dropped into it. Peel each egg and then dip it in just enough flour to cover the lower half of the egg. Place each egg in a slotted spoon and carefully lower it, floured side down, into the oil. Do not crowd the eggs. Fry until the bottom half is crisp and deeply golden while the top remains creamy white. Drain on paper towels.

Serve the eggs hot with the sauce spooned over the top.

10

CONTORNI

Vegetables

BRUGLIONE
Wild and Brown Mushrooms with Garlic and Potatoes

VERDURE A BUGLIONI
Tuscan Vegetable Stew

CARCIOFI ROMANI
Crispy Stuffed Roman Artichokes

CIAMBOTTO
A Mixture of Summer Vegetables

CICORIA LESSATA
Frisée or Dandelion Leaves Simmered in Broth

MELANZANE FARCITE
Eggplant Stuffed with Cheese and Basil

MELANZANE RIPIENE
Eggplant with a Filling as Soft as Mashed Potatoes

FUNGHETTI DI MELANZANE
Eggplants Cooked as If They Were Mushrooms

MELANZANE NEL RAGÙ CON MARSALA
Creamy Eggplant in a Marsala-Spiked Sauce

FAVE E FINOCCHIO
Fava Beans and Fennel

CECAMARITI
Blind Husbands, or Fried Morsels

PACCHETTI DI VERDURE
Vegetables Baked in Little Packages

PATATE E PEPERONI
Potatoes and Sweet Peppers with Olive Oil and Coarse Salt

PEPERONI RIPIENI
Stuffed Red and Yellow Peppers

POLPETTE DI PATATE
Potato Fritters

POMODORI RIPIENI
Tomatoes Filled with Rice

POMODORI CON LA RUCHETTA
Tomatoes with Arugula

SFORMATINO DI ZUCCHINE
Zucchini Baked in a Mold

TORTA DI VERDURA
Mashed Potato and Spinach Tart

ZUCCHINE DI GISA SOTIS
Zucchini with Red Onions and Basil

BRUGLIONE

Wild and Brown Mushrooms with Garlic and Potatoes

—

Serves 4 to 6

When porcini mushrooms appear in the Italian countryside, men set off before dawn, roving the hillsides in search of patches of the wild mushrooms with their intoxicating musky taste. Anna Marezza lives in Chianti where she makes bruglione with fresh porcini that grow in the woods and arrive in the markets of nearby Panzano. Few of us will be so lucky. Combining fresh brown or cremini mushrooms, which have a dark nutty flavor, with some dried porcini that have been soaked in warm water to release their flavor, is a splendid solution. This combination of mushrooms and potatoes cooked to a creamy stew is delicious with roast chicken, pork, and any simple meat dish. If dried porcini mushrooms prove hard to find, use French dried cèpes. If you can't find any dried mushrooms, use all fresh cremini or portobello mushrooms.

1 ounce dried porcini mushrooms

1½ cups warm water

1 pound fresh cremini, brown, or portobello mushrooms

3 tablespoons extra-virgin olive oil

2 garlic cloves, minced

2 large (about 1 pound) potatoes, peeled and cubed

1 teaspoon sea salt

¼ cup minced flat-leaf parsley

Soak the dried porcini in the warm water for at least 30 minutes. Scoop them up and rinse them under cold water. Drain them in a sieve lined with two layers of paper towels or cheesecloth and reserve the liquid for use later. Squeeze the porcini, letting any extra moisture fall back into the water in which they soaked. Rinse again, pat dry, and cut them in fine slices.

Wipe the fresh mushrooms with a damp paper towel or with a small damp brush to remove any dirt from their caps and stems. Cut in fine slices and set aside.

Warm the olive oil in a medium sauté pan, preferably nonstick, over medium-low heat. Add the garlic and sauté briefly until it is pale and lightly golden, no more than 2 minutes. Add the mushrooms, the drained porcini, the cubed potatoes, and 4 to 8 tablespoons of the porcini soaking water, depending on whether your pan is nonstick or not. Cook over medium heat for 30 to 35 minutes, until the potatoes are tender when pierced by the tip of a knife. Keep an eye on them and if the mixture becomes dry, drizzle in 3 to 4 more tablespoons of porcini liquid. Add salt, stir in the parsley, and cook another minute or two. Serve immediately.

MUSHROOMS (*Funghi*): Given a choice between culti-vated white mushrooms and old-fashioned brown mush-rooms, also known as cremini, Italian grandmothers much prefer the plump darker ones because their flavor is nuttier, richer, and more intense, their texture firmer. Portobello mushrooms are cremini mushrooms that have grown to maturity, their caps fully opening to reveal a fan of chocolate brown gills. To clean mushrooms, use a moist soft brush. Don't even think of washing them, because they soak up water like a sponge.

Italian grandmothers use meaty-tasting wild porcini mushrooms while they are fresh and then switch to dried ones the rest of the year. A good substitute for fresh porcini is a mixture of fresh cremini and a handful of the dried porcini. To reconstitute the porcini, soak them in tepid water for at least 30 minutes. Scoop them up in your hands, letting the water fall back in the soaking liquid. Rinse them several times and pat them dry. Strain the soaking water through cheesecloth or through paper toweling and save it for cooking.

VERDURE A BUGLIONE

Tuscan Vegetable Stew

—

Serves 6

Morena Spinelli has pictures of herself as a little girl at her family's produce stand in the San Lorenzo Market in Florence in the early 1930s. She vividly remembers when their grapes won a prize that was given by Mussolini himself.

Perhaps that early affinity for vegetables from the family orto was the inspiration for the thick vegetable buglione, a jumble of ingredients, which she serves like a stew. It is her rustic version of the classic buglione of the Sienese flatlands, which was traditionally made with a mixture of rabbit, lamb, and chicken, a dish that probably originates in the distant past when the poor cooked with whatever lesser cuts of meats were left over from the tables and kitchens of the signori. They knew how to coax all the flavor from what they had, so they boiled those meats, mixed them with aromatic vegetables and herbs from their kitchen gardens, sautéed them in olive oil, put them all in a pot covered with water, and cooked them until the mixture was thick and creamy.

When I asked Signora Spinelli about proportions for the various vegetables, she looked thunderstruck. "Whatever there is." The thought that I would write down amounts for each ingredient made her laugh. Just look in your garden, your pantry, or your refrigerator and use whatever mixture of vegetables that grow in high summer you have on hand to make this simple, imaginative, and delicious Tuscan vegetable stew. Don't, however, decide to make the dish with a preponderance of zucchini just because they have taken over your garden. You will need a balance of flavors or textures to make this tasty stew.

Salt
1 eggplant, peeled and cut in ½-inch-thick slices
2 medium-size red onions, sliced
¼ cup extra-virgin olive oil
3 Yellow Finn potatoes, peeled and diced
1 sweet red pepper, roasted, peeled, seeded, stemmed, and diced
2 tomatoes, peeled and chopped

2 to 4 tablespoons torn fresh basil leaves
Freshly ground black pepper

Salt the eggplant slices, set them in a colander over a plate for 1 hour, then drain and pat dry.

Put the onions and olive oil in a large, heavy skillet or sauté pan, preferably non-stick, and sauté over low heat until they are pale and limp, about 15 minutes. Add the eggplant, potatoes, and red pepper and cook for 10 minutes more, stirring and turning occasionally so they don't burn. Add the tomatoes, basil, salt, and pepper, partially cover, and continue cooking over very low heat for another 35 minutes, stirring and turning the vegetables from time to time, until they are a thick and creamy stew.

CARCIOFI ROMANI

Crispy Stuffed Roman Artichokes

—

Serves 6

When Andreina Pavani Calcagni turned seventy, she allowed someone else to do almost all the cooking for her birthday party. These delicious artichokes were the only exception—they are her specialty, the dish everyone looks forward to, and she has special tricks to make them both silky and crispy. They remind me of smaller Roman artichokes alla giudea, although these are filled with an herb mixture and are not fried.

Look for young medium-size artichokes. Italians know to find them by the length of their stems (the longer the stem, the younger the artichoke), but since most American artichokes come to market with their stems already drastically trimmed, it is harder to judge. Should you find them with stems, buy them!

The secret of the tenderness of these artichokes lies in the trimming and cutting of the leaves. You may feel scandalized by the amount you throw away, but that's the price for the artichoke's final silkiness.

Andreina puts the artichokes in water with lots of lemon slices in it and leaves them for at least 2 hours. First, though, she snaps off the leaves at the bottom and then uses a paring knife to cut away all the tough parts of those leaves so that even the exterior of the heart is pale green when she has finished. When she trims the artichokes, she turns and simultaneously cuts away at the leaves in an upward direction, a motion that resembles the action of a corkscrew. Perhaps if you have practiced this art with a knife for years, it comes easily, but for novices the technique can be daunting. I solved the problem by using scissors. Just remember: everything must be pale green and you won't have any tough leaves.

2 lemons

6 young medium artichokes

2 garlic cloves, preferably the flavorful red garlic, minced

2 teaspoons finely chopped fresh marjoram

2 teaspoons finely chopped flat-leaf parsley

¾ teaspoon finely chopped fresh mint

1 teaspoon freshly ground black pepper

Pinch of salt

1 cup extra-virgin olive oil

1 cup water

⅓ cup dry white wine

Fill a bowl with cold water, slice 1½ lemons and put them into it.

Starting with one artichoke, cut the stem flat to the bottom so it will stand up straight in the pot. Trim the remaining stem with a vegetable peeler and set it aside to prop up the artichokes in the cooking pot. Trim the artichoke itself by bending back the outer leaves at the base until they snap. Continue discarding more layers of leaves, pulling or cutting them off with a knife or scissors. Cut on an upward diagonal as you turn the artichoke in midair, cutting until the leaves are pale yellow at the base and pale green at the top. Be judicious; if you cut too much the artichoke won't have enough structure and it will fall apart in cooking. Adreina wipes her knife in the remaining cut lemon half and then keeps working, a great way to keep the artichoke from discoloring.

Turn the artichoke upside down and trim any remaining dark green fibrous parts from the base with a small paring knife. Finally, carefully open the center and use a small paring knife or sharp spoon to dig out the fuzzy choke. Rinse the cavity well and immediately rub the artichoke with the remaining lemon half. Put it into the acidulated water and leave for at least 2 hours. Repeat with the remaining artichokes.

To make the filling: Mix together the garlic, marjoram, parsley, and mint in a small bowl. Stir in the pepper, but be careful with salt, since the artichoke absorbs salt so easily. Divide the filling equally between the artichoke cavities.

Put the artichokes upright in a pot that will hold them securely. You can prop the stems between them to help them balance. Pour in a cup of water and all the white wine, which keeps them from turning dark green as they cook. Sprinkle about ⅓ cup of the olive oil over the filling of the artichokes, then pour the remaining ⅔ cup of the oil into the pot with the wine and water. Cover the pot and cook over medium heat until almost all the liquid has been absorbed, about 30 to 35 minutes. Keep your ears open; once all the water and wine have been absorbed, you will hear the oil bubbling as if it is frying. That is your cue that it is time to turn off the heat and remove the pot from the stove.

Be very, very careful as you turn the artichokes upside down and return them to the pot. I use a slotted spoon and tongs, not only because the artichokes are delicate but also because all the oil comes out of the interior cavity. Replace the cover, reduce the heat to low, and simmer until the artichoke tops look crispy and chocolate-colored, about 10 minutes. Adreina's special technique keeps them from steaming because there is no liquid, only the oil in the pot. Remove the pot from the heat, uncover it, and remove and invert the artichokes to upright position on paper towels for 1 hour. They will slowly reabsorb the oil.

TIPS:

- Italians have both white and light-pinkish-red garlic as well as fresh stalks of spring garlic that look like fat scallions. Most women use the white variety of garlic all year long, but Andreina Pavani Calcagni in Rome specifically prefers the red variety for its fuller flavor.
- Chopping garlic and herbs together means the flavor and tiny pieces of garlic cling to the herbs and don't get left behind on the chopping board.
- Using white wine in the cooking water keeps artichokes from turning the unappetizing gray-green color they often have at the end of cooking.

Profile of *Andreina Pavani Calcagni*

The minute she opens her front door, I know Andreina Pavani Calcagni is simpatica. She is seventy-three, a tall, good-looking woman with high cheekbones and extraordinarily fine posture. It is no time before she explains that her stately bearing owes a lot to the corset she wears for back trouble. It weighs something like 6 or 8 pounds— "See how well constructed it is," she says, knocking knuckles against ribs under her silk blouse and getting a strong thudding echo in response. "I set off metal detectors when I go into the bank."

Like the seven generations of her father's family who lived in Rome before her, Andreina is a real Romana, although hers is a Rome unfamiliar to most Americans. She lives in a large, impersonal postwar development with eight or ten identical high-rise towers off the via Nomentana, where the only visible individuality is the colorful laundry flapping on clotheslines all the way to the twelfth floor. She lives in the same fifth-floor apartment that she and her husband moved into forty-three years ago, only then it didn't have an elevator. Her mother-in-law moved with them and has been there ever since—forty-three years!

In the midst of such uninspired conformity, Andreina has planted a glorious garden on her tiny balcony where she grows beautiful begonias and all manner of herbs. Some of those herbs find their way into her version of Roman artichokes, which I had heard described as having the texture of silk. They were the lure that brought me to Andreina, and they were the reason I was standing in her sun-filled long, narrow kitchen watching her at work.

She started with *violette*, the conical, choke-free artichokes with violet-tinged leaves, and walked a mere two steps to the terrace to pinch off the sage and mentuccia (wild mint) leaves she needed for their flavoring. What she claimed was merely straightforward technique looked dazzling to me, sleight of hand performed by an expert. First she snapped off all the leaves at the bottom of the heart with a definitive gesture and then used a paring knife to cut away any tough parts so that even the exterior of the heart was pale green when she finished. She trimmed the artichokes like a magician,

Rome

simultaneously cutting away at the leaves and turning them in an upward direction in a corkscrew sort of motion. The first time I tried I ended up with a few forlorn leaves attached to a meaty heart but she wouldn't let me give up. "Just remember, everything must be pale green and you won't have any tough leaves."

Andreina puts the artichokes in water with lots of lemon squeezed into it and leaves them for at least 2 hours. Two more tricks: she uses white wine in the cooking water to keep the artichokes from turning dark green and is very sparing with salt because artichokes absorb it so readily.

Andreina learned to cook not from her Tuscan mother but from her Roman aunt, her father's sister, with whom she lived as a young woman, and she has remained devoted to Roman taste and traditions in the dishes she cooks. She goes all the way to Ostia, on the coast near Fiumicino, for her fish, because the fishmonger has such an varied and extremely fresh selection. She much prefers red garlic to white, because it is subtle and full-flavored, and never uses anything other than extra-virgin olive oil. "*Noi usiamo molto peperoncino, meno pepe*—We use a lot more hot red pepper than black pepper for seasoning."

Her father died in 1941 and her mother, a beautiful childlike woman, wasn't responsible, so Andreina, the eldest of eight and the only girl, took over and became the head of the house. It was the middle of the war, a terrible time, when there was, as she told me, "no heat, no sheets, no clothes, no food." She met her husband when she was twenty-seven and married him three years later. And then this strong, stoic woman described her forty-three years of working for the state as being so hard—*si stava male*—working all day and then coming home, washing, ironing, cooking, and taking care of her two children, Marco and Silvia, as well as her husband and preparing for the next day. "We were together much more before we married. If we had it to do all over again, we wouldn't get married because the minute we did, he got a job in the center of the city and couldn't come home at lunch, and anyway, I had to go to work, so we saw much less of each other." She adores her children, but when asked if she has grandchildren, "Oh, thank God, no," was the instant response.

Husband, wife, and mother-in-law still live together, and although Andreina has retired, she is once again a captive of home. Her ninety-seven-year-old mother-in-law is immobilized in a wheelchair and must be cared for like a child. Head bobbing, grinning broadly, the mother-in-law was anxious to tell me that her son had never let Andreina stay in the kitchen cooking for the entire family but insisted that she be at table with them for the meal. And, from the point of view of someone her age, such behavior probably does seem revolutionary, because women used to do all the cooking, then serve the men and boys, and only later go back into the kitchen to eat by themselves.

Generous, warm, flowing with feeling, it was clear that Andreina was under the strongest internal edict not to let her feelings about her captivity show too much. Under these circumstances, cooking has become even more strongly her passion, her way of expressing herself. She loves to entertain, often invites people right into the kitchen or leaves them to distribute themselves around the apartment, tasting all the dishes that flow forth from her hands. She cooks many traditional Roman dishes but she's also inventive, and has made up a pasta sauce with a big splash of vodka that was such a hit with her nephew that he asks for it for dessert as well as a main course.

CIAMBOTTO

A Mixture of Summer Vegetables

—

Serves 6

Everywhere I went in Molise and southern Lazio, people kept offering me versions of this delicious mixture of summer vegetables. Some cooks add potatoes, although most do not, and a few toss in a few peperoncini for their bite. One nonna explained that vegetables remain meatier when cooked over a high flame and become softer and almost melt over a low one. Take your choice. Serve this dish warm or at room temperature.

1 large globe eggplant, firm and glossy
6 tablespoons extra-virgin olive oil
1 garlic clove, peeled
12 ounces white onions, minced
3 sweet red peppers, seeded and cut in 1-inch chunks
2 ripe tomatoes, peeled, seeded, and roughly chopped

A handful of fresh leaves of basil
Salt
Freshly ground black pepper

Cut the eggplant in cubes, but do not peel it. Set the cubes in a large bowl covered with well-salted water and leave for 3 to 4 hours. Do not rinse or dry them, just drain and put in a deep pot with 3 tablespoons of the oil and a clove of garlic and cook over high heat, stirring and turning frequently, until they are pale and soft, 10 to 15 minutes. Discard the garlic clove.

In a separate heavy-duty skillet or nonstick sauté pan, warm the remaining olive oil, add the onions, and sauté until they are soft and limp, about 15 minutes. Stir in the sweet red peppers and cook over medium-high heat until they are almost tender, 15 to 20 minutes, stirring from time to time. Add the cooked eggplant and the tomatoes and continue cooking for another 15 minutes. Just before serving, tear the basil leaves into pieces, sprinkle them over the mixture in the pot, and cook another 2 or 3 minutes. Taste for salt and pepper. You can make this dish at any point earlier in the day and leave it covered. Serve at room temperature.

CICORIA LESSATA

Frisée or Dandelion Leaves Simmered in Broth

—

Serves 4 to 6

The bite of these bitter greens makes them a wonderful foil to pork dishes or to anything made with fava beans. The greens are delicious hot or at room temperature, so the dish can easily be made ahead, but do not refrigerate it and do not add the cheeses or oil until you are ready to serve it. I like to double the recipe, making more than I need, so I can use the leftovers for Cecamariti (page 347).

> 4 heads frisée or tender curly chicory or 4 bunches dandelion greens
> 2 cups water
> 2 cups chicken broth
> ½ teaspoon sea salt
> 1½ tablespoons freshly grated Parmigiano-Reggiano cheese
> 1½ tablespoons freshly grated pecorino cheese
> 3 tablespoons extra-virgin olive oil

Clean the frisée or curly chicory by removing the root end, discarding any wilted leaves, and cutting away any bruised spots. Wash them very well in several changes of cold water. If you are using dandelion greens, trim away the thick stalks and use only the leaves. Wash them in several changes of cold water as well.

Bring lightly salted water to a boil in a 3-quart pan, add the frisée, and simmer for about 5 minutes, turning and stirring them several times. Add the broth and continue simmering until the greens are tender, about 10 minutes longer.

Toss with the two grated cheeses and drizzle the olive oil over the top.

MELANZANE FARCITE

Eggplant Stuffed with Cheese and Basil

—

Serves 4 to 6

In this trompe l'oeil dish, the eggplant is essentially sliced and then formed again with some of the filling between each of the slices. Giuseppina Ianné Piazza loves this stuffed eggplant so much that she regularly makes two, one for her son and his wife, the other for herself. There are several varieties of eggplant in Sicily. She uses the so-called Tunisian eggplants, round, firm globes that have no bitterness and do not need to be salted, as opposed to the Turkish variety, which are oval and dark purple. We can use the familiar glossy dark purple globe eggplant and salt them to remove their bitterness, or the teardrop-shaped ones, which may not need to be salted. The signora says that all eggplants used to taste better than they do now, but she thinks the tomato sauce in this recipe compensates with its flavor.

These eggplants are filling enough to be a great single-dish meal. You could serve them as the center of a dinner or as the entirety of a supper with a little green salad and some good crunchy crusted country bread on the side.   *(continued)*

2 large purple globe eggplants (about 2 pounds), firm and glossy

Salt

½ onion, chopped very fine

1 garlic clove, minced

3 tablespoons finely chopped flat-leaf parsley

3 tablespoons minced fresh basil

½ cup grated pecorino cheese

3 to 4 tablespoons fresh bread crumbs

2 eggs, room temperature

Salt

Freshly ground black pepper

About 4 tablespoons extra-virgin olive oil

Salsa di Pomodoro Siciliana (page 430)

¼ cup warm water (optional)

Wash the eggplants, cut off the stems, and peel them. Cut the eggplants crosswise into ⅓-inch-thick slices. Salt and set them in a colander for 1 hour to drain the bitter juices. Rinse well, bathe in fresh water, and squeeze out the slices.

To make the filling: Combine the onion, garlic, parsley, basil, grated cheese, bread crumbs, eggs, salt, and pepper to form a thick paste. Let the mixture stand at room temperature for about 1 hour and it will become thicker.

When you have drained the eggplant slices, heat about 4 tablespoons of olive oil to film the bottom of a large, heavy sauté pan, preferably nonstick, and sauté the slices until they are tender and golden. Drain on paper towels.

Reconstruct the 2 eggplants by spreading some filling on each slice in the order in which it came from the eggplants and then reassembling the slices.

Preheat the oven to 350°F.

Bring the tomato sauce to a boil. Spoon a little over the bottom of a 12 × 7-inch gratin or baking dish On top of it set the reconstructed eggplants next to each other; they should be held firmly in place by the ends of the dish so that they maintain their shape. Pour the rest of the boiling sauce over the top. Sprinkle with ¼ cup of warm water if the sauce is too thick or the mixture seems too dry. Bake for 35 to 40 minutes until the eggplant is very tender when pierced with a sharp knife.

EGGPLANT: There are at least four kinds of eggplants commonly used in Italy, and all of them taste different from the eggplants raised before the Second World War, a unanimous opinion of the country's grandmothers. Globe-shaped, dark-purple-skinned Violetta di Firenze, called Turkish eggplants in Sicily, and the smaller purple ovals called Black Beauty in Italy resemble the two purple-skinned eggplants found in America. Signorine, as long and slender as the young women for whom they are named, are also called Violetta lunga and resemble Japanese eggplants. Larga Morada, or Tunisina in Sicily, are round and lightly striped with violet and white, while totally white-skinned eggplant are firm-fleshed and very sweet. No matter which kind they use, Italian grandmothers always buy firm, smooth eggplants with glossy skins.

The women have a variety of ways of dealing with eggplants. If the eggplants are young and have thin skins, they do not peel them at all. Some cooks rid eggplants of their bitter juices by using coarse salt on the slices. Others set eggplant slices in a bowl of highly salted water for somewhere between 15 minutes and 2 hours, then press out the water firmly so the eggplants won't turn dark or bitter. The water method keeps the eggplants from absorbing excess oil when they are sautéed, a genuine help, since eggplants can absorb an astonishing quantity of oil. Some eggplants, such as small, teardrop-shaped eggplants and Japanese eggplants, have no bitter seeds or juices and do not need to be salted.

MELANZANE RIPIENE

Eggplant with a Filling as Soft as Mashed Potatoes

—

Serves 6

*T*his dish of Giuseppina Peppino De Lorenzi's is a stunning example of rustic Italian cooking at its best. It begins with eggplant, that most humble of vegetables, which is filled with a mixture of the primary materials of everyday life in the southern region of Apulia: meaty ripe tomatoes, crumbs from wheels of full-flavored country bread, handfuls of freshly grated sheep's milk cheese, and capers that grow in the fissures of rock and wall. One taste of the filling, which is as soft as mashed potatoes, and it is obvious that Signora de Lorenzi's ingenuity has created a dish that is much more than the sum of its parts. Eat it hot or at room temperature.

Giuseppina
Peppino De Lorenzi

> 3 large globe (about 3 pounds) eggplants, firm and glossy
> Salt
> 3 tablespoons extra-virgin olive oil
> ½ white onion, diced
> 2 or 3 tomatoes, chopped
> 1 garlic clove, minced
> 3 tablespoons minced flat-leaf parsley
> 1¼ cups fresh bread crumbs, preferably homemade
> 1 cup (4 ounces) piquant freshly grated pecorino cheese, such as pecorino romano, plus extra for sprinkling
> 1½ teaspoons capers, preferably salt-cured, well rinsed and finely chopped
> Salsa di Pomodoro Pugliese (page 431)

Wash the eggplants. Bring a large pot of water to the boil, add salt, and cook the eggplants only until they are al dente, about 10 minutes, tender enough that a sharp knife can pierce the flesh but still firm enough to hold their shape well. Dry them and cut them in half crosswise, then use a sharp knife to scoop out the pulp, leaving a ¼-inch shell. Cut the pulp into dice, squeeze them well in a kitchen towel to eliminate any residual water, and set aside along with the eggplant shells.

Pour the oil into a sauté pan, add the onion and tomatoes, and sauté over low-medium heat until the onion is soft, about 10 minutes. Add the diced eggplant, garlic, and parsley and cook over low heat, stirring frequently, until the mixture is very soft and well blended, 10 to 20 minutes. Add warm water if it seems dry or stiff.

Preheat the oven to 325°F.

Meanwhile, make a thick paste of the bread crumbs, grated cheese, and capers. Mix the eggplant and bread crumb mixtures together to make a soft filling and use them to fill the eggplant shells. Place all the filled eggplant in an oiled baking pan that holds them securely. Pour the tomato sauce over the top and sprinkle with a little more cheese.

Bake for 50 minutes to 1 hour, until the filling is as soft as mashed potatoes and the eggplant shell is easily pierced by a sharp knife. Serve at room temperature or cold.

FUNGHETTI DI MELANZANE

Eggplants Cooked as If They Were Mushrooms

—

Serves 4

*H*ere's a wonderful dish based entirely on Italian imagination. It got its name and its inspiration from the Italians' passion for mushrooms. When there are none to be found, they invent whatever they can to re-create the tastes of the funghi from their hillsides. The dish, which I learned from Giuseppina Peppino De Lorenzi in Lequile just beyond Lecce, is every bit as simple and tasty as it appears.

> 2 large (2 pounds) globe eggplants, firm and glossy
> Salt
> 1½ tablespoons extra-virgin olive oil
> 1 onion, diced
> 1 garlic clove, minced
> 3 to 4 small tomatoes, peeled, seeded, and chopped
> 2 tablespoons drained capers, well rinsed and roughly chopped
> ¼ teaspoon red pepper flakes or freshly ground black pepper to taste
> 2 tablespoons finely chopped flat-leaf parsley

Peel the eggplants, discard the hard end piece near the stem, and cut into tiny cubes. Set the eggplant cubes in a medium-size bowl, cover with salted water to drain the bitter juices, and leave for at least 30 minutes. Rinse well and pat them dry.

Warm the oil in an earthenware pan or a heavy sauté pan, preferably nonstick, and sauté the eggplant, onion, garlic, and tomatoes. After 5 to 6 minutes, add the capers, cover, and continue cooking for another 15 or 20 minutes, checking from time to time to be sure nothing is sticking, until the eggplants are tender. Sprinkle with the red pepper flakes and parsley and taste for salt. Serve hot or at room temperature.

TIP: Gisa Sotis, Maria Michella Sorangelo, and Giuseppina Peppino De Lorenzi are three southern Italian grandmothers who don't salt eggplant to pull out its bitter juices. Instead, they leave slices of eggplant in salted water for 30 minutes to 2 hours and then press the water out firmly so the eggplant doesn't turn dark and so it doesn't soak up excessive olive oil while being sautéed or fried.

MELANZANE NEL RAGÙ CON MARSALA

Creamy Eggplant in a Marsala-Spiked Sauce

—

Serves 4 as a main course, 6 as a side dish

When Giovanna Passannanti was married in 1938, she went straight from her family home to her mother-in-law's house, as many young brides did at that time. The newlyweds lived in the countryside of Sicily six months of the year on an extensive farm where everyone worked together. "Even the old were strong and muscular," she remembers. It was an outdoor life in a small autonomous world. "We grew all our vegetables, had our own chickens and rabbits, our olive trees produced olives and oil, and our vines made wine."

She learned to cook from her mother and grandmother, both extraordinary cooks to judge from what she and her daughter-in-law made for me. Food has always been important in the family. When her brother was the mayor of Partinico, he sponsored festivals for which he brought cooks from Palermo, a real first.

This ambrosial creamy dish owes its haunting flavors and textures to the careful balance between the sweetness of the tomato sauce, the plump softness of the eggplant, and the seductive flavor of the Marsala. Make it early in the day, set it on a buffet table as a main-course dish, or serve it as the centerpiece of a lunch or a brunch.

1½ cups extra-virgin olive oil

2 globe eggplants, firm and glossy

½ red onion, diced

¾ cup Salsa di Pomodoro Siciliana (page 430),
    with the addition of ¾ cup chopped or torn fresh basil leaves

⅓ cup dry Marsala or red wine

2 cups water

½ teaspoon sea salt

Pinch of sugar (optional)

Heat the oil over high heat to 360°F. in a deep, heavy pot such as a Dutch oven and immerse the 2 whole eggplants in it. Reduce the heat to medium and cook for 15 minutes, turning the eggplants until they are entirely brown and distinctly soft. Carefully remove them from the pot and set them aside. Add the onion to the oil and sauté over medium heat until it is golden, 10 to 15 minutes. Stir in ¾ cup of the tomato sauce, reduce the heat to low, and cook, stirring frequently, until the sauce becomes very thick. At that point, add the Marsala and boil it down, stirring all the time. Now you can begin carefully adding 2 cups water, ½ cup at a time. At the beginning the mixture is very liquid, but it will reduce substantially in 10 minutes. Continue, adding all the water. At the end, add salt and bring to a boil.

Once the mixture is boiling hard, return the eggplants to the pot and keep at a low boil for about 30 minutes, turning the eggplants from time to time until the sauce is really thick. Taste for sweetness; you may want to add a little sugar. When the eggplants are done, you will see the oil rise to the top. Carefully move the eggplants to a platter and drain for at least 1 hour. Transfer the sauce to a bowl and set it in the refrigerator to allow all the oil to rise to the top. You can make the dish ahead to this point early in the day. Cover and leave at room temperature. Pour off the oil. Warm the sauce when you are ready. Serve the eggplants at room temperature.

FAVE E FINOCCHIO

Fava Beans and Fennel

—

Serves 4

*O*ne way to know that it's spring in the region of Apulia is seeing women in black dresses sitting at their front doors with their backs decorously to the street as they shell favas from their pods. This dish is usually prepared in the springtime when the fave have just appeared in the garden and their skins are so tender that they don't need to be peeled.

> 2 pounds fresh fava beans
> 3 tablespoons extra-virgin olive oil
> 1½ tablespoons finely minced pancetta or salt pork
> 3 whole garlic cloves, flattened
> ⅔ cup finely chopped wild fennel or finely chopped fennel tops and
>   ¼ to ½ teaspoon fennel seeds, lightly crushed
> ¼ to ½ teaspoon fennel seeds, crushed
> 3 tablespoons finely minced flat-leaf parsley
> 4 to 6 tablespoons dry white wine, broth, or water
> 1 teaspoon sea salt
> Freshly ground black pepper

Shell the fava beans. If they are not young and tender, remove the skins (see box, next page).

Warm the olive oil in a large, heavy skillet and cook the pancetta for 3 to 4 minutes or until almost crisp. Add the garlic, fennel leaves, fennel seeds, and parsley and sauté over medium-low heat only until the garlic is a pale gold, about 5 minutes. Add the fava beans and cook until they are tender, 3 to 5 minutes. Sprinkle with the white wine, turn the heat up to medium-high, cover, and cook until it has evaporated. Discard the garlic cloves, season with salt and pepper, and serve immediately.

FAVA BEANS (*Fave*): Also known as broad beans, fava beans are grown and eaten all over central and southern Italy. I saw several generations of Sicilian families sitting together, talking and shelling peas and fava beans, then stuffing them into freezer bags. In some cases the women collect the favas when they have dried on the plant, shell them, and leave them to dry longer. If they shell fresh favas, they often freeze them with their interior skins still on and peel them when they are ready to use them. All but the youngest fava beans must be peeled before they are cooked. To ease this arduous task, bring a pot of water to the boil, plunge in the favas and leave them very briefly, then drain; the fava skins should slip off easily.

WILD FENNEL: The succulent shoots of young fennel with their soft plume of fronds grow wild over much of California, but nowhere else in America, and they never appear in the markets. Do as Sicilians do when they visit—pick the plant from the hillsides and use the bulbs and seeds in a vast range of dishes. If you can't find wild fennel, use the delicate top leaves from cultivated fennel mixed with a small handful of fennel seeds.

CECAMARITI

Blind Husbands, or Fried Morsels

—

Serves 6

Here's a traditional country dish from Apulia based entirely on leftovers. Start with stale rustic bread, add greens and beans left over from the day before, cook them together, and what do you have? A true winter dish that gets its name from being so good that the husband eats outrageous quantities and goes blind!

Its provenance? Here's yet another inspired vegetable dish from the De Lorenzi family in Lequile.

If you don't have leftovers, cook frozen or fresh peas; if you use canned beans, drain and rinse them very well. If you can't find broccoli rabe, use broccoli.

¼ cup extra-virgin olive oil, plus extra for tossing
2 or 3 slices of stale country-style bread, cut into cubes
1 large or 2 small garlic cloves, whole but crushed to release their
    fragrance
1 small fresh hot red pepper, minced, or ⅛ to ¼ teaspoon red pepper flakes
10 ounces cooked peas or beans, such as fava beans or cannellini beans
1 pound broccoli rabe, previously boiled and/or briefly boiled, then sautéed
Sea salt
About 3 tablespoons water

Pour the oil into a medium-size heavy sauté pan, add the bread cubes, and sauté over medium-high heat until they are almost evenly browned all over. Add the garlic and hot pepper and sauté just until the garlic begins to turn pale golden, 2 to 3 minutes. Add the cooked peas, the broccoli rabe, salt, and about 3 tablespoons of water, and cook over a medium flame, stirring frequently, for 15 minutes. Remove the garlic, if you wish to emulate Signora De Lorenzi, or leave it in to complement the assertive vegetables in the dish. Toss with extra olive oil and serve.

PACCHETTI DI VERDURE

Vegetables Baked in Little Packages

—

Serves 4 to 6

*G*iulia Tondo cooks constantly when she isn't sewing, putting up preserves from the fruit in her garden in Rome, or dreaming up countless ways to be helpful to her children and grandchildren. Her recipes range from complicated sweet breads to dishes as easy as this one. There's nothing at all precise about the contents of these envelopes, so you should take her choice of vegetables as a mere suggestion. You could certainly double the number of peppers or onions and/or throw in a finely sliced fennel bulb, a few thin asparagus, or several finely sliced leeks. Use whatever you like or have on hand, but don't go overboard on any one ingredient. You can make the packets in the morning and cook them at mealtime. Refrigerate them and they keep well the next day.

1 small (¾ to 1 pound) eggplant, peeled and cut crosswise in ¼-inch-thick slices

4 cups cold water

2 tablespoons salt

1 or 2 Yellow Finn potatoes, peeled and diced

1 sweet red pepper, peeled and sliced thin

2 ripe tomatoes, peeled, seeded, and roughly chopped

1 large red onion, very thinly sliced

2 large garlic cloves, minced

½ cup finely minced flat-leaf parsley

2 zucchini, finely sliced (optional)

1 teaspoon sea salt

Freshly ground pepper

¼ teaspoon dried oregano

½ cup extra-virgin olive oil

Soak the eggplant slices in the water with 2 tablespoons of salt for at least 30 minutes, until the liquid is brown. Drain and pat them dry.

Preheat the oven to 375°F.

Combine the potatoes, red pepper, eggplant, tomatoes, onion, garlic, parsley, and zucchini in a large bowl. Mix the sea salt, pepper, oregano, and olive oil together well.

To make the packages, tear off six handkerchief-sized pieces of foil, each about 12 × 12 inches. Divide the vegetable mixture evenly among them and sprinkle the herb and oil mixture over the top. Close the packages by folding over the edges and then pinching them together very well. Close the top like a beggar's purse by pulling the foil into a knob and twisting it to seal it firmly. Repeat until you have used up all the vegetables. Place the packages on a baking sheet.

Bake for 20 to 35 minutes. You can test to see if the vegetables are done by opening a packet and inserting the tip of a sharp knife. If the potato is tender, everything is ready to serve.

PATATE E PEPERONI

Potatoes and Sweet Peppers with Olive Oil and Coarse Salt

—

Serves 4

What could be better than red peppers and potatoes tossed with good olive oil and a little coarse salt? Eat it hot, eat it warm, eat it at room temperature. Annita di Fonzo Zannella, the mother of the mayor of Campodimele, the village where almost all the people live into their late eighties and nineties, tosses this together in no time.

> 3 red sweet peppers
> 3 potatoes, preferably Yellow Finn or Yukon Gold
> 6 tablespoons extra-virgin olive oil
> 2 medium garlic cloves, minced
> 1 teaspoon coarse salt

Roast the sweet red peppers under a broiler or on a grill until they are evenly charred all over. Remove and place them in a paper bag to steam for about 30 minutes. When they are cool enough to handle, peel the peppers, remove the seeds and ribs, and slice the peppers into 1-inch-wide ribbons.

While the peppers are cooking, boil the potatoes in a large pot of salted water until they are tender, about 25 minutes. Peel and cut them into ⅜- to ½-inch-wide slices.

Warm all the olive oil over medium-low heat in a small, heavy pan and sauté the garlic only until it is pale and golden, 2 to 3 minutes. Do not let it burn. Combine the peppers, potatoes, garlic, oil, and the coarse salt. Toss them well to coat the vegetables evenly with the oil and the salt. Serve hot, although they are also delicious warm and at room temperature.

PEPERONI RIPIENI

Stuffed Sweet Red and Yellow Peppers

—

Serves 6

Antonina Lo Nardo comes from Palermo, where red and yellow sweet peppers are as intense in flavor as they are in color. The city's exuberant street markets, labyrinthine winding streets with vendors singing out the virtues of their wares, are full of the best products the island has to offer. There are sheep's milk cheeses—milky soft *tuma*, which becomes sharper *primo sale* after it has been salted and aged briefly, and wheels of pecorino aged for at least 6 months, meant for grating. There are juicy ripe tomatoes, and a plenitude of sausages and salami, all of which become part of the filling for Antonina's peppers.

Serve them as a first course, a main course, for brunch or for lunch. Serve them hot or serve them warm.

6 medium-size sweet peppers, 3 yellow and 3 red

FILLING

1 medium-size red onion, very finely chopped

¼ cup olive oil

⅓ cup (2 ounces) diced soppressata or other salami, tightly packed

½ cup (2 ounces) diced mortadella

1 cup bread crumbs, toasted

⅔ cup (2½ ounces) grated pecorino cheese

1 cup (4 ounces) finely diced young sheep's milk cheese, preferably caciotta or provola

2 cups Salsa di Pomodoro Siciliana (page 430)

Salt and freshly ground black pepper

12 (¼-inch) slices of caciocavallo cheese, to cover the tops of the peppers

Wash the peppers, cut them in half, and remove the seeds and ribs.

Preheat the oven to 375°F. Lightly oil a baking pan.

(continued)

Sauté the onion in olive oil over medium heat in a small sauté pan until golden and soft, about 10 minutes. Set aside to cool. Transfer to a bowl and stir in the diced soppressata, mortadella, toasted bread crumbs, grated pecorino, and young sheep's milk cheese. Stir in all but 3 to 4 tablespoons of the tomato sauce. Season with salt and pepper and spoon the mixture into the peppers. Lay a slice of caciocavallo cheese on top of each pepper as if it were a lid.

Set the peppers side by side in the prepared baking pan. Ladle the remaining tomato sauce over the top and bake for 50 minutes, adding water to the baking pan, if necessary, to prevent the sauce from burning. Serve warm or at room temperature.

POLPETTE DI PATATE

Potato Fritters

Makes 16

A friend tasted these polpette when Emma Grassi Bensi made them and exclaimed: *Supplì toscani!* Exactly! They are a Tuscan play on crispy Roman rice croquettes with strands of mozzarella hidden inside. Fried to a lightly crunchy golden brown, these potato fritters conceal a filling of buttery stracchino cheese that melts in their steamy interior.

If you can't find stracchino, look for taleggio or a similar creamy cheese. If you use Gorgonzola, which comes from the same family, be sure to pick the dolce-latte variety, not the much stronger-tasting aged cheese.

4 Yellow Finn or medium-size russet potatoes (about 2 pounds)
Salt
3 eggs, beaten
¾ teaspoon sea salt
1 large garlic clove, finely minced
6 tablespoons chopped flat-leaf parsley

Grated zest of 1 lemon

3 tablespoons plus 1 cup fine dry bread crumbs, preferably freshly grated

¼ cup (1 ounce) freshly grated Parmigiano-Reggiano cheese

4 ounces stracchino, taleggio, or a similarly creamy Italian cheese

2 to 3 cups olive or vegetable oil

Plunge the unpeeled potatoes in a medium-size pot of rapidly boiled salted water. Cook until they are tender when a knife easily pierces their interiors, about 25 to 30 minutes. Drain them well and set them aside to cool briefly, then peel them and mash or press through a ricer into a medium bowl. Transfer the potatoes to a pot, preferably nonstick, and cook over medium heat until they are dry. Set them aside to cool. Use a wooden spoon to mix in the eggs, sea salt, garlic, parsley, grated lemon zest, 3 tablespoons bread crumbs, and Parmesan cheese and blend well into a firm but still pliable mixture. Divide and shape with your palms into sixteen ovals, each the size of a large egg. Although Emma makes a small slit and adds a sliver of cheese to each fritter after it has been fried, I think it is much easier to slide a little piece of cheese into each polpetta before frying.

Place the remaining 1 cup bread crumbs on a dinner plate and roll the potato ovals in them to coat them thoroughly. Flatten them slightly so they are no more than 1 inch high.

Heat the oil to 350°F. in a heavy, high-sided sauté pan, and test that the oil is hot enough by dropping in a few bread crumbs; when they sizzle and dance immediately, you may proceed. Slip each fritter onto a slotted spoon and lower it into the hot oil, being careful not to crowd the polpette in the pan. Cook each one for 1½ to 2 minutes, until golden brown on both sides. Remove the polpette with a slotted spoon and drain on paper towels. Eat immediately.

POMODORI RIPIENI

Tomatoes Filled with Rice

—

Serves 10

*E*verything Andreina Pavani Calcagni does in this traditional Roman recipe goes against conventional wisdom. Cook tomatoes in an oven hot enough for pizza? Fill them with such a small amount of rice? It works magnificently. The extreme heat concentrates the flavor and sweetness of the tomatoes and brings out moisture that, along with the oil, cooks the rice perfectly.

Andreina slides individual slices of potato between the tomatoes to separate them in the baking pan. The olive oil cooks the potato slices; if you want, you can take the tomatoes out of the pan when they are done and continue to cook the potatoes until they are crispy.

> 14 small tomatoes or 10 medium tomatoes (3 pounds), all the same size, not too ripe
> 2 tablespoons chopped flat-leaf parsley
> ⅓ cup minced fresh basil
> 2 medium garlic cloves, minced
> 1 teaspoon minced fresh marjoram
> 5 leaves of fresh mint
> 1 teaspoon sea salt
> ¾ cup Arborio or Carnaroli rice
> 6 tablespoons extra-virgin olive oil
> 1 or 2 potatoes, peeled, cut in half crosswise, and then sliced lengthwise into ½-inch-thick segments
> ¼ teaspoon dried oregano

Preheat the oven to 450°F.

Wash and dry the tomatoes thoroughly. Cut a horizontal slice at the top of each one, but do not cut it through; it will be the flap that covers the tomato when it is cooked and served. Cut a tiny dime-sized piece out of the bottom so the tomato will balance easily. Use a small paring knife and spoon to scoop out the pulp carefully, leaving a shell about ¼ to ⅜ inch thick. Discard the seeds and juices. Salt the interiors of the tomatoes and let them drain upside down while you prepare the filling. Chop the pulp and put it in a bowl.

Mix the parsley, basil, garlic, marjoram, mint, and salt with the chopped tomato pulp. Stir in the rice and 4 tablespoons of the olive oil, and mix well.

Place the tomatoes in a lightly oiled baking pan that just holds them without crowding and tuck the potato slices between them. The potatoes help prop up the tomatoes, so slide them in anywhere you need them. Fill the interiors of the tomatoes with the rice filling. Don't worry if there is too much filling; it will overflow onto the potatoes and that is just fine. Drizzle the remaining olive oil over the tops of the tomatoes and potatoes and finish with the oregano. Put the flap of the tomato over the top to cover it.

Bake for 20 minutes, reduce the heat to 375°F., baste the tomatoes with liquid accumulated in the pan, and continue cooking for another 25 minutes. Pour or siphon off any excess liquid with a bulb baster. If the potatoes need extra cooking to become crisp, leave them in the oven for a few extra minutes or brown them quickly under the broiler. Serve hot.

Pomodori con la Ruchetta

Tomatoes with Arugula

—

Serves 4

Adele Rondini tosses this salad together in a flash and improvises if she's missing an ingredient. She says you should do the same. Don't have anchovies? Skip them. Can't find arugula? Substitute a few sprigs of finely chopped flat-leaf parsley with a handful of basil leaves and toss in an extremely finely sliced clove of garlic. I've also mashed two anchovies and mixed them right in with the olive oil, vinegar, and pepper, although I was careful to use the sea salt sparingly.

> 4 large ripe tomatoes
> 3 tablespoons extra-virgin olive oil
> 1 tablespoon red wine vinegar
> ¼ teaspoon sea salt
> Freshly ground black pepper
> ⅔ cup extremely finely cut ribbons of arugula
> 2 whole anchovies under salt, well rinsed and filleted,
>   or 4 anchovy fillets under oil, drained, optional

Cut the tomatoes in half and set them on a platter. Combine the olive oil, vinegar, salt, and pepper and sprinkle the mixture over the top. Cover the tomatoes with the arugula. Top with the anchovy fillets arranged in a star shape, if you want.

SFORMATINO DI ZUCCHINE

Vegetables Baked in a Mold

—

Serves 4

Hurray for Giulia Tondo. A sformatino is usually an elegant vegetable dish made with eggs and a béchamel sauce and served with a sauce. Not hers! No béchamel, no sauce, no ring mold: just the fresh sweet taste of zucchini layered with a combination of Parmesan cheese and bread crumbs under a melting crust of provolone cheese. Her sformatino could be the main course of a simple supper, a first course, or you could even cut it in tiny squares and serve it as part of an antipasto.

> 4 (about ¾ pound) young zucchini, cut into ¼-inch-thick rings
> Salt
> 1 onion, minced
> 1 tablespoon extra-virgin olive oil
> Freshly ground black pepper
> 6 tablespoons freshly grated Parmigiano-Reggiano cheese
> 2 tablespoons finely chopped flat-leaf parsley
> 6 tablespoons fine dry bread crumbs
> ½ pound provolone or caciocavallo cheese, cut in ⅛-inch-thick slices

Preheat the oven to 350°F. Lightly oil an 8-inch baking pan.

Blanch the zucchini rings in boiling salted water for no more than 1 to 2 minutes. Drain and set aside to cool.

Sauté the onion in the olive oil over medium heat until limp and translucent, about 8 to 10 minutes. Combine the zucchini and onion in a small bowl and season with salt and pepper.

Combine the Parmigiano-Reggiano, parsley, and bread crumbs. Salt and pepper them—remember that the cheese is salty—and mix well.

Cover the bottom of the prepared baking pan with a layer of the zucchini and onion, spread half the cheese mixture over them, and repeat, finishing with the cheese mixture. Cover the top with thin slices of provolone.

Bake for 20 minutes, until the cheese has melted and is lightly browned. Serve hot.

TORTA DI VERDURA

Mashed Potato and Spinach Tart

—

Serves 6

*H*ere's comfort food all dressed up for a party. Tall, thin, and elegant Laura Mansi Salom grew up in the Palazzo Mansi in Lucca with three cooks in the kitchen and a personal waiter for each family member. They sat down to multiple-course meals with four or five wines twice a day and stayed at table for hours on end.

"We've had a revolution," she exclaims with delight. She knows what the best food is and she loves to entertain with dazzling food, but refuses to spend much time in the preparation. This delicious savory tart is simply two layers of Parmesan-flavored mashed potatoes enclosing a filling of spinach, but what a presentation it makes! Cut into it and you discover a brilliant green layer hidden in the center. Serve it with any roast meat or roast chicken.

> 3½ pounds boiling potatoes, peeled
> Salt
> 3 egg yolks
> 2 eggs
> About 1 cup (4 ounces) freshly grated Parmigiano-Reggiano cheese
> ⅜ teaspoon freshly grated nutmeg
> ¾ teaspoon sea salt
> Freshly ground black pepper
> 4½ pounds spinach, stems removed
> 4 tablespoons unsalted butter

Preheat the oven to 350°F. Butter the bottom and sides of a 9-inch springform pan very well.

Plunge the potatoes into a large pot of rapidly boiling salted water and cook until they are tender when pierced with the tip of a knife, 20 to 25 minutes. Drain the potatoes and mash or press them through a ricer into a medium bowl. Set them aside to cool.

Stir the egg yolks, eggs, cheese, ¼ teaspoon of the nutmeg, and sea salt and pepper into the potatoes and combine them very well until they are like soft mashed potatoes.

Meanwhile, wash the spinach very well in at least three changes of water to remove all traces of dirt from the leaves. Set it in a large deep pot with only the water still clinging to the leaves, cover, and cook until barely tender, 7 to 10 minutes, stirring and moving them frequently so the large quantity of leaves cooks evenly. Drain the spinach leaves, then set them in the bowl of a ricer and press down just firmly enough to remove all the cooking water. Warm the butter in a heavy sauté pan and sauté the spinach briefly with the remaining ⅛ teaspoon nutmeg. Remove and chop the leaves finely with a mezzaluna or a knife. Do not use a food processor, because it will puree the spinach.

In the prepared pan, spread half the potatoes over the bottom and 1 inch up the sides of the pan and smooth the top so the layer is even. Cover with all the spinach and finish by spreading the rest of the potatoes over the top, smoothing it as above.

Bake the tart for 20 to 30 minutes, until the top is golden. Let it rest for about 5 minutes, then unmold by slipping the springform open and sliding the tart onto a platter. Serve hot, cut in wedges.

Tip: Use a potato ricer to squeeze the excess water out of freshly cooked spinach or chard.

Zucchini are often salted like eggplants and drained in a colander before being cooked. They are sometimes also dried in the sun, like tomatoes. Zucchini blossoms appear by the crateful in season, ready to be stuffed with any number of tempting fillings and then fried or sautéed.

ZUCCHINE DI GISA SOTIS

Zucchini with Red Onions and Basil

—

Serves 4 to 6

*G*isa Sotis has lived most of her life in the town of Minturno di Tufo, near the border between Lazio and Campania. She is both up-to-date—her freezer is full to the brim—and traditional—she grows her own olives and makes wine from her grapes—but she doesn't want to spend hours in the kitchen, not when her daughter, son-in-law, and two grandchildren, who all live with her, are part of her very full and active life. She is an excellent cook who can turn out several dishes in no time at all, including this simple zucchini with its intriguingly delicious taste. Her secret? Crumbling a chicken bouillon cube right into the mixture, a tiny trick that heightens flavor noticeably.

> 2 medium-size red onions, cut in half and thinly sliced
> 2½ pounds firm zucchini, washed, dried,
>   and cut into ½-inch rounds
> 2 to 3 tablespoons extra-virgin olive oil
> 1 chicken bouillon cube
> 7 leaves of fresh basil

Put the onion, zucchini slices, and oil in a large sauté pan, preferably nonstick, and cook them over medium heat until they are soft and lightly colored, 15 minutes. Crumble the chicken bouillon cube right on top of the mixture, stir it in, cover, and cook over medium heat until the zucchini and onion are lightly browned, about 5 minutes. Tear the basil leaves into small pieces and sprinkle them into the mixture about 2 minutes before the dish is finished. Taste for salt. Serve hot or at room temperature. You can also refrigerate the zucchini and serve them next day at room temperature.

11

DOLCI

Desserts

CREMA BACCHICA

Bacchus's Pudding

KOCK DI PANE CON SALSA DI PERE

Bread Pudding with Pear Sauce

CREMA

Creamy Soft Custard

BUDINO BELGA

Chocolate and Coffee Pudding from Mantua

PARADEL

Apple Bread Pudding

BUDINO DELLA NONNA

Grandmother's Custardy Chocolate Pudding

PASTA DI CROSTATA A QUADRATINO

Lattice Tart Filled with Jam

CROSTATA CON IL SAVOR

Latticed Fruit and Nut Tart

TORTA CON UN RIPIENO DI MANDORLE TRITATE E CIOCCOLATA

Chocolate Almond Tart

TORTA DELLA NONNA

Grandmother's Tart

TORTA DI MELE FRIULANA
Apple, Raisin, and Walnut Tart from Friuli

PASTATELLA
Almond, Chocolate, and Orange Tarts

TORTA DI RISO
Rice Pudding

TIMBALLO DI RICOTTA
Lemon-Flavored Ricotta Cake

TORTA DI CILIEGE
Cake Covered with Cherries

TORTA SBRISOLONA
Crumbly Cornmeal Cake from Mantua

TORTA DELLA ZUCCA
Pumpkin Tart

BENSONE
Crumbly Coffee Cake from Modena

TOZZETTI
Raisin and Nut-Studded Biscotti

DOLCE DI MANDORLE
Almond Cookies Wrapped Around a Wild Cherry

SPUMICINI
Almond-Flavored Meringue Cookies

SOFFICINI PORTOGHESI
Delicate Butter Cookies alla "Portuguese"

DOLCE PER I MORTI
"Day of the Dead" Cookies

BISCOTTI DI PRATO
Biscotti from Prato

DISCHI
Jam Sandwich Cookies

MARZAPANE
Lemon-Spiked Almond Cookies

CREMA BACCHICA

Bacchus's Pudding

—

Serves 6

Gianna Modotti promised me that this dessert would be completely different from any I've ever tasted, and she was right. Its evocative name may be slightly reminiscent of crème caramel and it does have a haunting resemblance, although wine adds an entirely different flavor and amalgamates differently from milk. People tend to be hesitant after their first bite: "How curious," they say, not quite knowing what to make of it. And then they plunge their spoons in again and again.

    4 eggs
    1¼ cups (4½ ounces) confectioners' sugar
    2⅓ cups sweet white wine, such as Riesling or Gewürztraminer
    ½ cinnamon stick
    3 whole cloves

Preheat the oven to 300°F.

Beat the eggs well, then set them aside to rest until the foam subsides. (You may do this as much as 4 hours ahead.)

Boil the confectioners' sugar and wine together with the cinnamon and cloves for about 5 minutes. Set the mixture aside to cool. Remove the cinnamon stick and cloves. Press the beaten eggs through a strainer to eliminate the rest of the foam and any impurities.

Pour the mixture into custard cups or ramekins and set them in a baking pan with boiling water that comes 1 inch up the sides of the cups. Bake for 55 minutes, until the puddings have set and a skewer comes out almost entirely clean. The tops remain the same golden color that they were originally, so don't expect them to brown in any way.

KOCK DI PANE CON SALSA DI PERE

Bread Pudding with Pear Sauce

—

Serves 6 to 8

*S*erve me any dessert that Gianna Modotti makes. This almond-studded bread pudding with a delicate pear-flavored sauce is stupendous—down-home and elegant all at once. It comes from the hilly eastern region of Friuli, where flavors bear the culinary imprint of a time when those lands were part of the Austro-Hungarian Empire. Gianna weaves the lessons of history into every Friulian dessert that she makes. The influence of Venice dances through her apple cake (page 382), while Slavic tastes imprint her cake covered with cherries (*Torta di Ciliege*, page 391).

FILLING

    3 or 4 slices of stale country-style bread, enough to make
        2 cups bread crumbs

    7 tablespoons sweet wine, such as Moscato, Aleatico, Recioto di Soave,
        or sweet Marsala

    5 tablespoons (2½ ounces) unsalted butter, room temperature,
        plus extra for the mold

    ⅓ cup (2½ ounces) sugar, plus extra for the mold

    2 egg yolks

    4 eggs, separated

    Grated zest of 1 lemon

    ¼ teaspoon cinnamon

    ½ cup (2½ ounces) tightly packed raw almonds, toasted for 10 minutes
        in a 350°F. oven and finely chopped

    A pinch of salt

SAUCE

    6 ripe pears

    2 tablespoons unsalted butter

    6 tablespoons sugar

    ⅓ cup pear eau-de-vie or pear liqueur

Preheat the oven to 350°F. Butter a 2-quart charlotte mold, soufflé dish, or other high-sided baking dish.

Grate the bread into a large bowl; you should have 2 cups of bread crumbs. Sprinkle with the sweet wine to soften them.

Cream the butter and sugar until light and fluffy. Add the 6 egg yolks one at a time, beating well to be sure that each is incorporated before adding the next. Stir in the grated lemon zest, cinnamon, and almonds. Combine with the bread crumbs in the large bowl.

Beat the egg whites to stiff peaks with a pinch of salt and gently fold them in.

Sprinkle the interior of the prepared mold with sugar to coat the bottom and sides. Spoon the filling inside.

Bake for 40 minutes, until the tip of a knife comes out clean. Serve warm.

While the bread pudding is in the oven, make the pear sauce. Peel and core the pears and cut them in small pieces. Melt the butter in a 2-quart heavy saucepan, stir in the sugar, and cook until the mixture is a caramel color, about 4 to 5 minutes. Add the pears and cook over very low heat until a fork pierces them easily. Remove the pears from the liqueur and puree by pressing them through a wire-mesh sieve or whirling them in a food processor or blender. Stir in the pear eau-de-vie and serve warm with the bread pudding. You can make this sauce ahead and reheat it gently.

CREMA

Creamy Soft Custard

—

Serves 6 to 8

*S*oft enough to be spooned on a plate, thicker than crème anglaise, and reminiscent of crème caramel without the topping, Luce Galante de Secly's incredibly creamy dessert is more delicate than, and at least as haunting as, any of those better-known dolci. One of the secrets of its smoothness comes from setting the baking dish on a kitchen towel as it cooks in a bagna maria (water bath). The little bit of insulation protects the crema from the effects of the heat and ensures that its texture remains creamy.

2 cups milk
⅔ cup (4½ ounces) sugar
Zest of 1 lemon, sliced in thin strips
½ vanilla bean, split lengthwise (optional)
1 tablespoon plus 2 teaspoons all-purpose flour
5 egg yolks
About 8 cups water

Preheat the oven to 350°F. Butter well a 2-quart soufflé dish. You may also use six ½-cup buttered ramekins.

Bring the milk, sugar, lemon zest, and optional vanilla bean to a boil in a 3-quart nonreactive saucepan over medium heat. As soon as the mixture comes to a boil, remove the pan from the heat and let the contents stand for 3 or 4 minutes. Remove the lemon zest and vanilla bean. Still off the heat, sift in the flour and whisk the mixture together.

Meanwhile, beat the egg yolks well in a medium bowl until they are light, creamy, and lemon-colored, about 5 minutes by a handheld mixer, 3 minutes by standing electric mixer. Whisk the warmed sweetened milk into the egg mixture in a slow, steady stream, being very careful not to pour too quickly so you don't cook the eggs. Whisk constantly until you have incorporated all the milk.

Strain the mixture through a sieve into the prepared baking dish. Cover the top with foil. Choose a slightly larger soufflé dish to use for a water bath. Fold a kitchen towel in half and lay it on the bottom of the pan. Set the baking pan with the custard on top of the towel to shield the custard from the harsh effects of the heat. Bring about 8 cups of water to a boil and carefully pour it into the baking pan to within ½ inch of the top of the baking dish.

Bake for about 50 minutes, or until a toothpick inserted near the edge of the custard comes out clean. Remove it from the oven and then from the water bath. Serve the crema at room temperature.

Budino Belga

Chocolate and Coffee Pudding from Mantua

—

Serves 8 to 10

*N*o one seems to know why this very old and much loved dessert is called a Belgian pudding. It has been cooked in the kitchens of ancient aristocratic families in Mantua for centuries and is so special that no one is willing to part with the recipe. Vanna Corbellani Camerlenghi, known in the city as an extraordinary cook, once served it as the pièce de résistance at a dinner party and was as amazed as the guest who slipped her spoon into it for a first taste and exclaimed in wonder, "This is what my mother made!" It was the first time she'd had it in years since the recipe had disappeared from her family treasures.

To make the dessert, you will need a 2-inch-deep 10-inch tube pan or savarin mold that has a hole in the center and a capacity of 11 or 12 cups. I recommend one with a nonstick surface because it is so easy to unmold. Do not substitute an angel food cake pan. Use instant espresso powder, not finely ground espresso coffee. When you make the caramel, be prepared to work very quickly to coat the sides of the pan. Caramel hardens with the speed of light.

This pudding is immensely delicious but it isn't sugary or overly sweet. You can make it early in the day or even the day before you plan to serve it.

(continued)

3½ ounces sweet or semisweet chocolate

1 quart heavy cream

½ cup (3½ ounces) sugar

1 tablespoon powdered instant espresso coffee

4 eggs, beaten well

CARAMEL

1 cup (7 ounces) sugar

4 tablespoons water

Preheat the oven to 350°F.

Shave the chocolate into flakes and set it in a 2-quart heavy-bottomed saucepan. Add the cream, sugar, and powdered coffee, set over very low heat, and melt the chocolate, stirring from time to time. Be very careful that the mixture doesn't boil. Once the chocolate has melted, set the mixture aside to cool to room temperature. Add the beaten eggs to the cooled chocolate mixture.

Caramelize the sugar by combining the sugar and water in a small heavy saucepan. Mix well over medium heat with a metal spoon only, then wipe down any crystals of sugar from the side of the pot with a brush dipped in cold water. Bring to a boil and cook without stirring until the mixture is a deep amber color and has caramelized, about 5 to 7 minutes. You will have to work very fast: pour immediately to coat both the sides and bottom of a 10-inch tube pan or savarin mold with an 11- or 12-cup capacity. Set aside to cool. Vanna says that when you hear the caramel making a crack-crack sound, it's time to pour in the egg mixture.

Place the filled tube pan in a baking pan, pour in simmering water to reach halfway up the sides of the tube pan, and cover the top of the baking pan with foil. Bake for about 1 hour and 10 minutes to 1 hour and 20 minutes, until the chocolate-colored top is set and a skewer comes out clean. If the pudding jiggles a bit, don't worry; it will become slightly firmer as it cools. Cool to room temperature, then cover with plastic wrap and refrigerate. To unmold, dip the mold very briefly in hot water. Loosen the top of the dessert by inserting the tip of a sharp paring knife between the pudding and the mold, about ¼ inch below the top of the pudding, and drawing it all around the interior of the mold. Place a platter on the dessert and invert to serve.

PARADEL

Apple Bread Pudding

—

Serves 6

High above Lake Como, the Valtellina stretches across a mountainous landscape that reaches almost all the way to Switzerland. Apple orchards dot the terrain, providing quantities of the fruits that have always found their way into the simple desserts of home. Lina Vitali learned this recipe from her mother-in-law and won first prize when she cooked it years later. No wonder: the apples become soft, the walnuts remain crunchy, and the bread is as tender as you could want it to be. If you have leftover walnut or raisin bread, the paradel will be particularly delicious.

5 large slices (5 ounces) of country-style bread, preferably stale
¾ cup milk
5 apples, preferably Golden or Red Delicious, peeled and cored
¼ cup (1¾ ounces) sugar
Grated zest of 1 lemon
⅓ cup (12) walnuts, toasted 10 minutes in 350°F. oven and chopped
1 egg, room temperature
1 teaspoon vanilla extract
1 tablespoon unsalted butter

About half an hour before you are ready to cook, break up the bread in your hands and put it in a large bowl. Pour the milk over the slices and leave them to soften.

Preheat the oven to 350°F. Butter a deep 9½-inch baking dish, such as a soufflé dish.

Cut the apples into thin slices and add them to the bread in the bowl. Mix in the sugar, lemon zest, and walnuts. Beat the egg and vanilla together and stir them into the apple and bread mixture.

Spread the mixture inside the prepared baking dish. Scatter flakes of butter over the top. Bake for 1 hour to 1 hour and 15 minutes until the apple slices are tender and the top is lightly crunchy and golden.

BUDINO DELLA NONNA
Grandmother's Custardy Chocolate Pudding
—
Serves 10

*I*f ever there was a chocolate dessert that typifies comfort food, this is it. Vittorina Seghesio blithely calls it an old-fashioned homemade dessert. I call it sublime and unforgettable.

Vittorina is so practiced and professional that she makes her caramel using only sugar. Emulate her if you have the skill; otherwise use some water to caramelize the sugar.

CARAMEL

> 1 cup (7 ounces) sugar
>
> 4 tablespoons cold water

PUDDING

> ¼ cup (1¾ ounces) sugar
>
> 12 eggs, room temperature
>
> ⅔ cup (2½ ounces) unsweetened cocoa
>
> 2 tablespoons sweet cocoa
>
> About 26 small amaretti, crumbled to make ⅔ cup crumbs
>
> 6 cups milk, room temperature

Caramelize the sugar by combining the 1 cup sugar and 4 tablespoons cold water in a small, heavy saucepan. Mix well over medium heat with a metal spoon only, then wipe down any crystals of sugar from the side of the pot with a brush dipped in cold water. Bring to a boil and cook without stirring until the mixture is a deep amber color and has caramelized, about 5 to 7 minutes. You will have to work very fast: pour immediately to coat both the sides and bottom of a 10-inch tube pan or savarin mold with an 11- or 12-cup capacity (one with a nonstick surface is ideal). You can also use a 10-inch (4-quart) soufflé dish. Set aside to cool.

Preheat the oven to 350°F.

Whisk together the sugar and eggs just until they are lightly frothy. Sift in the 2 cocoas and then gently whisk in the amaretti crumbs. Stir in the milk until it is well amalgamated.

Pour the mixture into the caramelized mold. Place the filled mold in a baking pan, pour in simmering water to reach halfway up the sides, cover the top with foil, and bake for about 1 hour and 20 minutes to 1 hour and 30 minutes, until the top is a chocolate-color and a tester comes out clean. Cool to room temperature. Unmold and invert to serve (see instructions for Budino Belga, p. 369).

PASTA DI CROSTATA A QUADRATINO

Lattice Tart Filled with Jam
—

Makes 2 crostate, one 9-inch and one 8-inch

*A*sked to name the archetypal grandmother dessert, the simple sweet that appears at the end of a meal at home, most Italians would answer in a flash: a crostata filled with jam. The dessert knows no regional boundaries: every Italian child grows up eating sweet pastry tarts filled with homemade preserves.

When Giulia Tondo makes this recipe, she makes ten crostate, but then, she does everything on a mammoth scale to feed all her children and grandchildren. No wonder nonne inspire such reverence in Italy; it can't be a coincidence that the word for lullaby, the comforting song of childhood, is *ninnananna*, a term born of the word for grandmother.

Since Giulia Tondo makes crostate frequently, she always saves a bit of the dough from the previous one and puts it in the freezer to pull out for the latticework on the next round of tarts. She lets the dough thaw in the refrigerator, so that when she takes it out, it is easy to roll with her fingers and she doesn't need a rolling pin.

You will probably not be in the same kind of production that Giulia Tondo is, but you can make this dough ahead and leave it in the refrigerator for a day or freeze it for up to a month.

(continued)

2¾ scant cups (12½ ounces) unbleached all-purpose flour
    plus extra tablespoons for rolling

½ cup (3½ ounces) sugar

1 teaspoon baking powder

A pinch of salt

4 tablespoons (2 ounces) unsalted butter, room temperature,
    cut in small pieces

Grated zest of ½ lemon

2 large eggs, room temperature

2 tablespoons Cointreau or Grand Marnier

1 teaspoon vanilla extract

3 tablespoons extra-virgin olive oil

FILLING

3½ cups fruit preserves, such as apple and grape preserves (page 419)
    or any jam of your choice; use 2 cups for the 9-inch crostata and
    1½ cups for the 8-inch

EGG WASH

1 egg beaten with 1 teaspoon water

Combine the flour, sugar, baking powder, and salt in a large bowl. Scatter the pieces of butter over the top and cut in with a pastry blender or rub in with your fingers until the mixture has the consistency of coarse cornmeal. Sprinkle the lemon zest over the top. Blend together the eggs, Cointreau, vanilla, and olive oil, and mix them into the dry ingredients until a dough is formed. Knead briefly until it is smooth. Divide the dough into two pieces, one slightly larger than the other.

Set a piece of plastic wrap on your work surface, sprinkle it with a tablespoon of flour, take one of the pieces of dough, flatten it into a square, sprinkle a little flour over the top, cover with another piece of plastic wrap, and press down with the weight of your body to flatten it a bit. Repeat with the second piece of dough. You may set them in the refrigerator now for 1 hour or 1 day or freeze for up to a month.

When you are ready to bake, preheat the oven to 400°F and set the rack on the middle shelf. Lightly oil a 9-inch baking pan.

Set the larger piece of dough on a lightly floured work surface. Cut off a piece that is slightly less than one-quarter of the dough and set it aside. Use a rolling pin to roll out the remaining dough into a 10½-inch circle. Fold the piece in half and then in half again and set it in the center of the prepared baking pan. Gently open the segments of the dough; they should cover the bottom and sides of the baking pan entirely. Press them firmly into place with your fingers and trim any pieces that are hanging over the edges. Collect any scraps and incorporate them into the reserved small piece of dough.

Spread 2 cups of the preserves to cover the bottom of the dough.

Lightly flour your work surface. Roll the reserved dough into an 8 × 12-inch rectangle and use a pizza cutter to cut twelve 1½-inch-wide strips for the lattice. Paint the strips with the egg wash. Save any excess dough for the second pastry shell. Arrange six of the dough strips across the filling in each direction to form a diagonal latticework. Using a knife to loosen the dough that covers the rim of the pan, Giulia folds that dough down over the edges of the crostata in a free-form and charmingly homemade way.

Repeat with the second piece of dough but roll it to a 9-inch circle and set it in a well-oiled 8-inch pie pan. Proceed as above.

Just before baking, brush all the exposed dough with the egg wash. Bake for about 20 minutes until the dough is golden brown. Cool on a rack.

Profile of *Giulia Tondo*

Ten crostate, six pizze Friulane: Giulia Tondo's recipes are calibrated to feed her four children, their spouses, and their six children. She grows peaches, apricots, pomegranates, pears, plums, and mandarin oranges in the garden of her house in the center of Rome. And what does she do with the fruit? She turns it into fifty bottles of fruit syrup so that her grandchildren always have *bibite*, soft drinks, when they come to visit. Basketfuls of apricots, plums, and peaches become jams for the center of their crostate. In mid-January she even offers them peaches that taste as if they had just been picked off the trees, because Giulia freezes fruits at the height of their summer juiciness and saves them to brighten life during the dreary winter months.

(continued)

Viterbo
Rome

Giulia learned to cook when she discovered that her very handsome surgeon husband was regularly eating lunch with one of the fifteen nurses he saw every day. Ernestina, a gorgeous blond, was an excellent nurse who also happened to cook extremely well, and each evening when he came home, Dr. Tondo described what she had made for him that day. "I didn't know how to make anything," Giulia remembered. She herself had trained as a nurse but quit on her fiancé's instruction: young mothers didn't have time for careers. So she set herself on a different kind of training: "I learned to cook," she said, "because I was jealous." She went into the kitchen at seven in the morning and stayed there until he arrived home at one. Every day.

Today Giulia Tondo's recipe file is a jumble of index cards taped to the inside of one kitchen cabinet door. The rest is readily available in her head. "My father used to say, 'Don't buy meat if you don't know the butcher as well as you know your brother.'" She clearly took his advice to heart, because although she lives in Rome, she buys almost all of her meat in Vetralla, near Viterbo, where the family has long kept an apartment. She is particularly committed to the sausages she buys there, convinced that their superb taste comes from the pigs' having been raised in a forest of oaks, eating the acorns and chestnuts that fall to the ground. She buys the sausages when they are fresh, hangs them to dry at room temperature before putting them in the refrigerator, and keeps them to flavor tomato sauce and home-fried potatoes. She wouldn't eat a prosciutto that was cured for less than 18 months, a pig that wasn't killed during a north wind when the temperature was low, or a piece of veal from a calf whose life history she doesn't know.

Greeting me warmly at her garden gate, Giulia instantly took my arm and tucked it into hers, resting it comfortably at the waist of her soft seafoam-green knit dress. Iron-gray hair pulled back into a bun framed her strong, square face. She walked me with purpose through the garden into the large, modern family apartment. A still-warm iron rested at the end of the ironing board, ready to press heaps of napkins, tablecloths, and soft absorbent towels she made for various family members. They were not brand-new; not only does Giulia make them but she launders them as well for children and grandchildren. Giulia seems the embodiment of the family-centered nonna, one who does everything possible for her children and grandchildren and is deeply involved in their daily lives. She sews for them, knits for them, and cooks endlessly for them. Giulia gets her sense of self from being in perpetual motion, even though she is past seventy-five. She wears no makeup and little jewelry, since they might demand time or interfere with her whirlwind motion. She makes special food for her grandchildren to take to school and on trips, and she fills tins with the hazelnut biscotti one son loves, sending them to him in Sardinia.

For her pizza Friulana, a complicated panettone-like bread from Friuli, the northern region where she was born, Giulia still makes her dough with four different additions of flour, milk, and butter. And she makes dozens of crostate a month, turning out that most favored of all homemade desserts with astonishing finesse. Her directions and observations are crystal clear and often expressed with an instinctive feeling for the tactile—she loves the silky feeling of pasta dough—and the sensual: she squeezes a starter through her fingers, stirs with her hands, scoops up dough with her whole being. Rolling out pastry dough on a simple cloth she herself cut and hemmed—it keeps the dough from slipping—she slides the dough into a round baking pan, spreads homemade jam or marmalade over the bottom, sets a latticework of dough over the jam, and then folds the raggedy edge over the top. "It doesn't have to be perfect around the edges," she remarks reassuringly. "The homemade look is part of its charm."

Surrounded by all the food she was preparing, Giulia suddenly put down her rolling pin and disappeared. When she returned, she held up a black silk dress accented by triangular insets of flowered fabric at the tapered waist. It was unmistakably the dress for a smaller Giulia. "You lose your shape when you stop smoking," she said, "when you get sick and have to take cortisone, and especially when your husband dies. Loving gives you everything, releases everything."

She clearly adored her husband. Her love for him still spills over into every facet of her life, warms and embraces every member of her family. She lives for regular phone calls from her children, which she says are like water for plants. If her husband inspired her phenomenal cooking, her children and grandchildren continue to encourage it. When Giulia went to visit her daughter and son-in-law in Houston, she carried a prosciutto inside a box that once housed Perugina chocolates and wrapped three *guanciali* (preserved pork jowl, a pancetta-like specialty of Lazio) in one of her silk dresses. She swears she cooked for half of Houston. Her daughter's friends wanted her to stay so much that they found her a location for a restaurant and promised to patronize it eternally.

Giulia Tondo grew up in a house where both food and culture were important. Her father was a veterinarian who spoke many languages and the family had, as she enumerates them, four horses, three maids, and two motorcycles. But after fascism came, her father took his wife and six children to Argentina rather than compromise people he cared about. The family returned twelve years later. Giulia's love for Italy is clear, as is her immense pleasure in feeding her family. "It's simple," she says. "When I see someone dipping bread into sauce, I'm happy."

Crostata con il Savor

Latticed Fruit and Nut Tart

—

Makes one 8- or 9-inch tart

When Ida Lancellotti was five or six, she would take bread dough made by her mamma and wrap it around an apple, making a little basket. Then she took a little more dough and made it into a handle, put it in the oven, and baked it. She laughed: "I also made it in the shape of a big salami, patting lots of dough around the apple. My sister and I were in a real competition. I'd improve the taste of the bread dough if I could filch a little butter or add a little milk to brush over the top of the dough."

Clearly her talents evolved early. This crostata is what a mince pie might aspire to if it were meatless and made in Emilia Romagna. Ida Lancellotti suggests making the filling the day before you want to use it. If your savor is too stiff, my solution, although it is hardly traditional, is to add a bit of quick pear apple preserves (page 420) or some applesauce to thin it to the proper texture.

PASTRY DOUGH

2 cups (10 ounces) unbleached all-purpose flour

½ teaspoon baking powder

¾ cup (5 ounces) sugar

A pinch of salt

1 stick plus 3 tablespoons (5 ounces) unsalted butter, room temperature

1 egg

1 egg yolk

½ teaspoon vanilla extract

FILLING

2 cups (18 ounces) Savor (page 423)

6 dried figs, roughly chopped

¼ cup walnuts, toasted in a 350°F. for 10 minutes and roughly chopped

¼ cup (2 ounces) crumbled simple biscotti or Marie biscuits

About 8 small (3½ ounces) amaretti, crumbled

Fine dry bread crumbs (optional)

By hand: To make the dough by hand, place the flour, baking powder, sugar, and salt in a bowl and stir to mix. Cut the butter in small pieces and cut it into the flour mixture with a pastry blender or two knives until the mixture resembles coarse meal. Slowly stir in the first egg and then the egg yolk, mixing thoroughly. Then stir in the vanilla. Gather the dough together and knead it roughly and briefly on a lightly floured work surface just until the dough comes together. Flatten it into a disk, wrap it in plastic wrap, and refrigerate for at least 1 hour but no longer than 1 day.

By heavy-duty electric mixer: Cream the butter and sugar in a mixer bowl with the paddle until pale and creamy. Add the egg, egg yolk, and vanilla, in two additions, mixing thoroughly after each addition. Add the flour, baking powder, and salt and mix until the dough comes together and is consistent but still soft. Be careful not to overmix or the dough will be tough. Gather the dough into a ball, flatten it into a disk, wrap it in plastic wrap, and refrigerate for at least 1 hour but no longer than 1 day.

To make the filling: Scoop the savor into a bowl, stir in the figs, walnuts, and biscotti and amaretti crumbs and mix well. Add some bread crumbs, if you need them; the mixture should have the texture of pumpkin pie filling. You may refrigerate the filling for up to 24 hours.

Shaping: Let the dough stand at room temperature for 30 to 45 minutes before rolling it out. Knead it briefly on a lightly floured surface to make it supple enough for rolling. Divide the dough into two pieces, one twice as large as the other. Cover the smaller piece. On a lightly floured work surface roll the larger piece to an 11-inch circle and ease the dough into a lightly buttered 8- or 9-inch tart pan with a removable bottom. The dough should drape over the sides. Fill with the savor filling.

Preheat the oven to 400°F.

Roll the remaining dough on the very slightly floured work surface into a large oval. Use a ravioli cutter to cut eight strips that are ½ inch wide. Arrange the strips in a diagonal lattice over the filling (four in each direction) and press hard onto the edges, pinching the strips lightly onto the tart shell. Ida takes tiny pieces of the remaining dough and rolls them into balls and puts them in alternating squares of the filling between the lattice strips.

Bake for 25 to 30 minutes, until the pastry is golden.

TORTA CON UN RIPIENO DI MANDORLE TRITATE E CIOCCOLATA

Chocolate Almond Tart

———

Makes 1 10-inch tart and 4 2-inch tartlets

*T*his spectacular tart comes from the handwritten recipe journal of the mother of Signora Giovanna Passannanti, a Sicilian woman in her mid-eighties. I have substituted candied orange peel for the candied squash called for. The combination of almonds, chocolate, lemon zest, and candied orange is so delicious that most people find it almost impossible to confine themselves to a single helping. Even more unbelievably, this tart keeps for 7 days and still tastes as if I'd baked it that day!

You must use the filling when you make it; it stiffens as it cools and is too hard to spread. Should that happen to you, add a little warm water to soften and proceed from there.

DOUGH

    1¾ cups plus 2 tablespoons (9 scant ounces) unbleached all-purpose flour

    ¼ cup plus 2 teaspoons (2 ounces) sugar

    ¾ teaspoon baking powder

    A pinch of salt

    6 tablespoons (3 ounces) best-quality lard or unsalted butter

    1 egg

    ¼ cup dry Marsala

    Butter for the tart pan

FILLING

    4½ cups (18 ounces) blanched almonds

    1½ cups (10 ounces) sugar

    Juice and grated zest of 2 lemons

    5 ounces bittersweet chocolate, grated or shaved

    6 tablespoons candied orange peel or candied citron peel

Although no traditional grandmother would do so, I sometimes make this dough in the food processor because it is so easy. Just place the flour, sugar, baking powder, and salt in the processor bowl fitted with the steel blade and pulse several times to sift. Scatter the pieces of lard over the top and pulse until the mixture has the consistency of coarse cornmeal. Combine the egg and Marsala in a cup with a spout and, with the motor running, pour down the feed tube, mixing until the dough comes together.

By hand: Sift the flour, sugar, baking powder, and salt into a large bowl. Scatter the lard over the top and rub it in until the mixture has the consistency of coarse cornmeal. Make a hole in the middle, pour in the egg and Marsala, and slowly work them in until a dough is formed.

Shape the dough into a thick disk, wrap it in plastic, and place it in the refrigerator for at least 1 hour. It will keep for 24 hours in the refrigerator or for a month in the freezer.

Preheat the oven to 350°F. Prepare a well-buttered 10-inch tart pan.

Shaping: To shape the tart dough, cut off and set aside about one fifth of the dough for the lattice that will go on top of the tart. Wrap it in plastic and put in the refrigerator while you roll out the dough for the tart pan. On a lightly floured work surface roll the rest of the tart dough into an 11-inch circle. Carefully fold it in half in order to slip it into the prepared tart pan. Trim any excess dough and save it.

To make the filling: Grind the almonds to a powder in small batches using a blender or a nut grinder. You will get a completely different texture if you use the processor, but should that be your only option, place 2 tablespoons of the sugar used in the filling into the bowl with the almonds and pulse until the almonds are ground. Put the remaining sugar and lemon juice in a 3-quart saucepan, preferably one with a non-stick coating, over medium heat and when the sugar has dissolved in the lemon juice, add the lemon zest, ground almonds, chocolate, and candied peel. Stir the mixture over low heat until it is well mixed but still moist. You must use this filling while it is warm and spreadable. If you set it aside to reheat later, it will thicken and you may need to add warm water before being able to spread it in the tart shell.

Spread the filling over the dough, being sure that it reaches no higher than the edge of the tart shell. Roll out the remaining dough and any scraps to an 11-inch square. Use a ravioli or pizza cutter to cut it into ten 1-inch-wide strips. Moisten the dough on the rim of the tart pan with water and attach five strips in each direction, pressing the edges of the strips lightly onto the rim and forming a diagonal lattice. Trim the edges of the dough so they are even with the top of the pan.

Bake the tart for 35 to 40 minutes and the tartlets 22 to 25 minutes, until the crust and lattice are golden.

Torta di Mele Friulana

Apple, Raisin, and Walnut Tart from Friuli

—

Serves 6 to 8

$\mathcal{G}$ ianna Modotti grew up with her grandparents in the Carnia mountains of Friuli, although she has lived most of her life in Udine, the largest city in the region. She went to the Scuola Istituto di Economia Domestica and completed all the courses required for a regular university degree plus others in gastronomy. Her passion for cooking is unquenchable, her knowledge is remarkable, and her recipes are impeccable.

This walnut- and raisin-studded apple tart is a perfect example. Simple and straightforward to make, it is the quintessence of a delicious Italian equivalent of apple pie.

DOUGH

    1¾ cups plus 2 tablespoons (9 ounces) all-purpose flour

    ¼ cup (2 scant ounces) sugar

    1½ teaspoons baking powder

    A pinch of salt

    1 stick plus 3 tablespoons (5 ounces) unsalted butter, room temperature

    1 egg

    4 teaspoons rum

    1 teaspoon vanilla extract

    4 teaspoons water

FILLING

    2 tablespoons raisins

    1 tablespoon rum

    3 medium (about 1 pound) Golden Delicious apples

    ¼ cup finely chopped walnuts or dry bread crumbs

    Grated zest of 1 lemon

    ¼ cup (2 scant ounces) sugar

    ½ teaspoon cinnamon

    Confectioners' sugar for sprinkling

To make the dough by hand: Place the flour, sugar, baking powder, and salt in a bowl and stir to mix. Cut the butter into small pieces and cut it into the flour with two knives or rub it in with your fingers until the mixture resembles coarse meal. Slowly stir in the egg, mixing thoroughly. Then stir in the rum, vanilla, and water. Gather the dough together and knead it briefly. Flatten and wrap in plastic wrap, and refrigerate for at least 1 hour. Let the dough come to room temperature when you are ready to use it.

By heavy-duty electric mixer: To make the dough in a heavy-duty mixer, cream the butter and sugar in a mixer bowl with the paddle until pale and creamy. Add the egg, rum, vanilla, and water, one at a time, mixing thoroughly after each addition. Add the flour, baking powder, and salt and mix until the dough comes together and is consistent. Gather the dough together and knead it briefly. Flatten and wrap in plastic wrap, and refrigerate for at least 1 hour. Let the dough come to room temperature when you are ready to use it.

Preheat the oven to 350°F. Butter a 9-inch baking pan, preferably a square one with a detachable bottom.

To make the filling: While the dough is resting, set the raisins in a small bowl, pour the rum over them, and steep for at least 30 minutes. Toast the walnuts in the 350°F. oven for 10 to 12 minutes. Peel the apples and grate them with a grater or the grating disk of a food processor. Put the apples in a large bowl and mix in the walnuts, raisins and rum, lemon zest, sugar, and cinnamon.

Set the dough on a lightly floured work surface, and divide it in half. Roll each piece to a 10- or 11-inch square. If the dough feels soft or starts to tear, enclose it between two largish pieces of plastic wrap to roll it. Don't worry, however, because the dough is very forgiving and is easily pressed out and patched right in the pan.

Line the prepared pan with the first piece of dough so it covers the bottom and drapes over the sides. Spread the filling evenly over the dough. Cover with the second piece of dough, pinch the edges together, and prick the top with a fork.

Baking: Set the pan on the lower or middle rack of the 350°F. oven and bake for 45 minutes, or until golden. Remove to a rack for 20 to 30 minutes. Cut the torte in squares and sprinkle with confectioners' sugar. Serve warm or at room temperature.

TORTA DELLA NONNA

Grandmother's Tart

—

Serves 8

*E*veryone in Italy knows that a torta della nonna is a two-crusted pie filled with pastry cream and decorated with a few pine nuts sprinkled over the top. Lisa Contini Bonacossi, a nonna with thirteen grandchildren of her own, has dreamed up a dazzling alternative to tradition by adding ricotta to the filling to make it softer, putting the pine nuts inside instead of on the top, and flavoring it all with the Vin Santo that she makes in her vineyard. One taste and everyone wants to be adopted. Lisa used to make a cake every day for her seven children when they came home from school. She gave each cake a different name, but the children finally figured out that they were all the same cake, changed only by what she put inside—ricotta one day, jam another. The whole family now lives at the Capezzana winery, which is the oldest property in Tuscany that has been in continual rental. The first lease was signed in 804 under the reign of Charlemagne! Now the members of three generations gather daily around the table in the light-filled dining room, which was once the stable, eating under the spell and the care of a remarkable nonna.

To make the recipe in steps: The pasta frolla dough is very buttery, so it must be well chilled. Best results come with rolling it out between pieces of plastic wrap. The dough can be made a day ahead, wrapped, and refrigerated for several days or frozen for up to a month.

The pastry cream can also be made a day ahead. Cover and refrigerate until you are ready to assemble the torta.

PASTA FROLLA

    12 tablespoons (1½ sticks, 6 ounces) unsalted butter, room temperature

    ¾ cup (5 ounces) sugar

    1 egg

    1 egg yolk

    1 teaspoon vanilla extract

    2 cups (10 ounces) all-purpose flour

A pinch of salt

Zest of 1 orange

PASTRY CREAM

2 cups milk

¾ cup (5 ounces) sugar

Zest of 1 lemon, in thin strips

3 egg yolks

A pinch of salt

4 tablespoons (1¼ ounces) all-purpose flour

1½ teaspoons vanilla extract

FILLING

2½ cups (1⅓ pounds) ricotta, drained

All the pastry cream (see above)

⅓ cup (2 scant ounces) pine nuts, chopped

½ cup (2 scant ounces) walnuts, toasted for 10 minutes in a 350°F. oven,
and chopped

3 to 3½ tablespoons Vin Santo (optional, but highly recommended;
if unavailable, you may substitute rum)

Confectioners' sugar for sprinkling

To make the dough by heavy-duty electric mixer: Beat the butter until it is soft and then beat in the sugar in a steady stream. Continue beating until the mixture lightens. Add the egg and the egg yolk one at a time, beating until the mixture is very smooth. Stir in the vanilla. Mix the flour and salt together and grate the zest from the orange right over the top. Beat into the butter and sugar mixture only until absorbed, being careful not to overmix. Flatten into a disk, wrap in plastic wrap, and let rest in the refrigerator for at least 1 hour.

By hand: Work the butter in your hands until it is very malleable and place in a bowl. Beat in the sugar. Add the egg and egg yolk and then the vanilla. Grate the zest from the orange over the top. Add the flour and salt and bring the dough together. Flatten into a disk, wrap in plastic, and let rest in the refrigerator for at least 1 hour.

To make the pastry cream: Slowly bring the milk and half the sugar to a boil in a nonreactive pan; add the lemon zest. In a separate bowl, beat together the egg yolks, the remaining sugar, and a pinch of salt until thick but still golden. Sift the flour directly into the egg and sugar mixture and then whisk it in well to prevent any lumps from forming. Whisk ½ cup of the hot milk into the egg mixture, then stir the rest of the egg mixture into the milk. Continue whisking over medium heat until it thickens, about 2 to 3 minutes. When it comes to a boil, whisk immediately to smooth it, reduce the heat, and stir for 1 minute. Remove from the heat and discard the lemon zest. Stir in the vanilla extract. Pour the pastry cream into a heatproof glass or stainless-steel bowl and press plastic wrap directly against the surface of the cream. Chill immediately in the refrigerator.

Preheat the oven to 375°F. Butter and flour a deep 9½- or 10-inch springform pan, preferably one with a nonstick surface.

To make the filling: Press the ricotta through a wire-mesh sieve into the bowl of a heavy-duty electric mixer, being sure to discard any liquid. Little by little add the chilled pastry cream and mix in well using the paddle attachment. Stir in the nuts and the Vin Santo.

Divide the chilled dough in two pieces, one twice the size of the other. On a lightly floured work surface, roll the first piece into a 13-inch circle. To do this, it is easiest to roll the dough into about an 8-inch circle, then cut a large piece of plastic wrap, and flour it lightly. Set the circle of dough on the plastic wrap, flour it lightly, and cover it with a second piece of plastic wrap. Now, continue rolling the dough into a 13-inch circle. Carefully peel the dough off one side of the plastic wrap, drape it over your rolling pin, and lower it into the prepared springform pan to line it. If some of the dough breaks, do not worry. The dough is very forgiving and is easily patched. Press the dough with your fingertips evenly over the bottom and up the sides almost to the top of the pan. Pour in the filling. Using the same system with the plastic wrap, roll out the second piece of dough to a 10½-inch circle and carefully lower it over the filling. Trim the overhanging dough, press the two edges together, and crimp decoratively, sealing the edges. Prick the top crust with a fork to allow the steam to escape (Lisa Contini Bonacossi uses a *fumaiolo*, a little tube set under the top crust, to do the same thing).

Baking: Bake until the top is golden, about 1 hour. The center will still be a bit jiggly, but a tester will come out clean. It is important not to overbake the torta or the filling will become watery and soak through the bottom crust. Turn the oven off with the cake inside and leave the door ajar for 10 minutes. Sprinkle the surface with confectioners' sugar as soon as it comes out of the oven. Cool on a rack. This cake is so delicious served slightly warm that I urge you to bake it 2 or 3 hours before serving.

PASTATELLA

Almond, Chocolate, and Orange Tarts

—

Makes 14 (4-inch) tarts or 6 (4-inch) tarts and 1 (8-inch) tart

*M*arzia Buontempo in Ururi has loved eating pastatella all her life—who could blame her?—but she only succeeded in wresting the recipe from her cousin, who had sole possession for years, when the woman finally announced that she'd given up baking. The recipe for the tart with its orange-flavored chocolate filling has been secretly guarded by generations of her mother's family.

This is an excellent dessert for the holidays because it keeps so well and because it is best made in advance. You must make the filling several hours ahead on the day you are baking or, preferably, the evening before. You can make the pasta frolla at least 1 hour before you plan to bake, but it keeps 1 day in the refrigerator and a month in the freezer.

FILLING

    2 scant cups (9 ounces) chopped toasted raw almonds

    1¼ cups (9 ounces) sugar

    1 whole egg plus 1 egg yolk, beaten together in a small bowl

    3½ ounces semisweet chocolate, grated or shaved

    ¾ cup (3½ ounces) finely chopped candied orange or citron peel

    1 tablespoon unsweetened cocoa

    About 5 tablespoons tepid water

    5 egg whites, room temperature

    A pinch of salt

PASTA FROLLA

    2 cups (10 ounces) all-purpose flour

    ⅓ cup (2½ ounces) sugar

    ½ teaspoon baking powder

    A pinch of salt

    5 tablespoons (2½ ounces) unsalted butter, room temperature

    2 eggs

    ½ teaspoon vanilla extract

    Grated zest of 1 lemon

(continued)

To make the filling: At least 6 hours before you plan to bake, but preferably the night before, grind the almonds and sugar in a nut grinder or a food processor and process until the mixture is a fine powder. Move it to a large mixing bowl and stir in the egg and yolk. Mix in the chocolate, candied peel, and cocoa. Stir in just enough water to make a smooth thick batter. The mixture should be creamy but not liquid. You will not need the egg whites and the salt until the last minute of preparation, but be sure the whites are at room temperature.

To make the pasta frolla: Blend the flour, sugar, baking powder, and salt in a bowl. Using a pastry cutter or your fingertips, cut or blend in the butter until you have the consistency of coarse meal. Add the eggs, then the vanilla. Sprinkle the lemon zest over the top and bring the dough together. Flatten into a disk, wrap in plastic wrap, and rest in the refrigerator for at least 1 hour.

Preheat the oven to 425°F. Prepare fourteen 4-inch fluted tart shell forms with removable bottoms, or six 4-inch fluted tart shell forms and one 8-inch tart form, by brushing them with butter or oil.

Divide the dough in half and cover the half you are not using. Roll the dough on a lightly floured work surface to an 11-inch square that is about ⅛ to ¼ inch thick. Cut the dough with a 5-inch cookie cutter and put each dough circle into one of the fluted 4-inch forms. Repeat with the second piece of dough or use some for the 8-inch tart form. Reroll the scraps and use all the dough.

Just before you are ready to put the filling into the forms, beat the 5 egg whites with the pinch of salt until they are stiff and add to the filling mixture.

Fill the prepared forms two-thirds full with the filling.

Baking: Bake for about 25 minutes until the pastry and the filling are brown and a toothpick inserted into the filling comes out smooth.

Torta di Riso

Rice Pudding

—

Serves 8 to 10

$\mathcal{R}$ice pudding is home cooking at its most evocative, a dessert made by generations of grandmothers like Vittoria Genovese in the tiny Ligurian town of Nicola. The
top is pale golden, its interior fragrant with the flavor of lemon and a hint of rum. As
it cooks, the pudding separates so that the rice sinks to the bottom and a creamy layer
of custard rises to the top. It is best served at room temperature, still warm from the
oven. If you must refrigerate it, reheat it in a 325°F. oven for 20 minutes before serving.

If you can find it, please use the short-grain Italian rice called originario to produce the right creamy texture, although Arborio will work too. You can cook the rice
ahead and make the rest of the pudding when you are ready.

4¼ cups water
½ cup (3½ ounces) short-grain Italian rice
10 eggs, room temperature
2 cups (14 ounces) sugar
4 to 5 tablespoons rum or Sambuca
4¼ cups milk
1 tablespoon grated lemon zest
1 teaspoon vanilla extract
A pinch of salt
1 tablespoon unsalted butter for the baking dish

Heat the water and rice to a gentle simmer in a medium-size heavy saucepan. Reduce
the heat to low, cover tightly, and cook for about 10 to 15 minutes, until the rice is
barely tender, still a bit al dente, because it will cook more in the final cooking. Drain,
set aside, and cool to room temperature.

Preheat the oven to 350°F. Butter a 10-inch soufflé or baking dish.

Beat the eggs and sugar together only until the sugar has dissolved. Vittoria says
the real secret of this rice pudding is that the eggs and sugar should be creamy but not

frothy or foamy. Stir in the rum, then the milk, lemon zest, vanilla, and salt, always being careful to fold them in gently. Carefully add the rice to the egg mixture.

Ladle the rice mixture into the prepared baking dish carefully. Stir it around; some rice will sink to the bottom.

Bake for 1 hour and 20 minutes to 1 hour and 25 minutes, until the pudding shrinks away from the sides of the dish and a tester comes out clean. The pudding still shakes a bit, but don't worry; it will set as it cools.

TIMBALLO DI RICOTTA

Lemon-Flavored Ricotta Cake

—

Serves 6

*S*omewhere between a cake and a pudding, this dessert from Le Marche is distinguished by the lemon glaze that is poured over the top just before it is served. Do not be alarmed that the cake shrinks away from the sides of the cake pan as it cools or that it falls, losing almost half its height before your very eyes. I assure you it will lose none of its delicate and creamy lemon-infused flavor.

> Unsalted butter and fine dry bread crumbs for lining the pan
> 3 eggs, separated
> ¾ cup (5 ounces) sugar
> 4¼ cups (2 pounds) fresh ricotta cheese, drained
> ¼ cup rum
> 3 tablespoons all-purpose flour
> Grated zest of 1 lemon
> 1 teaspoon vanilla extract
> A pinch of salt

GLAZE
> ¼ cup lemon juice
> 2 tablespoons sugar

Preheat the oven to 350°F. Thoroughly butter a 1½-quart soufflé dish or leakproof 9-inch springform pan and coat the interior with fine bread crumbs.

Beat the yolks with the sugar until light, creamy, and lemon-colored. Process the ricotta with several pulses in a food processor until smooth, whirl in a blender, or press it through a wire-mesh sieve into the bowl with the egg mixture. Mix them together well until they are smooth. Stir in the rum, flour, lemon zest, and vanilla, and blend them in well. Beat the egg whites and salt in a separate bowl until the soft peaks are formed, then fold them carefully into the egg mixture with a rubber spatula.

Spoon the mixture into the prepared baking dish. Smooth the top with a rubber spatula. Bake until the top is golden, although the cake will be slightly jiggly when you lightly shake the baking dish, about 1 hour to 1 hour and 15 minutes. Let it cool for 5 minutes.

Meanwhile make the glaze by mixing together the lemon juice and sugar until the sugar dissolves. Spoon 2 or 3 tablespoons over the top of the cake, wait 5 minutes, and spoon as much over again. Serve with a little of the topping spooned over each slice of cake.

TORTA DI CILIEGE

Cake Covered with Cherries

—

Serves 8

This cake is as easy to make as it is delicious to eat. It starts with a simple batter over which you must scatter handfuls of cherries and then watch half of them slowly sink into the interior, creating a rustic sweet that is at home at brunch, lunch, or a supper. Gianna Modotti uses dark cherries from the Veneto or from Friuli, where she lives, and you should find the meatiest dark ripe red cherries you can. Use a deep baking pan because the dough rises up over the top of a standard tart pan.

(continued)

1 stick plus 3 tablespoons (5 ounces) unsalted butter, room temperature

¾ cup (5 ounces) sugar

3 eggs, room temperature, separated

3 tablespoons milk

1 teaspoon vanilla extract

1 cup plus 2 teaspoons (5 ounces) all-purpose flour

1½ teaspoons baking powder

A pinch of salt

1 pound meaty ripe red cherries, pitted

2 to 4 tablespoons sugar, depending on the sweetness of the fruit

Preheat the oven to 350°F. Butter and flour a deep 9½-inch tart pan or springform pan.

Cream the butter and sugar by hand or by electric mixer until they are light and fluffy, about 5 minutes. Add the egg yolks one at a time, beating thoroughly after each addition. Stir in the milk and the vanilla. Mix together the flour and baking powder and sift them directly into the bowl. Finally, beat the egg whites and a pinch of salt until they stand in soft peaks. Stir a quarter of the egg whites into the butter and sugar mixture, then carefully fold in the rest.

Spread the dough into the prepared pan. It will come halfway up the sides. Combine the cherries and sugar and sprinkle them over the top.

Bake for 50 to 60 minutes, until the top is golden and a knife inserted comes out clean. You will probably need to test in more than one place in case you hit a cherry. Cool in the pan for 15 to 30 minutes, then unmold onto a rack to cool completely.

TORTA SBRISOLONA

Crumbly Cornmeal Cake from Mantua

—

Serves 6

*T*his delicate dessert from Mantua is a cake like no other. The light crunch of cornmeal, the hint of lemon, the flavor of almond all combine to create a rich, slightly
crumbly textured dolce. Luisa Cappelli may be from Tuscany, but she is more than
willing to cross regional lines to make this for family and friends. The secret of its success lies in the unusual sequence of combining the ingredients. Do not be afraid of
using your hands as you mix; it is important that the dough be barely and gently
brought together.

> 1 cup (7 ounces) sugar
>
> A pinch of salt
>
> Grated zest of 2 large lemons
>
> 1 teaspoon vanilla extract
>
> 2 eggs
>
> 1 stick plus 7 tablespoons (7 ounces) unsalted butter, room temperature
>
> 1¾ cups (8½ ounces) all-purpose flour
>
> ¾ cup plus 2 tablespoons (4 ounces) stoneground cornmeal or polenta
>
> 1 cup plus 1 tablespoon (4 ounces) fine-grind cornmeal
>
> 1⅓ cups (7 ounces) raw almonds, coarsely chopped
>
> 2 tablespoons turbinado sugar

Preheat the oven to 350°F. with the rack on the middle shelf. Butter and lightly flour a
9-inch square cake pan.

Put the sugar in a large bowl and make a well in the center. Add the salt and
grated lemon zest. Beat the vanilla and eggs together and whisk them in, mixing well.
Begin adding the butter, a small piece at a time, mixing in each piece before you add
the next. In a separate bowl combine the flour and cornmeals and then start adding
them to the sugar mixture, first mixing them in with a rubber spatula and then, about
halfway through, with your hands. Add the chopped almonds to the crumbly mixture,

working them into the light granular dough with your hands. Be careful not to press too firmly. Don't even try to use a mixer because it will ruin the texture.

Drop the mixture into the prepared pan in clumps. Use the palms of your hands to even the top. Sprinkle the turbinado sugar over the top.

Bake for about 30 to 40 minutes, being careful not to open the oven door before the time is over. To be sure that it is done, test that a toothpick comes out clean. You may need to bake it slightly longer. Do not take the pan out of the oven. Pull out the oven shelf and use a knife to cut the cake immediately in rhomboids or in long narrow strips. Cut slowly because you are likely to hit an almond or two on your way. Or you could be truly authentic and "cut" the cake in the traditional way by banging on the middle with the side of your fist and letting the cake fall into crumbly bites.

Let the cut sbrisolona sit at room temperature for an hour before serving.

Torta della Zucca

Pumpkin Tart

—

Serves 8

Everyone who has tasted this delicious pumpkin pudding cake wants more, but no one, not a single person among them, has ever guessed that mixing butternut squash with apple, dark rich cocoa, and cookie crumbs is the source of its tantalizing creamy taste. After eating a slice or two, however, they are all believers.

Signora Vitali pulverizes the cookies with a rolling pin, although a food processor does an equally good job. She specifically calls for a Reinette apple with its matte russeted skin; if you can't find one, use a fragrant Fuji or Gala.

The torta della zucca is a perfect example of an entrancing dessert made of absolutely simple ingredients. Serve it for Thanksgiving, if you want to give a slightly Italian inflection to the archetypal American day, but don't let that keep you from baking it for almost any other meal in your life.

2¼ pounds butternut squash or pumpkin

1⅓ cups milk

A pinch of salt

2 cups (7 ounces) crumbled amaretti

9 (3½ ounces) Marie biscuits or any simple cookies, crushed

1 egg, lightly beaten

2 tablespoons sugar

Grated zest 1 lemon

3 tablespoons cocoa

1 apple, peeled, cored, and grated

1 tablespoon unsalted butter

Preheat the oven to 400°F. Set the rack in the middle level of the oven. Butter a 10-inch springform or tart pan with a removable bottom.

Peel the butternut squash, remove the seeds, and cut the pulp into thin slices. Put them in a 9- or 10-inch baking pan, cover with the milk and a pinch of salt, and place it in the oven. Cook, mashing the squash from time to time with a spoon, until they are easily pierced with a fork. Bubbles appear in the milk and it becomes thick; continue cooking until the milk is almost absorbed, about 1 hour.

Puree the squash in a food processor or press through a ricer or sieve. Place in a large bowl and stir in 1⅔ cups of the amaretti and all the crushed Marie biscuits to incorporate them well. Add the egg, sugar, and grated lemon zest and mix well. At the end, sift in the cocoa, and finally stir in the grated apple. Mix the ingredients together to form a thick batter. Pour into the prepared pan. Distribute small flakes of butter over the top and sprinkle with the ⅓ cup reserved amaretti crumbs.

Bake for about 1 hour and 10 minutes to 1 hour and 20 minutes, until the torta pulls away from the sides of the pan and a skewer comes out almost entirely clean. Serve warm or at room temperature.

BENSONE

Crumbly Coffee Cake from Modena

Serves 8

*I*talians indulge their fierce love of sweets in any number of ways—notice how many spoonfuls of sugar they heap into tiny cups of espresso—but they also have a real passion for simple homemade cakes like bensone, a traditional dessert that crumbles in the fingers and melts in the mouth. This simple S-shaped cake is not overly sweet, but it is easy to make and easy to eat.

DOUGH

> 3 scant cups (14 ounces) all-purpose or pastry flour, plus extra for kneading
>
> ¾ teaspoon baking powder
>
> ¾ teaspoon baking soda
>
> ¾ cup (5 ounces) sugar
>
> A pinch of salt
>
> Grated zest of 1 lemon
>
> 7 tablespoons (3½ ounces) unsalted butter, room temperature, cut into small pieces
>
> 2 eggs, room temperature
>
> 6 tablespoons milk
>
> 1 teaspoon vanilla extract
>
> 2 tablespoons unsalted butter for the baking sheets

GLAZE

> ¼ cup milk
>
> 2 tablespoons turbinado or raw sugar

Preheat the oven to 350°F. You will need two 13 × 17-inch baking sheets and two pieces of parchment paper.

Sift the flour, baking powder, baking soda, and sugar together into a large ceramic or glass bowl. Stir in the grated lemon zest. Scatter the pieces of butter over the top and rub them in with your hands a bit at a time until the mixture has the texture of coarse cornmeal. Mix together the eggs, milk, and vanilla, make a well in the center of the dry ingredients, and pour them in, mixing gently until a dough is formed. Knead the dough lightly in the bowl, adding sprinkles of flour as needed, and mix until it is smooth and very soft. You can make the dough and refrigerate it up to 24 hours before baking.

Divide the dough into two equal pieces on a lightly floured work surface. Roll each into a cylinder that is about 2 inches wide and 18 inches long. Flatten the surface and neaten the edges. Set a piece of parchment paper on each of the baking sheets, warm them for about 1 minute in the oven, and then rub a tablespoon of butter on each piece of parchment. Set a log of dough on the center of each baking sheet, twist it into an S shape, and use a sharp knife to make three parallel cuts on the top of the dough. Finish by brushing the surface of each one first with the milk and then sprinkling the turbinado sugar over the top.

Set the baking sheets on the middle shelf of the oven and bake for 25 to 30 minutes, until the top of the bensone is golden and a toothpick comes out clean. Be careful not to overbake. Transfer to a rack. Slice and serve warm or at room temperature with a sweet wine, such as Lambrusco Amabile or Moscato d'Asti, or with coffee as a mid-afternoon merenda.

TOZZETTI

Raisin- and Nut-Studded Biscotti

—

Makes 6 dozen biscotti

*I*t is hard to believe these delicious tozzetti began life as a Lenten dessert, compensation, perhaps, for deprivation in the dark winter months before the arrival of spring. Tozzetti may be as squat and stubby as their name suggests, but a single bite of the orange-flavored cookies and you'll be astonished by their tantalizing elegance. Nella Galletti, her daughter, and her granddaughter in Todi all make the cookies, which disappear in a flash. Six dozen? A mere nothing. Be warned. They are hard to resist.

> ⅓ cup (scant 2 ounces) dark raisins
>
> 1 tablespoon curaçao or cognac
>
> About 2¾ cups (14 ounces) all-purpose flour
>
> 1 cup (7 ounces) sugar
>
> 1½ teaspoons baking powder
>
> ¼ teaspoon salt
>
> 5½ tablespoons (3 ounces) unsalted butter or best-quality lard,
>   or half of each, room temperature
>
> 3 egg yolks
>
> ¾ cup milk
>
> 2 tablespoons pine nuts
>
> 2 tablespoons chopped candied orange peel
>
> ½ scant cup (2 scant ounces) raw almonds, toasted in a 350°F. oven
>   for 10 minutes, and roughly chopped
>
> ¼ teaspoon aniseeds

EGG WASH

> 1 egg beaten with a little water

Soak the raisins in the curaçao or cognac for 30 minutes. Squeeze the raisins and drain, reserving the liquid.

Preheat the oven to 350°F. Lightly grease and flour 2 baking sheets.

To make the tozzetti by hand: Sift together the flour, sugar, baking powder, and salt into a large mixing bowl. With your fingers, rub in the butter until the mixture has the texture of coarse cornmeal. Make a well in the center. Beat together the egg yolks, the reserved liqueur, and the milk and pour them into the well. Gradually draw the dry ingredients into the egg mixture, turning the bowl and working from the outside toward the center. When the dough is evenly mixed, scrape it onto a lightly floured work surface and flatten it into a rectangle. Scatter half the raisins, pine nuts, candied fruit, and almonds over the dough, sprinkle on half the aniseeds, and fold the dough over on itself several times to distribute them evenly. Very lightly flour the work surface so the dough won't stick, and repeat the process by sprinkling the remaining raisins, nuts, candied peel, and aniseeds over the top.

By heavy-duty electric mixer: Combine the flour, baking powder, and salt and set aside. In the mixer bowl cream the butter and sugar and beat for about 3 minutes until the mixture is light and creamy. Add the egg yolks one at a time, waiting until each is incorporated before adding the next. Stir in the liqueur and milk. Sift the flour mixture over the top and incorporate it at the lowest speed. Add the rest of the ingredients by hand.

Shaping: Lightly flour both the work surface and your hands and divide the dough into six equal pieces. Shape each into a 9×2-inch log. If the dough is too soft to roll, cover and refrigerate it for 1 to 2 hours. Transfer the logs to the prepared cookie sheets, setting them at least 2 inches apart. Flatten the tops to even them and brush them with the beaten egg.

Baking: Bake until pale golden and barely firm, about 20 minutes. Remove the logs from the pan, let them cool until they are comfortable to handle, about 10 minutes, then cut each one on the diagonal at ½-inch intervals. Set the slices in a standing position on the cookie sheets, leaving ¼-inch space between them, and bake until they are deeply golden and firm, about 15 to 18 minutes. You may also lay them on their sides and turn them after 7 minutes. Cool on a rack.

DOLCE DI MANDORLE

Almond Cookies Wrapped Around a Wild Cherry

—

Makes 3 dozen cookies

*N*o one has ever eaten just one of these cookies, says Marzia Buontempo, a phenomenal home baker who now makes wedding cakes and all manner of sweets for brides and grooms where she lives in Molise. The combination of tastes—the tiny crunch of the almonds and the startlingly wild taste of the cherries—makes peoples' eyes fly open in amazement as their hands reach for another. And another. The cookies are as easy to make as she assured me they would be, certain that I could whip them up by myself in no time. Anyway, she shrugged, "*Tanti occhi non vengono bene*—Too many cooks spoil the broth," or, in this case, the cookies.

> 2 egg whites
> ¾ cup plus 2 tablespoons (6 ounces) sugar
> 2⅓ cups (12½ ounces) blanched almonds
> ½ teaspoon cinnamon
> Grated zest of 1 lemon
> 2 teaspoons rum, crème de cacao, or Sambuca
> 36 amarena cherries (See Source Guide to Ingredients)
> About 1 cup confectioners' sugar

Preheat the oven to 300°F. Prepare 2 parchment paper–lined baking sheets.

Beat the egg whites in a mixer bowl until soft peaks are formed. Continue beating, gradually adding ¾ cup of the sugar until the peaks are stiff and glossy. Grind the almonds with the remaining 2 tablespoons of sugar in the food processor until they are like fine crumbs. Fold the nuts into the egg white mixture, then stir in the cinnamon, lemon zest, and rum.

Place a bowl of cold water nearby in which to dip your hands. Pinch off a piece of the dough about the size of a walnut. Moisten your hands and then roll the dough into a ball. Flatten the ball in one hand, place a cherry in the center, and roll the dough to cover it completely. Sift the confectioners' sugar onto a dinner plate and roll the ball in it to cover. Repeat with the rest of the dough and cherries. Place about 1½ inches apart on the prepared baking sheets.

Bake for about 30 to 35 minutes, until the cookies are pale brown but firm when tested with a fingernail and still very slightly soft inside.

SPUMICINI

Almond-Flavored Meringue Cookies
—

Makes 16 to 18 (2½-inch) cookies or 80 little cookies baked in petit four cups

*M*aria Andriani started making these phenomenal lemon-flavored almond cookies to use up leftover egg whites, but the results are much greater than the inspiration would imply. They are more than a delicious twist on traditional meringues and they are certainly more than compensation for a surfeit of egg whites. I prefer baking lots of tiny cookies in petit four cups, but Maria makes fewer and larger ones in muffin papers.

9 ounces blanched almonds; 3 cups when ground
1¼ cups (9 ounces) superfine sugar
Grated zest of 1 lemon
6 egg whites
A pinch of salt

Preheat the oven to 300°F.

Use a nut grinder, coffee grinder, or blender to grind the almonds to a fine flour. You may also grind the almonds in a food processor with 2 tablespoons of the sugar. Transfer them to a large bowl, add the sugar and the grated lemon zest, and mix in well. Beat the egg whites to stiff peaks with a pinch of salt and fold into the almond mixture.

Spoon 1 teaspoon of the dough into petit four cups or fill 2½-inch paper muffin cups with the mixture and set them on baking sheets.

Bake until the tops are set and are lightly browned, about 30 minutes for the smaller size or 40 to 45 minutes for the larger ones.

Maria Andriani talks about La Badessa, which was once the largest landholding in Apulia, with conflicting emotions. Maria was born in a nearby agricultural village, but she really grew up at La Badessa, when the estate belonged to the Neapolitan Conte Caracciolo di Forino and his French wife. When Maria arrived just after the war, its immensity so amazed her that she thought it must be a village.

At first Maria came during the day to do the laundry, arriving with her cousin, Nicolino, who brought her on the handlebars of his bicycle, even when the ground was carpeted with snow. Her mother was a laundress who also worked in the fields, her father an invalid with tuberculosis. As soon as they saw that their children were old enough to work, they sent the sons to factories in Germany and Maria and her older sister, although totally untrained, were consigned to La Badessa. It wasn't long until her sister left to study with the nuns, leaving Maria, a small scrawny girl, on her own. It was the first time she had lived in a room by herself, the first time she had slept in a bed by herself, and the first time she was totally without family, but she was determined to succeed.

She remembers the death of the Conte, whose funeral included a procession with two horses, one black and one white, and his faithful dog. She also remembers that Nicolino, who is slightly older than she, wore short pants until the Conte persuaded him to exchange them for the trousers of a man. Nicolino was three years younger than François, the son and heir of the count, who married a beautiful young woman from New York in 1955, the year before Maria married Nicolino. François immediately moved to La Badessa with his exquisite and intelligent wife, Shirley, who resembled a Henry James heroine suddenly transposed to this remote property deep in the heel of the Italian boot.

Like a feudal village, La Badessa was almost self-sufficient. The staff, made up of four or five families, included a man who took care of the sheep and cows and another who looked after the large stable of horses. There was a carpenter as well as a seamstress, gardener, and cook. From the milk of the cows and sheep they made cream, sour cream, and cheese, and they spun the wool of the sheep into yarns that became blankets and capes and coats. Maria and Nicolino helped to harvest the olives, which were made into enough oil to last the year.

The Austrian governess who had raised the Caracciolo children was in charge of the kitchen. Cold and demanding, "worse than a wartime soldier," she commanded Maria to prepare all the ingredients and whenever anything went wrong, pointed the finger of blame at her. When the governess finally left, Maria was on her own. She learned to cook from the Contessa, who taught her French and Austrian recipes, from which she had first removed every trace of garlic and onion. Imagine food in southern Italy without garlic or onion! The tiny girl would move huge pots around on an enormous tiled stove with brass knobs and stick her hand in the oven to measure its heat. She made 30 to 40 pounds of jam at a time. She cooked meals for so many people who came to dinner that when the Caracciolo family left La Badessa in 1962, she and Nicolino were besieged with offers to work as a couple.

In the ensuing years, Maria, the gracious and elegant-looking gray-haired woman who greeted me in Squinzano, near Lecce, not far from La Badessa, had become a mother and grandmother. She and Nicolino built their spacious house two rooms at a time, and it is now as warm and welcoming as they are. The kitchen in which Maria performs her alchemy has all the equipment a cook could want, and the dining room, with beautiful cabinets full of china and silver, seats eight comfortably. In the garden lemons and oranges thrive along with more exotic citrus plants such as mandarancio and Chinese mandarin oranges, all of whose peels Maria candies for her baking. Herbs grow in profusion, ready to flavor her Apulian dishes.

Maria is a walking lexicon of local dishes. Amazingly, she had never cooked a single Apulian dish until she left La Badessa and was able to make these foods for her husband. I think that she must have cooked most of them for me.

Maria makes *cavatelli*, a typical Apulian pasta, and tosses it with broccoli rabe that has been sautéed on the side. She begins by rolling out a fine sheet of pasta dough made of half durum and half wheat flour kneaded with very warm water. From it she breaks off short pieces, about 2 inches long, rolls each one around a rod of metal the thickness of a fine knitting needle, then with a quick yank pulls it out, and *ecco!* small spirals of pasta with a fine hole in the center. When she makes ear-shaped orecchiette, she cooks them in the same water with the broccoli rabe to infuse them with the vegetable flavor, and while they bubble together, sautés garlic and anchovy fillets in olive oil in a small pan, tosses the drained pasta in the anchovy mixture, grates ricotta salata over the top, and then serves her extraordinary, immensely tasty version of Apulia's archetypal pasta.

Her meatballs are the size of walnuts and because she fries them in oil so hot it is almost smoking, they are done in seconds, bouncing as they cook and absorbing so little oil that they remain light and delicate. Her preserved eggplant, mushrooms, and artichokes have none of the raw, acidic taste of others I have tasted. The secret: bringing equal amounts of water and vinegar to a boil and plunging the vegetables in only very briefly before draining and then setting them aside to cool before covering them with oil.

If a native of Apulia were asked to name the typical dish of the region, there would be but one answer: the *tiella*, a lovely construction made of layers of mussels, yellow-fleshed potatoes, tomatoes, cheese, and sprinkled over the top of it all, the light crunch of rice, all baked in the broth of the mussels. Every nonna, I daresay every cook, in Apulia makes tiella. Maria's version is especially delicious and remarkably easy to make.

Maria and Nicolino are clearly devoted to each other. They take enormous pride in their attractive daughter, who lives nearby, and their very successful son, who lives with his wife and two children in Treviso, north of Venice. Maria remains devoted to the Caracciolos and still stays in touch with la Contessina, as she has always called François's bride. "They are like my second family," she said, remembering how much they brought to her life when they arrived at La Badessa forty years ago. Their affection was deeply important to her then and it remains so today, an ongoing relationship intimately woven into her memories and her life.

SOFFICINI PORTOGHESI

Delicate Butter Cookies alla "Portuguese"

—

Makes about 2 dozen cookies

Whenever her son and his family come to visit in Squinzano, near Lecce, deep in the south of Apulia, Maria Andriani makes these cookies for them to take back to their home in the north. A couple of years ago, when he still had the sealed tin with him, her son saw a sign for a dessert contest in Treviso. He walked in, surrendered the cookies, and they walked away with first prize. Maria was flattered but not surprised. Her friends have been asking for the recipe for years, but until now, she has never given it to anyone. "It's as secret as the formula for Coca-Cola," says her daughter.

6 tablespoons (2½ ounces) sugar

1 stick plus 1½ tablespoons (5 ounces) unsalted butter

2 egg yolks

Grated zest of 1 lemon

1½ scant cups (7 ounces) all-purpose flour

A pinch of salt

GLAZE

1 egg yolk beaten with 1 teaspoon water

Beat the sugar and butter together until they are light and fluffy, about 5 or 6 minutes with a handheld mixer or 4 or 5 minutes with a heavy-duty electric mixer. Beat in the egg yolks one at a time, incorporating one thoroughly before adding the next. Stir in the lemon zest and blend well until smooth. Sift the flour and salt together directly into the bowl and stir into the butter mixture until a dough is formed. Wrap the dough in plastic wrap and chill for 1 hour in the refrigerator.

Preheat the oven to 350°F. Prepare buttered or parchment paper–lined baking sheets.

Divide the dough in half and cover the portion you are not using. Place the dough on a lightly floured surface and roll it out into a ¼-inch-thick rectangle. Cut out disks with a 2½-inch cookie cutter. Repeat with the second piece of dough and then reroll the scraps. Don't worry if they seem ragged; this dough is very malleable and forgiving. Set the circles on the prepared baking sheets.

Brush the tops with the egg yolk glaze. Make a decorative pattern by drawing the tines of a fork across the top of the cookies in both directions.

Bake for about 15 minutes or until lightly golden.

Dolce per i Morti

"Day of the Dead" Cookies

—

Makes 5 to 6 dozen cookies

*O*ne glance at the ingredients that Marzia Buontempo uses to make these crispy spice- and chocolate-laced cookies makes it easy to guess that they come from an ancient tradition. Ammonium bicarbonate, a leavening that has the side effect of promoting dryness, gives the cookies an extra crunch. You can buy it at pharmacies and from a few mail-order suppliers; see the Source Guide to Ingredients at the back of the book. You can also use the equivalent quantities of baking powder and baking soda. I have substituted currant jelly for the saba Marzia uses (see page 418 if you want to make it yourself and the Source Guide if you want to order some). But I haven't done anything to take away from the tantalizing taste of the nut- and espresso-flavored cookies.

The cookies were always made for the Day of the Dead in the region of Molise. Be sure to take them out of the oven when they are still a bit soft because they harden at room temperature in no time.

> 3¾ cups (18 ounces) all-purpose flour
>
> ½ cup plus 1½ tablespoons (4½ ounces) sugar
>
> 2 teaspoons ammonium bicarbonate or 2 teaspoons baking powder
>   and 2 teaspoons baking soda
>
> 1 teaspoon cinnamon
>
> ½ teaspoon ground cloves
>
> Zest of 1 lemon
>
> Zest of 2 mandarin or navel oranges
>
> 1 scant cup (4½ ounces) blanched almonds, toasted in a 350°F. oven and
>   diced
>
> 3½ ounces fondant chocolate, shaved or grated
>
> ½ scant cup brewed espresso coffee, room temperature, sweetened with
>   1 tablespoon sugar
>
> 1 cup (about 10 ounces) currant jelly
>
> 2 to 3 tablespoons olive oil
>
> Confectioners' sugar for sifting

Preheat the oven to 350°F. Prepare 4 parchment paper–lined baking sheets.

Mix together the flour, sugar, ammonium bicarbonate, cinnamon, and cloves in a large bowl. Grate the lemon and orange zests directly into the mixture. Stir in the almonds and chocolate shavings. Mix in the coffee and the currant jelly and work them in well. If you don't mind using your hands, you'll see they are really helpful in combining the moist ingredients. Add the olive oil at the very end, starting with the smaller amount, stirring it in quickly, then adding more if necessary.

Since the dough may be sticky, keep a bowl of water nearby. Moisten your hands as you break off walnut-sized rounds of the dough, roll them into little balls, and set them about 1 inch apart on the prepared baking sheets. Flatten the balls a bit with the back of a moistened spoon and neaten the edges with your fingers.

Bake for about 15 minutes, until the cookies are firm but not hard and are only slightly browned at the edges. Sift confectioners' sugar over the tops immediately after you remove them from the oven. Cool on racks.

BISCOTTI DI PRATO

Biscotti from Prato

—

Makes 4 dozen biscotti

*L*isa Contini-Bonacossi lives at Capezzana, her family's great wine estate, with three generations in a large handsome house with an extra-ordinary view over the entire Tuscan valley where Carmignano wine is produced. She is half Venetian and half Tuscan, but admits *"mi sento più toscana"* ("I feel more Tuscan"). Her father's family tree hangs on one dining room wall. It includes almost every great Italian family and cur-rently has 480 members! Tintoretto painted an earlier family portrait.

Lisa Contini-Bonacossi

Lisa is a woman of many talents, not the least being her passion for cooking. Lucky are the family members who eat with her daily and lucky the students who learn to cook Tuscan food. Her biscotti di Prato are *eccessionale*. If you make them in a heavy-duty standing mixer, reserve 1 egg yolk until you have put the dough together. It may not be necessary.

3¾ cups (18 ounces) all-purpose flour

1½ cups (10 ounces) sugar

2⅛ teaspoons baking soda

2⅛ teaspoons baking powder

1 teaspoon sea salt

7 tablespoons (3½ ounces) unsalted butter, melted, room temperature

4 eggs

3 egg yolks

1 teaspoon vanilla extract

Grated zest of 2 oranges (1½ teaspoons)

Scant ⅞ cup (3½ ounces) whole raw almonds, toasted for 10 minutes in a
    350°F. oven and roughly chopped

GLAZE

1 egg yolk

Preheat the oven to 350° F. Butter and flour two baking sheets that are at least 15 inches long.

Combine the flour, sugar, baking soda, baking powder, and salt in a large mixing bowl and stir well to mix them. Use your fingers to rub in the cooled melted butter until the mixture has the texture of cornmeal. Whisk the eggs, egg yolks, and vanilla with the grated orange zest and gradually work them into the flour, mixing with your hands until you have a smooth dough. Knead in the almonds thoroughly, sprinkling with additional flour, if necessary. Do not overwork the dough or it will get tough.

Divide the dough into quarters. On a lightly floured surface roll each piece into a flat log that is 2 to 2½ inches wide and place the logs on the prepared baking sheets. Beat the egg yolk and brush over the tops of the dough.

Bake the logs for about 35 minutes, until they are golden and firm to the touch. Remove from the oven and reduce the temperature to 325°F. Remove the logs from the pans to racks to cool until they are comfortable to handle. When they are cool, use a sharp serrated knife to slice through the logs diagonally at ¾- to 1-inch intervals. Lay them, cut side up, on the baking sheets and return to the oven for another 10 to 15 minutes, depending on how crispy you like your biscotti. Cool on racks.

DISCHI

Jam Sandwich Cookies

Makes about 30 cookies

*T*hese charming sandwich-like cookies that are filled with jam are from Vasto in Abruzzo. Marzia Buontempo, who taught me how to make them, cuts them out with a drinking glass, the traditional implement found at home, although I prefer a cookie cutter. Marzia once made 330 pounds of them for a wedding, working night and day over the course of a week, and then taking them to the town's communal oven to bake after the bread had come out, when the temperature was just right for cookies.

It is important to roll the dough without any tears so the jam can't escape during the baking. If it does, simply sift a heavier veil of confectioners' sugar over the top.

> 3¾ cups (18 ounces) all-purpose flour
> 1½ teaspoons baking powder
> ¾ cup (5 ounces) sugar
> A pinch of salt
> 1¾ sticks (14 tablespoons) cold unsalted butter or 7 tablespoons cold
>   unsalted butter and 7 tablespoons cold best-quality lard
> 2 eggs
> 2 egg yolks
> 2 teaspoons vanilla extract
> 1 cup thick jam
>
> Confectioners' sugar for sprinkling

No nonna would use a food processor for making dough, but I do and you can, since it's so easy. Put the flour, baking powder, sugar, and salt in the processor fitted with the steel blade and process several times. Scatter chunks of the cold butter over the top and process until the mixture resembles coarse cornmeal. Mix together the eggs, egg yolks, and vanilla and pour down the feed tube with the motor running. Mix only until a rough dough is formed. Take out of the processor and knead briefly on a work surface.

Flatten into a thick disk, wrap in plastic wrap, and chill in the refrigerator for at least 1 hour.

Preheat the oven to 350°F. Prepare 2 or 3 greased or parchment paper–lined baking sheets.

Divide the dough in half and cover the part you are not using. Roll the dough on a lightly floured work surface to ⅛- to ¼-inch thickness. Be sure to roll in one direction only, starting from the middle of the dough and rolling to the edge, then return to the middle and roll toward the edge of the other half. Use a 3-inch cookie cutter to cut the disks from the dough. Save the scraps to reroll. Brush any excess flour from the bottom of the dough.

Dip a brush into water to wash the edges of the bottom disks. Put a scant tablespoon of jam in the center, leaving a 1-inch margin, cover with a second disk of dough as for a sandwich, and press the edges firmly together to close the cookies well. Set them 1½ inches apart on the prepared cookie sheets, because they spread in cooking. Repeat with the second portion of dough. Reroll the scraps left from both times and proceed as above.

Bake until the edges are golden, 10 to 12 minutes. Immediately sprinkle with confectioners' sugar. Move to a rack and let cool to room temperature.

MARZAPANE

Lemon-Spiked Almond Cookies

—

Makes 2½ to 3 dozen cookies

*L*emon and almond: an unbeatable combination from Maria Andriani. She has great tricks as well: use a bread knife instead of a rolling pin to press the sticky dough into a rectangle and moisten it with lemon juice so it won't stick to the dough.

If you can find parchment paper, you'll be happy that you have it when making the cookies. If you don't have any, remove the cookies from the oven and from the cookie sheets without any delay.

> 2 cups (10 ounces) blanched almonds
> Grated zest of ½ lemon
> ¾ teaspoon vanilla extract
> 2 egg whites
> 1 cup (7 ounces) sugar (or 14 tablespoons, if using a processor)

Preheat the oven to 350°F. Prepare 2 parchment paper–lined baking sheets.

Toast the almonds in the oven for 10 minutes, then set them aside to cool. Grind the almonds in a nut grinder, a meat grinder, or a blender; if you use a processor, add 2 tablespoons of the sugar to the processor bowl and grind only until the mixture is the consistency of coarse cornmeal. Transfer to a medium bowl and stir in the lemon zest and vanilla.

Beat the egg whites in a mixer bowl until they form soft peaks. Continue beating, gradually adding the sugar until the peaks are stiff and glossy. Set aside 2 tablespoons of this mixture. Gently mix the rest of the egg white mixture into the almonds.

Sprinkle a little flour on your work surface. If the mixture seems very sticky to work with, moisten your hands slightly and pat the dough into a rough rectangle. Using the half lemon whose zest went into the dough, squeeze some juice on both sides of a bread knife. Then use the knife almost as if it were a rolling pin and press out the sticky marzapane dough into a rectangle that is about 10 × 6 inches. The lemon juice keeps the knife from sticking, so use a bit more and cut the dough diagonally in 1-inch strips in each direction, forming diamonds or rhomboids. Squeeze a little more lemon juice on a spatula and use it to transfer the cookies to the prepared baking sheets. Spread a little of the reserved sugar and egg white mixture on top of each cookie.

Bake until light brown, about 15 to 22 minutes. Cool on a rack.

12

DISPENSA

Pantry

SABA
Fresh Grape Syrup

MARMELLATA DI UVA E MELE
Apple Jam Made with Fresh Grape Syrup

MARMELLATA ESPRESSA
Quick Pear and Apple Preserves

PERATA
Pear Conserve

SAVOR
Apple, Quince, and Grape Conserve

FICHI AMMANDORLATI
Dried Figs Filled with Almonds and Grated Orange Peel

FUNGHI SOTT'OLIO
Mushrooms Preserved Under Oil

MELANZANE SOTT'OLIO
Giuseppina de Lorenzi's Eggplant Under Olive Oil

SALSA DI VERDURE
Summer Vegetables Preserved in Oil

SUGO FINTO
"Fake" Sauce

POMMAROLA
Summer Tomato Sauce

SALSA DI POMODORO SICILIANA
Tomato Sauce from Sicily

SALSA DI POMODORO PUGLIESE
Tomato Sauce from Apulia

LIMONCINO
Lemon Liqueur

NOCINO
Walnut Liqueur

SABA

Fresh Grape Syrup

Makes about 2½ cups

*L*ong before Italian women ever used sugar, they had saba, a natural sweetener like honey. They took armloads of grapes collected at the end of the wine harvest, pressed and stemmed them until their juices ran free, and then cooked them slowly, reducing them to a thick syrup with a deep earthy sweetness. Saba has a complex provocative taste with none of the cloying sweetness of sugar, as if molasses were stirred into raisins that had cooked into a syrup.

Ida Lancellotti makes saba every fall and preserves it for use through the arc of the year. It is traditional to serve a great dome of hot soft polenta poured onto a communal plate and allow everyone to scoop out a hollow in the portion in front of them, and pour in a portion of saba for flavor. Children love saba mixed with snow—the original snow cone—and Signora Lancellotti has a particularly compelling use for saba in making savor, a fruit conserve combining apples, pumpkins, and quince.

> **4¼ pounds (16 cups) ripe red grapes; if you can find wine grapes, please use them; otherwise use the tastiest red table grapes you can find**

Wash the grapes, remove their stems, and then mash them in a bowl with a pestle or press them through a food processor using the shredding disk. Drain and press through a sieve, saving the liquid in a 5-quart heavy saucepan. Set over very low heat, skimming off any foam, and slowly simmer to concentrate the flavor, about 1 hour. Turn up the heat and cook at a vigorous boil until you have a thick syrup. Saba keeps for 4 to 5 days in the refrigerator. It can also be preserved in jars or frozen.

MARMELLATA DI UVA E MELE

Apple Jam Made with Fresh Grape Syrup

—

Makes 2 cups

*T*his jam is almost as dark as molasses. It is thick and deep tasting with rich apple overtones in its flavor. It is not sweet, which is why it is particularly delicious as a filling for a crostata. The recipe comes from Lina Morasini in Pergola near San Lorenzo in Campo nelle Marche. She starts with *Saba* (page 418). You may follow her example or buy *saba* ready to use—please see the Source Guide to Ingredients at the end of the book.

1½ cups *Saba* (page 418)
3 Golden Delicious apples, peeled, cored, and chopped
3 large strips of lemon zest
½ cup (3½ ounces) sugar

Put all the ingredients into a 2- or 3-quart nonreactive pan, preferably nonstick. Let them cook very slowly over the lowest possible heat for about 1½ to 2 hours. Skim the foam from the top from time to time and make sure that the mixture is not sticking. When it has been reduced to a thick jam-like consistency, test it by letting drops run from the side of a cool metal spoon. If they coalesce in a ribbon instead of individual drops, the jam is ready.

You may use the jam immediately to fill a crostata or pour it into a hot sterilized jar with a pint capacity, screw on a lid and band, and seal.

Marmellata Espressa

Quick Pear and Apple Preserves

—

Makes five (8-ounce) jars

*I*magine a velvety combination of pears and apples cooked thick enough to spread inside a tart, a layer cake, or pastries. Adele Rondini simply puts all the ingredients into one pot and simmers them together until they are tender. Although Italians don't eat applesauce, I'd serve this smooth fruit mixture just that way. If you can find some unripe pears, include them for their natural pectin.

> 6 cups (2 pounds, 3 ounces) unpeeled firm pears, cut into chunks
> 6 cups (2 pounds, 3 ounces) cut-up unpeeled apples, cut into chunks
> ½ cup dry Marsala
> ½ cup white wine
> ¾ teaspoon cinnamon
> Grated zest of 1 lemon
> ¾ cup (5 ounces) sugar

Place all the ingredients in a nonreactive pan, preferably one that is nonstick. Cover and simmer, letting the mixture bubble slowly over medium heat for about 1 to 1¼ hours; peek under the lid and stir fairly regularly, making certain that the mixture is not sticking. When it is thick and the pieces of fruit are tender, press them through a sieve or food mill or puree them in a blender. Do not use a food processor. The mixture keeps well in the refrigerator for a week.

To keep longer, sterilize the jars in your dishwasher and fill while they are hot, or wash, then boil them in a large pot of water for at least 10 minutes. Wash the screwbands and metal lids very well. The screwbands can go into the boiling water with the jars, but the lids should be dried and set aside.

To keep, pour the jam into the jars, leaving ½-inch headroom, close the jars well, and process in a boiling-water bath for 20 minutes.

PERATA

Pear Conserve

—

Makes six (8-ounce) jars

When Luce Galante de Secly makes this delicious pear jam, she uses intensely perfumed rosy-colored Italian petruccine pears that are firm, juicy, and sweet. They appear in June and July, the earliest pears of the year, and are so small that until recently most Italians routinely fed them to the pigs. It was just too much trouble to bother with the seeds and cores. Luce peels her pears but most women do not.

To reproduce the extraordinary taste of Luce's jam as closely as possible, I have used both fresh French butter pears and dried pears. French butter pears, also known as Pear Hardy, taste deeply of pear and are more delicate than the Italian petruccini, but are firm enough to be shipped all over the country in the early fall. The fruit of Lecce and the Salentine Peninsula basks in the strong Apulian sun; with so little rain, it develops immense natural sweetness. In Lecce the jam cooks until it is rosy-colored; we cannot ask that much of our pears, so they retain their pale golden color.

> 7 ounces dried pears, organically grown
> 4½ pounds French butter pears
> 3¾ cups (1 pound, 9 ounces) sugar
> 2 tablespoons lemon juice

Be sure that you have at least six canning jars, screwbands, and metal lids with a red rubber seal. Wash the jars in your dishwasher so that they will be sterilized and hot; or clean the jars very well, bring a very large pot of water to the boil, and set them in it at a gentle simmer for at least 10 minutes or until you are ready to use them. Wash the screwbands and metal lids very well. The screwbands can go into the hot water with the jars, but the lids should be dried and set aside.

Soak the dried pears in warm water to cover for 20 to 30 minutes. Drain and chop them very fine.

Wash the pears thoroughly. Peel, and remove their stems, cores, and seeds. Cut the pears into small pieces. You should have about 6 cups. Place the pears, the dried pears, the sugar, and the lemon juice together in a bowl and let stand for 2 to 3 hours. Move them to a nonreactive kettle and bring to a boil. Luce says the secret of her success is using a large wide-mouthed pot and cooking only a small amount at a time. You will find the mixture dry at first but lots of juice appears as it heats up. Cook at a boil, skimming off the foam that appears, and continue to boil just until the jam mixture begins to set, when it falls off the side of a cool metal spoon in thick drops that begin to form a sheet. At this point turn to the lowest possible heat and continue cooking, stirring continually with a wooden spoon, until the syrup is dense. To get the texture of Luce's jam, I put the pear mixture into the food processor or blender and puree until it is smooth. The mixture keeps well in the refrigerator for a week.

To keep longer, remove the jars from the water and drain them on towels. Dry the screwbands and lids. Fill the jars leaving ¼- to ½-inch headroom, close well, and process in a boiling water bath for 20 minutes.

SAVOR

Apple, Quince, and Grape Conserve

—

Makes about 4 cups

*I*da Lancellotti begins to make savor when she collects the last grapes at the harvest, puts them into a big cauldron, and boils them down to make *Saba* (page 418). That done, she adds apples, quince, and a sweet pumpkin—our butternut squash makes a fine substitute—to the pot with the *saba* and cooks them together slowly until they have a texture similar to chutney or applesauce. You can treat savor like a chutney and serve it with boiled meats and sausages such as cotechino, you can use it as a filling for cookies, or—and here's my choice—you can make Ida Lancellotti's crostata with a mixture of savor, dried figs, walnuts, biscotti, and amaretti. If mince pie were meatless and made in Emilia-Romagna, it would hope to be as good as Signora Lancellotti's *Crostata con il Savor* (page 378).

If you don't want to make *saba*, you can buy an outstanding import from Reggio Emilia (see the Source Guide to Ingredients). Bekmez, grape molasses made from concentrated grape juice, can be found in Middle Eastern stores.

2 cups Saba (page 418)
3 or 4 (about 2 pounds) Golden Delicious apples, peeled, cored, and thinly sliced
1 small quince, peeled, cored, and thinly sliced
1 tablespoon sugar
5 ounces butternut squash or pumpkin, peeled, seeded, and grated

Put all the ingredients in a heavy 3-quart kettle or casserole, preferably one that is nonstick. Simmer the mixture slowly for 2 to 3 hours, skimming any foam that rises to the top from time to time, and making sure that the mixture is not sticking to the bottom of the pot. When it has been reduced to about one-third or one-quarter the original volume and has the texture of applesauce or a light chutney, it is done.

Use in the next few days or put in sterile jars, seal, and process in a boiling water bath for 20 minutes.

FICHI AMMANDORLATI

Dried Figs Filled with Almonds and Grated Orange Peel

—

Makes 5 dozen

*H*ow are delicious plump white figs dried in Italy? Quantities of local Italian varieties are picked, set in the sun for a whole day, and then slipped into a slow oven for 15 minutes. In Ururi, an Albanian community in Molise, the women toast an almond to fill each fig, then sprinkle a little Sambuca over the top, while in Matera they add a little more flavor by grating orange zest and crushing fennel seeds to join the almonds in the cavity of the figs. They are perfect with espresso at the end of dinner. You can make quantities of the figs, keep them in an airtight tin for months, and give them as Christmas presents—if you can bear not to eat them all first.

Since we don't have dried white Italian figs, use plump Calmyrna figs instead.

60 (about 2 pounds) dried figs, preferably soft and plump Calmyrnas
60 raw almonds, toasted for 10 minutes in a 350°F. oven
2 tablespoons finely grated orange zest
½ to 1 teaspoon fennel seeds, lightly crushed with the side of a cleaver
Red wine or Sambuca

Preheat the oven to 400°F.

Cut off the hard stem of the fig. Cut an opening in the fig large enough to accommodate the almond, but do not cut the fig all the way through. First sprinkle a little orange zest and a few fennel seeds in the cavity, then press in the almond. Press the fig closed as tightly as you can. Repeat with the remaining figs.

Set the filled figs on a baking sheet, drizzle them with a little red wine or Sambuca, and bake for about 5 minutes, just enough to caramelize a little. If you can resist eating the figs, put them in an airtight tin and they will keep for months.

Funghi Sott'Olio

Mushrooms Preserved Under Oil

—

Makes two (8-ounce) jars

*M*aria Andriani in Apulia and Teresa Frate in Molise give mushrooms a brief bath in water and vinegar and then put them up under olive oil. They keep easily for a year.

1½ pounds fresh brown mushrooms, stems removed
3 cups water
3 cups white wine vinegar
1½ teaspoons coarse sea salt
2 bay leaves, preferably European
2 garlic cloves, halved
1 cup extra-virgin olive oil

Clean the mushrooms by wiping them with a moist paper towel.

Bring the water, vinegar, and coarse sea salt to a boil in a 2-quart nonreactive pot. Add the mushrooms. When the mixture comes back to the boil, immediately remove the mushrooms with a slotted spoon and drain them well in a colander. Weight the mushrooms with a plate to drain out the excess liquid—you may leave them for hours this way—and set them aside to cool. They should be at least as cool as cool room temperature and a cooler pantry temperature would be even better.

Pack the mushrooms in two sterilized jars with the bay leaves and halved garlic cloves, and push them down firmly with your fingers. Fill the jars with olive oil, then slide a small paring knife around the sides, making sure that no air bubbles remain in the oil. Close the jars tightly and set aside for at least 6 weeks.

VARIATION: Use several mint leaves and small pieces of peperoncino, strong red chili pepper, in place of the bay leaf.

MELANZANE SOTT'OLIO

Eggplant preserved under olive oil

—

Makes 3 (8-ounce) jars

2 globe eggplants, about 2 pounds
3 tablespoons coarse sea salt
For the jars: small pieces of hot red pepper, 1½ teaspoons dried oregano,
    4 garlic cloves, finely chopped

Peel and cut the eggplants into ⅛-inch-thick slices, discarding the stem ends. Place the slices in a bowl, sprinkle each layer with coarse salt, and weight down with several heavy cans for 12 hours.

Drain the eggplants and press out all the bitter juices by squeezing them firmly in a kitchen towel. Proceed following the mushroom recipe (page 425) through the cooling.

Pack the eggplants in three jars with the hot red pepper pieces, dried oregano, and garlic cloves.

SALSA DI VERDURE

Summer Vegetables Preserved in Oil

—

Makes three (1 pint) jars

*I*da Lancellotti puts up summer vegetables in August, when they are at their most plentiful, so she can have them on hand through the cold winter months. Don't jump to conclusions: that doesn't mean that they have the usual acid flavor of vegetables poached in vinegar. Contrary to all expectations, these vegetables retain the crunch and sweetness of their beginnings and have just the loveliest tantalizing hint of a bite. I serve them with sliced meats, such as the pistachio-studded turkey sausage on page 235.

Ida Lancellotti

10 ounces green beans, cut in 1-inch lengths
10 ounces carrots, diced
1 large onion, diced
1 tablespoon sugar
½ cup olive oil
1 tablespoon sea salt
3¼ cups white wine vinegar
1⅓ pounds sweet red peppers, diced
Olive oil to cover

Be sure that you have three wide-mouthed pint canning jars, screwbands, and metal lids with red rubber seals. Wash the jars in your dishwasher to sterilize them or clean the jars very well and put in a large pot of gently boiling water for at least 10 minutes, or until you are ready to use them. The screwbands can go into the hot water with the jars, but the lids should be washed separately, dried, and set aside.

Put all the ingredients except the red peppers and the final olive oil in a large, heavy stockpot and simmer for 15 minutes. Add the sweet red peppers and cook for another 7 minutes. Set aside to cool. Transfer the vegetables to the wide-mouthed glass jars and cover them with olive oil. Screw the tops on tightly and set aside in your pantry until you are ready to use.

SUGO FINTO

"Fake" Sauce

—

Serves 4

*T*his tomato sauce comes with the unlikely name of *finto* ("pretend or fake") because it is made just like a meat sauce, although there isn't a hint of beef or veal to be found in it. In a country in which meat has been a rare treat and vegetables a daily pleasure, it's just one more clever way that Italian grandmothers deal with scarcity. Toss with pasta or serve with polenta.

> 4 tablespoons extra-virgin olive oil
> 1 medium white onion, diced very fine
> 1 carrot, diced very fine
> 1 celery rib, diced very fine
> 1 branch of fresh rosemary, needles minced
> 3 leaves of fresh sage, chopped
> 5 leaves of fresh basil
> ¼ cup finely chopped flat-leaf parsley
> 2 or 3 (14 to 16 ounces) juicy ripe tomatoes, peeled, seeded, and chopped
>   or 1 (14-ounce) can Italian plum tomatoes, drained and chopped
> Salt
> Freshly ground black pepper

Warm the olive oil in a large, heavy-bottomed sauté pan or nonstick skillet over moderate heat. Add the onion, carrot, celery, rosemary, sage, basil leaves, and parsley and sauté over low-medium heat until the onion is soft and translucent but not brown, about 10 to 15 minutes. Add the tomatoes and salt, cook until the juices start to boil, then reduce to a simmer and cook for 20 to 30 minutes, until the sauce is thick and dense, adding hot water as necessary if it becomes too condensed. Remove from the heat and stir in the pepper.

TUSCAN VARIATION: You can add ⅓ cup dry red wine once the vegetables have been sautéed. Bring the wine to a boil and let it cook down until a few tablespoons of wine are left in the pan, 5 to 10 minutes. Continue as above.

POMMAROLA

Summer Tomato Sauce

—

Serves 6

*T*here may be as many tomato sauces in Italy as there are cooks, but what distinguishes this summer sauce from others is the fact that the vegetables and herbs aren't sautéed before the tomatoes are added. Just toss everything into the pot and cook over very low heat until you have a thick sauce.

> 2½ pounds ripe, fresh tomatoes, preferably plum tomatoes
> 1 yellow onion, sliced
> 1 carrot, sliced
> 1 celery rib, sliced
> 1 small garlic clove, lightly crushed
> 3 leaves of fresh basil
> 5 sprigs of flat-leaf parsley
> 1 teaspoon sea salt
> Sugar (optional)

Wash the tomatoes very well. Remove and discard the stems. Cut the tomatoes in half if they are small, in quarters if they are large. Place the tomatoes, onion, carrot, celery, garlic clove, basil leaves, and parsley in a heavy saucepan large enough to hold them comfortably. Stir the mixture with a wooden spoon to mix the ingredients well and then cook, covered, over very low heat for 1 to 1½ hours. When the tomatoes have been reduced to a fairly thick mass, put the contents of the pan through the large disk of a food mill. If you don't have a food mill, try pressing them through a sieve just enough to hold back the seeds and skin that add bitterness to the sauce. You can then put the contents in a blender or food processor. Taste for seasoning; add extra salt and a little sugar, if needed.

SALSA DI POMODORO SICILIANA

Sicilian Tomato Sauce

—

Makes about 2 cups, enough for 1 pound of pasta

*W*atching Giovanna Passannanti make her exceptional tomato sauce was a revelation. She commented in a very off-hand manner: "I cook with my nose. The minute you smell the garlic, use it." She always sets a lid slightly ajar over the mixture as it simmers and always presses the tomatoes through a food mill or sieve to remove the skin and seeds, which may be bitter.

> 2½ pounds ripe tomatoes, preferably plum tomatoes, roughly chopped
> 1 small white onion, finely chopped
> 4 garlic cloves: 3 whole and 1 minced
> 2 to 3 tablespoons extra-virgin olive oil
> ½ to ¾ cup of fresh basil, torn into small pieces
> ½ to ¾ teaspoon sea salt
> Sugar (optional)

Cook the tomatoes, onion, and whole garlic cloves in a large, heavy nonreactive saucepan over medium heat with the lid set slightly ajar. Stir to mix them together. Signora Passannanti sets a wooden spoon under the the cover to prop the lid open a bit. After 10 minutes press the mixture through a food mill with a coarse blade or a sieve with colander-sized holes. This will hold back most of the seeds and skin that can give a bitter taste to the sauce.

Meanwhile, drizzle the olive oil into a small sauté pan and add the minced garlic. The minute you smell the familiar scent of garlic, turn off the heat. Stir this combination into the sieved tomato mixture. Add the basil leaves and simmer for another 10 minutes. Taste the sauce and add the sea salt and a little sugar if the tomatoes need the sweetness.

SALSA DI POMODORO PUGLIESE

Tomato Sauce from Apulia

—

Makes 2 cups

*O*ne more wonderful tomato sauce for all seasons. Maria Andriani's version has white wine, which gives it a special flavor.

> 8 medium-size ripe red tomatoes, roughly chopped
> 2 to 3 tablespoons extra-virgin olive oil
> 1 onion, finely chopped
> ⅓ cup white wine
> 7 leaves of fresh basil, torn
> Salt

Cook the chopped tomatoes in a 3- to 4-quart heavy nonreactive saucepan over medium heat for 10 minutes. Then rub them through a sieve or food mill to eliminate the skin and seeds.

While the tomatoes are cooking, warm the olive oil in a sauté pan, add the onion and sauté over medium heat until it is golden, about 10 minutes. Add the white wine, turn up the heat, bring it to a lively bubble, and cook until it has evaporated. Stir in the tomato sauce and basil and cook 15 to 20 minutes longer over very low heat, until it has thickened. Taste for salt.

Profile of *Luce Galante de Secly*

Luce Galante de Secly's serene presence and soft voice draw people to her as naturally as light draws a moth. She strokes everyone to whom she speaks, pale tones and light fingers drawing them closer, closer to her warm, comforting, quiet presence. She is beguiling, moving, a tender and slightly mysterious woman. She still lives in her mother's childhood house, an immense and beautifully furnished palazzo in Lecce with library after library filled with books, one room opening into the next. Her father, an important book collector, was the editor of the great newspaper of the south, *La Gazetta del Mezzogiorno*. His leather-bound first editions claim shelf after shelf. Luce's dynamic husband, a highly distinguished surgeon, is now retired, although he never stops moving, thinking, doing. He collects art books, which are everywhere in this big, comfortable house—on tables, on shelves, stacked on the floor. He is passionate about music and opera; he paces from room to room finding records, laying hands on pamphlets, books, and articles to be displayed and discussed.

Luce dresses in the conservative dark silks of wealthy well-bred women. She loves the house with its beautiful hand-painted Neapolitan tiles on the floor, its fine old family portraits and oils, its fine furniture. The house itself, built on ancient ruins at the end of the fifteenth century, was the property of various noble families, all of whom had the pleasure of its proximity, via a door whose key they hold, to a second-century Roman theater in the garden. Luce tends the masses of geraniums planted in ancient marble containers parading across the balcony, the first spot of color you see upon entering the courtyard, before your eye falls on the great nineteenth-century carriage parked in the shadows. There are roses as well, called millefoglie, dense with petals that Dr. Galante's grandmother cultivated. His family, too, is old and rooted. He tells stories of his ancient aunt talking about the food that his grandmother made.

Moving through the house, with its mysteriously circular plan, showing it off with quiet pride, Luce arrives at the kitchen, three enormous rooms, one opening to the next. She is deeply attached to these rooms. One holds a refrigerator given over entirely to jams and preserves. Another has a long rectangular wooden table polished by the fingers and hands of many cooks and eaters, a huge marble sink with a long drainboard, and cupboards full of culinary implements. She loves food and she loves to cook. She has had the same cook for 37 years, and he knows her recipes and her desires by heart, but she still is in the kitchen frequently, and her friends wait for her invitations. She makes magnificent jams—bitter orange marmalade and pear jam from tiny deep-tasting petruccini pears—puts up limoncino liqueur and other fruit infusions from the citrus trees in the garden, and makes a dazzling rosy-colored cotognata, molded quince paste served with coffee as an end-of-meal sweet. "We never use cultivated fruit or vegetables. We just wait for the season to arrive and then cook what has grown." Her grandmother was totally enveloped in thinking about food and the household, a pattern her mother continued, and Luce does the same, although she says she isn't so bound up as they were. Nevertherless, she loves to talk about food. She says of the apricots in the market, especially Spanish ones, that they have no flavor, but the apricots in the countryside of Lecce are perfumed, full of aroma and taste. She serves phenomenal food—a soft creamy pudding with irresistable texture and delicate flavoring with the deceptively simple name crema; cookies called *muffettati* filled with jam made from their white grapes and topped with finely wrought delicate tendrils of dough. We spend hours poring over her mother's notebooks, full of recipes from much earlier in this century.

Rosella, her deep-voiced daughter, arrives with her husband and their fourteen-year-old son, who is clearly deeply attached to Luce and to things of the family. He hunts down an old photograph album and can describe all the people, every scene, and every event in it, even if these events occurred before he was born. He lives with his family in a separate, but not detached, house of this great palazzo. Luce's son and his family live in a similar wing on the other side, so the entire family lives under one very large roof. The grandson goes to school every morning via Luce's kitchen. "Oh yes," he says, his eyes widening, "I always see the big pot with something cooking in it, with the big ladle, stirring, stirring."

A smile, a crescent of pleasure, appears on Luce's moon-shaped face. What Rosella says ironically again and again is true: "This is still a society that lives in the flavor and fragrance of its sauces, its dolci, its marmellate."

LIMONCINO

Lemon Liqueur

—

Makes 2½ pints

A delicious digestivo from Luce Galante de Secly, who grows all manner of lemons in her garden in Lecce, including the *limoni veraci* that she uses for this liqueur. A walk through the garden, with its numerous citrus trees, is a dazzling experience, as is the view from the small gate beyond the oranges, lemons, and citrons where the original Roman theater sits at the edge of the property, confirmation of the importance of the city of Lecce millennia ago. Today Lecce is full of baroque palazzi, villas, and churches sculpted of the local golden stone in the late seventeenth and early eighteenth centuries.

> **5 ripe lemons, organically grown, if possible**
> **2⅛ cups vodka**
> **2½ cups (17½ ounces) sugar**
> **2 cups water**

Wash the peel of the lemons well and meticulously cut the zest away from the inner white pith of the peel. Discard the white pith and put the zest in a quart glass jar or bottle. Pour the vodka over the top. Cover and let stand in the sun for 8 days.

Prepare a sugar syrup with the sugar and water. Bring them to a boil in a heavy saucepan, stirring to dissolve the sugar, and cook at 175°F. to make a syrup. Simmer for 10 minutes, then set aside to cool.

Filter the vodka and lemon liquid by pouring it through cheesecloth or paper coffee filters. Pour the filtered liquid back into the jar and stir in the sugar syrup. Mix well, and leave for at least 10 to 15 days before drinking, although Luce leaves it for months and it tastes exquisite.

NOCINO

Walnut Liqueur

Makes 1 quart

*E*very country family in Emilia Romagna has its special nocino recipe, and they all begin with soft green walnuts that have not yet developed their shells. They are picked on the Feast of San Giovanni, June 24, after they have been bathed by the dew of the previous evening. The number of walnuts infusing the liquore varies from recipe to recipe but it usually has some ritual significance. This one has 21, a particularly powerful number since 3 is the number of the Trinity and 7 of the cardinal virtues.

Nocino was evidently first made in the Garfagnana, the beautiful green hilly region of Tuscany above Lucca, but it has long been associated with Emilia Romagna. This particular recipe comes from Modena, where people have long drunk it on festival days after they've indulged in good food and wine. Some country people keep nocino from generation to generation and add to it every year.

Since it is illegal to buy pure alcohol in America, you can substitute grappa, aquavit, or 80-proof vodka. To give you an idea of how much ritual is involved in the making of nocino, I am told that the juniper branch should come from an adult cultivated tree, that it should be snapped off, not cut, and it should be about the same diameter as a thumb.

Although it isn't at all traditional, I use a little nocino when I make pasta alle noci; it gives a definite zip to the walnut-flavored sauce.

21 soft green walnuts, tender enough to cut easily with a knife
4¼ cups 80-proof vodka, grappa, or aquavit
4 cloves
½-inch cinnamon stick
Zest of 1 orange, in strips
1 branch of fresh juniper, 3 inches long
2 cups (14 ounces) sugar
1¼ cups water

(continued)

Clean, but do not wash, the walnuts. Cut each into quarters. Put them in a 6-cup wide-mouthed glass jar that has a tight seal. Pour in the vodka, add the cloves, cinnamon stick, strips of orange zest, and juniper branch, and stir well to mix them together. Set the jar in the sun and leave it from 40 days to 2 months, shaking well every 3 days. Do not be surprised that the mixture inside turns dark brown very soon. At the end of that time, filter the liquid by pouring it through cheesecloth into a large bowl.

Prepare a sugar syrup with the sugar and water. Bring them to a boil in a heavy saucepan, stirring to dissolve the sugar. Skim the surface, then cook at a simmer for 10 minutes. Set aside to cool.

Pour the filtered liquid back into the jar, stir in the sugar syrup, return the juniper branch to the mixture, and mix very well. Close the jar tightly and leave indoors until Christmas. Taste from time to time, and remove the juniper after 1 month.

Remove the walnuts; you can eat them, if you want, because they are so soft, or you can put them in another bottle, cover them with Marsala for 3 or 4 weeks, and serve as a light cordial.

At Christmas, filter the mixture once again and leave it until Easter, according to one nonna, or until the next Christmas, according to another. At the end of the chosen time, pour the nocino into wine bottles. It is now ready to drink.

Selected Bibliography

Aiolfi, Maria Teresa. *1900 to 1923: Vent'anni di civiltà contadina in un paese del Cremasco*. Milano: Giuffre Editore, 1988.

Barbagli, Marzio. *Sotto lo stesso tetto: Mutamenti della famiglia in Italia dal XV al XX secolo*. Bologna: Il Mulino, 1984.

Barber, Elizabeth Wayland. *Women's Work: The First 20,000 Years*. New York: Norton, 1994.

Beevor, Kinta. *A Tuscan Childhood*. London: Viking, 1993.

Bimbi, Franca. *Il genere e l'età*. Milano: Franco Angeli, 1993.

Bimbi, Franca, and Grazia Catellano. *Madri e Padri*. Milano: Franco Angeli, 1993.

Birnbaum, Lucia Chiavola. "The Long History of Sicilians" in *Through the Looking Glass: Italian and Italian American Images in the Media*. Edited by Mary Jo Bona and Anthony Julian Tamburri. Staten Island, N.Y.: American Italian Historical Association, 1996.

Boni, Ada. *La Cucina Romana*. Rome: Newton Compton Editori, 1983.

Bugli, Tiziano, Antonelle Chiadini, and Morena Morelli. *Ricette in Soffitta*. Forli: Edizioni Speedgraphic, 1993.

Caico, Louise. *Sicilian Ways and Days*. London: John Long Ltd., 1910.

Caldwell, Lesley. "Italian Feminism: Some Considerations" in *Women and Italy: Essays on Gender, Culture and History*. Edited by Baranski, Zygmunt G., and Shirley W. Vinall. New York: St. Martin's, 1991.

Camporesi, Piero. *Alimentazione, folclore, società*. Parma: Practiche Editrice, 1980.

Casale Cipriano. *Pizza e Pezze: La storia dei senza storia: Costumanze, superstizioni e credenze della gente molisana*. Pescara: Arz Prandi, Edizioni Alberti, n.d.

Cicioni, Mirna, and Nicole Prunster. *Visions and Revisions: Women in Italian Culture*. Providence, R.I., and Oxford: Berg Publishers, 1993.

Gamacchio, Roberti Chiey. *Riconoscimento e use delle piante selvatiche*. Sommacampagna: La Casa Verde, Demtra S.r.l., 1990.

Gambogi, Anna Maria. *Ieri e l'altro ieri.* Lucca: Maria Pacini Fazzi Editore, 1990.

Gianni, Guido, ed. *Quando la cucina si chiamava "casa."* Sapori perduti ritrovati degli alunni delle scuole elementari e medie della provincia di Arezzo. Cortona: Ingrocart Edizioni, Accademia Italiana della cucina, n.d.

Grande enciclopedia illustrata della gastronomia. Milan: Selezione al Reader's Digest, 1990.

Gray, Patience. *Honey from a Weed.* New York: Harper & Row, 1987.

INSOR (Istituto nazionale di sociologia rurale). *Gastronomia e società.* Milan: Franco Angeli Editore, 1984.

Mafai, Miriam. *Pane Nero.* Milan: Oscar Mondadori, 1987.

Mannocchi, Luigi. *Folk-lore di Fermo e circondario*: Etnografia illustrata, vol. 9. Fermo: Fondazione Cassa di Risparmio di Fermo, 1993.

Manzon, Domenico. "Poesia del ragù." *L'Accademia* no. 42, 1994.

Marini, Marino. *La cucina bresciana,* Padua; Franco Muzzio Editore, 1993.

Menesini, Renzo. *Le erbe aromatiche in cucina.* Lucca: Maria Pacini Fazzi Editore, 1992.

Muratore, Maria Rosaria Stoja. *La cucina salentina.* Galatina: Congedo Editore, 1993.

Parenti, Giovanni Righi. *Il Buon Mangiare.* Siena: Edizioni ALSABA, 1988.

Pitkin, Donald S. *The House that Giacomo Built.* Cambridge: Cambridge University Press, 1985.

Porta, Nella Credaro. "Una cucina in movimento: storia, strumenti di cottura, ingredienti." Talk given at Regional Fair on the products of the Lombard mountains, Morbegno, October 7, 1995.

Quintavalle, Arturo Carlo. "Contadini: fiaba sistema storia" in *I Paisan: Immagini di fotografia contadina della bassa padana* by Giuseppe Morandi. Milan: Mazzotta, n.d.

Revelli, Nuto. *L'anello forte. La donna: storie di vita quotidiana.* Turin: Einaudi, 1985.

Rondini, Adele. *S'l'arola.* Rome: Club Culturale "Le Rondini," 1991.

Ruffini, G. D. *Doctor Antonio.* London: David Stott, 1891.

Sada, Luigi. *The Food of Puglia.* Rome: Newton Compton Editori, 1994.

Sammarco, Daniela, and Maria Angela Marramaldo. *Polizzi: Generosa anche a tavola.* Edizioni Grifo, n.d.

Sorcinelli, Paolo. *Gli Italiani e il cibo: Appetiti, digiuni e rinunce della realtà contadina alla società del benessere.* Bologna: CLUEB, 1995.

Zanini de Vita, Oretta. *The Food of Rome and Lazio,* translated by Maureen Fant. Rome: Alphabyte Books, 1993.

Source Guide to Ingredients
—

OLIVES AND OLIVE OILS, VINEGARS, PASTAS, POLENTA, DRIED PORCINI MUSHROOMS AND OTHER ITALIAN SPECIALTY FOODS

Balducci's Mail Order, 42–26 12th Street, Long Island City, NY 11101; 800–225–3822

Colavita Home Delivery Service, P. O. Box 9143, Elizabeth, NJ 07202 Fax: 908–862–4382

Convito Italiano, 1515 Sheridan Road, Wilmette, IL 60091 847–251–3654; fax 847–251–0123

Corti Brothers, 5810 Folsom Blvd, Sacramento, CA 95829 916–736–3800; fax 916–736–3807

Dean & DeLuca Mail Order, 560 Broadway, New York, NY 10012; 800–221–714, ext. 223 or 270

G. B. Ratto International Grocer, 821 Washington Street, Oakland, CA 94507; 800–228–3515 in California; out of state 800–325–3483

Il Cibo di Lidia, P. O. Box 4461, Grand Central Station, New York, N.Y. 10163; 800–480-CIBO; fax 212–935–7687

Manganaro Foods, 488 Ninth Ave., New York, N.Y. 10018; 212–563–5331; 800–472–5264

Pasta Shop, 5665 College Avenue, Oakland, CA 94618 510–547–4005

Vivande, 2125 Fillmore Street, San Francisco, CA 94115; 415–346–4430

Wally's, 2107 Westwood Boulevard, Los Angeles, CA 90025; 800–8-WALLYS

Williams-Sonoma Catalogue, P.O.Box 7465, San Francisco, CA 94120; 800–541–2233; fax 415–421–5153

Zabar's Mail Order Catalogue, 2245 Broadway, New York, N.Y. 10024 212–787–2003; 800–221–3347

Zingerman's Delicatessen, 422 Detroit St., Ann Arbor, MI 48104; 313–769–1625; fax 313-769–1235

DRIED HERBS AND SPICES

The Spice House, 1048 N. Old World Third Street, Milwaukee, WI 53203; 414–272–0977

The Sandy Mush Herb Nursery, Route 2, Surrett Cove Road, Leicester, N. C. 28748; 704–683–2014: Live herbs and herb seeds

DRIED BEANS

Dean & DeLuca

Grace's Marketplace, 530 East 119th Street, New York, NY 10035; 212–737–0600

Phipps Country, growers and distributors of heirloom beans including borlotti, cannelini, 2700 Pescadero Road, P.O. Box 349, Pescadero, CA 94060; phone: 415–879–0787; fax 415–879–1622

Vivande

ANCHOVIES AND CAPERS UNDER SALT

Balducci's, Vivande, Zingerman's

PROSCIUTTO DI PARMA, SALAMI, SAUSAGE

Balducci, Dean & DeLuca, Williams-Sonoma, Zingerman's

PANCETTA, OUTSTANDING PROSCIUTTO, SAUSAGES

Hobbs' Applewood Smoked Meat Company, 1201 Andersen Drive, San Rafael, CA 94901; 415–453–0577; fax 415–453–1653

B & L Specialty Foods,
P.O. Box 80068,
Seattle, WA 98108;
800–EAT PASTA

ORGANIC TOMATO PUREE (PASSATA), TOMATO PASTE, PEELED ITALIAN TOMATOES

Colavita, Dean & DeLuca, Pasta Shop,
Vivande

SHELLED FAVA BEANS

Sultan's Delight, Box 090302,
Brooklyn, NY 11209;
718–745–6844 or 800–852–5046

FRESH ITALIAN-STYLE BREADS

Balducci's, Williams-Sonoma,
Zingerman's

SHEETS OF FRESH EGG PASTA (SOMETIMES)

Pasta Shop, Williams-Sonoma

FRESH VEGETABLES

Balducci's: broccoli rabe

Williams-Sonoma: Yukon Gold potatoes

MOZZARELLA, PARMIGIANO-REGGIANO, PECORINO, AND OTHER CHEESES

Balducci's, B & L Specialty Foods,
Dean & DeLuca carry handmade
fior di latte and imported mozzarella di bufala, aged
Parmigiano-Reggiano, pecorino
romano and ricotta salata,
scamorza, and provolone

Mozzarella Company (handmade fior
di latte mozzarella, ricotta, other
handmade cheeses, fresh and
aged), 2944 Elm Street, Dallas,
TX 75226; 214–741–4072;
800–798–2954

Murray's Cheese, 257 Bleecker Street,
New York, N.Y. 10014;
212–243–3289; fax 212–243-
5001

Williams-Sonoma, Vivande,
Zingerman's

WHEAT FLOUR, IMPORTED CORNMEAL, POLENTA, POLENTA TARAGNA, DURUM, SEMOLINA

The Baker's Catalogue, P.O. Box 876,
RR 2, Box 56, Norwich, VT
05055; 800–827–6836

Balducci's, Dean & DeLuca

Gray's Grist Mill, P.O. Box 422,
Adamsville, RI 02801;
508–636–6075

Kenyon Cornmeal Company: white
and yellow cornmeal,
Usquepaugh, West Kingston, RI
02892; 401–783–4054

G. B. Ratto

Todaro Brothers, 557 Second Avenue,
New York, NY 10016;
212–679–7766

Vivande, Zingerman's

FARRO

Dean & DeLuca, Pasta Shop,
Zingerman's

SPELT

Purity Foods Inc., 2871 West Jolly
Road, Okemos, MI 48864;
517–351–9231

ITALIAN RICE

Balducci, Dean & DeLuca, Pasta Shop,
Todaro Brothers, Vivande,
Zingerman's

FOR DESSERTS: OUTSTANDING CITRUS OILS, VANILLA EXTRACT, COCOA, NUTS

The Baker's Catalogue, Dean &
Deluca, Grace's Marketplace,
Todaro Brothers, Williams-
Sonoma, Zingerman's

AMARENA WILD CHERRIES

Zingerman's

SABA OR SAPA

Corti Brothers

AMMONIUM BICARBONATE

The Baker's Catalogue

Source Guide to Equipment

—

BAKING STONES, WOODEN PEELS FOR BREAD AND PIZZA, EQUIPMENT FOR BREAD BAKING AND DESSERT MAKING

The Baker's Catalogue (see above) has
everything for the home baker

Sur La Table, 84 Pine Street, Pike
Place Farmers' Market, Seattle,
WA 98101; 800–240–0853

RIDGED SKILLET AND GRILL PAN, FOOD MILL, FLAME TAMER, POTATO RICER

The Baker's Catalogue, Sur La Table,
Williams-Sonoma, Zabar's

Index